INTERIORS
NOW

INTERIORS
NOW 3

EDITED BY
MARGIT J. MAYER

TEXT BY
IAN PHILLIPS

TASCHEN

POSH NEUTRAL LIKE AN ART GALLERY; MADCAP CONSERVATIVE, OR NEO-MINIMALIST— GREAT INTERIORS MAKE THEIR OWN RULES

At first glance, it looks like a pulsating sun, but the disc-shaped Marc Quinn painting on the cover of this book is, in fact, a portrait—a painstakingly created depiction of a human iris. Coincidentally, it's a picture that, in terms of symbolism, could hardly be more appropriate for our purposes. After all, the constant viewing of and selecting from information, the need to see our actions in the context of a galaxy of similarly discerning peers, the focus on individuality as a potent natural source of power—in short, the things that make this global digital era so novel and occasionally stressful—also affect the way great interiors are created. Gone are the days when a glance at the homes of wealthier neighbors was enough to tell us how we should furnish our own. Nowadays, we have the whole world to draw on, and all of history, too. With such vast amounts of visual content at our fingertips, the range of decorating options available to us has exploded. And lest we are tempted to avoid such complexity by simply appointing an interior designer and letting them get on with it, decorator extraordinaire Jacques Grange's approving description of his world-famous clients —the Coppolas— as "easy to work *with*" (and not work *for*) would suggest that this, too, is a thing of the past.

The following pages thus feature numerous projects that are coproductions between creative clients and their interior designers, not to mention a great many combinations of space, furniture, and art that blur the boundaries of geography and time. You'll find a Berlin apartment whose exposed roof structure is more reminiscent of Venice, an Indian dining room with Kaare Klint chairs, and a New York loft that, with its mix of shoji screens, smooth wood surfaces, and flower-print fabrics, calls to mind the sophisticated innocence of Charles and Ray Eames's Pacific Palisades residence.

My heartfelt thanks goes to all the designers, photographers, stylists, and their agents without whom this third edition of TASCHEN's *Interiors Now* series would not have been possible. To those whose projects didn't make it into the book, all I can say is: Please don't hold it against us. There is always next time. I'd also like to thank the owners who were willing to share their private sanctums with interior design fans around the world—and to apologize for any inconvenience caused by our various requests. Just how irksome such a photo shoot can be for the home's occupants is made abundantly clear by Tiina Laakkonen and Jon Rosen's cat, whose tail can be seen protruding from beneath the coffee table on page 146. Dear Monkey, please forgive the intrusion—it was all in a very good cause. MARGIT J. MAYER

◀ The welcoming contours of Jean Royère's *Polar Bear* armchair contrast with the austerity of Joseph Dirand's mainly black-and-white scheme for this Paris apartment. • Mit seinen einladenden Konturen kontrapunktiert Jean Royères *Eisbär*-Sessel die Strenge dieses von Joseph Dirand weitgehend schwarz-weiß gehaltenen Pariser Apartments. • Les contours accueillants du célèbre fauteuil *Ours Polaire* de Jean Royère contrastent avec le décor austère, majoritairement noir et blanc, créé par Joseph Dirand dans cet appartement parisien. *Photographed by Adrien Dirand, page 68ff.*

NOBEL NEUTRAL WIE EINE GALERIE, SPLEENIG TRADITIONELL ODER NEOMINIMALISTISCH: GUTE INTERIORS MACHEN IHRE REGELN SELBST

Das Rundbild des britischen Künstlers Marc Quinn auf dem Cover dieses Bandes erinnert an eine pulsierende Sonne, ist aber ein Porträt. Es zeigt die minutiös nachgemalte Iris eines Menschen. Purer Zufall, und doch hätte ich mir kein besseres Symbolmotiv für diesen Sammelband wünschen können. Individualität als natürliches Kraftwerk, schauen, auswählen, und sich dabei als Teil einer Galaxie von ebenfalls im Wahrnehmungsmodus befindlichen Sternen wissen: Was das Leben in der digital-globalen Ära so neu und oft anstrengend macht, hat auch Auswirkungen auf die Art, wie großartige Wohnungen entstehen. Vorbei die Zeiten, als ein Blick zu wohlhabenderen Nachbarn genügte, um zu wissen, wie man sich einrichten sollte. Heute ist die ganze Welt unsere Nachbarschaft, und die Historie sowieso. Mit dem Zugriff auf unendliche Bildwelten haben sich die Optionen vervielfacht. Zu kompliziert, lieber einen Interiordesigner beauftragen und alles ihr oder ihm überlassen? Wenn selbst der Großmeister dieser Zunft, Jacques Grange, seine weltweit berühmten Auftraggeber namens Coppola dafür lobt, wie „leicht das Arbeiten *mit* ihnen" war (und nicht etwa *für* sie), dann weiß man: Auch das ist von gestern.

Und so finden sich auf den folgenden Seiten viele Koproduktionen zwischen kreativen Klienten und Innenarchitekten, dazu jede Menge zeitliche wie örtliche Grenzüberschreitungen beim Kombinieren von Raum, Mobiliar, Kunst. Da erinnert die offene Dachkonstruktion eines Berliner Apartments an Venedig, in Indien wird auf Stühlen von Kaare Klint diniert, und in einer New Yorker Loftwohnung verbinden sich Shoji-Schiebewände, viel Holz und Stoffe mit Streublümchen zu einer *sophisticated innocence,* die an das Privathaus von Charles und Ray Eames in Pacific Palisades denken lässt.

Mein Dank gilt allen Designern, Fotografen, Stylisten und Agenten, die TASCHEN bei dieser dritten Folge der *Interiors Now*-Serie unterstützt haben. Jene, deren Projekte es nicht ins Buch geschafft haben, bitte ich um Verständnis und Geduld: Es gibt immer ein nächstes Mal. Ebenfalls bedanken möchte ich mich bei den Eigentümern, die ihre Privatsphäre mit Interiorfans in aller Welt zu teilen bereit waren, sowie bei deren Mitbewohnern. Wie nervig so ein Fotoshoot sein kann, demonstriert der Kater von Tiina Laakkonen und Jon Rosen auf Seite 146: Nur sein Schwanz lugt noch unter dem Coffeetable hervor. Lieber Monkey, bitte verzeih uns, es war wirklich für einen guten Zweck. **MARGIT J. MAYER**

▶ Prints galore: John Loecke and Jason Oliver Nixon adopted a characteristically exuberant approach to the decoration of the spare room in their Brooklyn row house. The chair is part of their Madcap Cottage Custom line. • Muster en masse: Beim Einrichten des Gästezimmers in ihrem Reihenhaus in Brooklyn gingen John Loecke und Jason Oliver Nixon mit charakteristischem Überschwang ans Werk. Der Sessel ist aus ihrer Madcap-Cottage-Kollektion. • Des imprimés à gogo : Dans la chambre d'amis de leur maison à Brooklyn, John Loecke et Jason Oliver Nixon ont opté pour l'exubérance. Le fauteuil fait partie de leur ligne de mobilier Madcap Cottage Custom. *Photographed by John Bessler, page 164ff.*

DU CHIC NEUTRE FAÇON GALERIE D'ART AU CLASSIQUE DÉJANTÉ OU AU NÉO-MINIMALISME, CES DÉCORS INVENTENT LEURS PROPRES RÈGLES

La peinture circulaire de Marc Quinn en couverture de ce livre ressemble à un soleil vibrant, mais c'est en réalité un portrait, ou plutôt la représentation minutieuse d'un iris humain. Sur le plan symbolique, on ne saurait concevoir image plus juste pour illustrer notre propos. Car le flot incessant d'informations consultées et triées, le besoin de considérer nos actes dans le contexte d'une constellation de semblables, la priorité accordée à l'individualité en tant que source de puissance naturelle – bref, tout ce qui rend notre ère numérique planétaire si novatrice, et parfois si stressante – affectent également la manière de concevoir les beaux intérieurs. Fini le temps où il suffisait d'un regard dans les demeures de nos voisins fortunés pour savoir comment meubler la nôtre. Aujourd'hui, nous avons le monde entier pour nous inspirer, ainsi que toute l'Histoire. La gamme d'options décoratives est aujourd'hui gigantesque. Nous pourrions être tentés de contourner une telle complexité en donnant carte blanche à un spécialiste ; mais si l'on s'en tient à l'avis du grand décorateur Jacques Grange, qui préfère travailler « avec » plutôt que « pour » ses célèbres clients les Coppola, cette alternative appartient au passé.

Les pages qui suivent présentent de nombreux projets réalisés en tandem par des clients créatifs et leurs décorateurs, ainsi que de nombreux agencements d'espaces, de meubles et d'œuvres d'art qui brouillent les frontières de la géographie et du temps. On y découvre, entre autres, un appartement berlinois dont les poutres apparentes évoquent Venise ; des chaises de Kaare Klint dans une salle à manger indienne ; et un loft new-yorkais qui, avec son mélange de *shôji*, de bois et d'imprimés fleuris, rappelle l'innocence raffinée de la résidence de Charles et Ray Eames à Pacific Palisades.

Je remercie les décorateurs, les photographes, les stylistes et leurs agents qui ont rendu possible ce troisième volume de la collection *Interiors Now* de TASCHEN. Pour ceux dont les projets ne figurent pas ici, ce n'est que partie remise. J'exprime également toute ma gratitude aux propriétaires qui ont accepté de partager leur sanctuaire avec des professionnels et des amateurs de décoration du monde entier. Les séances de photos sont parfois perturbantes pour les occupants des lieux, à l'instar du chat de Tiina Laakkonen et de Jon Rosen, dont la queue dépasse sous la table basse en page 146. Cher Monkey, pardonne-nous cette intrusion, c'était pour une très bonne cause.　　MARGIT J. MAYER

◀　White walls and minimalistic furniture bring serenity to the library of Peter Heimer's Berlin apartment. A black-and-white photo by Martin Boyce hangs above a Clemens Tissi *Lichtkiste* lamp. • Der Bibliothek in Peter Heimers Apartment in Berlin geben weiße Wände und Minimal-Mobiliar gelassene Klarheit. Eine Schwarz-Weiß-Fotografie von Martin Boyce hängt über einer *Lichtkiste* von Clemens Tissi. • Les murs blancs et le mobilier minimaliste créent une atmosphère sereine dans la bibliothèque de l'appartement berlinois de Peter Heimer. Une photo en noir et blanc de Martin Boyce est accrochée au-dessus d'un luminaire *Lichtkiste* de Clemens Tissi. *Photographed by Achim Hatzius, styled by Stephan Meyer, page 108ff.*

CONTENT

FOREWORD	4
JONATHAN ADLER & SIMON DOONAN THEIR WEEKEND GETAWAY ON SHELTER ISLAND	12
TATIANA BILBAO AN APARTMENT IN MEXICO CITY THAT HONORS LATIN AMERICAN MODERNISM	24
JAVIER CARRASCO GONZÁLEZ & JUAN DE MAYORALGO A GUESTHOUSE IN LISBON	32
ALEX COCHRANE A SMARTLY RENOVATED HISTORIC BOATHOUSE IN BERKSHIRE, U.K.	42
CHRISTOPHER COLEMAN & ANGEL SANCHEZ THEIR DUPLEX IN BROOKLYN	50
FRANCIS D'HAENE A LODGE IN MONTANA	58
JOSEPH DIRAND AN APARTMENT IN PARIS	68
MARINA FAUST HER *ATELIERWOHNUNG* IN VIENNA	78
MICHAEL FUCHS HIS APARTMENT IN A MONUMENT OF 1920s JEWISH BERLIN	88
ALAIN GILLES HIS FAMILY HOME IN BRUSSELS	98
PIERRE JORGE GONZALEZ & JUDITH HAASE AN APARTMENT FOR ART IN BERLIN	108
JACQUES GRANGE A HOTEL FOR FRANCIS FORD COPPOLA IN BERNALDA, ITALY	116
BIJOY JAIN A WEEKEND RESIDENCE IN HARMONY WITH INDIA'S HERITAGE	126
MATHIAS KISS AN ARTISTIC APARTMENT IN PARIS	136
TIINA LAAKKONEN & JON ROSEN THEIR HOUSE IN AMAGANSETT, LONG ISLAND	144
INEZ VAN LAMSWEERDE & VINOODH MATADIN THEIR COCOON OF COOL IN NEW YORK	152
JOHN LOECKE & JASON OLIVER NIXON THEIR MADCAP HOME IN BROOKLYN	164

SALLY MACKERETH A FLAMBOYANT BACHELOR PAD IN LONDON	176
ADAM McCULLOCH & EMMA SLOLEY THEIR *CASA CÁRDENAS* IN MÉRIDA, MEXICO	186
PAULO MENDES DA ROCHA A CONCRETE HOUSE IN SÃO PAULO	196
DOUG MEYER A TRIUMPH OF D.I.Y. DECORATING IN NEW YORK	208
JOHN MINSHAW A HOUSE IN KENT	218
CECILIA MORELLI PARIKH AN APARTMENT FOR HERSELF AND HER HUSBAND IN MUMBAI	228
MELINDA RITZ A MANSION FOR A FAMILY IN BEVERLY HILLS	238
JOHN ROBSHAW HIS MULTI-CULTI APARTMENT IN NEW YORK	250
BEATRICE ROSSETTI & PIERO GEMELLI THEIR PHOTO-STUDIO-CUM-HOME IN MILAN	258
HECTOR RUIZ VELÁZQUEZ A SMALL WONDER IN MADRID	266
SHAMIR SHAH HIS MULTI-CONTINENTAL FLAT IN NEW YORK	274
LAURENCE SIMONCINI HER RHAPSODY IN GRAY NEAR PARIS	282
FAYE TOOGOOD A SOPHISTICATED RENOVATION IN LONDON	294
JORGE VARELA A HOUSE IN MADRID THAT GIVES ORNAMENT A NEW LEASE OF LIFE	304
BERNHARD WILLHELM A FASHION DESIGNER'S *ROSENHEIM* PIED-À-TERRE IN PARIS	316
PIERRE YOVANOVITCH HIS COOLLY SENSUAL APARTMENT IN PARIS	324
FABIO ZAMBERNARDI HIS "METROPOLITAN RETRO" DUPLEX IN MILAN	334
PHOTOGRAPHERS / DESIGNER CONTACTS	344
IMPRINT	354

JONATHAN ADLER & SIMON DOONAN

THEIR WEEKEND GETAWAY ON SHELTER ISLAND

WHO Adler *(above left)* is a New York-based home-furnishings guru and decorator who started out as a potter. Doonan is creative-ambassador-at-large of Barneys New York department stores and the author of several books on life and style. **WHAT** A 307 m² (3,300 sq. ft.), three-bedroom, new-built bungalow. **WHERE** On the Atlantic shore of Shelter Island. **COLLABORATORS** The pair worked with the Connecticut firm Gray Organschi Architecture ("kindred spirits") and Hamptons builder Carlos Routh ("enthusiastic, intelligent, patient"). **BIG HONOR** In 2009, Doonan was invited by President Obama and the First Lady to decorate the White House for the holidays. **TV FAME** Adler was a judge on the Bravo show *Top Design.* Doonan's memoir, *Beautiful People,* was adapted into a BBC series. **FOUR-LEGGED FRIEND** When naming their perky Norwich terrier, "Liberace", the couple—who were married in California in 2008—had a not-so-hidden agenda: "It's important to keep alive the memory of eccentric funsters," says Adler.

PHOTOGRAPHED BY RICHARD POWERS   PRODUCTION BY DOMINIC BRADBURY

13 Adler created the retro-style fireplace with its conical steel hood and concrete base. Sheepskins are draped over a pair of 1950s wicker-and-iron chairs from the Paris flea market. • Adler entwarf den Retro-Kamin mit Betonsockel und kegelförmiger Stahl-Esse. Schaffelle bedecken zwei Korbstühle auf Eisenkufen aus den 1950er-Jahren vom Pariser Flohmarkt. • La cheminée rétro avec sa hotte conique en acier et sa base en béton sont des créations d'Adler. Les chaises des années 1950 en osier et en fer ont été dénichées aux Puces de Paris.

◄ He also put his talents to good use on a terrace with views of Gardiners Bay. The ceramic wall and cushions are all his design. • Von seiner Kreativität profitierte auch eine Terrasse mit Blick auf die Gardiners Bay: Keramikwand und Kissen sind selbst designt. • Pour la terrasse donnant sur Gardiners Bay, Adler a dessiné le mur en céramique et les coussins.

▲ In one corner of the living room, a vintage burled live-edge table and a 1960s armchair bought in Palm Beach stand on a Peruvian wool rug by Adler. • Im Wohnzimmer stehen ein Vintage-Tisch aus Wurzelholz und ein Sixties-Sessel aus Palm Beach auf einem Adler-Teppich aus peruanischer Wolle. • Dans le séjour, une table basse en bois brut et un fauteuil des années 1960 acheté à Palm Beach sur un tapis en laine péruvienne dessiné par Adler.

16–17 The sofa, brass coffee tables, and aerated concrete screen of the conversation pit are all custom. The yellow cone lights are another Paris find. • Sofa, Messingtischchen und der Raumteiler aus Schaumbeton wurden eigens für die Sitzsenke angefertigt. Die gelben Pendelleuchten sind Fundstücke aus Paris. • Le canapé, les tables basses en laiton et la cloison en béton du coin salon sont des créations personnelles. Les suspensions jaunes ont été dénichées à Paris.

▲ In one of the guestrooms, a Leila Jeffreys photo of a budgerigar watches over a ceramic gramophone and the *Whitaker* chair and ottoman by Adler. • In einem der Gästezimmer wacht ein Wellensittich – eine Fotografie von Leila Jeffreys – über ein Keramik-Grammofon und Adlers *Whitaker*-Stuhl. • Dans une chambre d'amis, une perruche photographiée par Leila Jeffreys contemple, un gramophone en céramique ainsi que le fauteuil *Whitaker* d'Adler et son repose-pieds.

▶ New York-based artist and designer John-Paul Philippé painted a stylized bird motif onto the kitchen counter. The collection of animals is glass. • Der New Yorker Künstler und Designer John-Paul Philippé malte ein stilisiertes Vogelmotiv auf die Küchentheke. Darauf eine Glas-Menagerie. • L'artiste et designer new-yorkais, John-Paul Philippé, a peint des oiseaux stylisés sur le comptoir de la cuisine envahi par une collection d'animaux en verre.

◄ *(clockwise)* Richard Schultz furniture by Knoll on the dining terrace; the master bathroom features the artwork *Mishegas* (Yiddish for "crazy") by Danny Balgley; a blue Adler console and rug give a maritime Pop feel to one guest room; in the master bedroom, an exotic feather headdress serves as a wall sculpture. • *(im Uhrzeigersinn)* Richard-Schultz-Möbel von Knoll auf der Essterrasse; im Bad erfreut morgens Danny Balgleys Arbeit *Mishegas* (Jiddisch für „verrückt"); Sideboard und Teppich in Blau, beide von Adler, geben einem der Gästezimmer maritimen Pop-Look; im Schlafzimmer wurde ein exotischer Feder-Kopfputz zur Wandplastik. • *(Dans le sens des aiguilles d'une montre)* Meubles de Richard Schultz pour Knoll sur la terrasse ; dans la salle de bains principale, une œuvre de Danny Balgley, *Mishegas* (« folie » en yiddish) ; la commode et le tapis bleus d'Adler donnent à l'une des chambres d'amis un look à la fois pop et marin ; une coiffe en plumes devenue sculpture murale dans la chambre principale.

▲ Black beauty: for the couple, the charcoal exterior helps the house blend in with the surroundings. • *Black Beauty:* Dank kohlschwarzer Außenhaut verschmilzt das Haus besser mit der Umgebung, findet das Paar. • « Noir, c'est noir » : grâce à ses murs anthracite, la maison se fond dans son environnement.

22 A chandelier from Rewire gallery in Los Angeles hangs above a set of vintage Warren Platner chairs and Adler's *Ravello* cocktail table with crackle-glass tile inlay. The daybed is another of his designs. • Ein Lüster aus der Galerie Rewire in Los Angeles hängt über Vintage-Sesseln von Warren Platner und Adlers Cocktailtisch *Ravello* mit einer Mosaikplatte aus Craquelé-Fliesen. Das Daybed ist ebenfalls sein Entwurf. • Un lustre de la galerie Rewire est suspendu au-dessus de sièges de Warren Platner ; la table basse *Ravello* avec sa plaque en céramique incrustée et le lit de repos sont d'Adler.

"THIS HOUSE SITS ON THE MOST QUINTESSENTIALLY PERFECT SPOT I COULD EVER IMAGINE." JONATHAN ADLER

"I was attracted to the location because I'm a human being," states Adler. With its sweeping sea views, the site of his and Simon Doonan's retro-fun getaway on Shelter Island is breathtaking. The house itself is also quite something. Its inspirations include Adler's parents' Scandinavian-style home, "Big Sur bohemian," and "rich Ibiza hippie." The couple, meanwhile, decided to paint the exterior black as a wink to houses in Japan. "Our neighbor likened the result to Darth Vader's coffin," quips Doonan. For the interiors, they wanted something innately casual. Adler describes the result as "dreamy, rustic, low-tech, and luxe." "It's every designer's dream to build a house," he adds. "It was a magical project for me." He created many pieces himself and counteracted the austere exterior with warm colors, mixing in vintage finds and family heirlooms. Chief among them is a hanging sculpture fondly named *Granny's Dangler* as it once belonged to his grandmother.

„Dieses Haus liegt an der absolut idealsten Stelle, die man sich nur vorstellen kann", da ist sich Jonathan Adler sicher. „Ich habe mich hier sofort wohlgefühlt, einfach weil ich ein menschliches Wesen bin." Tatsächlich bietet das Grundstück, auf dem er und Simon Doonan ihr Getaway errichtet haben, ein atemberaubendes Meerespanorama. Und erst das Haus! Sein Retro-Fun-Look verbindet so unterschiedliche Einflüsse wie den skandinavischen Stil von Adlers Elternhaus, Boheme à la Big Sur und den Chic reicher Ibiza-Hippies um 1970. Den schwarzen Außenanstrich hingegen übernahm das Paar von japanischer Architektur. „Unser Nachbar fühlt sich davon an Darth Vaders Sarg erinnert", lacht Doonan. Die Einrichtung sollte möglichst unkompliziert sein – Adler nennt sie „verträumt, rustikal, *low-tech* und luxuriös". Und setzt hinzu: „Jeder Designer träumt davon, ein Haus zu bauen. Es war ein magisches Projekt für mich." Viele Möbel entwarf er selbst, setzte der strengen Fassade warme Farben entgegen und rundete das Ganze mit Vintage-Funden und Erbstücken ab. Der Star unter letzteren ist *Granny's Dangler*, eine Hängeskulptur aus dem Besitz seiner Großmutter.

« On ne pourrait imaginer un emplacement plus parfait. Quel être humain y résisterait ? », déclare Jonathan Adler. Le refuge au charme rétro plein d'humour qu'il partage avec son compagnon Simon Doonan sur Shelter Island jouit, certes, de vues éblouissantes sur la mer. La maison, tout aussi exceptionnelle, mêle les influences scandinaves de la demeure des parents d'Adler à l'esprit « bohème californien » et « hippy chic d'Ibiza ». L'extérieur a été peint en noir, clin d'œil aux maisons japonaises. « Notre voisin trouve que ça ressemble au cercueil de Darth Vader », s'amuse Doonan. L'intérieur est, selon Adler, « onirique, rustique, simple et luxueux ». « Ce fut pour moi un projet magique. Tout décorateur rêve de bâtir sa propre maison. » Il a contrebalancé l'austérité de la façade avec des couleurs chaudes, des pièces de son cru, des trouvailles chinées et des objets de famille, dont le clou est une sculpture suspendue qui appartenait jadis à sa grand-mère, baptisée le « pendouillis de mémé ».

TATIANA BILBAO

AN APARTMENT IN MEXICO CITY THAT HONORS LATIN AMERICAN MODERNISM

WHO Mexican architect. **WHAT** A 220 m² (2,368 sq. ft.), three-bedroom apartment in a 1946 building designed by Mario Pani. **WHERE** In the central neighborhood of Polanco. **CAPITAL CHOICE** Bilbao loves the vibe of Mexico City. To experience it fully, she installed her offices on its main artery, Paseo de la Reforma. **FAMILY FIRST** Her sister, Catia, is both a partner in her firm and its financial director. **ON THE GROUND** Her projects to date have included a botanic garden in Culiacan and a funeral home in San Luis Potosi. Several of her models and sketches have been acquired by Centre Pompidou in Paris. **IN THE SKIES** Bilbao calculates she has clocked up over 1 million kilometers (620 thousand miles) of travel for her work. Her favorite airline? "Lufthansa. It's comfortable, always very clean, and as straightforward as many Germans."

PHOTOGRAPHED BY CHRISTIAN SCHAULIN   PRODUCED BY KERSTIN ROSE   PORTRAIT BY ALBERTO GIULIANI

25 Bilbao made the wood veneer pendant in the foyer herself. • Die Pendelleuchte im Entree fertigte Bilbao selbst aus Furnierstreifen. • Bilbao a réalisé elle-même le lustre en placage de bois du vestibule.

▲ Visitors access the building via a garden that still has its original paths. • Den Vorgarten durchziehen noch die originalen Wege. • Le jardin qui mène au bâtiment a conservé ses allées d'origine.

▶ Furnishings in the living room include a vintage Mexican sofa and cocktail table, a Paola Lenti rug and Héctor Esrawe's bench. Cantera fireplace, 1940s. • Sofa und Tisch vor dem Cantera-Kamin sind mexikanisches Vintage, die Bank ist von Héctor Esrawe. Teppich von Paola Lenti. • Dans le séjour, une table basse et un canapé mexicains vintage, un tapis de Paola Lenti et un banc « mille-pattes » d'Héctor Esrawe. La cheminée en pierre volcanique date des années 1940.

◄ Bright and white: "I like clean things," explains Bilbao, and this kitchen proves it. The concrete counter with embedded gas range was cast on site. • *Bright and white*: „Ich mag es *clean*", erklärt Bilbao – diese Küche belegt es. Die Betontheke mit eingefügtem Gasfeld wurde vor Ort gegossen. • Blanc et lumineux : « J'aime les espaces nets », déclare Bilbao. La cuisine en est l'illustration même. Le comptoir en ciment avec la gazinière intégrée a été moulé sur place.

▲ Iconic Brazilian furniture by Joaquim Tenreiro inspired the forms of the custom Tzalam wood dining table and chairs. Pendant by Verner Panton. • Joaquim Tenreiros brasilianische Klassiker waren Inspiration für den eigens getischlerten Esstisch mit Stühlen aus Tzalam-Holz. Lüster von Verner Panton. • Le mobilier emblématique du designer brésilien Joaquim Tenreiro a inspiré les formes de la table et des chaises en bois de tzalam. Le lustre est de Verner Panton.

31   The walnut of the headboard contrasts with the original Monteclaro parquet in the master bedroom. "There were very few places in the flat to store things," says Bilbao, who decided to add the shelving, which continues into the dressing room to the right. • Das Nussbaumholz des Betthaupts kontrastiert im Masterbedroom mit dem originalen Monteclaro-Parkett. „Es gab in der Wohnung nur sehr wenig Stauraum", bemerkt Bilbao. Sie fügte deshalb ein Regal ein, das sich in der Ankleide (rechts) fortsetzt. • Dans la chambre principale, la tête de lit en noyer contraste avec le beau parquet d'origine. « Il y avait peu d'espace de rangement », explique Bilbao. Les étagères qui s'étirent jusque dans le dressing contigu sont des ajouts.

"THE BUILDING IS BY MARIO PANI – FOR ME, MEXICO'S MOST IMPORTANT MODERNIST ARCHITECT." TATIANA BILBAO

"It's a sexy, super-interesting building," Bilbao continues. Although Pani became famous as an urbanist who planned multistory blocks for 15,000 residents, this project was for the genteel middle class. Commissioned by the son of a Supreme Court judge, it houses six nearly identical flats—two per floor, each a mirror image of the other. Bilbao loves the way it mixes Art Deco with Functionalism, sensuous curves with rationalist straight lines. "Pani's interiors are very well thought out," the architect asserts. Thus, when she restored one of the units, she decided to keep as many original details as possible. These include a Cantera stone fireplace wall and the most vivid feature—the Monteclaro wood floors. She sanded and polished the latter, installed a new kitchen and bathrooms, and added storage. Walls were left starkly white in keeping with Pani's original intent and furnishings chosen with care. As Bilbao says, "The space itself is so strong, it doesn't need much."

„Das Haus hat Mario Pani gebaut – für mich Mexikos wichtigster Architekt der Moderne", sagt Tatiana Bilbao. „Es ist extrem interessant." Pani, der sich mit für 15 000 Bewohner konzipierten, vielstöckigen Blocks eher als Stadtplaner einen Namen machte, entwarf hier für die bürgerliche Mittelklasse. Das Gebäude besteht aus sechs Einheiten – je zwei pro Etage, spiegelverkehrt, doch sonst nahezu identisch geschnitten. Bilbao gefällt, wie sich Art déco und Funktionalismus verbinden, sinnliche Kurven und gerade Linien. „Panis Ausstattung ist sehr durchdacht", meint die Architektin. Als sie das Apartment renovierte, erhielt sie deshalb viele Originaldetails, darunter den Kamin aus Cantera-Vulkanstein und – auffälligstes Element – das Monteclaro-Parkett. Sie ließ es polieren, baute Küche und Bad neu ein und erweiterte den Stauraum. Die Räume wurden, wie schon bei Pani, weiß gestrichen und sorgsam möbliert. „Die Architektur ist so stark", meint Bilbao, „sie braucht nicht viel."

« C'est un bâtiment super intéressant construit par Mario Pani qui est, selon moi, le plus grand architecte moderniste du Mexique », déclare Tatiana Bilbao. Si Pani s'est rendu célèbre comme urbaniste pour avoir conçu de grands ensembles d'habitation pour 15 000 personnes, cet immeuble-ci s'adressait à une classe moyenne raffinée. Commandé par le fils d'un juge de la Cour suprême, il accueille six appartements quasi identiques sur trois étages. Bilbao adore la façon dont il marie Art déco et fonctionnalisme, courbes sensuelles et lignes droites rationalistes. « Les intérieurs de Pani sont très bien pensés », explique l'architecte. Dans cette unité, elle a préservé le plus possible les détails originaux, dont une cheminée en pierre volcanique et un précieux parquet de Monteclaro. Bilbao a poncé et verni ce dernier, refait la cuisine et les salles de bains, créé des zones de rangement et choisi le mobilier avec soin. Conformément au concept original de Pani, les murs sont restés blancs. Comme le dit Tatiana Bilbao : « Un espace aussi puissant n'a pas besoin de grand-chose. »

JAVIER CARRASCO GONZÁLEZ & JUAN DE MAYORALGO

A GUESTHOUSE IN LISBON

WHO Lisbon-based Spanish decorating duo. **WHAT** Baixa House, an 18th-century building that was renovated by local architect José Adrião and has been transformed into a guesthouse with 12 serviced apartments, ranging in size from 55–90 m² (592–969 sq. ft.). **WHERE** In the heart of the historic Baixa District. **CLIENT** Spanish landscape designer Jesús Moraime, who owns the hotel. **DAFT FOR CRAFT** De Mayoralgo, *above right,* trained in traditional weaving techniques at a factory in the Alentejo region, while his partner perfected his sewing skills with a Lisbon tailor. **COMPLETED PROJECTS** They include apartments in Madrid and the Swiss Alps, a villa on La Palma in the Canary Islands, and the soberly chic Altair restaurant in Mérida, Spain. **THEIR LISBON TIP** To first-time visitors, Carrasco González, *above left,* recommends a fado cabaret evening in Alfama – "Nothing represents better the spirit of the Portuguese people." De Mayoralgo suggests "a boat trip on the Taj to see the city from a completely different perspective."

PHOTOGRAPHED BY ANA PAULA CARVALHO   STYLING AND PORTRAIT BY MARÍA ULECIA

33 Fluffy *cobertores de papa* blankets made from Iberian sheep wool cover the beds, as here in the Fronteira guest apartment. The 1960s botanical posters come from a German school. • *Cobertores de papa* aus der Wolle einer alten iberischen Schafrasse liegen auf den Betten, hier im Fronteira-Apartment mit alten botanischen Tafeln aus einer deutschen Schule. • Dans la suite Fronteira : *cobertores de papa* en jetés de lit ; au fond des planches botaniques allemandes des années 1960.

▶ In the Principe Real apartment, two outdoor iron chairs stand in front of a photo of jacaranda trees in bloom. Guests can watch the tramway roll by on Rua da Conceiçao. • Zwei Gartenstühle vor einem Foto des Parks, nach dem das Apartment benannt ist: Principe Real. Auf der Rua da Conceiçao rollt die Straßenbahn vorbei. • Dans l'appartement Principe Real, deux chaises de jardin sous une photo de jacarandas. La fenêtre donne sur la Rua da Conceiçao et son tramway.

◀ The two wooden chairs in the Fronteira entry probably belonged to a school. On the first floor, this flat is among the largest of Baixa House and has two bedrooms. • Auch die Stühle im Fronteira-Flur standen wohl einst in einer Schule. Mit zwei Schlafzimmern ist das Apartment im ersten Stock eines der geräumigsten im Haus. • Deux chaises d'école dans l'entrée. Avec ses deux chambres, l'appartement Fronteira, au premier étage, est l'un des plus grands.

▲ Each living room features a striped shepherd's rug. The simple bench, here used as a coffee table, is one of the numerous items the designers found at Lisbon's Feira da Ladra flea market. • In allen Wohnzimmern liegen gestreifte Schäferteppiche. Die Bank, die hier als Tisch dient, entdeckten die Designer auf dem Feira-da-Ladra-Flohmarkt. • Chaque séjour a son tapis en grosse laine. Le banc portugais reconverti en table basse vient du marché aux puces de Lisbonne, la Feira da Ladra.

▶ Keeping with the botanical theme, a Svenskt Tenn wallpaper by Josef Frank decorates the entry of the Bélem apartment. The green bench was found in a Madrid market. • Schon im Entree des Belém-Apartments greift die Josef-Frank-Tapete von Svenskt Tenn das Botanik-Thema auf. Grüne Bank von einem Markt in Madrid. • Un papier peint Svenskt Tenn de Josef Frank décore l'entrée du Bélem. Le banc vert a été chiné sur un marché madrilène.

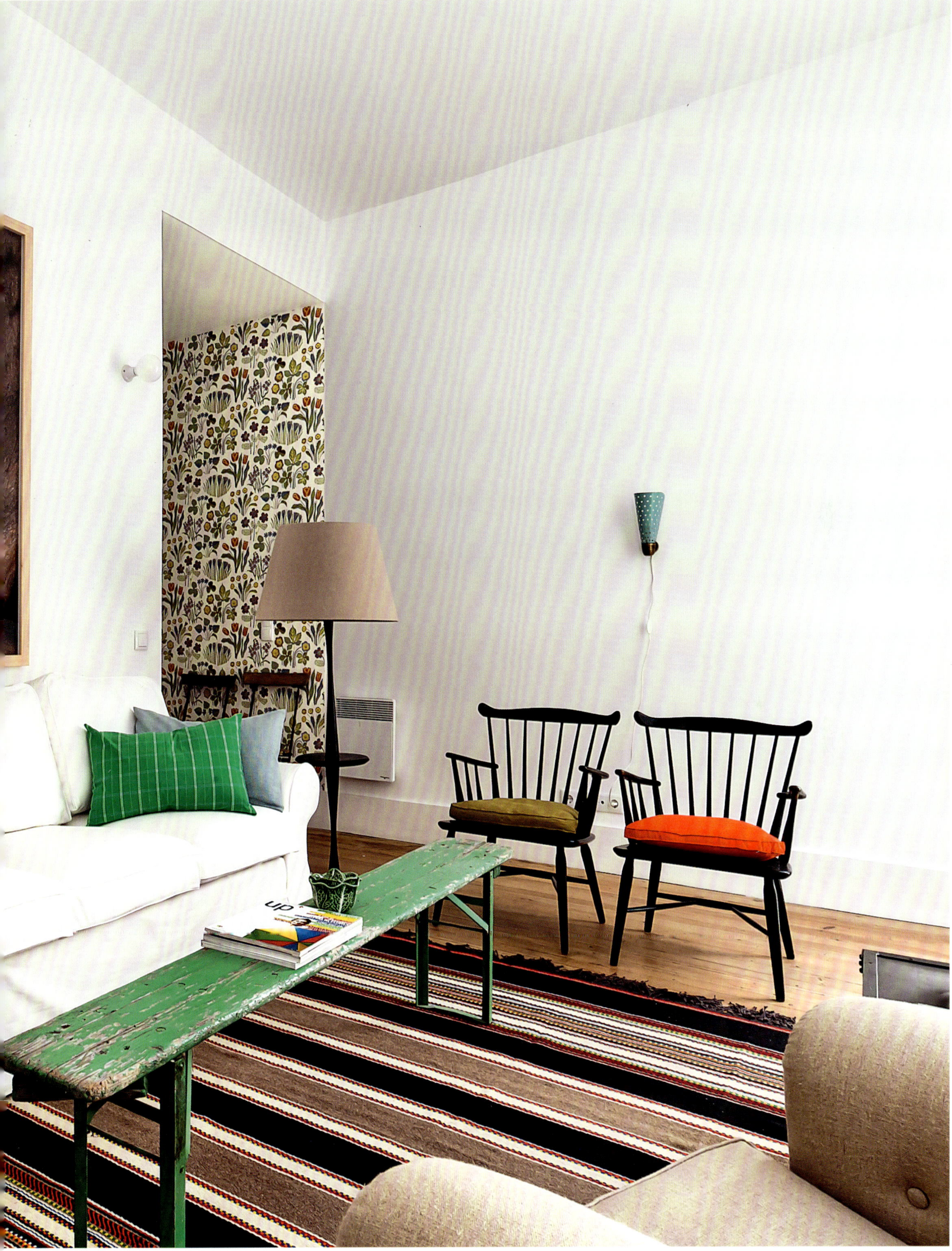

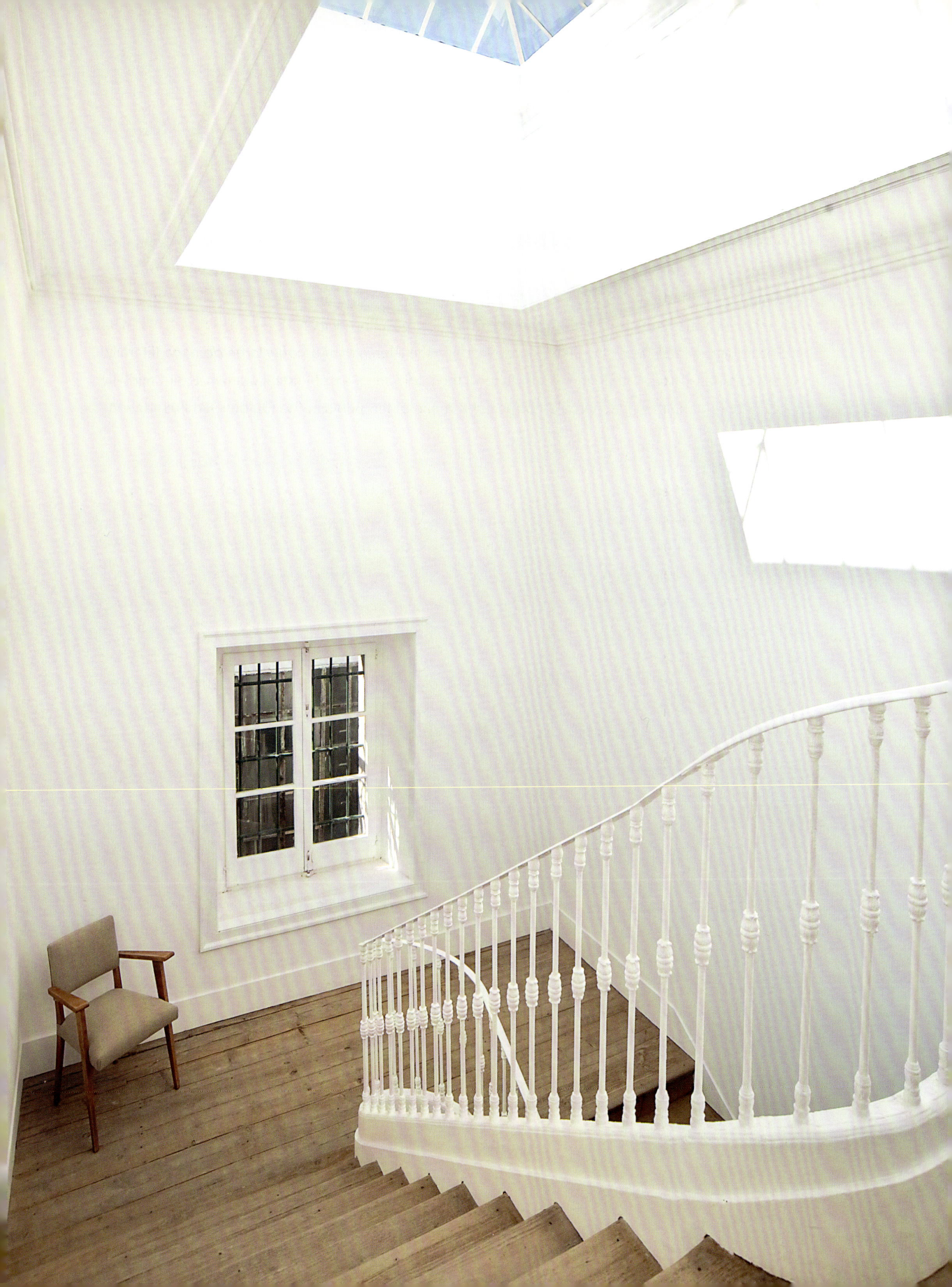

"The idea was that the gardens of Lisbon be represented in these apartments," explains interior designer Juan de Mayoralgo. The horticultural theme is close to the heart of the owner of Baixa House, landscape architect Jesús Moraime. He thought it would be particularly fitting given that the 12-apartment guesthouse is located in the only district of the Portuguese capital without its own public park. With architect José Adrião, he salvaged as many of the building's original features as possible—floorboards, doors, and *azulejos* (handmade tiles)—and highlighted them by painting the walls white. The starting point for the decoration was a series of large-format photos of Lisbon's gardens (each apartment bears the name of one of them). They in turn inspired De Mayoralgo and Carrasco González to integrate outdoor furniture and 1960s botanical posters. There is an emphasis on Portuguese crafts, with shepherd's rugs made in the Alentejo, and *cobertores de papa* (literally father's blankets) from the Beira region. Among the many flea market finds, meanwhile, are midwife stools and iron chairs whose circular forms echo those of the pools at the Gulbenkian Foundation.

„Unser Leitgedanke war, die Gärten von Lissabon in den Interieurs zu spiegeln", erklärt Juan de Mayoralgo – ein Thema ganz nach dem Geschmack von Eigentümer Jesús Moraime. Besonders gefiel dem Landschaftsarchitekten die Idee, weil das Baixa House mit seinen zwölf Gästeapartments im einzigen Viertel ohne öffentlichen Park liegt. Gemeinsam mit Architekt José Adrião bewahrte er viel Originales – Dielen, Türen, *azulejos* – und hob es durch weiße Wände hervor. Ausgangspunkt der Einrichtung waren Moraimes Großformate von Lissabons Gärten; Carrasco González und de Mayoralgo bezogen sich mit Outdoor-Möbeln und botanischen Schautafeln aus den 1960er-Jahren darauf. Eine wichtige Rolle spielte auch traditionelles Handwerk wie gestreifte Schäferteppiche aus Alentejo oder *cobertores de papa*-Decken aus der Gegend um Beira. Unter den vielen Flohmarktfunden sind Hebammenhocker und Eisenstühle, die an die Teiche in der Gulbenkian-Stiftung erinnern.

« LA DÉCORATION INTÉRIEURE REND HOMMAGE AUX JARDINS PUBLICS DE LISBONNE. » JUAN DE MAYORALGO

C'est un thème cher au propriétaire, un paysagiste espagnol nommé Jesús Moraime, d'autant plus que sa *guesthouse* se trouve dans le seul quartier de Lisbonne qui n'en possède pas. Avec l'aide de l'architecte José Adrião, il s'est efforcé de préserver les détails architecturaux d'origine tels que les parquets, les portes et les *azulejos*, mis en valeur par des murs blancs. Les décorateurs Carrasco González et de Mayoralgo sont partis de grandes photographies de jardins de la capitale prises par Moraime (qui ont donné leur nom à chacun des douze appartements), qu'ils ont complétées avec des planches botaniques des années 1960 et des meubles de jardin. Ils ont également mis l'accent sur les matières naturelles et l'artisanat portugais. Les tapis en grosse laine viennent de l'Alentejo, les *cobertores de papa* (couvertures de papa) de la région de Beira. Parmi les nombreux objets chinés ici et là, on remarque des tabourets de sage-femme et des chaises en métal aux formes arrondies qui rappellent les bassins de la Fondation Gulbenkian.

38 So light, so white: sun flows into the main stairwell via a skylight that is original to the late-18th-century building. • So hell, so gut: Das Oberlicht, durch das Sonnenlicht ins Treppenhaus flutet, wurde schon beim Bau des Hauses im 18. Jahrhundert angelegt. • Une idée lumineuse : le soleil inonde la cage d'escalier principale grâce à la verrière d'origine du 18e siècle.

▲ The *azulejos* under the kitchen window in the Alorna apartment date from the 19th century and add graphic interest to all-white contemporary cupboards. • Die *azulejos* aus dem 19. Jahrhundert unter dem Küchenfenster setzen im Alorna-Apartment einen grafischen Kontrapunkt zu den komplett weißen neuen Einbauten. • Dans l'appartement Alorna, les *azulejos* sous la fenêtre de la cuisine au mobilier moderne datent du 19e siècle.

◀ French literature books from the 1970s sit on a shelf whose metal wall supports were found at the Feira da Ladra flea market. • Metallkonsolen vom Flohmarkt tragen das unregelmäßig geformte Holzbord mit Ausgaben französischer Literatur aus den 1970er-Jahren. • Des livres de littérature française des années 1970 sur une étagère fixée par des équerres anciennes chinées à la Feira da Ladra.

◂ A photo that owner Jesús Moraime took of the Jeronimos monastery park hangs in the eponymous apartment above a wicker sofa bought on eBay.
• Das Foto über dem Korbsofa (eine eBay-Trophäe) machte Jesús Moraime im Park des Jerónimos-Klosters, nach dem das Apartment benannt wurde.
• Une photo du monastère Jerónimos prise par Jesús Moraime, le propriétaire, est accrochée dans l'appartement du même nom au-dessus d'un canapé en rotin acheté sur eBay.

ALEX COCHRANE

A SMARTLY RENOVATED HISTORIC BOATHOUSE IN BERKSHIRE, U.K.

WHO A London-based architect. WHAT A 70 m² (753 sq. ft.) weekend retreat for him and his wife on the top floor of an 1820s boathouse, thought to have been designed by George IV's favorite architect, Jeffry Wyatville. WHERE On Virginia Water lake, at the southern edge of Windsor Great Park. PEDIGREE Cochrane spent his early years in the Lebanon. He returned there in 1995 and worked for a year at Pierre El-Khoury Architects before completing his studies at the Architectural Association in London. He is married to Alannah Weston, the Creative Director of Selfridges. ARTISTIC LINKS The couple live in a Chelsea studio once inhabited by painter Augustus John. GREEN CREDENTIALS The boathouse is heated by a lake-generated pump system. SHHHH! Cochrane recently created a "Silence Room" in Selfridges—a no-noise environment meant as an antidote to the hustle and bustle of the department store.

PHOTOGRAPHED BY RACHAEL SMITH©THE WORLD OF INTERIORS   PORTRAIT©ALEX COCHRANE ARCHITECTS

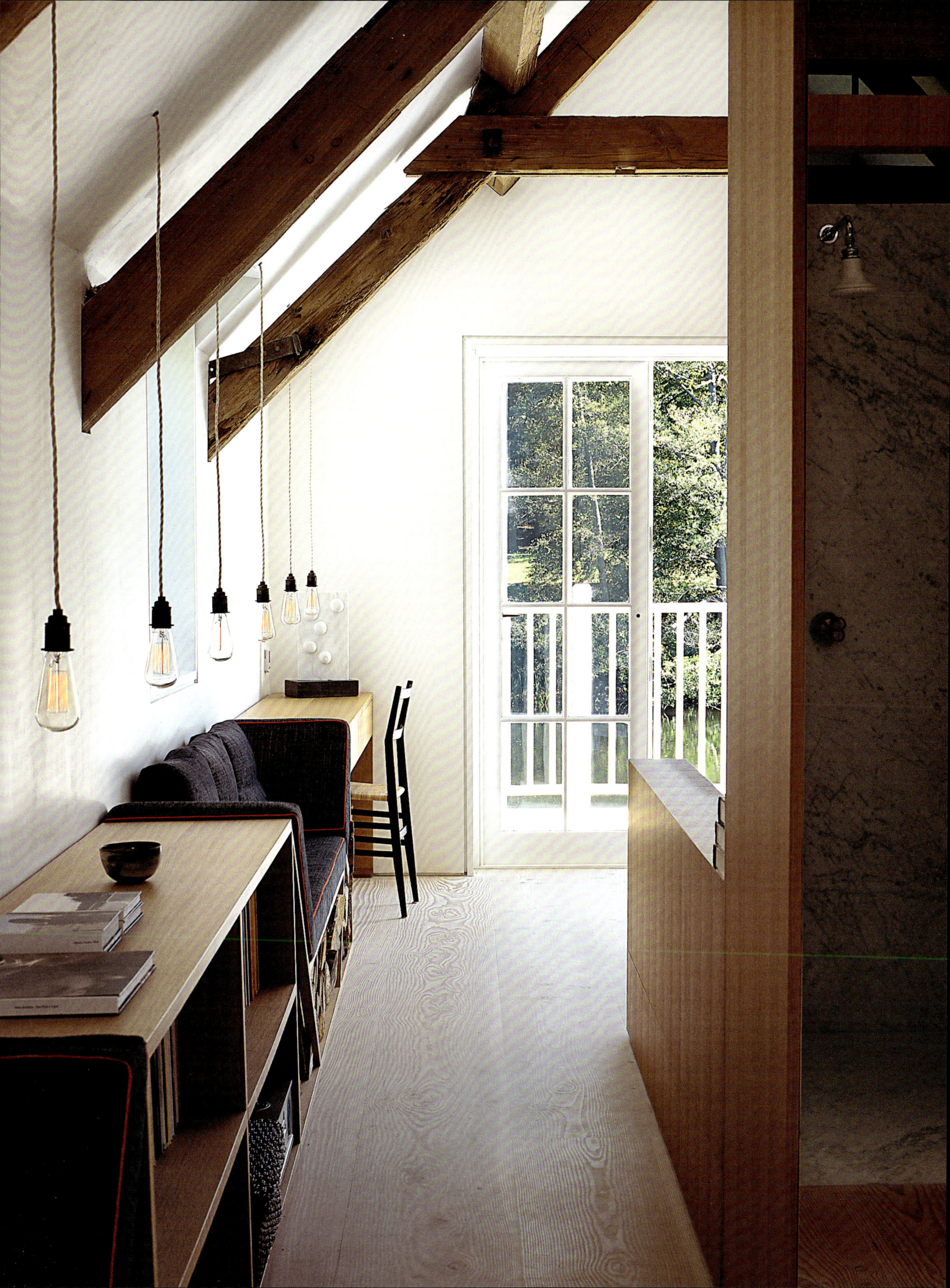

43 A set of bulbs from the Historic Lighting Company hangs above the multipurpose unit, at the end of which stands a small William Peers marble sculpture. • Glühlampen der Historic Lighting Company reihen sich über dem multifunktionalen Einbau; hinten Marmorskulptur von William Peers. • Une série d'ampoules de la Historic Lighting Company sont suspendues au-dessus du long meuble polyvalent au bout duquel se trouve une petite sculpture en marbre de William Peers.

▲ The oak-veneer built-ins were designed to fit underneath the A-frame of the sandblasted original rafters. Ceramics by Fiamma Colonna Montagu. • Die Dachbalken wurden sandgestrahlt und überspannen nun eichenfurnierte Funktionseinheiten. Keramiken von Fiamma Colonna Montagu. • Les modules plaqués en chêne ont été conçus pour se glisser sous la charpente d'origine en A dont les poutres ont été poncées. Les céramiques sont signées Fiamma Colonna Montagu.

◀ View of the boathouse across Virginia Water. When created in 1753, the lake was the largest man-made body of water in England. • Blick auf das Bootshaus über das Virginia Water – 1753 angelegt, war es damals der größte künstliche See in England. • Vue du hangar à bateaux depuis le Virginia Water. Créé en 1753, le lac était alors le plus grand plan d'eau artificiel d'Angleterre.

▶ A seascape photograph entitled *Hurricane* by Clifford Ross hangs above the master bed, which can be easily separated into two chaise longues. • Clifford Ross' Fotografie *Hurricane* hängt über dem Doppelbett, das sich in zwei Chaiselongues aufteilen lässt. • Une photographie de mer de Clifford Ross intitulée *Hurricane* est fixée au-dessus du lit principal, qui peut se séparer facilement pour former deux méridiennes.

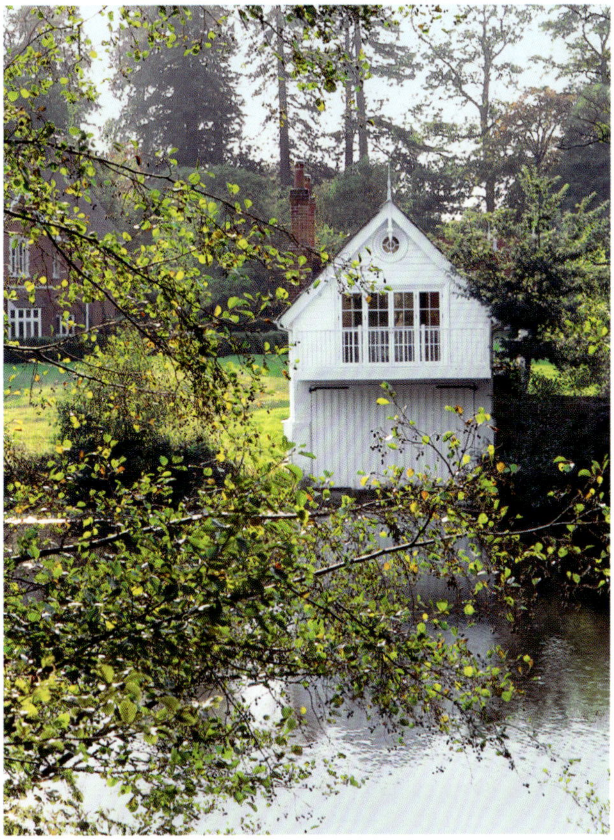

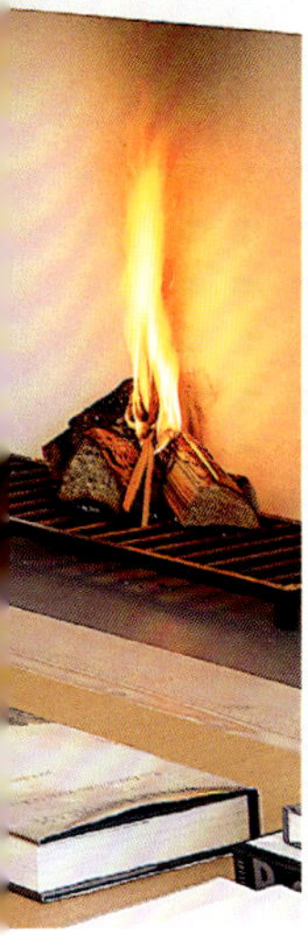

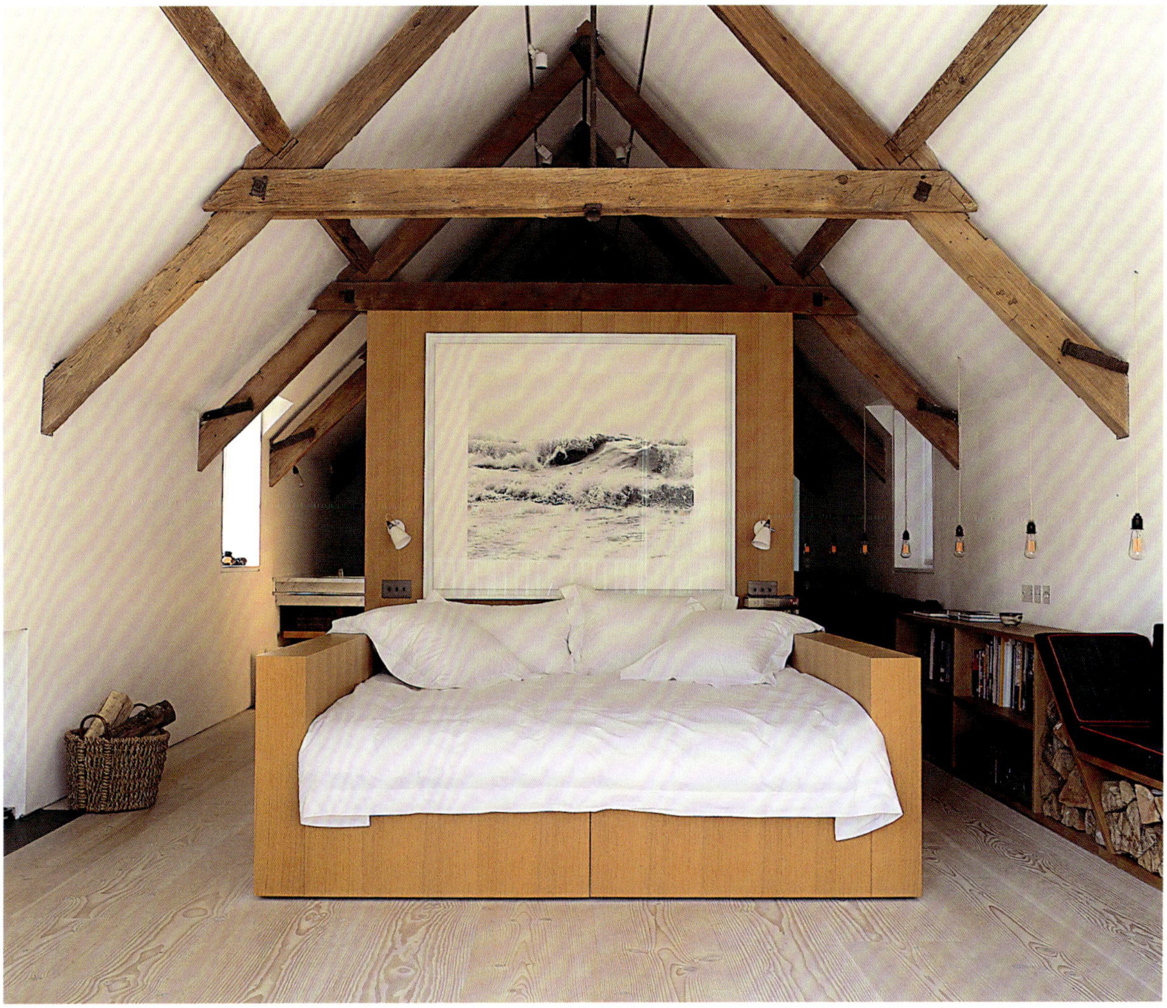

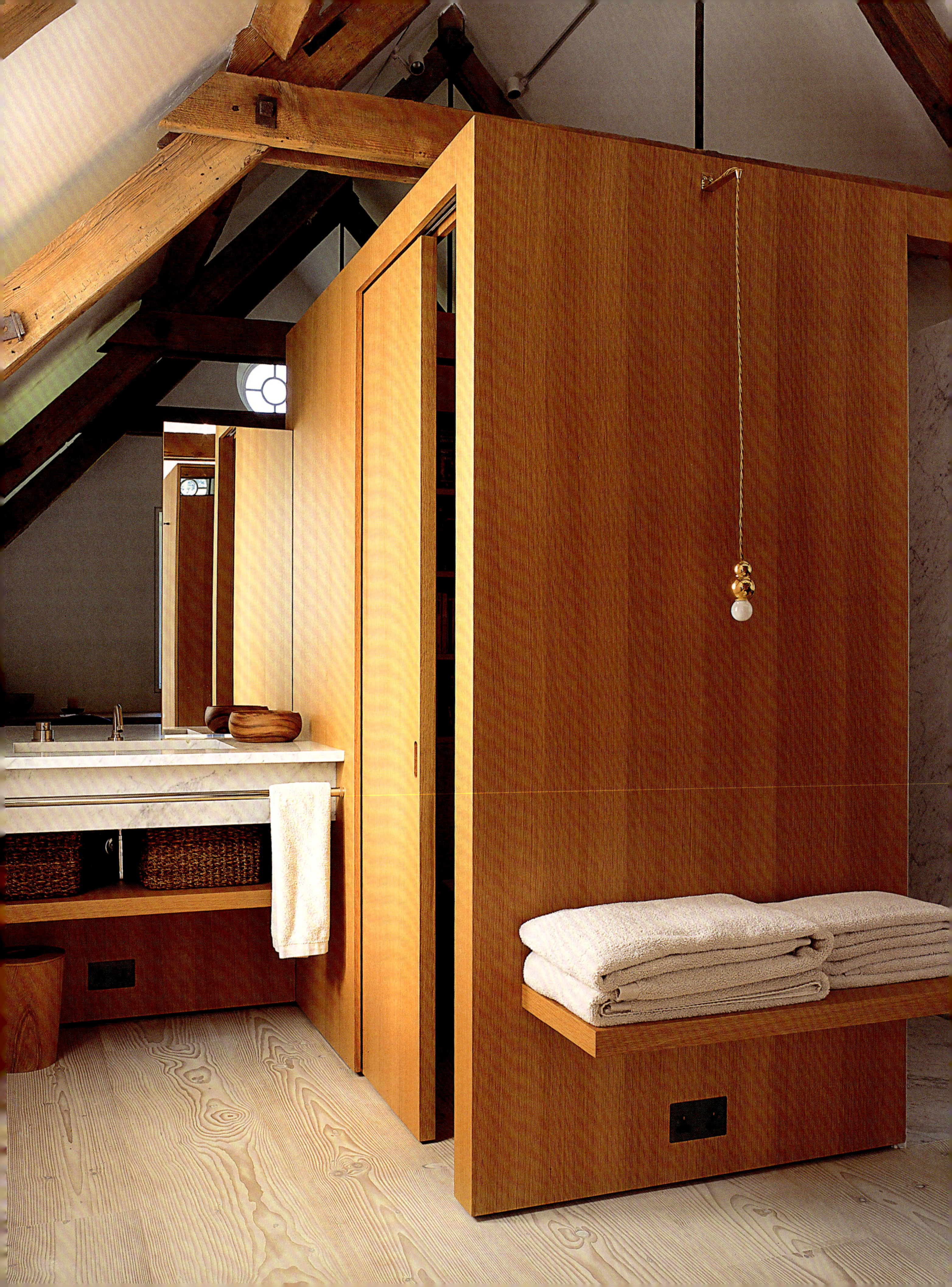

Probably once a dwelling for the royal boat-keeper, the upper floor of this historic building had remained uninhabited for at least 80 years. As architect Alex Cochrane puts it, the space "was previously very compartmentalized and cellular," meaning three pokey, dark rooms. He enlarged the windows, added a balcony (which involved inserting steel beams into the rather flimsy structure), and stripped the interior. In doing so, he discovered a stunning wooden A-frame, which he celebrated by creating an open-plan arrangement. Now there are finely crafted freestanding units, track lighting by Erco, and carefully chosen furnishings. Design classics by Hans Wegner, Norman Cherner, and Gio Ponti join custom-built pieces that often are multi-purpose. The double bed that looks out onto the lake, for instance, can split up into two chaise longues, while a unit running down the whole length of one side provides seating, firewood storage, and a desk. For Cochrane and his wife, Alannah, it's the perfect place to escape to read or write. "Windsor Great Park is a haven of peace and tranquility," he rejoices. "You're 40 minutes from London, but you could easily be hours and hours away."

„LONDON LIEGT NUR 40 AUTOMINUTEN ENTFERNT, ABER HIER IM PARK IST ES SO FRIEDLICH ALS WÄREN ES EINIGE FLUGSTUNDEN." ALEX COCHRANE

In ihrem Häuschen im Windsor Great Park können sich der junge Architekt und seine Frau Alannah wunderbar Auszeiten zum Lesen und Schreiben nehmen. Über 80 Jahre stand der historische Bau, den wohl einst Bootsleute in Diensten Ihrer Majestät bewohnt hatten, zuvor leer. „Kleinteilig und zellenartig" fand Alex Cochrane das Obergeschoss – es bestand aus drei dunklen Kammern. Er vergrößerte die Fenster, fügte einen Balkon an und entfernte Decke und Wände. Der neue offene Grundriss bringt den prächtigen Dachstuhl gut zur Geltung, freistehende Einheiten definieren nun die Wohnbereiche. Erco-Strahler beleuchten Klassiker von Hans Wegner, Norman Cherner und Gio Ponti, die von Maßschreinerei ergänzt werden: Das breite Bett mit Blick auf den See lässt sich in zwei Chaiselongues teilen, und ein langgezogener Einbau vereint Bänke mit Polsterauflagen, eine Schreibtischplatte und Stauraum für Brennholz.

Après avoir probablement hébergé les employés de Sa Majesté chargés de l'entretien des bateaux, le premier étage de ce bâtiment historique est resté inhabité pendant plus de huit décennies. Comme l'explique l'architecte Alex Cochrane, « l'espace était très compartimenté », à savoir, composé de trois pièces minuscules et sombres. Il a agrandi les fenêtres, ajouté un balcon et abattu toutes les cloisons, découvrant une superbe charpente qu'il a mise en valeur en créant un espace ouvert désormais modelé par de beaux modules indépendants, un éclairage sur rail d'Erco et un mobilier parcimonieux. Des éléments sur mesure sont associés à des classiques du design signés Hans Wagner, Norman Cherner ou Gio Ponti. Le grand lit faisant face au lac peut se scinder en deux méridiennes tandis qu'un meuble bas s'étirant tout le long d'un mur sert de banc, de réserve à bûches et de bureau. Pour Cochrane et son épouse Alannah, « le Grand Parc de Windsor est un havre de paix et de tranquillité », un lieu idéal pour la lecture et l'écriture. « On est à quarante minutes de Londres et on se croirait à l'autre bout du monde. »

46 Michael Anastassiades's gold-plated Ball Light lamp hangs above a bench in the bathroom. The Dinesen Douglas fir floors are heated. • Über der Bank im Bad baumelt ein Ball Light von Michael Anastassiades. Die Douglasien-Dielen von Dinesen sind von unten beheizt. • Dans la salle de bains, une suspension Ball Light plaquée or de Michael Anastassiades est placée au-dessus d'un banc. Le plancher en douglas de chez Dinesen cache un chauffage par le sol.

▲ Logs for the two fireplaces are stacked under a sofa bench upholstered in linen from Designers Guild. • Das Brennholz für die beiden offenen Kamine lagert unter der eingebauten Bank; ihre Polster sind mit Leinen von Designers Guild. bezogen • Les bûches servant à alimenter les deux cheminées sont astucieusement stockées sous un canapé tapissé d'un tissu en lin de chez Designers Guild.

◀ Never without books: clever storage solutions include the built-in bookshelves over the toilet. Cochrane used straight-grained American oak throughout. • Nicht ohne meine Bücher: Zu Cochranes cleveren Staulösungen gehören Borde über der Toilette. Alle Einbauten sind aus schlicht gemaserter Eiche. • « Jamais sans mes livres » : une solution de rangement astucieuse dans les W.-C. Dans tout l'appartement, Cochrane a utilisé du chêne américain à fil droit.

▶ The shower is sandwiched between the living and dining areas. Its walls are lined with the same Carrara marble that was used for the washbasin and kitchen counter. • Die Duschnische liegt zwischen Wohn- und Essbereich. Sie ist aus dem gleichen Carrara-Marmor wie Waschtisch und Küchenplatte • La douche est nichée entre le séjour et le coin repas. Ses murs sont revêtus du même marbre de Carrare que le lavabo et le comptoir de la cuisine.

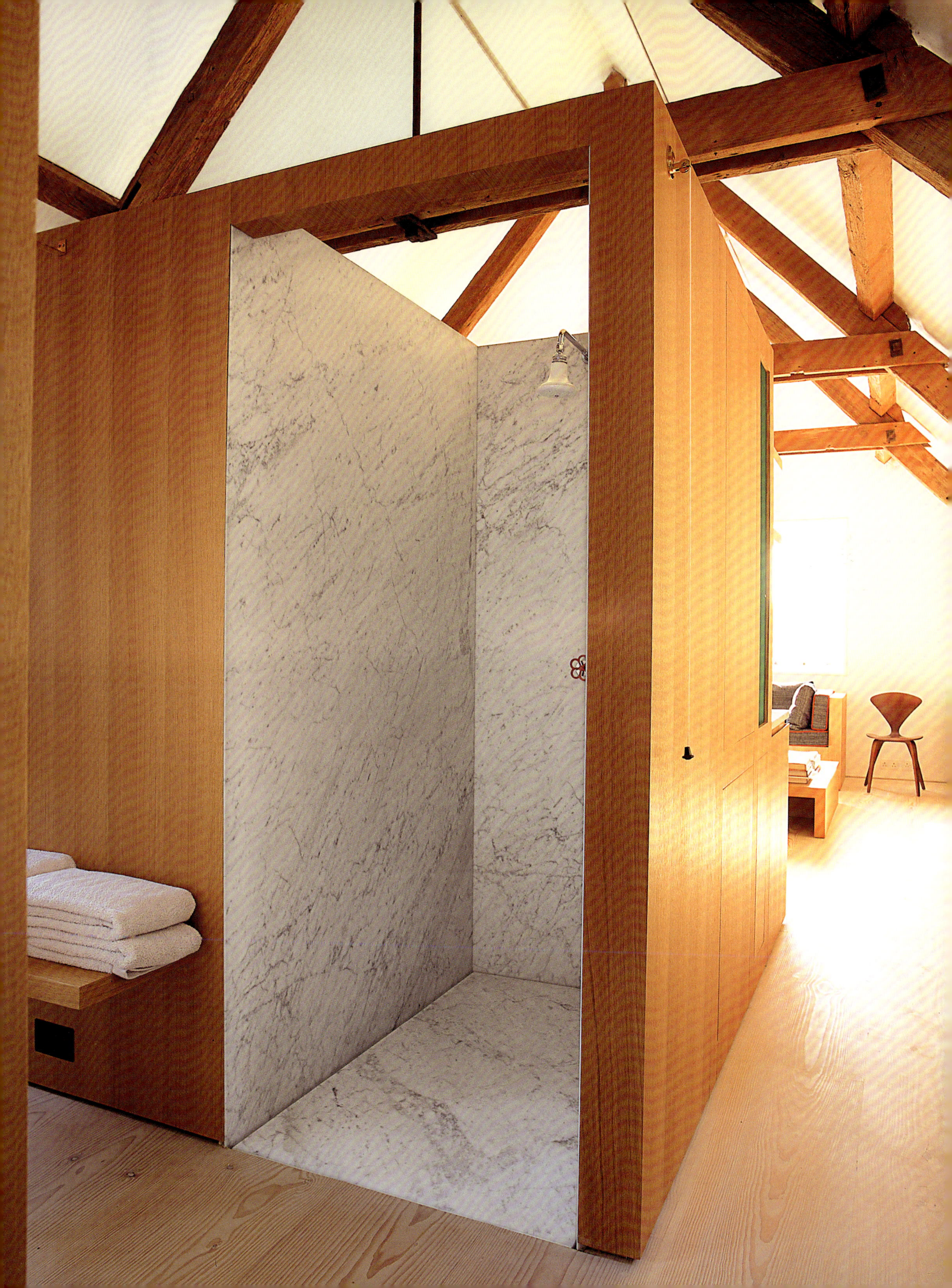

CHRISTOPHER COLEMAN & ANGEL SANCHEZ

THEIR DUPLEX IN BROOKLYN

WHO Coleman, *above right,* is a New York-based decorator; Sanchez is a Venezuela-born fashion designer. **WHAT** A 115 m² (1,237 sq. ft.), one-bedroom flat in a new development. **WHERE** Williamsburg, Brooklyn. **THE NEIGHBORHOOD** Coleman calls it "very hip, very young," adding: "It's got a big music and art community. I always joke that nobody wakes up until 11 o'clock." **CLAIM TO FAME** Sanchez has designed wedding dresses for Sandra Bullock and Eva Longoria. Other fans include Salma Hayek, Giselle Bündchen, Beyoncé, and Iman. **PROJECTS** Coleman has completed residences in New York, the Hamptons, and Martha's Vineyard, plus a table tennis club on 23rd Street in Manhattan. **QUIRKIEST INTERIOR** The pair created a Nurse Jackie-themed room for the Kips Bay showhouse that featured a hospital-style bed and pill-patterned wallpaper.

PHOTOGRAPHED BY JONNY VALIANT/TRIPOD AGENCY   STYLED BY IAN PHILLIPS

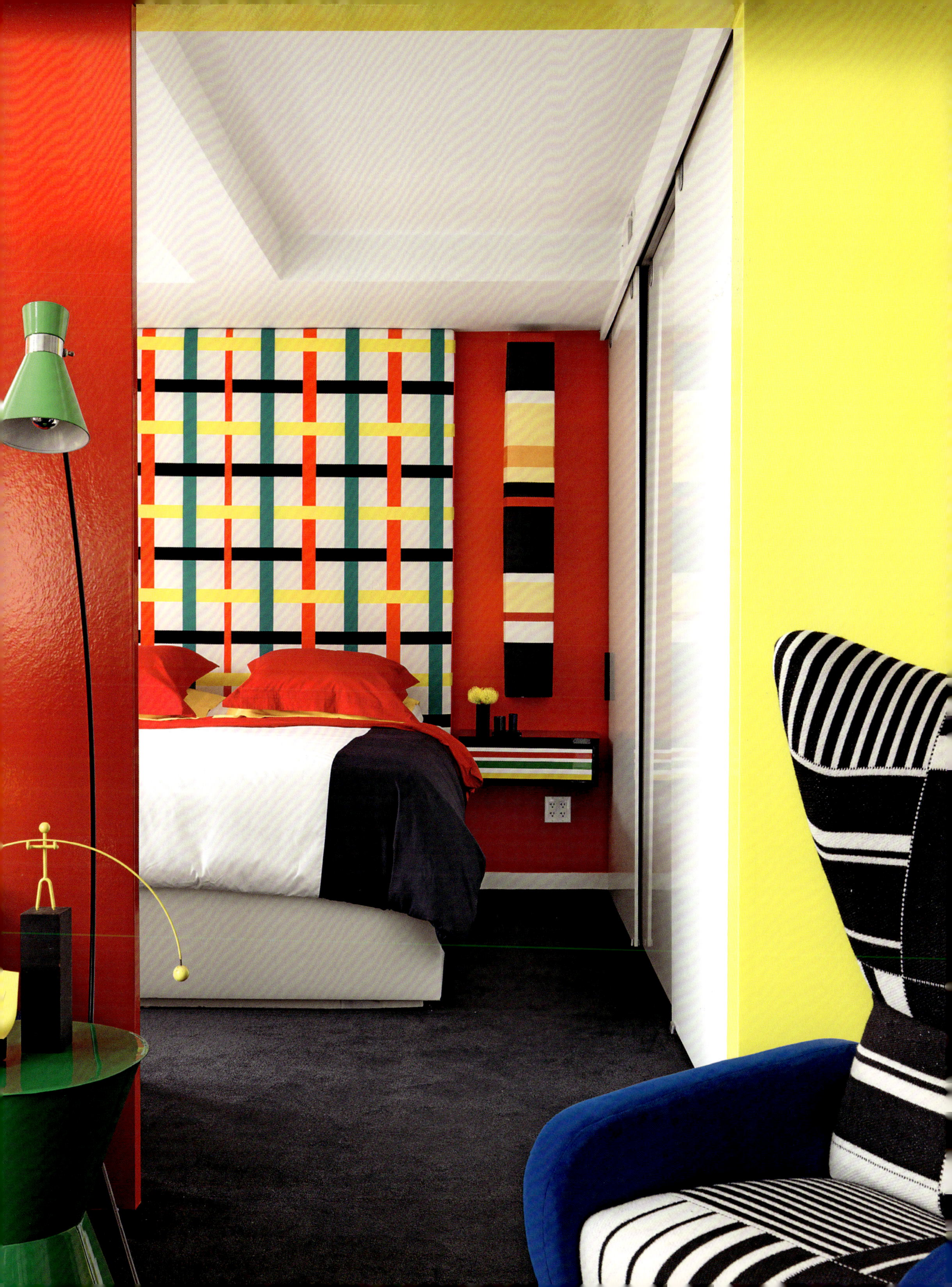

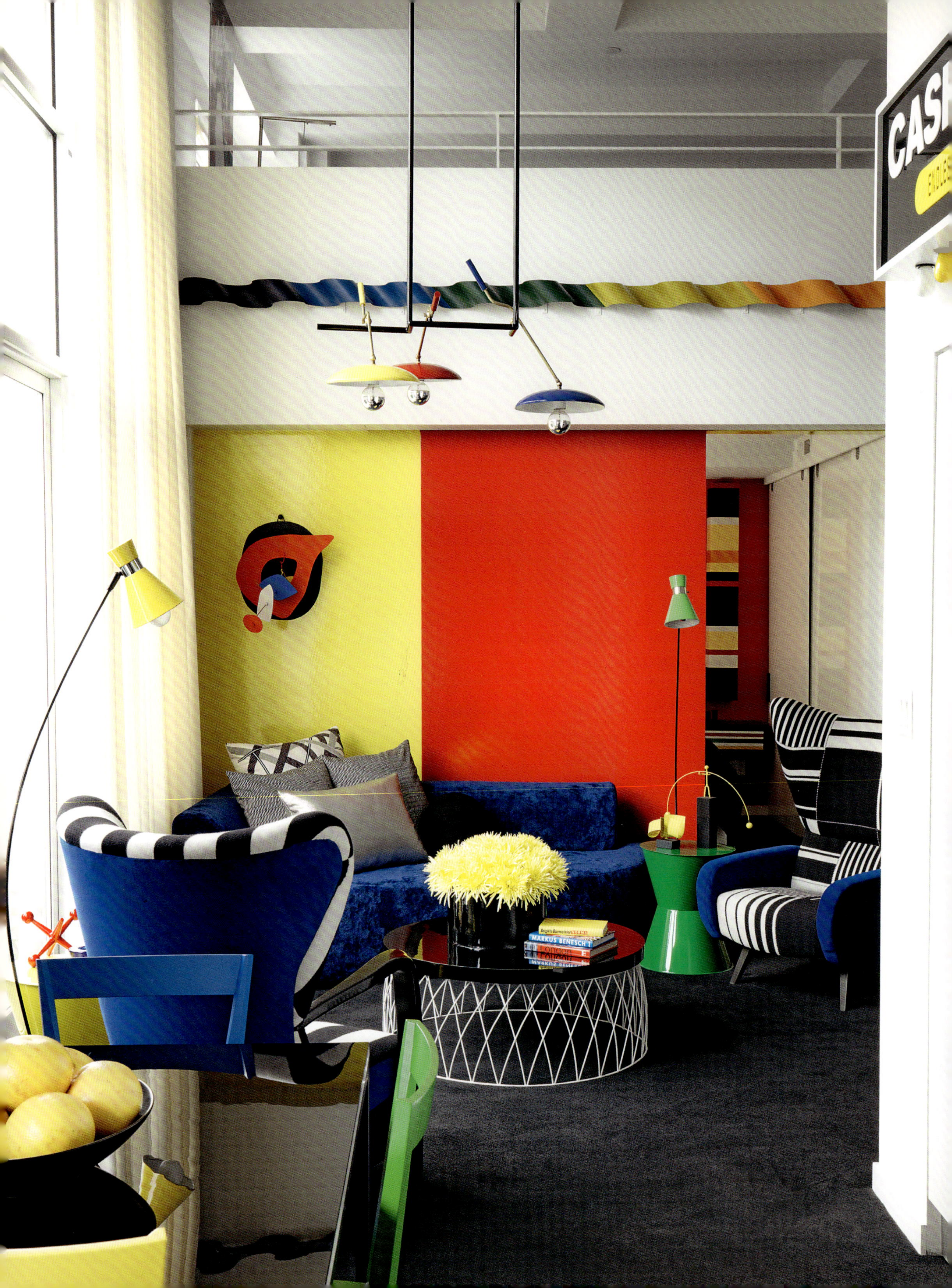
MARKUS BENESCH

51 A view into the bedroom, where Coleman combined patterns. The boxy silk sconces were originally created for a Miami Beach showhouse. • Blick ins Schlafzimmer, dessen Muster sich ergänzen. Die Wandleuchten aus Seide wurden für eine Dekor-Show in Miami Beach entworfen. • Dans la chambre, Coleman a juxtaposé les motifs. À l'origine, les longues appliques en soie ont été conçues pour un décor éphémère à Miami Beach.

◄ Coleman used red and yellow leatherette on the living room walls. The 1950s Czech armchair to the right was covered in a rug he found in the south of France. • Die Wohnzimmerwände sind mit rotem und gelbem Kunstleder verkleidet. Der tschechische Fifties-Sessel rechts ist mit einem Teppich aus Südfrankreich bezogen. • Les murs du séjour sont recouverts de skaï rouge et jaune. Un tapis acheté dans le sud de la France recouvre le fauteuil tchèque des années 1950 (à droite).

▲ The striking wallpaper in the kitchen was designed by Sanchez and produced by Wolf Gordon. Re-edition Gio Ponti chairs from L' Abbate complete the Milanese look. • Die auffällige Tapete in der Küche designte Sanchez für Wolf Gordon. Ponti-Stühle von L' Abbate vervollkommnen den Mailand-Look. • Dessiné par Sanchez, le papier peint de la cuisine a été fabriqué par Wolf Gordon. Des rééditions de chaises de Gio Ponti complètent le look milanais.

▲ At the bottom of the stairs sits the prototype of a screen made by Coleman from colored acrylic blocks. The sliding door leads into the bathroom. • Am Treppenaufgang steht der Prototyp eines Wandschirms, den Coleman aus farbigen Acryl-Fliesen zusammenfügte. Hinter der Schiebetür liegt das Bad. • Au pied de l'escalier, un prototype de paravent réalisé par Coleman avec des carreaux en acrylique coloré. La porte coulissante donne accès à la salle de bains.

◄ Calder, anyone? The playful painted-metal wall sculpture was picked up by the couple in Hudson, New York. • *Calder, anyone?* Die verspielte Wand-Installation aus lackiertem Metall entdeckte das Paar in Hudson, New York. • Vous reprendrez bien un peu de Calder ? Le couple a déniché cette amusante sculpture en métal peint à Hudson, dans l'État de New York.

► In the mezzanine office, an Andrew Martin chair and a collage by German artists C.neeon. The rug was made from old T-shirts by Project Alabama. • Das Mezzanin-Büro mit Sessel von Andrew Martin und Collage des Berliner Modeduos C.Neeon. Teppich aus alten T-Shirts: Project Alabama. • Dans le bureau en mezzanine, un fauteuil d'Andrew Martin et un collage des artistes allemands C.neeon. Le tapis de Project Alabama a été réalisé avec de vieux t-shirts recyclés.

56 Coleman turned a dining table top into a wall panel (left) and placed it above a Jean-Charles de Castelbajac Lucite chair. Carpet from ABC Home. • Coleman machte eine Tischplatte zum Wandpaneel (links), davor ein Acrylglas-Stuhl von Jean-Charles de Castelbajac. Teppich von ABC Home. • Coleman a transformé un plateau de table en panneau mural (à gauche) et l'a placé au-dessus d'un fauteuil en Plexiglas de Jean-Charles de Castelbajac. Tapis d'ABC Home.

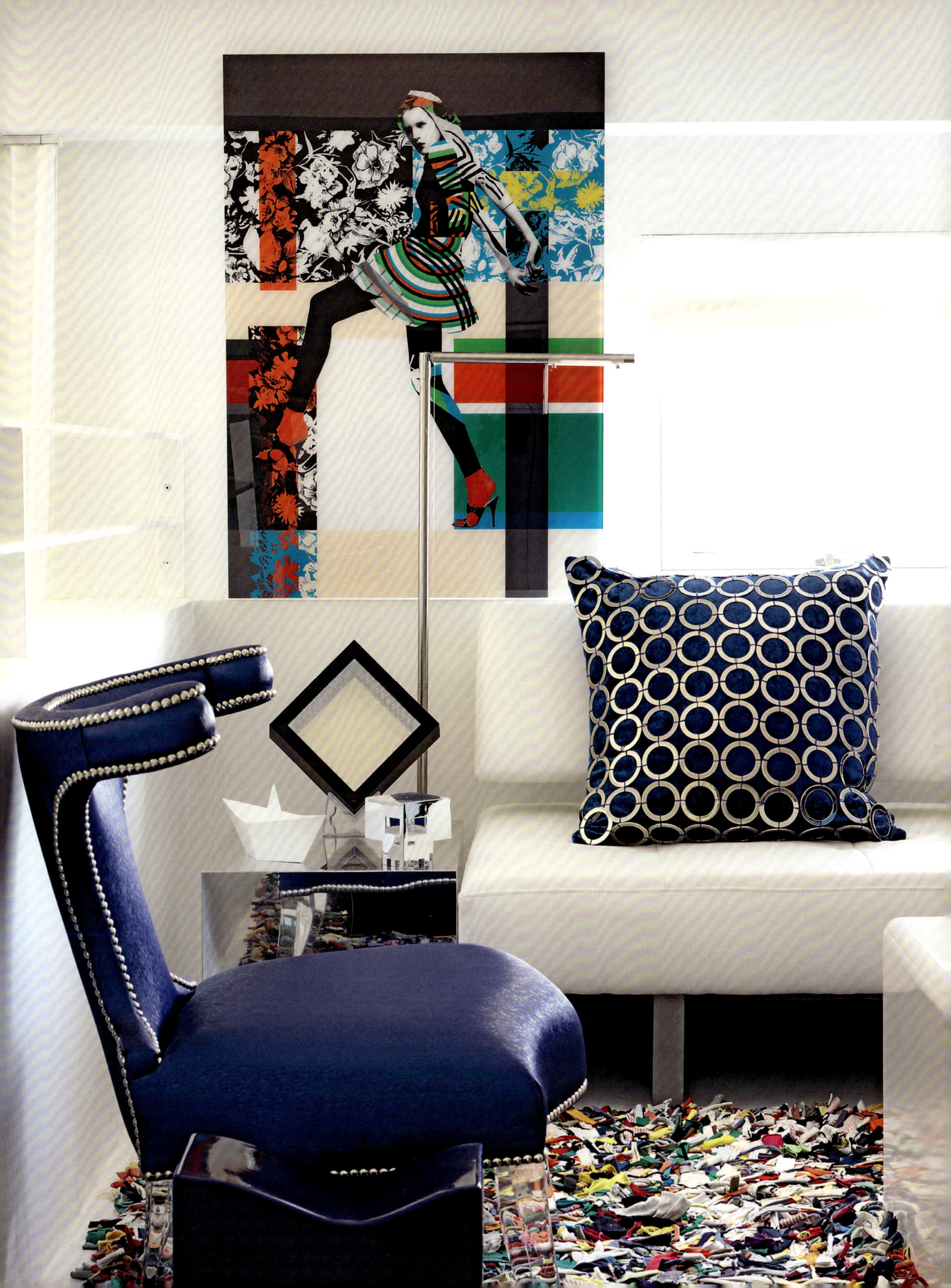

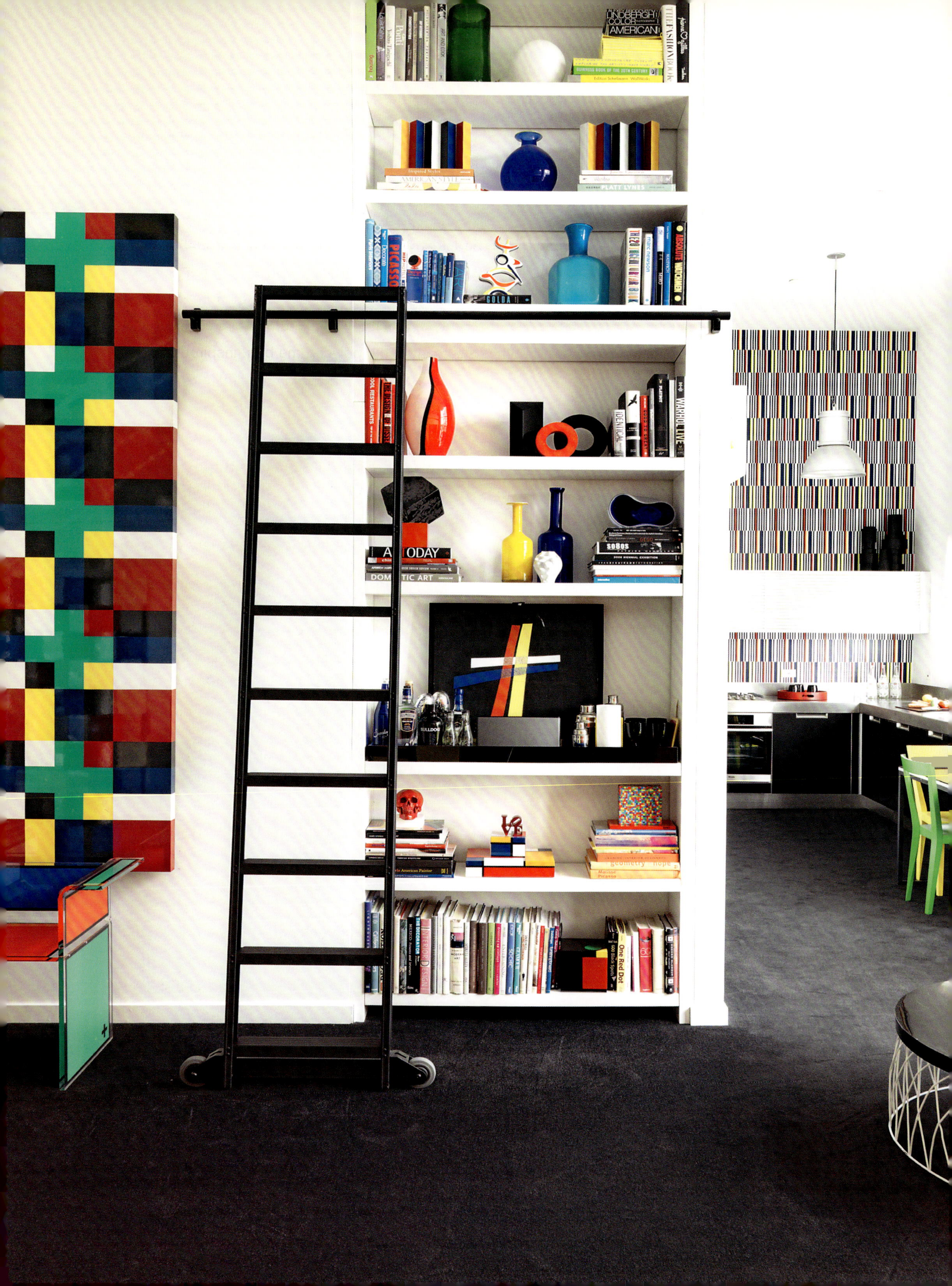

"In the beginning, I was really a black-and-white-person," admits Angel Sanchez. "I was afraid of color." That was before he met his partner, Christopher Coleman, more than a decade ago. The interior designer is a big fan of bright hues. "I find them uplifting, an essential part of life," he asserts. Their apartment features not just a blue sofa, yellow and green side tables, and a sliding door covered in shiny red leatherette, but also a bedroom that is a riot of pattern—the lights and bedside tables are adorned with stripes, and the wall behind the bed is covered in a multihued checked fabric from Liberty of London. It's the kind of environment in which Ettore Sottsass would no doubt have spent a restful night. Coleman describes his style as "playful," yet there is also geometric rigor to it. "I'm not a design snob," he insists. "If I like the shape of a table, I'll send it to an automobile shop and have it lacquered in a fun color." Promptly, Sanchez also caught the polychrome bug: inspired by the work of 1950s Latin American artists, he designed the Op Art-style wallpaper in the kitchen.

„Früher haben mir Farben Angst gemacht", gesteht Modedesigner Angel Sanchez. „Ich war ein richtiger Schwarz-Weiß-Typ". Doch dann lernte er vor gut zehn Jahren Christopher Coleman kennen. Der Interiordesigner kann von leuchtenden Tönen nicht genug bekommen: „Sie heben meine Stimmung, ich möchte nicht ohne sie leben." Im Apartment der beiden finden sich ein blaues Sofa, gelbe und grüne Beistelltische sowie rotes Glanzkunstleder an einer Schiebetür, und im Schlafzimmer wetteifern diverse vielfarbige Streifen- und Karomuster miteinander. Ettore Sottsass hätte hier sicher entspannte Nächte verbracht. Coleman nennt seinen Stil „verspielt", dennoch hat das Resultat auch etwas Geometrisch-Strenges. „Ich bin kein Design-Snob", betont er. „Wenn mir die Form eines Tischs gefällt, dann stört mich die falsche Farbe nicht – ich lasse ihn einfach in einer Autowerkstatt knallig lackieren." Wie sehr diese Begeisterung auf seinen Partner abgefärbt hat, zeigt die Küche: Die von lateinamerikanischer Kunst der 1950er-Jahre inspirierte Op-Art-Tapete dort entwarf Sanchez.

« AU DÉBUT, J'AVAIS PEUR DE LA COULEUR. J'ÉTAIS PLUTÔT ADEPTE DU NOIR ET BLANC. » ANGEL SANCHEZ

C'était il y a plus de dix ans, avant que le créateur de mode ne rencontre son compagnon, le décorateur Christopher Coleman. « Les tons vifs m'inspirent et constituent une partie essentielle de la vie », observe ce dernier. Dans leur séjour se côtoient un canapé bleu, des tables basses jaunes et vertes ainsi qu'une porte coulissante en skaï rouge. Leur chambre est une débauche de motifs : les luminaires et les tables de chevet sont rayés, et le mur derrière le lit tendu d'un tissu à carreaux multicolores de chez Liberty of London. Ettore Sottsass s'y serait senti chez lui. Le style ludique de Coleman n'est pas sans rigueur géométrique. « Je ne suis pas snob en ce qui concerne le design », précise-t-il. « Si la forme d'une table me plaît, je l'envoie chez un carrossier et la fait laquer dans une couleur amusante. » Sanchez a lui aussi attrapé le virus de la polychromie : inspiré par les artistes latino-américains des années 1950, il a dessiné le papier peint op'art de la cuisine.

FRANCIS D'HAENE

A LODGE IN MONTANA

WHO The Belgian-born principal of the New York-based architecture firm D'Apostrophe. **WHAT** A 743 m² (8,000 sq. ft.), five-bedroom chalet built in 2007 by architect Carl Erickson. **WHERE** The members-only Yellowstone Club in Montana. **THE CLIENTS** A family of five. **CLAIM TO FAME** The club covers some 13,600 acres (5,500 hectares) and alleges to be "the only private ski resort in the world." It has attracted the likes of Bill Gates, Justin Timberlake, and Leonardo DiCaprio. **SPECIALTY** Many of D'Haene's projects have links to the art world. Among them are the offices of the Calder Foundation, as well as the Skarstedt and Stellan Holm galleries in Manhattan. **SNOW-HOW** In his youth, D'Haene skied often in Zermatt: "It's impossible to beat in terms of authenticity." **RECENT COMMISSIONS** Residential projects in TriBeCa, Brooklyn, Sagaponack, and the Bahamas and a Madison Avenue gallery for Dominique Lévy and Emmanuel Perrotin.

PHOTOGRAPHED BY GREGORY HOLM   PORTRAIT BY BART MICHIELS

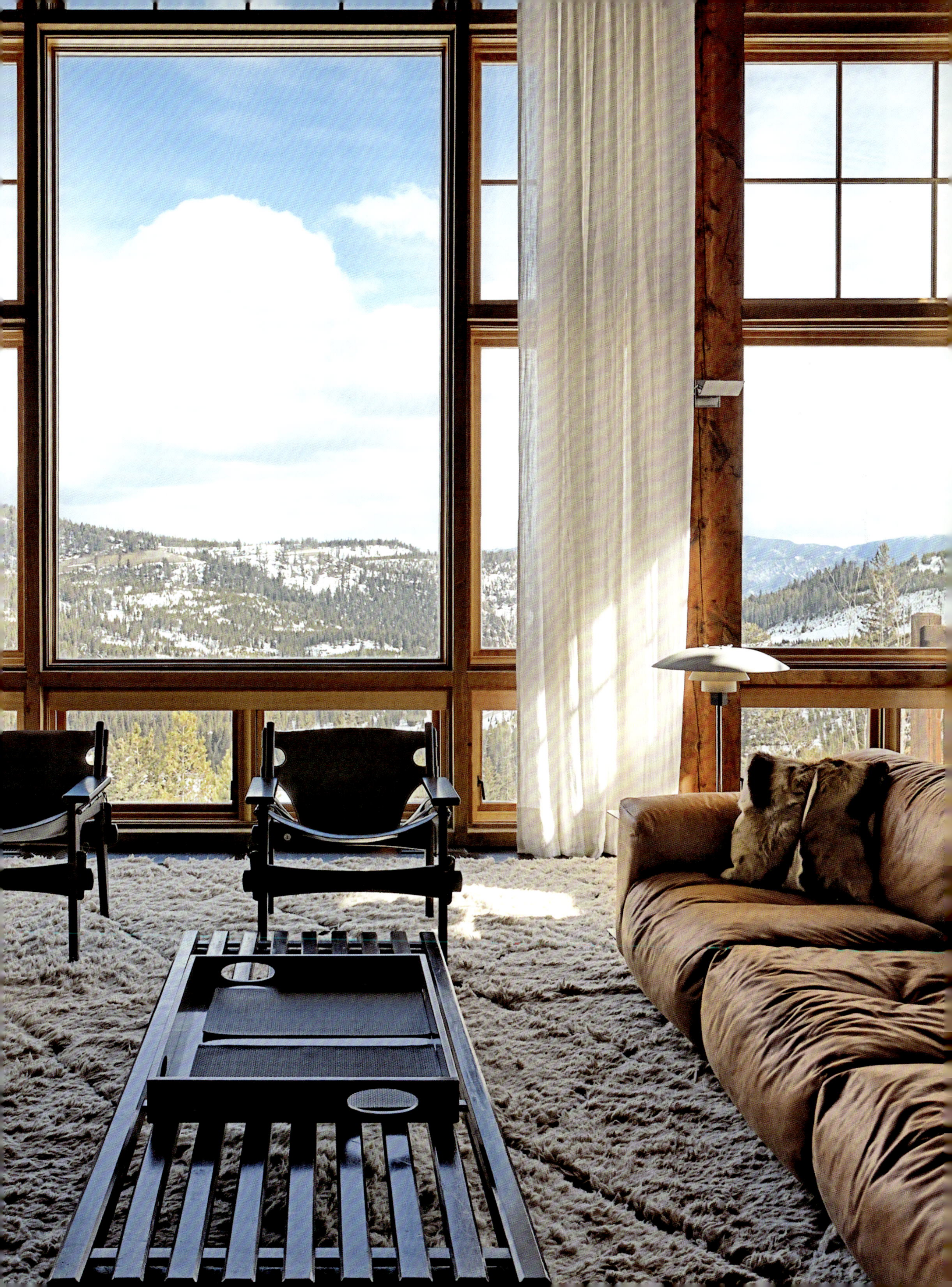

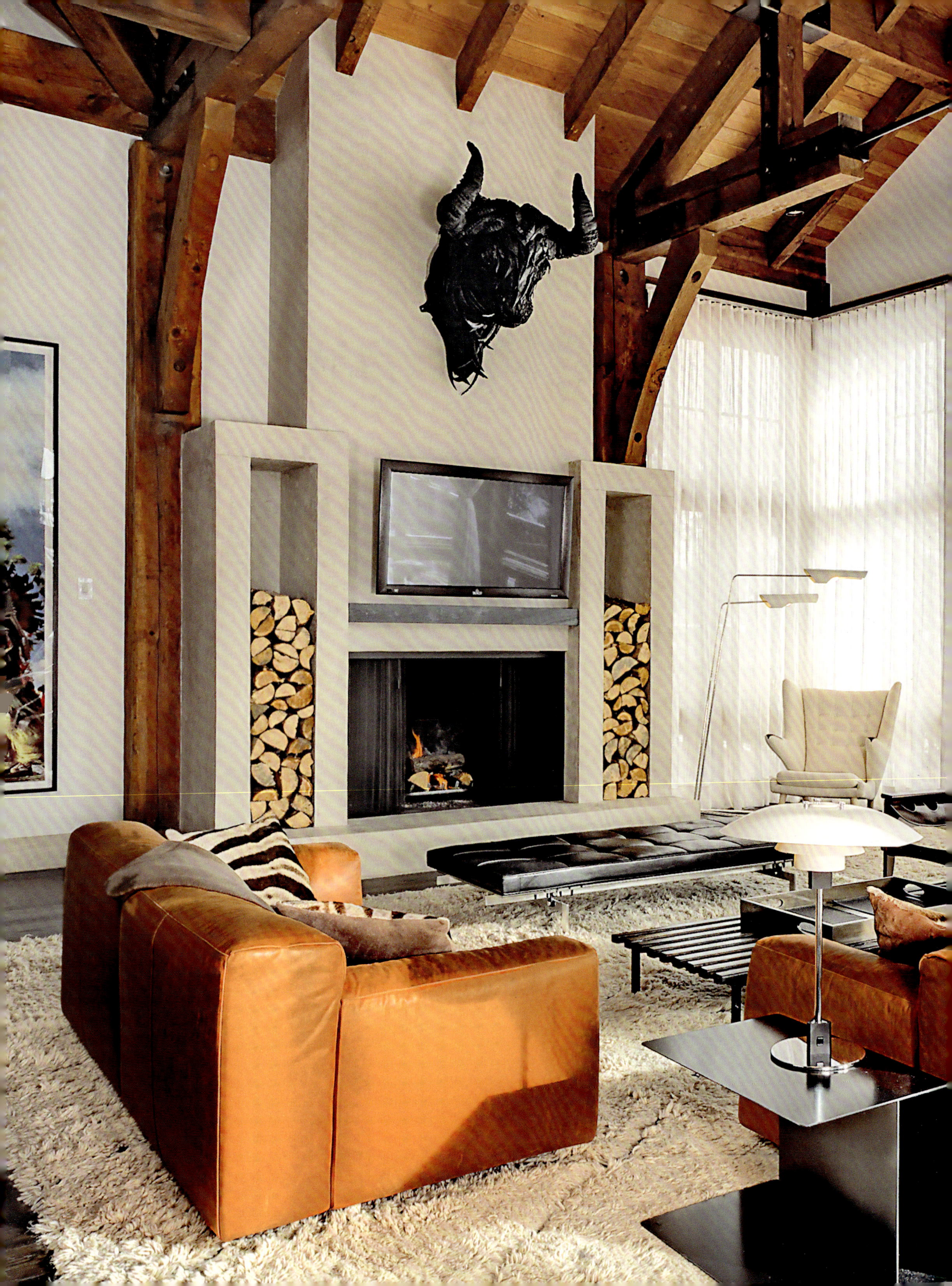

◀ and **59** A buffalo's head made from tires by artist Yong Ho Ji looks down on design classics, Piero Lissoni sofas by Living Divani, and a Moroccan carpet in the living room. • Im Wohnzimmer blickt ein Büffelkopf aus Autoreifen von Yong Ho Ji auf Designklassiker, Piero Lissonis Sofas für Living Divani und einen Teppich aus Marokko. • Dans le séjour, une tête de bison de Yong Ho Ji en fragments de pneus domine des canapés de Piero Lissoni pour Living Divani et un tapis marocain.

▶ The kitchen, designed by the house's architect, Carl Erickson, features white oak millwork and Pietra del Cardoso sandstone counters. • Der Architekt des Hauses, Carl Erickson, entwarf die Küche mit ihren Fronten aus Amerikanischer Weißeiche und Arbeitsplatten aus grauem Pietra del Cardoso. • La cuisine a été conçue par Carl Erickson, l'architecte de la maison, avec des éléments en chêne blanc et des paillasses en grès Pietra Cardosa.

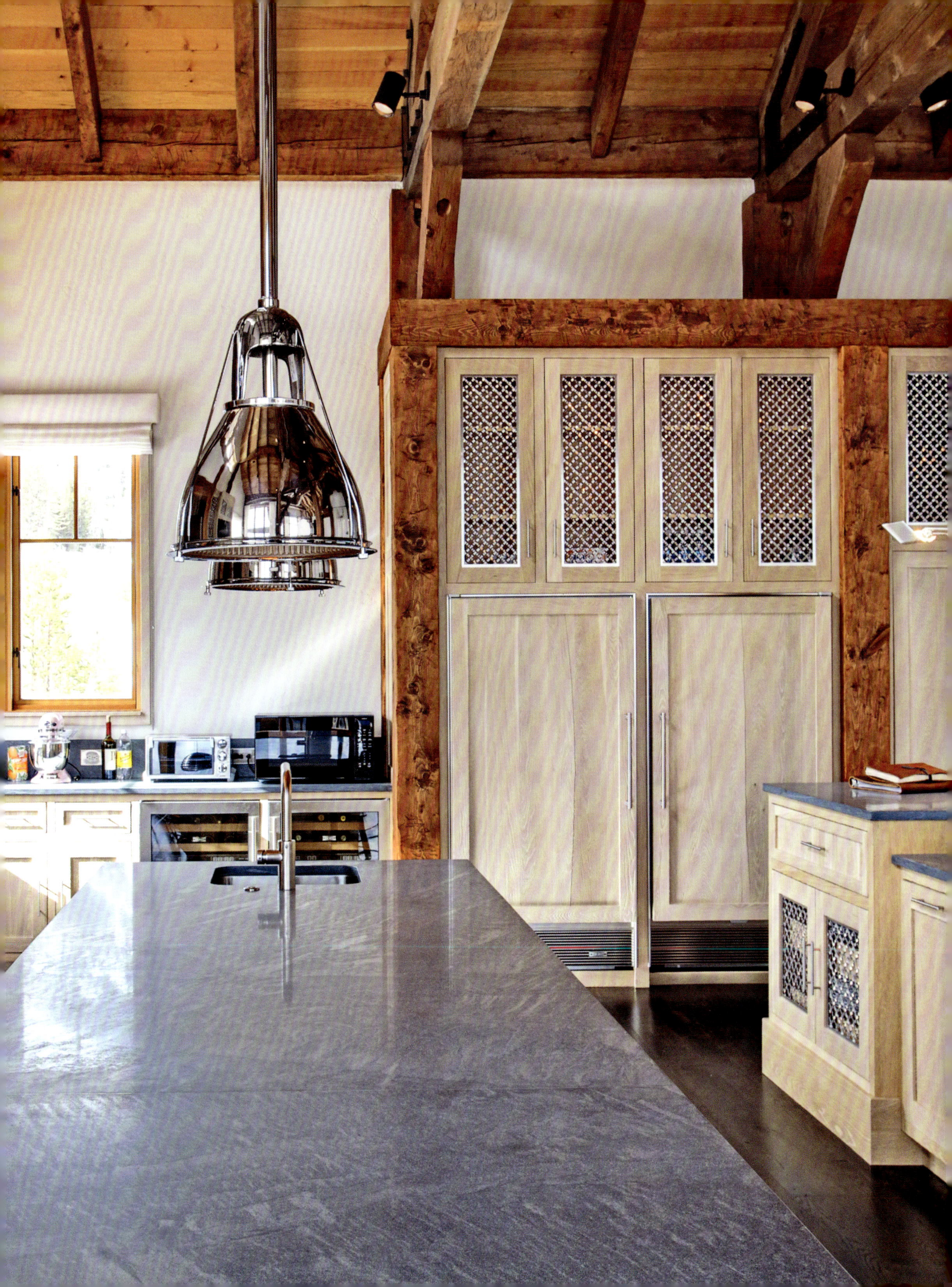

▲ The staircase with its whitewashed oak handrail leads up to the living room, master suite, and one child's bedroom on the top floor. • Über die Treppe mit Geländer aus gebleichter Eiche erreicht man das Obergeschoss mit Wohnzimmer, Mastersuite und einem der Kinderzimmer. • L'escalier muni d'une rambarde en chêne blanchi à la chaux mène au dernier étage où se trouvent le séjour, la chambre principale et une chambre d'enfant.

◀ Built in 2007, the ski-in, ski-out chalet lies at the heart of possibly the most select winter resort in the world. • Vor der Tür beginnt die Piste: Das 2007 erbaute Chalet liegt im Herzen des vielleicht exklusivsten Skiresorts der Welt. • Construit en 2007, le chalet « au pied des pistes » se trouve au cœur de ce qui est probablement la station de ski la plus sélecte du monde.

▶ Flyin' high: *Nasa Meatball Logo, Color* by Tom Sachs hangs in the media room with Edra's Boa sofa. A Ross Lovegrove table is used for playing board games. • Höhenflug: Im Mediaroom hängt Tom Sachs' *Nasa Meatball Logo, Color*. Am Tisch von Ross Lovegrove trifft man sich zu Brettspielen, vorn Edras Boa-Sofa. • Dans le salon de détente, un canapé Boa d'Edra côtoie une œuvre de Tom Sachs, *Nasa Meatball Logo, Color*. La table de jeux est de Ross Lovegrove.

66 Michael Anastassiades's *Tube Chandeliers* shine on Sergio Rodrigues chairs and a custom oak table designed by D'Haene for the dining area. • Michael Anastassiades' *Tube Chandeliers* beleuchten Stühle von Sergio Rodrigues und den Esstisch, den D'Haene aus Eiche tischlern ließ. • Dans le coin repas, des *Tube Chandeliers* de Michael Anastassiades illuminent une table en chêne dessinée par D'Haene. Chaises de Sergio Rodrigues.

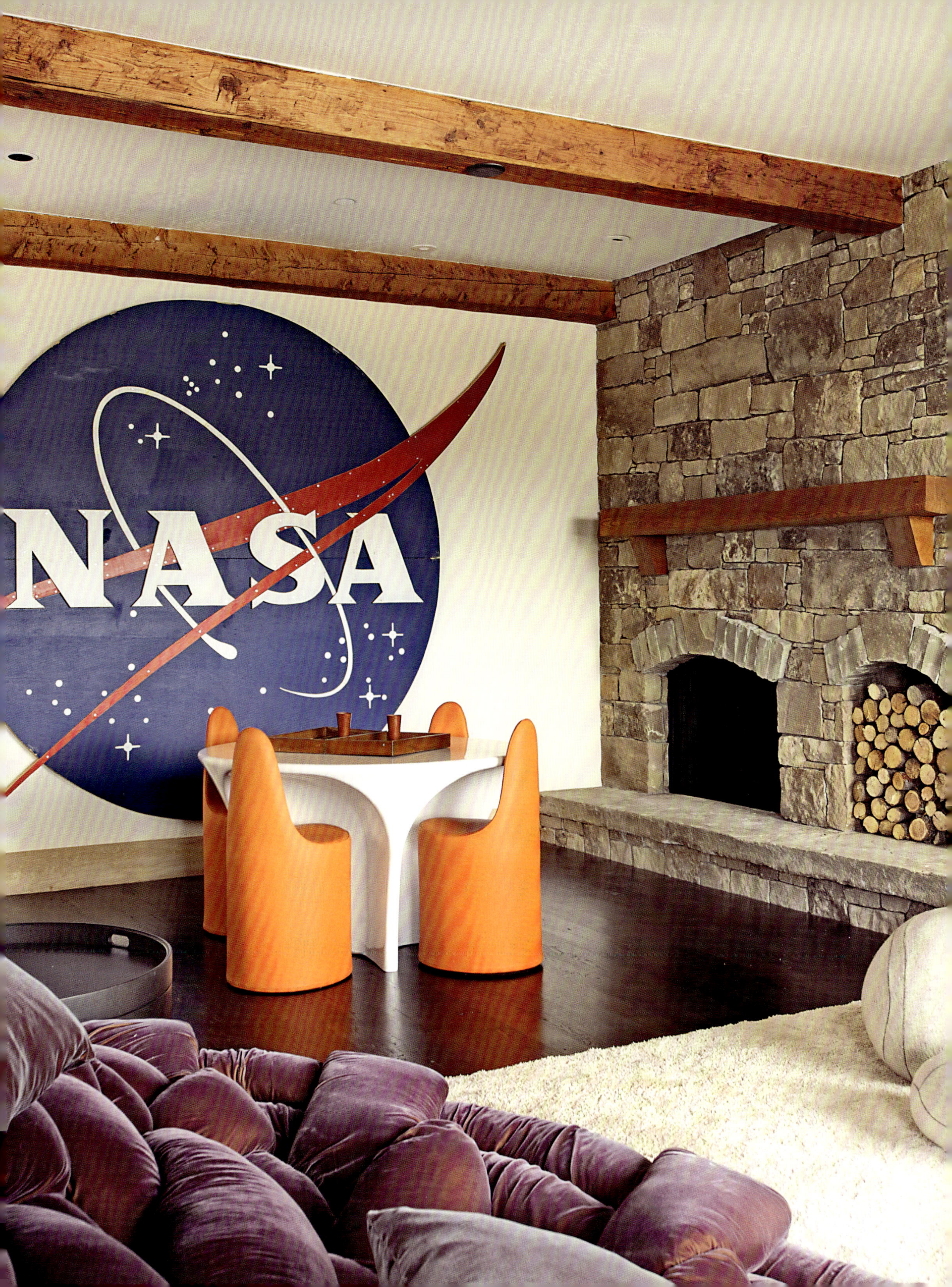
NASA

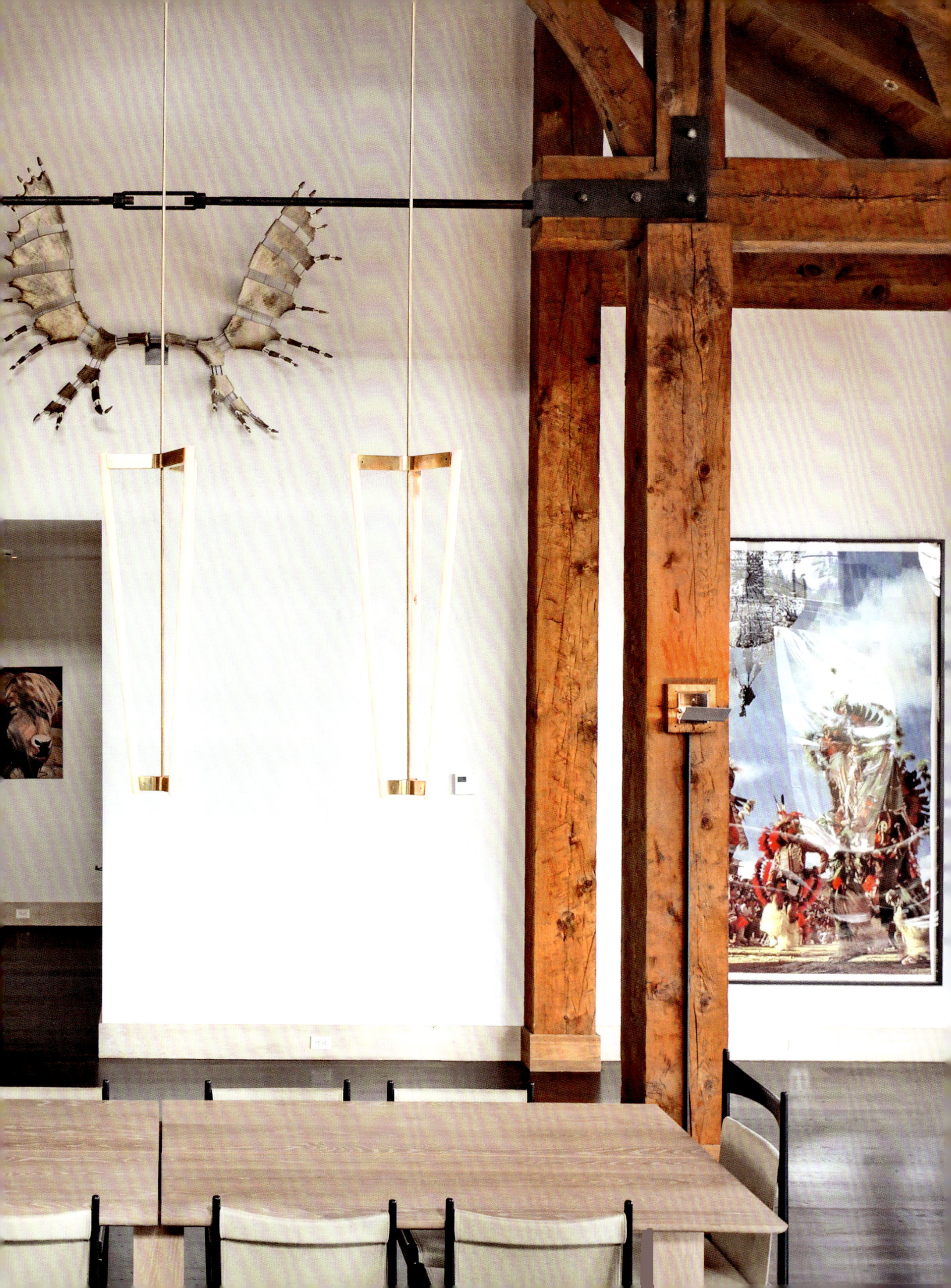

"We wanted minimalism that still feels warm and cozy," states Francis D'Haene. He also wanted to steer away from clichés. "Houses out here are often Western-themed," he notes. "The architecture was going in that direction. So we scaled it down." The New York-based architect removed moldings and favored white plaster walls over the traditional wood. He also accentuated the Rocky Mountain views by placing the living room on the top floor and installing sheer white drapes along the window wall. "The main appeal," he says, "is definitely the surrounding nature." Local references were incorporated in more sophisticated ways, with Sergio Rodrigues armchairs in cowhide and leather area rugs. There are also numerous touches of humor. Instead of hunting trophies, D'Haene placed a buffalo's head made from pieces of tire above the fireplace and a Michael Joo artwork of stainless steel and antlers that recalls a gigantic moth in the dining area. Just as surreally playful is the *Cow Bench* by London-based designer Julia Lohmann—it is shaped like a headless resting bovine.

„Wir wollten einen Minimalismus, der etwas Warmes, Behagliches hat", sagt Francis D'Haene. Außerdem wollte er vermeiden, in die Klischee-Falle zu tappen. „Die Häuser hier draußen sehen oft nach Wildem Westen aus", bemerkt der New Yorker Architekt. „Von außen geht auch dieses in die Richtung. Also haben wir es innen etwas entschlackt." Er entfernte alle Gesimse und ließ die Holzwände verputzen. Um den Blick auf die Rocky Mountains zu optimieren, verlegte er das Wohnzimmer ins Obergeschoss und rahmte das Panoramafenster mit schlichten weißen Stores. „Die Hauptrolle", sagt er, „spielt definitiv die Natur." Auf regionale Traditionen bezieht sich die Einrichtung eher subtil: Leder ist allgegenwärtig, etwa auf Sesseln von Sergio Rodrigues oder als Bodenbelag. Und statt Jagdtrophäen platzierte D'Haene über dem Kamin einen Büffelkopf aus Reifenresten und im Essbereich eine Plastik aus Edelstahl und Geweihteilen. Ebenso verspielt surreal ist die *Cow Bench* der in London arbeitenden Deutschen Julia Lohmann – sie hat die Form einer kopflosen Kuh.

«NOTRE OBJECTIF ÉTAIT DE CRÉER UNE ATMOSPHÈRE MINIMALISTE QUI SOIT CHALEUREUSE ET DOUILLETTE.» FRANCIS D'HAENE

L'architecte new-yorkais souhaitait également éviter les clichés. «Les maisons ici sont souvent dans le style Far West. L'architecture de la maison l'était déjà, alors nous l'avons atténuée», explique-t-il. Il a ôté les moulures, préféré les murs en plâtre blanc aux boiseries traditionnelles, privilégié les vues sur les Rocheuses en aménageant le séjour au dernier étage et en installant des voilages blancs d'une grande sobriété sur toute la longueur des baies panoramiques. «Le principal attrait du lieu, c'est la nature.» Les références locales revêtent une forme plus sophistiquée, avec une profusion de peaux de bêtes, notamment des fauteuils en peau de vache de Sergio Rodrigues et des tapis en cuir, le tout agrémenté d'un brin d'humour. En guise de trophées, D'Haene a accroché une tête de bison en fragments de pneus au-dessus de la cheminée et une œuvre de Michael Joo en inox et bois de cerf qui évoque un papillon de nuit géant dans le coin repas. Le banc de la designer londonienne Julia Lohmann est tout aussi surréaliste et drôle : il a la forme d'une vache sans tête couchée.

JOSEPH DIRAND

AN APARTMENT IN PARIS

WHO Paris-based interior designer born with a discerning eye. His father, Jacques Dirand, was a famous interiors photographer whose work appeared in numerous books and magazines including *The World of Interiors*. **WHAT** A 150 m² (1,615 sq. ft.), two-bedroom apartment. **WHERE** Directly on the Left Bank of the Seine, with breathtaking postcard views of Paris. **THE CLIENT** An American tech investor, who is also Dirand's business associate. **COLORS** Black and white: "They allow you to capture the essence of a space." **INSPIRATION** Movies—for his Distrito Capital hotel in Mexico City, for instance, he referenced Jacques Tati's *Playtime*. **PET OBJECT** He is currently crazy for a spherical pendant light created by Danish architect Louis Weisdorf in the 1960s for Lyfa. **FRIEND OF FASHION** Dirand has designed the new store concepts for Alexander Wang, Emilio Pucci, and Chloé.

PHOTOGRAPHED BY ADRIEN DIRAND   STYLED BY MARIE KALT

I FYOUCAN
T TAKE
AJOKEYOU
CANGETHE
THEFUCK
OUT FUCK
OUTOF OF
MYHOUSE

ALEXANDRE NOLL
CHARLOTTE PERRIAND
CHARLOTTE PERRIAND
BASQUIAT
CHRISTOPHER WOOL
ALBERTO BURRI
BASQUIAT
ART DECO

69 In the living room, Christopher Wool's *If You* painting hangs behind a 1961 black-stained mahogany desk by Charlotte Perriand. • Im Wohnzimmer hängt Christopher Wools Gemälde *If You* hinter einem von Charlotte Perriand entworfenen Tisch von 1961 aus schwarz gebeiztem Mahagoni. • Dans le séjour, l'œuvre *If You* de Christopher Wool domine un bureau en acajou teinté en noir de 1961 signé Charlotte Perriand.

◄ Instead of applying wooden baguettes to the walls in the traditional fashion, Dirand went negative—he created the "paneling" by hollowing out plaster. • Statt wie üblich hölzerne Zierleisten an den Wänden anzubringen, wählte Dirand das Negativprinzip – er schälte die „Täfelung" aus dem Gipsputz. • Pour créer l'effet boiserie, plutôt que d'appliquer des baguettes en bois à la manière traditionnelle, Dirand a creusé les moulures dans le plâtre.

▲ The arched shape of the living room window is echoed in the rounded forms of a Jean Prouvé table and Jean Royère seating. Above the 1940s fireplace, a Cy Twombly got its own plaster frame. • Der Prouvé-Tisch und die Sitzgruppe von Royère greifen den Bogenschwung des Fensters auf. Über dem Kamin aus den 1940ern bekam ein Cy Twombly den passenden Gipsrahmen. • Dans le séjour, les arrondis de la table de Prouvé et des sièges de Royère rappellent la fenêtre en arceau. Au-dessus de la cheminée des années 1940, un Cy Twombly.

72–73 A Wim Wenders photograph dominates the master bedroom. The slate coffee table was created by Jannie van Pelt, c. 1958. • Das Schlafzimmer beherrscht eine Fotografie von Wim Wenders. Schiefer-Tisch von Jannie van Pelt, ca. 1958. • Dans la chambre principale, une photographie de Wim Wenders et une table basse en ardoise créée par Jannie van Pelt vers 1958.

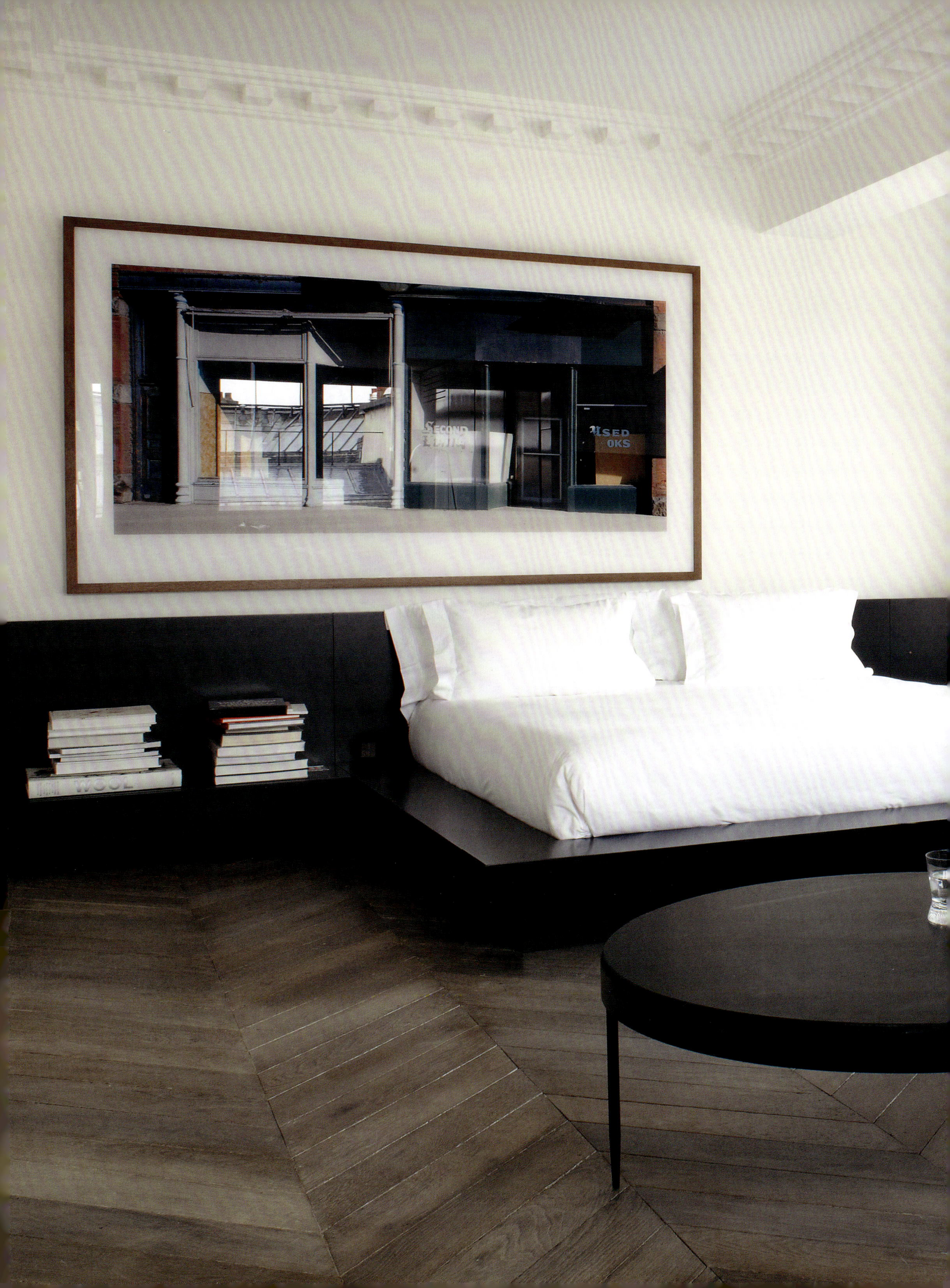
SECOND
USED
WOOL

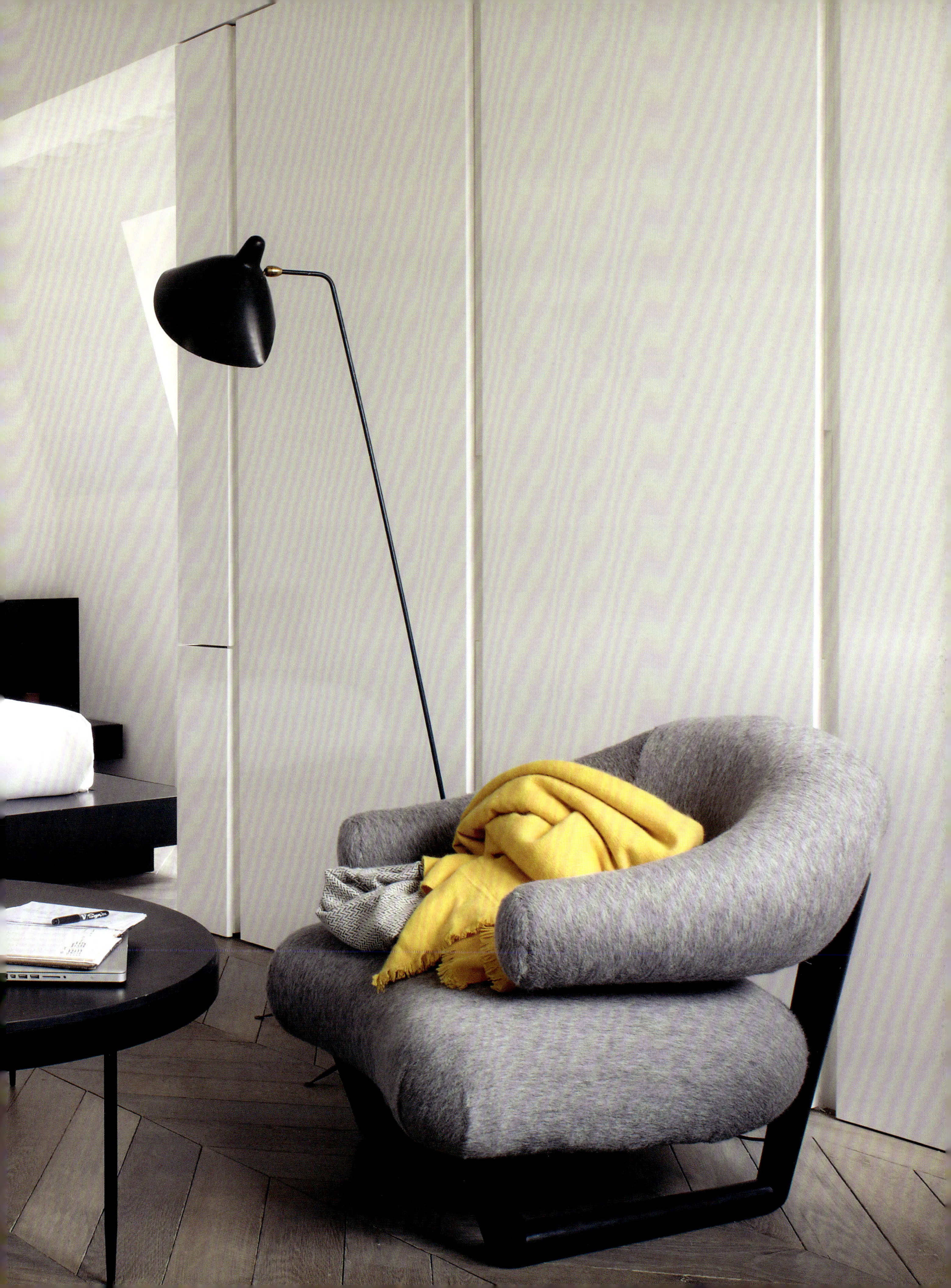

▲ The view from the flat's balcony is unbeatable—here you can see the Pont de la Concorde and, in the distance, the gigantic glass dome of the Grand Palais. • Die Aussicht vom Balkon ist unschlagbar – über die Pont de la Concorde blickt man bis zu den imposanten Glasgewölben des Grand Palais. • Depuis le balcon, la vue est imprenable. On aperçoit le pont de la Concorde et, plus loin, les verrières gigantesques du Grand Palais.

76 Black and white allows Dirand to find a form of spatial quintessence, exemplified here in the elegant linear geometry of the master bathroom. • Die elegante Geometrie des Bads zeigt es aufs Schönste: Indem Dirand auf Farbe verzichtet, verdichtet er die Raumwirkung zur Quintessenz. • Le noir et le blanc permettent à Dirand de trouver « une forme de quintessence spatiale », comme en témoigne l'élégante géométrie linéaire de la salle de bains.

▲ ▶ In the dining room, icons of European midcentury design happily mingle. On top of the Perriand/Jeanneret sideboard sits a Jean-Michel Basquiat drawing from 1985. Charlotte Perriand's rare *Forme Libre* table has a black Formica top. The Poul Kjærholm chairs are among the few pieces retained from the previous decor. • Das Esszimmer vereint Ikonen des europäischen Midcentury-Designs. Das Sideboard entwarfen Perriand und Jeanneret; darauf eine Zeichnung von Jean-Michel Basquiat von 1985. Den seltenen Perriand-Tisch mit Formica-Platte umgeben Stühle von Poul Kjærholm; sie gehörten schon vor Dirands Update zur Einrichtung. • La salle à manger accueille un assortiment de design du milieu du 20ᵉ siècle. Sur un buffet de Perriand et Jeanneret, un dessin de Jean-Michel Basquiat de 1985. La table *Forme libre* de Charlotte Perriand, une pièce rare, possède un plateau en formica noir. Les chaises de Poul Kjærholm comptent parmi les quelques éléments préservés de l'ancien décor.

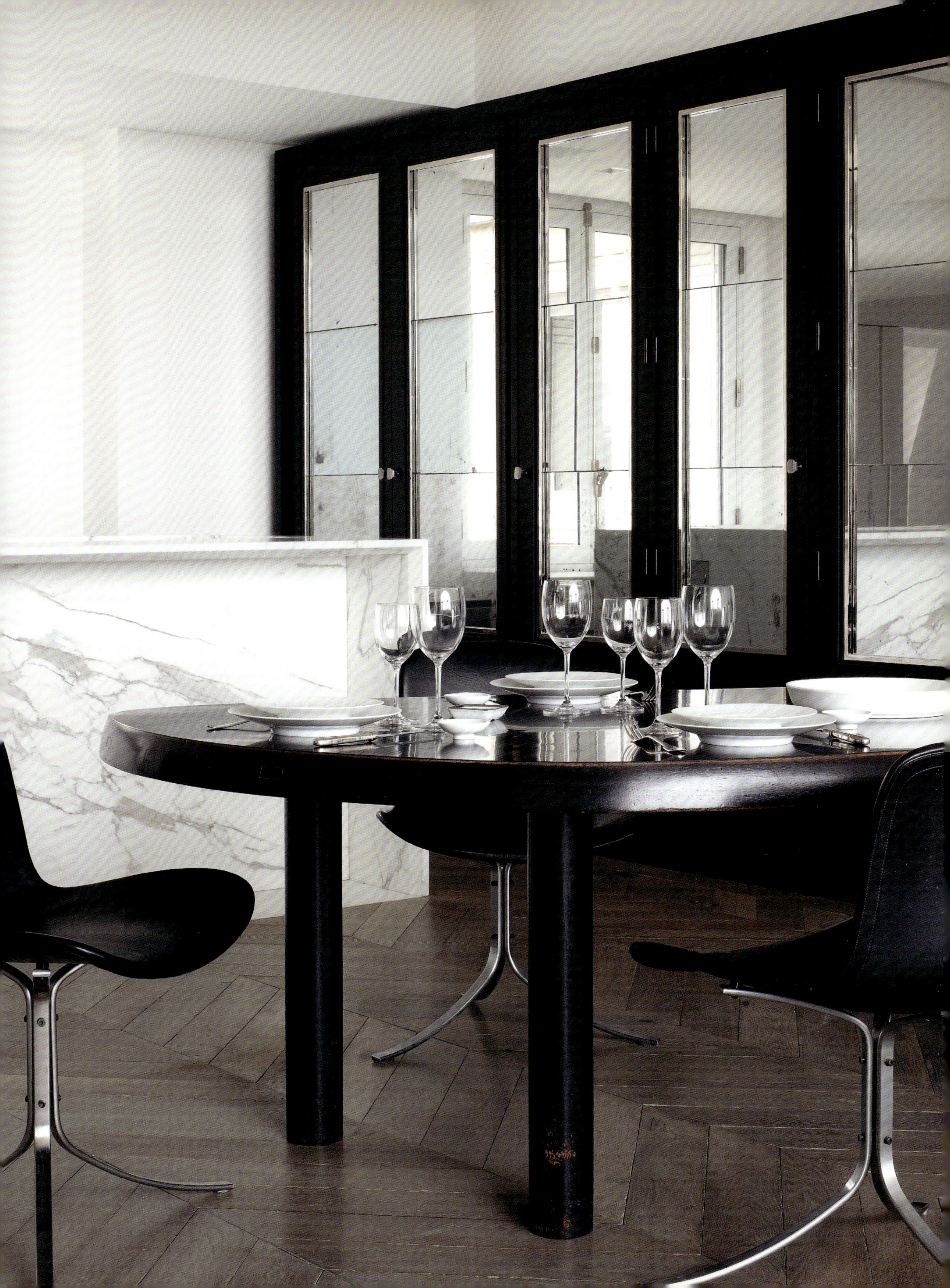

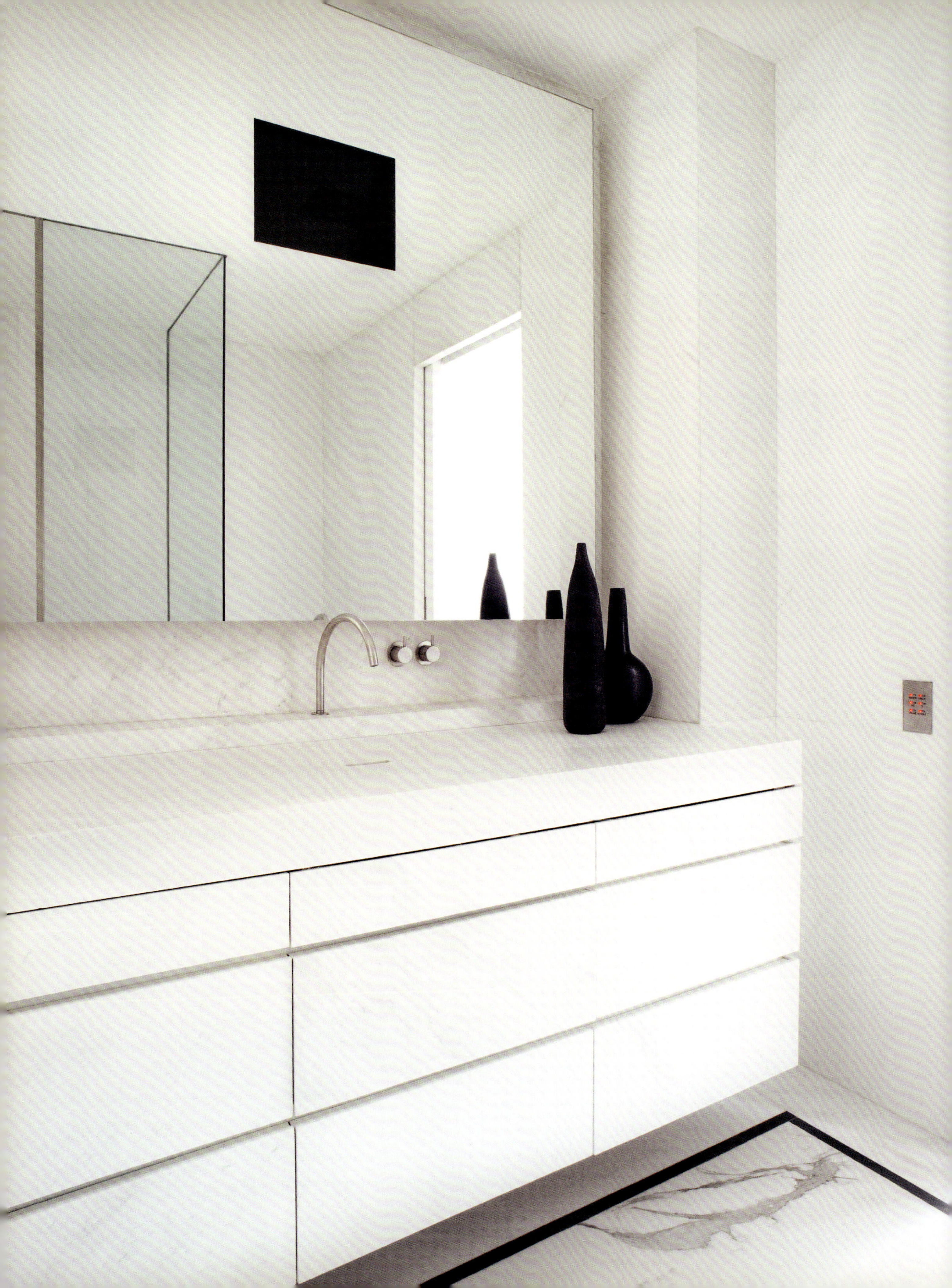

"THERE ARE ONLY TWO KNOWN SPECIMENS OF PERRIAND'S *FORME LIBRE* TABLE IN THE WORLD—AND ONE IS STANDING IN THE DINING ROOM." JOSEPH DIRAND

Even the best interiors have to change with the times. Joseph Dirand initially decorated this flat back in 2005; featured as "WDL Apartment" in TASCHEN's *New Paris Interiors* book, it was "conceptual" and "a sort of statement." Back then, its austere, angular lines and minimal decor were perfect for his client's single lifestyle. When the man in question became a father, however, he decided it was time for a revamp. Dirand stuck to his signature black-and-white-palette but transformed a former TV room into a second bedroom and incorporated slightly more decorative architectural elements. A purist version of an 18th-century cornice was installed and trompe-l'œil paneling created by gouging geometric lines out of the plaster walls. The precious contemporary art remained, while rounder, more family-friendly forms were introduced via the furniture, which includes Jean Royère's *Polar Bear* sofa and armchairs and a very rare vintage table by Charlotte Perriand. "It was really quite a scoop to find such a magical piece," notes Dirand with a smile.

Selbst die besten Interieurs müssen sich mit der Zeit verändern. Dieses Apartment gestaltete Joseph Dirand ursprünglich 2005 – es sei „konzeptuell", „ein Statement", so wurde es damals beschrieben und in TASCHENs *New Paris Interiors* präsentiert. Strenge, kantige Konturen und ein Dekor, das gegen Null tendierte, passten zum Single-Leben des Bewohners. Als dieser jedoch Vater wurde, erschien ihm die Zeit reif für ein Update mit dem ursprünglichen Interiordesigner. Dirand blieb seinem charakteristischen Schwarz-Weiß treu, wandelte jedoch den Mediaroom in ein zweites Schlafzimmer um und fügte dezenten Wandschmuck hinzu – angedeutete Boiserien sowie die Puristenversion eines Stuckgesimses im Stil des 18. Jahrhunderts. Die wertvolle Gegenwartskunst blieb, dafür wurde das Mobiliar um rundere Formen ergänzt, darunter Jean Royères *Ours-Polaire*-Sofa und -Sessel sowie ein sehr rarer Vintage-Tisch von Charlotte Perriand. „Das war ein echter Coup, denn weltweit gibt es nur zwei Exemplare dieses Möbels", konstatiert Dirand lächelnd.

Même les meilleurs décors doivent évoluer. Joseph Dirand avait réalisé cet appartement en 2005. Publié dans *Nouveaux intérieurs parisiens* de TASCHEN, il était «conceptuel», «une sorte de statement». À l'époque, ses lignes austères et son atmosphère minimaliste convenaient à la vie de célibataire du propriétaire. Celui-ci étant devenu père, il était temps de changer. Fidèle à sa palette noir et blanc, Dirand a transformé la salle de télévision en deuxième chambre et a incorporé des éléments plus décoratifs : une version épurée d'une corniche du 18e siècle et une boiserie en trompe-l'œil réalisée en creusant des lignes dans les murs en plâtre. Les œuvres d'art contemporain côtoient des meubles aux formes plus accueillantes et arrondies dont le canapé et les fauteuils *Ours Polaire* de Jean Royère et une très rare table «Forme libre» de Charlotte Perriand. «Il n'en existe que deux dans le monde; et l'une d'elles se trouve dans la salle à manger», déclare Dirand avec un sourire.

MARINA FAUST

HER *ATELIERWOHNUNG* IN VIENNA

WHO Austrian artist and photographer. **WHAT** A 200 m² (2,153 sq. ft.), two-bedroom penthouse apartment. **WHERE** On Ringstrasse boulevard, which circles the city's feudal center. **STAYING PUT** Faust has lived in the 1910–14 building since 1956. In the late 1950s, her parents swapped their apartment on the third floor for the former photography studio at the top of the building: "My mother always dreamt of having terraces where she could be in the sun," Faust explains. **ART** She met Franz West while teaching at the École des Beaux-Arts in Paris: "It was the beginning of a wonderful friendship." A West show at Gagosian Gallery in London, which opened right after his death in 2012, included a collaboration between the two entitled *Talk Without Words*. **FASHION** Faust chronicled Martin Margiela's work in backstage reportages and on film from 1989 until the designer's early retirement. **INTERIORS** She photographed for the U.S. edition of *Architectural Digest* for 25 years. Still, her favorite shoot ever "was for the magazine's German edition—the house of Austrian writer Thomas Bernhard in Ohlsdorf."

PHOTOGRAPHED BY MARINA FAUST   STYLED BY STEPHAN MEYER   PORTRAIT BY LUC FREY

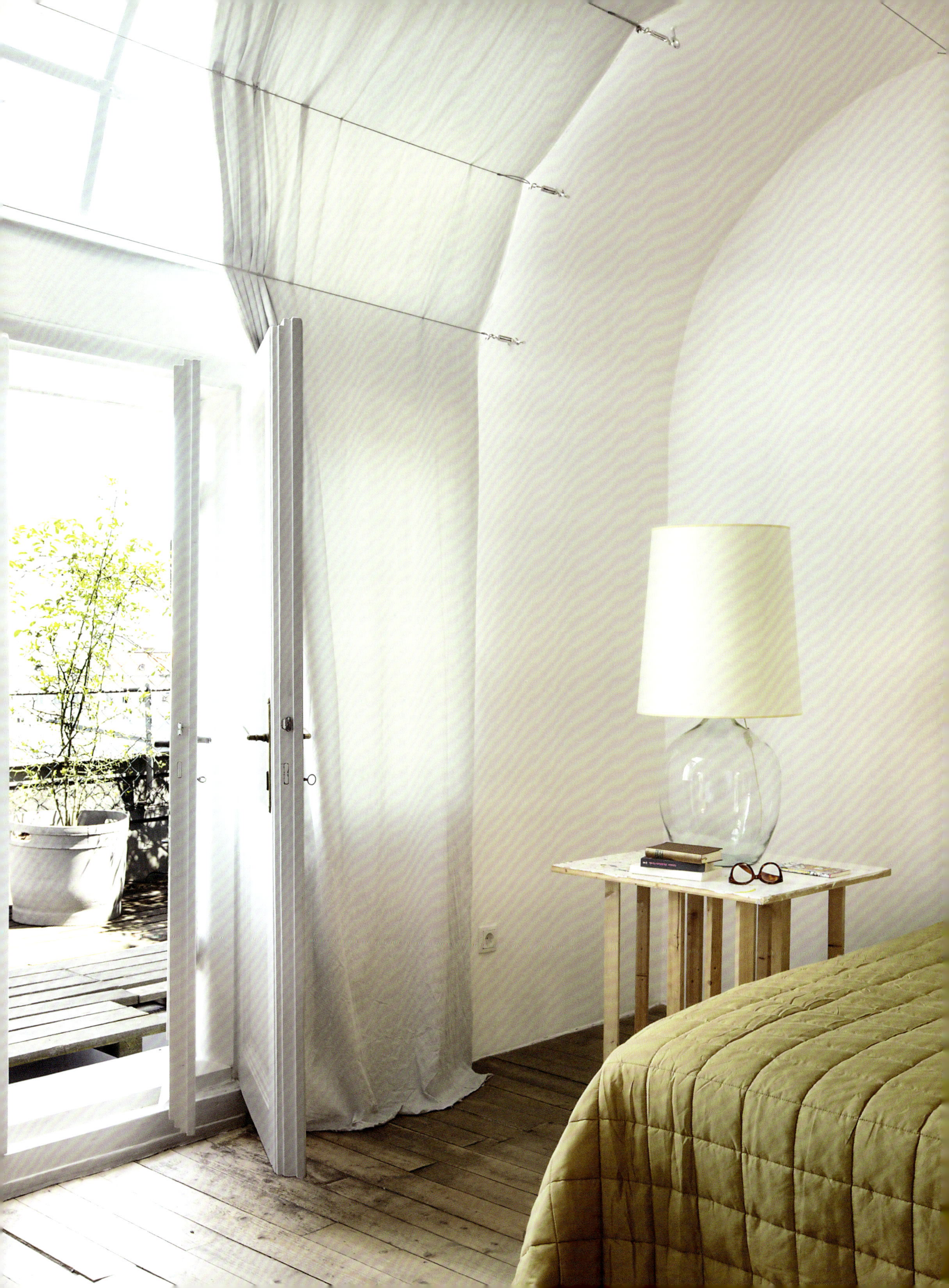

79 A lamp made by Faust's mother from a blown-glass jar stands on one of artist Franz West's sculpture plinths in the master bedroom. • Eine Leuchte, die Fausts Mutter aus einem Einweckglas machte, steht im Schlafzimmer auf einem Postament des Künstlers Franz West. • Dans la chambre principale, une lampe réalisée par la mère de Faust avec un bocal en verre soufflé est posée sur un piédestal de Franz West convertie en table de chevet.

▲ In the living room, a Carl Auböck floor lamp is placed next to a screen created by West from rebar steel, wood and acrylic paint. Faust inherited the tables and chairs from her parents. • Die Tische und Stühle im Wohnzimmer erbte Faust von ihren Eltern. Eine Carl-Auböck-Leuchte steht neben einem Paravent von West aus Betonstahl, Holz und Acrylfarbe. • Dans le séjour, un lampadaire de Carl Auböck près d'un paravent de West en acier d'armature, bois et acrylique. Faust a hérité des tables et des chaises de ses parents.

◀ In the atelier, works from Faust's *Shelf* series are stored alongside part of her father's extensive book collection. • Arbeiten aus ihrer *Shelf*-Serie in Fausts Atelier, in dem auch ein Teil der umfangreichen Bibliothek ihres Vaters lagert. • Dans l'atelier, des œuvres de la série *Shelf* de Faust sont entreposées parmi une impressionnante collection de livres de son père.

▶ The back terrace is nicknamed Twin Peaks Terrace due to the rustic wooden furniture, which reminds Faust of David Lynch's iconic TV series. "I was crazy about it," she smiles. • Die hintere Terrasse heißt Twin-Peaks-Terrasse, wegen der groben Holzmöbel, die Faust an David Lynchs TV-Serie erinnern. „Ich war verrückt danach", erklärt sie. • À l'arrière de l'appartement, la terrasse « Twin Peaks » avec ses meubles rustiques en bois, baptisée ainsi par Faust en clin d'œil à la célèbre série TV de David Lynch. « J'en étais folle », confie-t-elle.

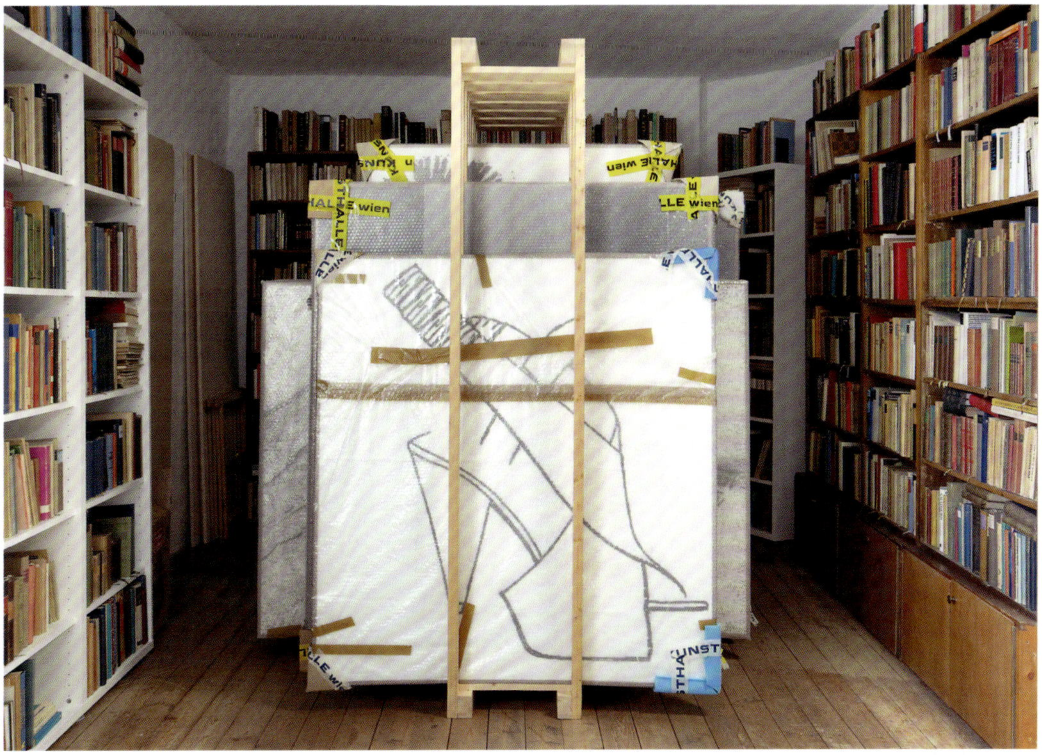
LLE wien

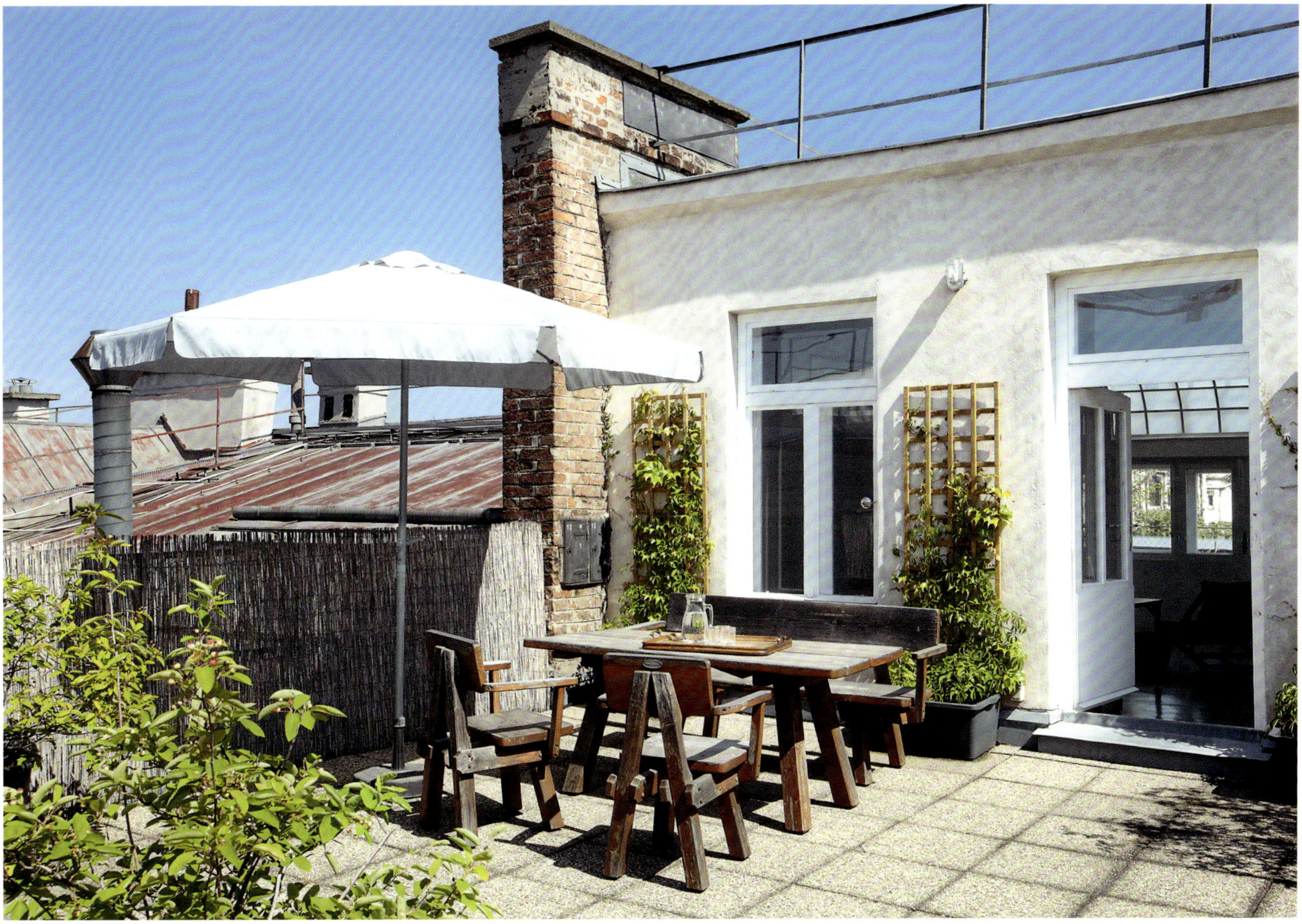

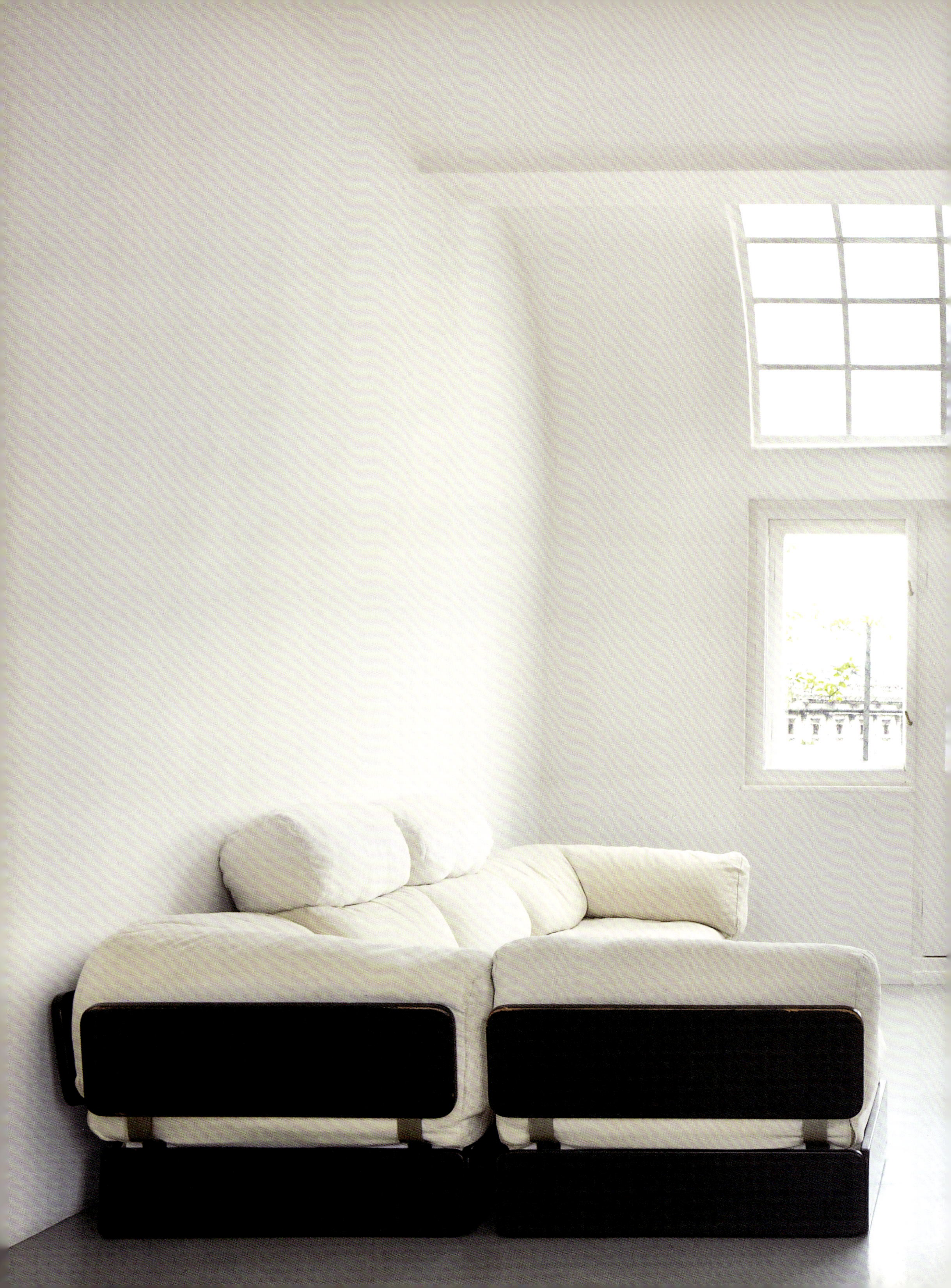

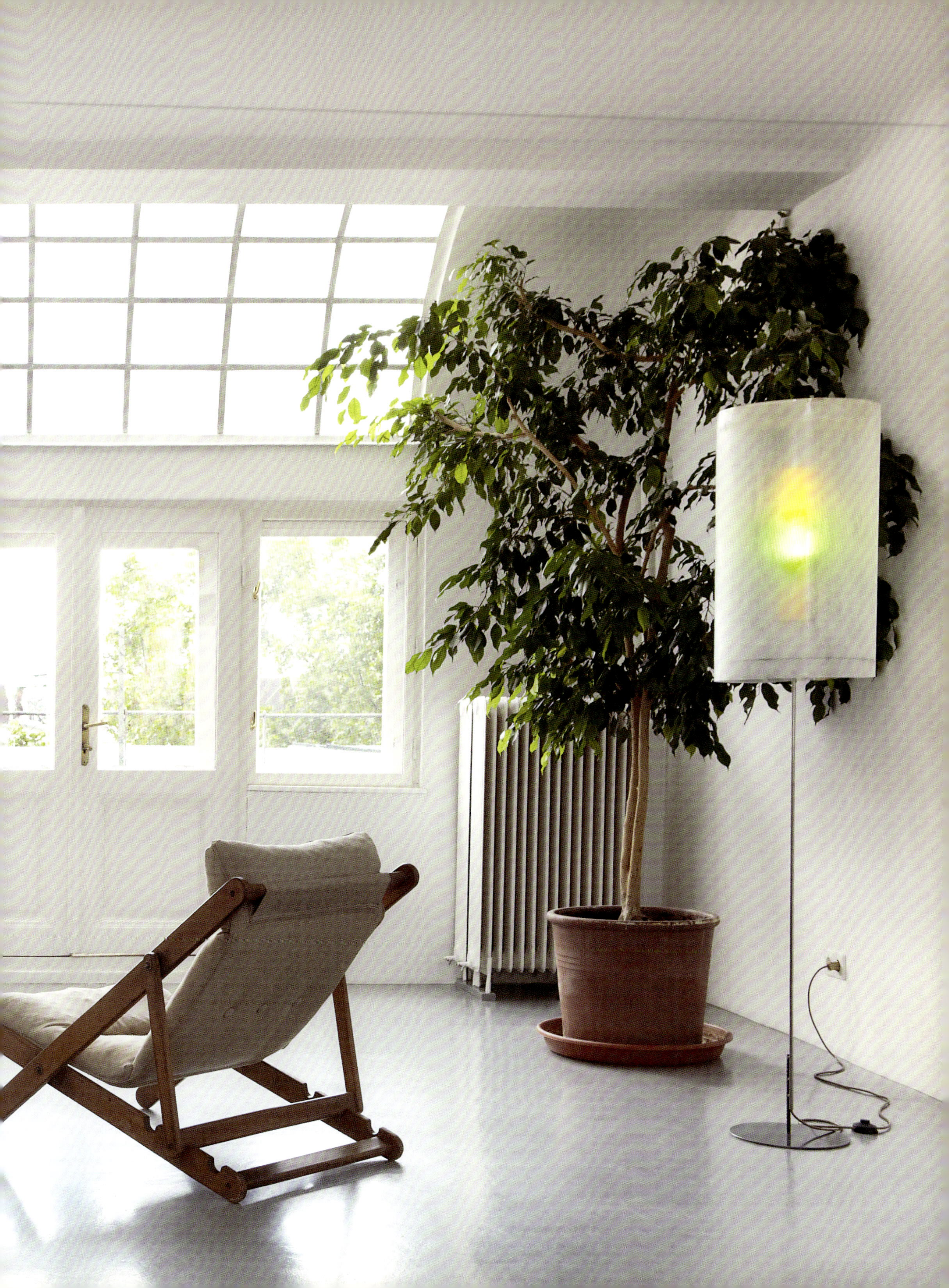

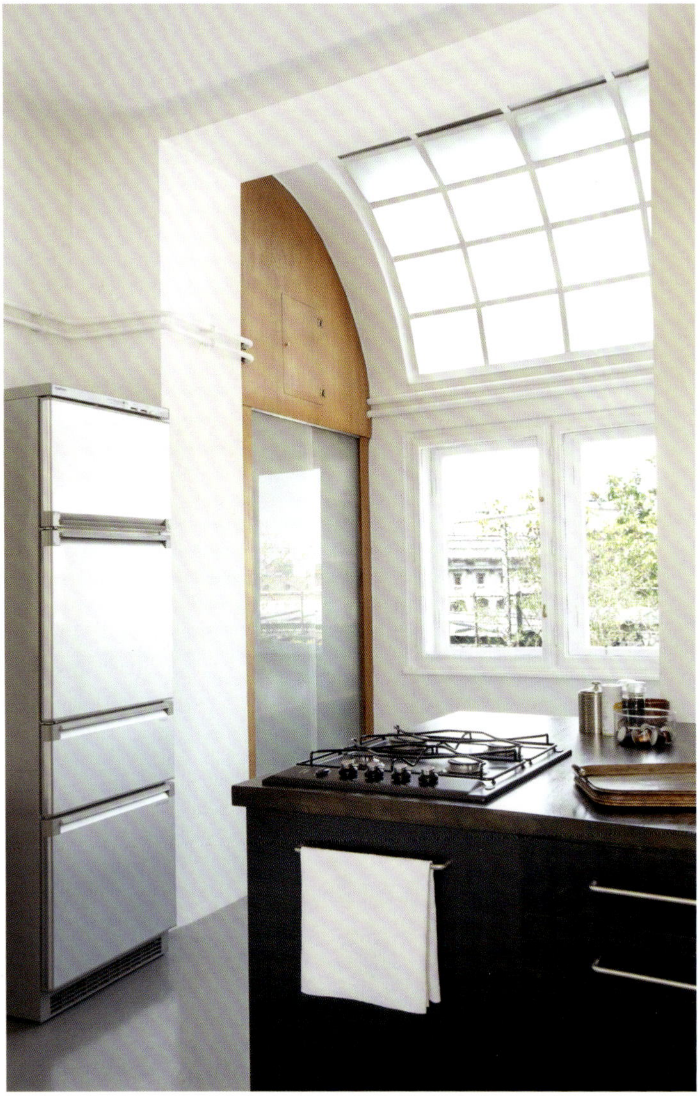

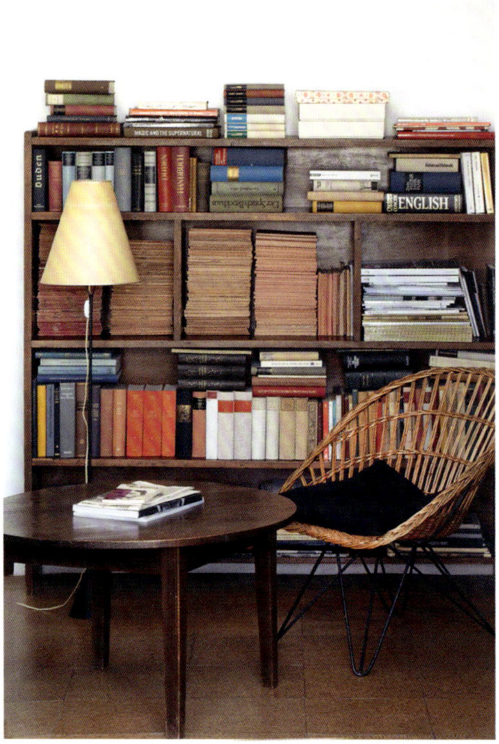
Duden
ENGLISH

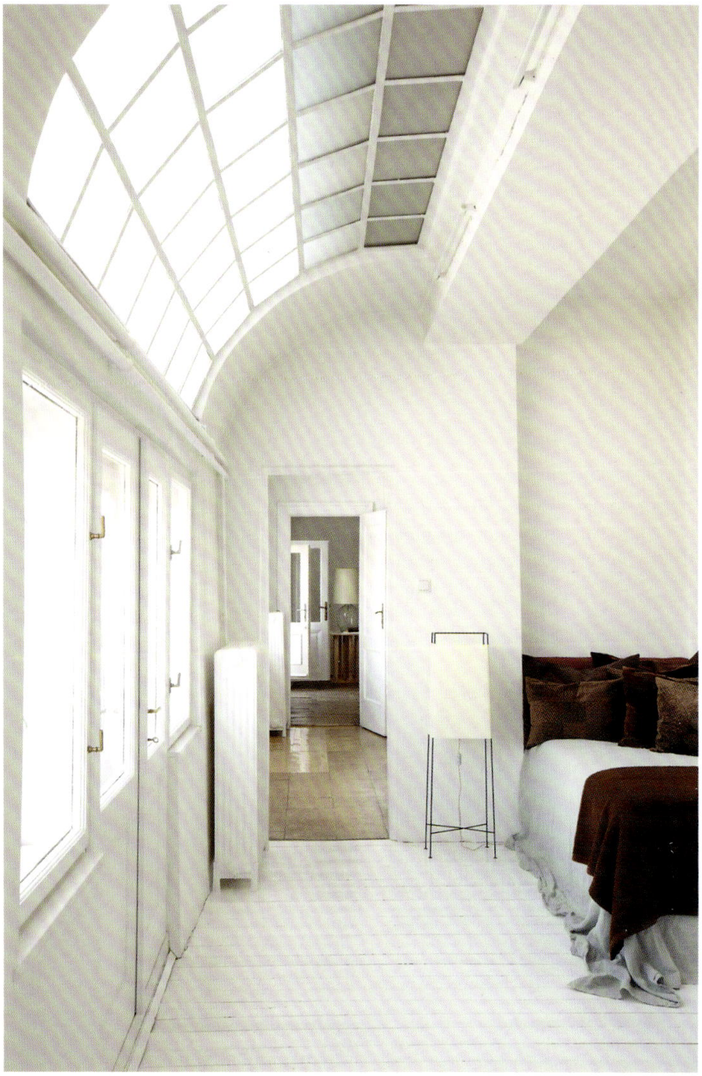

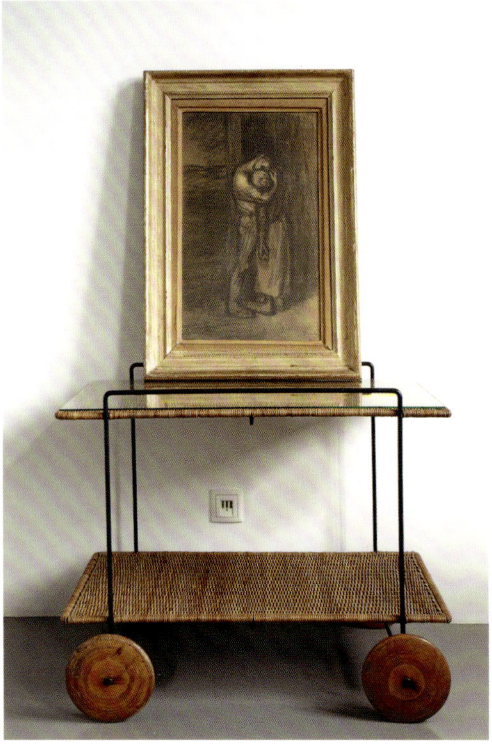

82–83 The 1970s sofa was bought by Faust's mother at auction in Munich. The Franz West floor lamp is made from steel and acrylic glass. • Das Sofa aus den 70ern ersteigerte ihre Mutter in München. Franz Wests Stehleuchte besteht aus Stahl und Acrylglas. • Le canapé des années 1970 provient d'une vente aux enchères à Munich. Le lampadaire de Franz West est en acier et en verre acrylique.

◀ *(clockwise)* Faust's kitchen with vintage fridge; her father's complete collection of Karl Kraus's journal *Die Fackel*; skylights recall the prewar use of the space as a photo studio; a Theophile Steinlen drawing rests on a Carl Auböck wicker trolley. • Fausts Küche mit Vintage-Kühlschrank; ihres Vaters komplette Sammlung von Karl Kraus' *Die Fackel*; Oberlichter erinnern daran, dass die Wohnung einst ein Fotostudio war; Zeichnung von Theophile Steinlen auf einem Auböck-Servierwagen. • Le frigo vintage dans la cuisine ; la collection complète de la revue *Die Fackel* héritée de son père ; avant la guerre, l'espace était un studio de photographe, comme le rappelle le puits de lumière ; dessin de Theophile Steinlen sur un chariot en osier de Carl Auböck.

▲ The view from Faust's front terrace takes in the Hofburg complex and the spire of St. Stephan's Cathedral. • Auf der vorderen Dachterrasse hat man die Hofburg und die Turmspitze des Stephansdoms im Blick. • La terrasse située à l'avant de l'appartement offre une vue sur le complexe de la Hofburg et le clocher de la cathédrale Saint-Étienne.

87 In the guest room, a chair from Franz West's studio stands near an Auböck coat rack. From left, art by Nicolas Jasmin, Clegg & Guttmann, and Pierre Leguillon. • Im Gästezimmer steht ein Stuhl aus Franz Wests Studio, die Garderobe ist von Auböck. Kunst von Nicolas Jasmin, Clegg & Guttmann und Pierre Leguillon. • Dans la chambre d'amis, une chaise de l'atelier de Franz West côtoie un portemanteau d'Auböck. Sur les étagères, des œuvres de Nicolas Jasmin, Clegg & Guttman, et Pierre Leguillon (de gauche à droite).

"I'm not a person who buys design furniture," asserts artist and photographer Marina Faust. Instead, her apartment in Vienna is furnished mainly with possessions she inherited from her parents. There is part of her father's stunning book collection, a vintage American refrigerator with drawers, and several pieces by Austrian midcentury designer Carl Auböck, who was a family friend. The look today is much sparer than when her parents lived here. "I like whiteness," Faust admits. "I love empty walls. It's a kind of freedom." But not everything is perfectly pristine. "My atelier space in the back is full of stuff. Sometimes I need both chaos and order," she says. Among the things she added are several objects by her friend, the late artist Franz West. In the living room is a monochrome screen that she views and uses as both an artwork and room divider. She also has one of West's centipede wooden sculpture plinths, which acts as a bedside table. On top of it is a simply chic glass lamp made by her mother around 1960. The act of bold, impromptu creation, it would seem, is in the genes.

„ICH WAR NIE JEMAND, DER SICH NEUE DESIGNERMÖBEL KAUFT." MARINA FAUST

Stattdessen ist das Wiener Apartment der Künstlerin und Fotografin vor allem mit Erbstücken ausgestattet – man entdeckt zahllose wertvolle Bände aus der erstaunlichen Bibliothek ihres Vaters, einen amerikanischen Kühlschrank mit Schubladen und mehrere Objekte des legendären österreichischen Midcentury-Designers Carl Auböck, der ein Freund der Familie war. Der heutige Look ist allerdings viel karger als zu Zeiten ihrer Eltern. „Ich habe es gern weiß", gesteht Faust. „Ich liebe leere Wände. Das ist eine Art Freiheit." Doch das gilt nicht überall. „Mein Atelierbereich ist vollgestopft", erzählt sie. „Irgendwie brauche ich beides, Chaos und Ordnung." Zu den Dingen, die sie zur Einrichtung hinzufügte, gehören mehrere Arbeiten ihres verstorbenen Freunds Franz West, darunter ein monochromer Wandschirm – für Faust Kunstwerk und Raumteiler in einem. Sie besitzt auch eines von Wests vielbeinigen Postamenten, das nun als Nachttisch dient. Die so simple wie schicke Glas-Leuchte darauf baute ihre Mutter um 1960. Das Talent zum kühnen Impromptu steckt offenbar in den Genen.

« Je ne suis pas du genre à acheter du mobilier design », prévient l'artiste et photographe Marina Faust. Effectivement, son appartement viennois est aménagé principalement avec ce que lui ont laissé ses parents. On y trouve l'impressionnante bibliothèque de son père, un vieux réfrigérateur américain à tiroirs et plusieurs pièces des années 1950 du designer autrichien Carl Auböck, un ami de la famille. Le décor y est plus dépouillé que du temps de ses parents. « J'aime le blanc et les murs nus, c'est une forme de liberté », confie Faust. Toutefois, tout chez elle n'est pas immaculé. « Mon atelier à l'arrière est plein à craquer. En fait, j'ai besoin à la fois du chaos et de l'ordre. » Elle a ajouté au décor des œuvres de son ami disparu Franz West. Dans le séjour, l'écran monochrome de ce dernier fait à la fois office de sculpture et de cloison. Un de ses piédestaux « mille-pattes » sert de table de chevet. Dessus, Faust a placé une lampe en verre à l'élégante simplicité réalisée par sa mère vers 1960. À croire que le sens de la création spontanée est un trait de famille !

Franz West
Cy Twombly
FRANZ WEST SCHRIEB
GERHARD RICHTER
WITTGENSTEIN
CLAES OLDENBURG
THOMAS BERNHARD
BETTIE KLINE

MICHAEL FUCHS

HIS APARTMENT IN A MONUMENT OF 1920s JEWISH BERLIN

WHO Art dealer. **WHAT** A 450 m² (4,844 sq. ft.), two-bedroom apartment. **WHERE** Top floor of the Ehemalige Jüdische Mädchenschule (Former Jewish Girls School), built by architect Alexander Beer in 1927/28, in Berlin-Mitte's Auguststraße. Fuchs renovated the redbrick building with Grüntuch Ernst Architekten. **ON-SITE DINING** The former sports hall houses the chic Pauly Saal bar and restaurant. Also on the ground floor is Mogg & Melzer Delicatessen. **LIVING ABOVE THE SHOP** In his gallery on the fourth floor, Fuchs shows the likes of Howard Hodgkin, Frank Stella, and Bernar Venet. The building is also home to Museum The Kennedys, CWC Gallery, and Eigen + Art Lab. **MOST MEMORABLE DESIGN ENCOUNTER** "Sharing a bottle of wine with Verner Panton, in the great Dane's spaceship of a living room in Basel, Switzerland." **PEDAL POWER** Right after moving in, Fuchs rode his bike down the 40m (130-feet)-long corridor. "I felt like eight or nine years old, doing something my parents definitely shouldn't know about," he says with a laugh.

PHOTOGRAPHED BY HIEPLER, BRUNIER STYLED BY STEPHAN MEYER

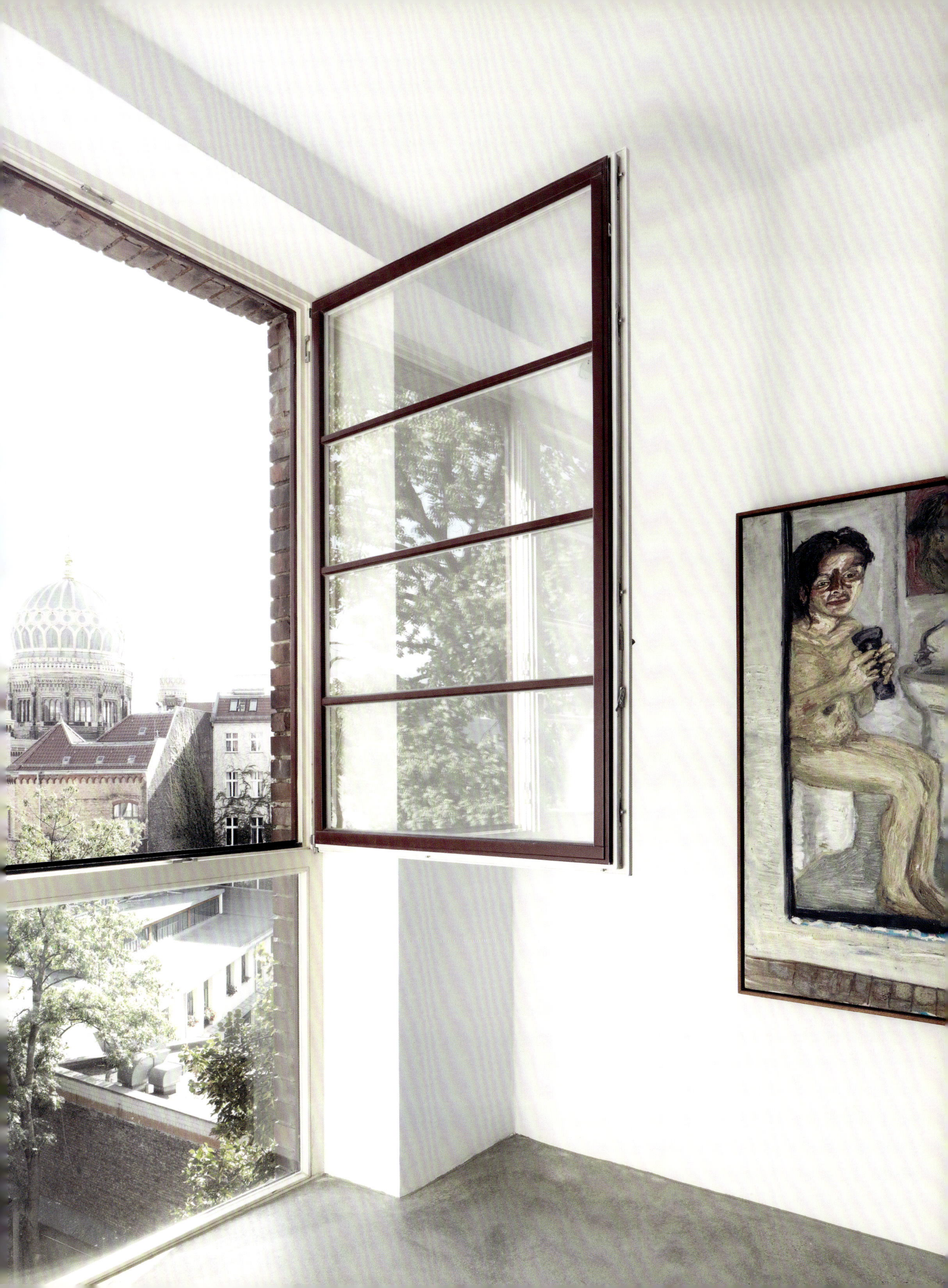

89 At the end of what was once a school corridor awaits a stunning view of Mitte's Neue Synagoge (New Synagogue). Oil painting *Lichtung*, 2003, by Gustav Kluge. • Am Ende des früheren Schulflurs wartet der beeindruckende Blick auf die Neue Synagoge. Ölbild *Lichtung*, 2003, von Gustav Kluge. • L'extrémité de cet ancien couloir d'école offre une vue superbe sur la Nouvelle Synagogue de Berlin. La peinture à l'huile, *Lichtung* (2003), est de Gustav Kluge.

▲ The Former Jewish Girls School was built in the New Objectivity Style. It originally comprised 14 classrooms, a gymnasium, and a rooftop garden. • Die Ehemalige Jüdische Mädchenschule, erbaut im Stil der Neuen Sachlichkeit, besaß neben 14 Klassenzimmern eine Turnhalle und einen Dachgarten. • Cette ancienne école juive pour filles a été construite dans le style de la Nouvelle Objectivité. Elle comportait à l'origine 14 classes, un gymnase et un jardin sur le toit.

◀ Hans Wegner seating is paired with Verner Panton carpets and cocktail tables. The painting is by Andreas Golder, an artist Fuchs represents. • Sofa und Sessel von Hans Wegner treffen auf Verner Pantons Teppiche und Cocktailtische. Gemälde von Andreas Golder, den Fuchs' Galerie vertritt. • Dans le séjour, des sièges de Hans Wegner et des tables basses sur des tapis de Verner Panton. L'œuvre au mur est d'Andreas Golder, un artiste exposé par Fuchs.

▲ In the entry hall, a Bernar Venet sculpture below a Leiko Ikemura painting. The stroller with bird trap is a work by Andreas Slominski. • Im Entrée steht eine Plastik von Bernar Venet unter einem Gemälde von Leiko Ikemura. Der Kinderwagen mit Vogelfalle ist von Andreas Slominski. • Dans le hall d'entrée, une sculpture de Bernar Venet est posée au sol sous une peinture de Leiko Ikemura. La poussette avec un piège à oiseaux est d'Andreas Slominski.

92–93 The main room showcases a painting by Johannes Kahrs and Fuchs's vintage furniture, including a black Gio Ponti *Distex* chair. When the brick ceiling was discovered during renovation work, Fuchs decided to expose it and built a new insulated roof structure on top. "Quite an effort," he admits, "but worth it." • Im Hauptraum kommt das Gemälde von Johannes Kahrs ebenso gut zur Geltung wie die Vintage-Möbel, etwa Pontis schwarzer *Distex*-Sessel. Beim Renovieren wurde die Ziegeldecke freigelegt und mit einem isolierten Dach überbaut. „Viel Aufwand", so Fuchs. „Aber es hat sich gelohnt." • Dans la pièce principale, un tableau de Johannes Kahrs côtoie des meubles vintage, dont un fauteuil noir *Distex* de Gio Ponti. Lors de la rénovation, Fuchs a mis au jour le plafond en briques et a décidé de le conserver en construisant un nouveau toit isolant par-dessus. « Ce fut tout un travail, mais cela en valait la peine », déclare-t-il.

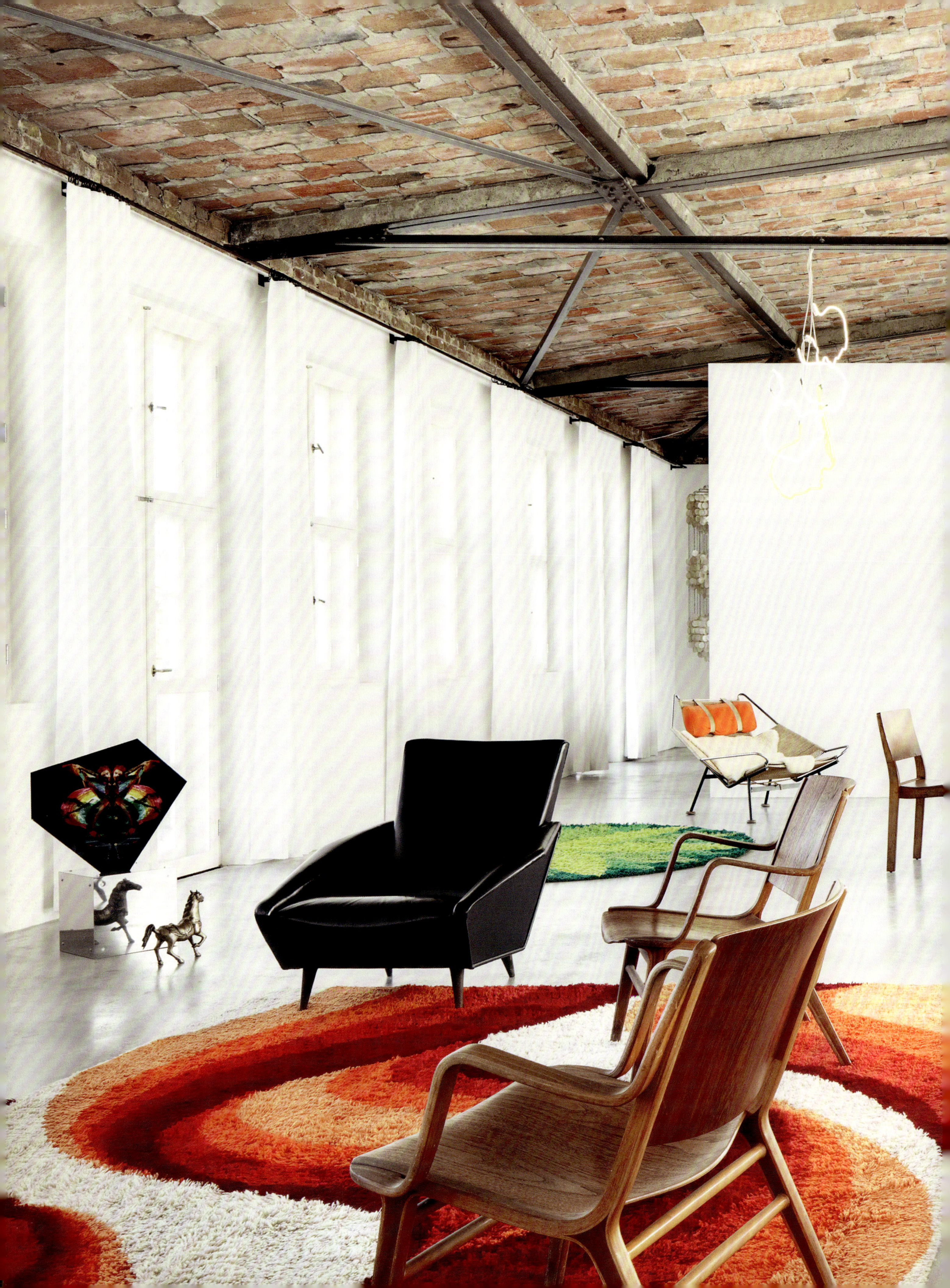

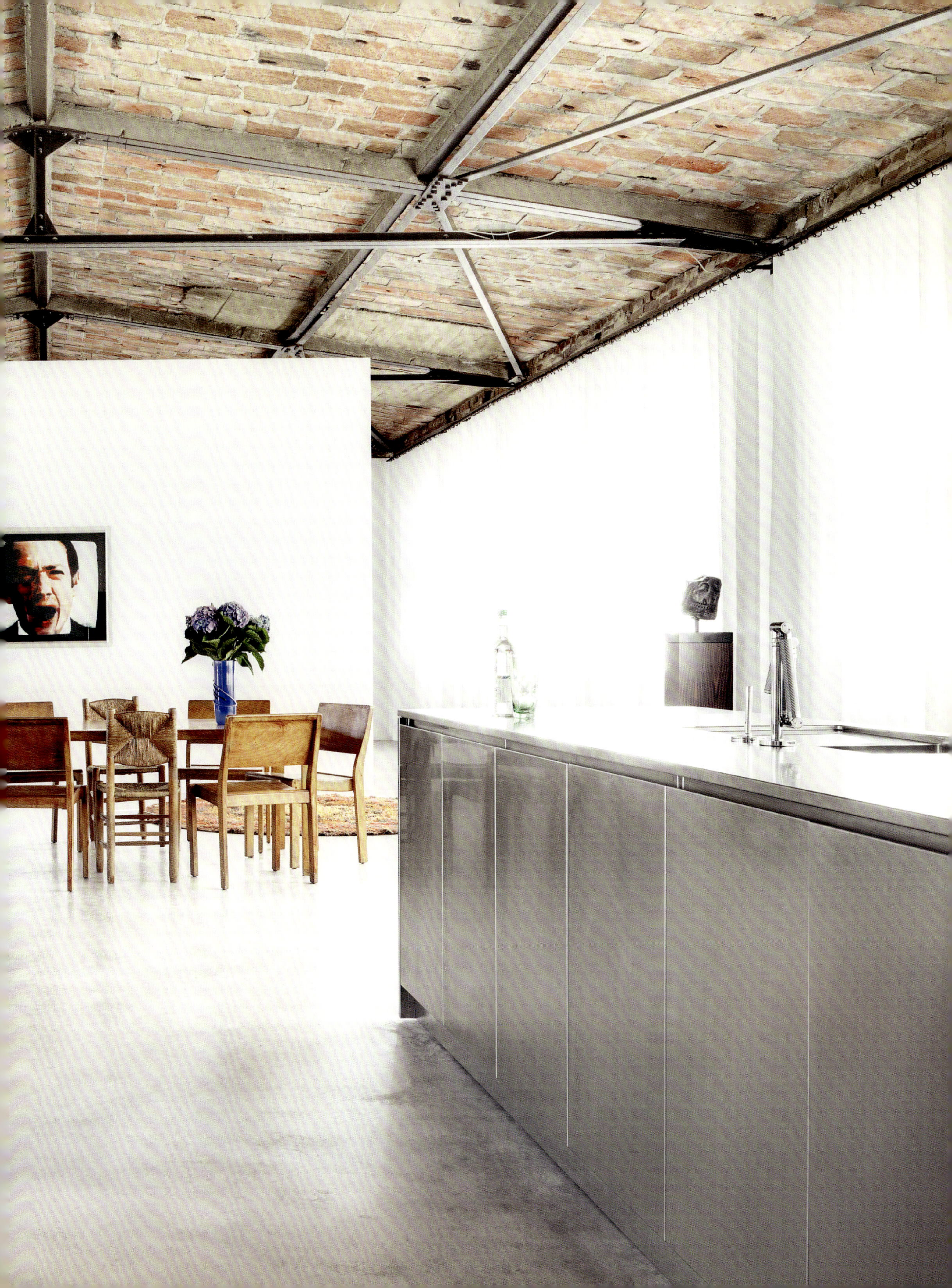

▲ The lengthy corridor, which runs down a side wing of the building, is used to exhibit artworks including Paul Hosking's *Rorschach Portrait (Teal),* front right. • Der lange Flur in einem Seitenflügel bietet Raum zur Präsentation von Kunst wie Paul Hoskings *Rorschach Portrait (Teal)* vorn rechts. • Le long couloir qui court tout le long d'une aile du bâtiment sert à exposer des œuvres, dont le *Rorschach Portrait (Teal)* de Paul Hosking, au premier plan à droite.

◀ In the master bathroom, Fuchs opted for a dramatic change of atmosphere, which allowed him to integrate the 19th-century daybed he inherited from his grandmother. He stripped the vintage tub of its paint and placed an original backlit Piero Fornasetti mirror above it. • Im Masterbad ändert sich die Atmosphäre radikal – so schuf Fuchs den passenden Rahmen für ein Daybed aus dem 19. Jahrhundert, ein Erbstück seiner Großmutter. Über die historische Wanne, deren Lackierung entfernt wurde, hängte er einen Spiegel von Piero Fornasetti.
• Dans la salle de bains, la tonalité est radicalement différente. Fuchs y a installé un lit de repos du 19ᵉ siècle hérité de sa grand-mère. Il a décapé la baignoire ancienne et a placé au-dessus un miroir vintage de Piero Fornasetti illuminé par l'arrière.

◀ The bedcover is another heirloom that belonged to his grandmother. Archival photographs by Dussart, most famous for his images of Brigitte Bardot. • Auch die Überdecke ist von seiner Großmutter. An der Wand Archiv-Aufnahmen von Dussart, den seine Set-Fotos von Brigitte Bardot bekannt machten. • Le dessus-de-lit est un autre héritage de sa grand-mère. Au mur, des photographies d'archives de Dussart, surtout connu pour ses portraits de Brigitte Bardot.

▲ ▶ The office is furnished with a Jean Prouvé desk and cafeteria table, and a bookshelf by Moebel Horzon. Artworks by Gregory Crewdson and (on floor) William Copley. • Im Büro stehen Desk und Tisch von Prouvé sowie ein Regal von Moebel Horzon. Kunst von Gregory Crewdson und William Copley (auf dem Boden). • Dans l'espace de travail, bureau et table de cafétéria de Jean Prouvé et une bibliothèque de Moebel Horzon ; œuvres de Gregory Crewdson (mur) et de William Copley (au sol).

"THE AIM OF OUR RENOVATION WAS TO LET BOTH THE SPACE AND MY COLLECTION SPEAK FOR THEMSELVES." MICHAEL FUCHS

"That's why the very straightforward, clean style of Grüntuch Ernst Architekten of Berlin was just ideal," states Fuchs, who has long lived in gallery-like spaces. "I didn't want to have a decorator going nuts and putting in some mirrored walls." Fuchs collects both works by artists he represents and others he admires. In the latter category are the Andreas Slominski stroller in the entry hall and paintings by William Copley and Johannes Kahrs. He also has a small selection of drawings by Tiepolo. "Many look perfectly contemporary," he explains. "You can put them next to work by Cecily Brown and have a hard time figuring out who did what." His flat is also filled with major vintage furniture by the likes of Prouvé, Panton, Perriand, and Aalto. The bedroom and bathroom, meanwhile, offer a dramatic change of atmosphere. There, Fuchs incorporated Rubelli brocade drapes and a couch à la Sigmund Freud he inherited from his grandmother. It seems even modernists need a comfort zone.

„Der geradlinige Stil von Grüntuch Ernst Architekten war ideal für das Ziel unserer Renovierung der Ehemaligen Jüdischen Mädchenschule in Berlin", sagt Michael Fuchs. „Am Ende sollten die Räume und die Kunst für sich sprechen können. Verrücktes Interiordesign mit verspiegelten Wänden war da keine Option." Der Galerist sammelt nicht nur Arbeiten von Künstlern, die er vertritt, sondern auch von anderen, die er bewundert. In die zweite Kategorie gehören der Kinderwagen von Andreas Slominski (mit Vogelfalle statt Baby) im Entrée sowie Gemälde von William Copley und Johannes Kahrs. Auch einige Tiepolo-Zeichnungen besitzt Fuchs: „Manche davon haben etwas sehr Zeitgenössisches. Deutlich wird das, sobald man sie neben eine Arbeit von etwa Cecily Brown hält." Außer Bildern jeder Dimension begegnet man in seiner Wohnung vor allem Entwürfen mit bester Provenienz von Prouvé, Panton, Perriand und Aalto. Nur Schlafzimmer und Bad halten sich nicht ans loftige Konzept: Dort finden sich Vorhänge aus Rubelli-Brokat und eine Couch à la Freud, die Michael Fuchs von seiner Großmutter geerbt hat. Auch Modernisten brauchen eine *comfort zone*.

« Le style très net et dépouillé du cabinet berlinois Grüntuch Ernst Architekten me convenait parfaitement », explique Michael Fuchs. « Je ne voulais surtout pas d'un décorateur farfelu qui me mette des murs en miroir. » Le galeriste berlinois collectionne à la fois les artistes qu'il expose et d'autres qu'il admire. Parmi les œuvres de ces derniers, la poussette d'Andreas Slominski (avec un piège à oiseaux au lieu d'un bébé), ainsi que des toiles de William Copley et de Johannes Kahrs. Il possède aussi une petite sélection de dessins de Tiepolo. « Beaucoup paraissent très modernes. On peut les placer à côté d'une œuvre de Cecily Brown et se demander qui a fait quoi. » Son appartement est rempli de meubles design signés Prouvé, Panton, Perriand ou Aalto, entre autres. Dans la chambre et la salle de bains, l'atmosphère est radicalement autre. Fuchs y a intégré des rideaux en brocart de Rubelli et un divan à la Sigmund Freud hérité de sa grand-mère. Apparemment, même les partisans du style loft ont besoin de leur petit coin douillet !

ALAIN GILLES

HIS FAMILY HOME IN BRUSSELS

WHO Belgian product and furniture designer. **WHAT** A 500 m² (5,382 sq. ft.), two-story loft in a former workshop dating back to the 1920s. **WHERE** In the working-class neighborhood of Schaerbeek, a 15-minute walk from the historic center of Brussels. **SETTING THE FRAME** Gilles collaborated on the project with Olivier Bastin, co-founder of the architecture cooperative L'Escaut. **LATE BLOOMER** At the age of 32, Gilles left his job in finance at J. P. Morgan to study design. **UNUSUAL INFLUENCES** He claims his love of color is derived from classic Belgian comic strips, especially Edgar P. Jacobs's *Blake and Mortimer*. When designing, he enjoys listening to electronic music by Mr. Oizo, Amon Tobin, and Funki Porcini. **REBEL, REBEL** He and his wife, Rama, got married in Las Vegas. **RECOGNITION** Gilles was named Designer of the Year 2012 at the hip and happening Biennale Interieur in Kortrijk, Belgium.

PHOTOGRAPHED BY SERGE ANTON/LIVING INSIDE   PORTRAIT BY THOMAS DE BOEVER

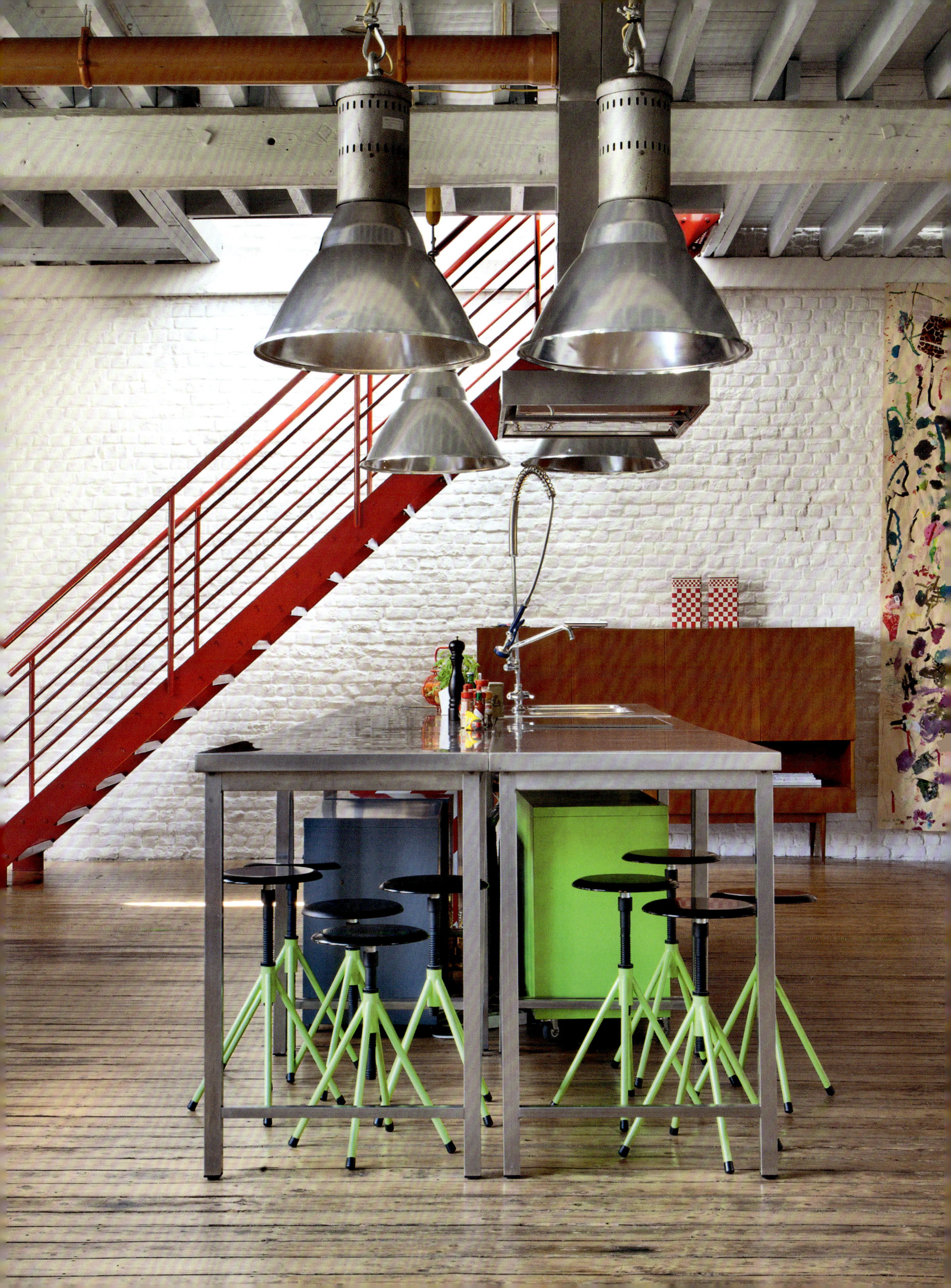

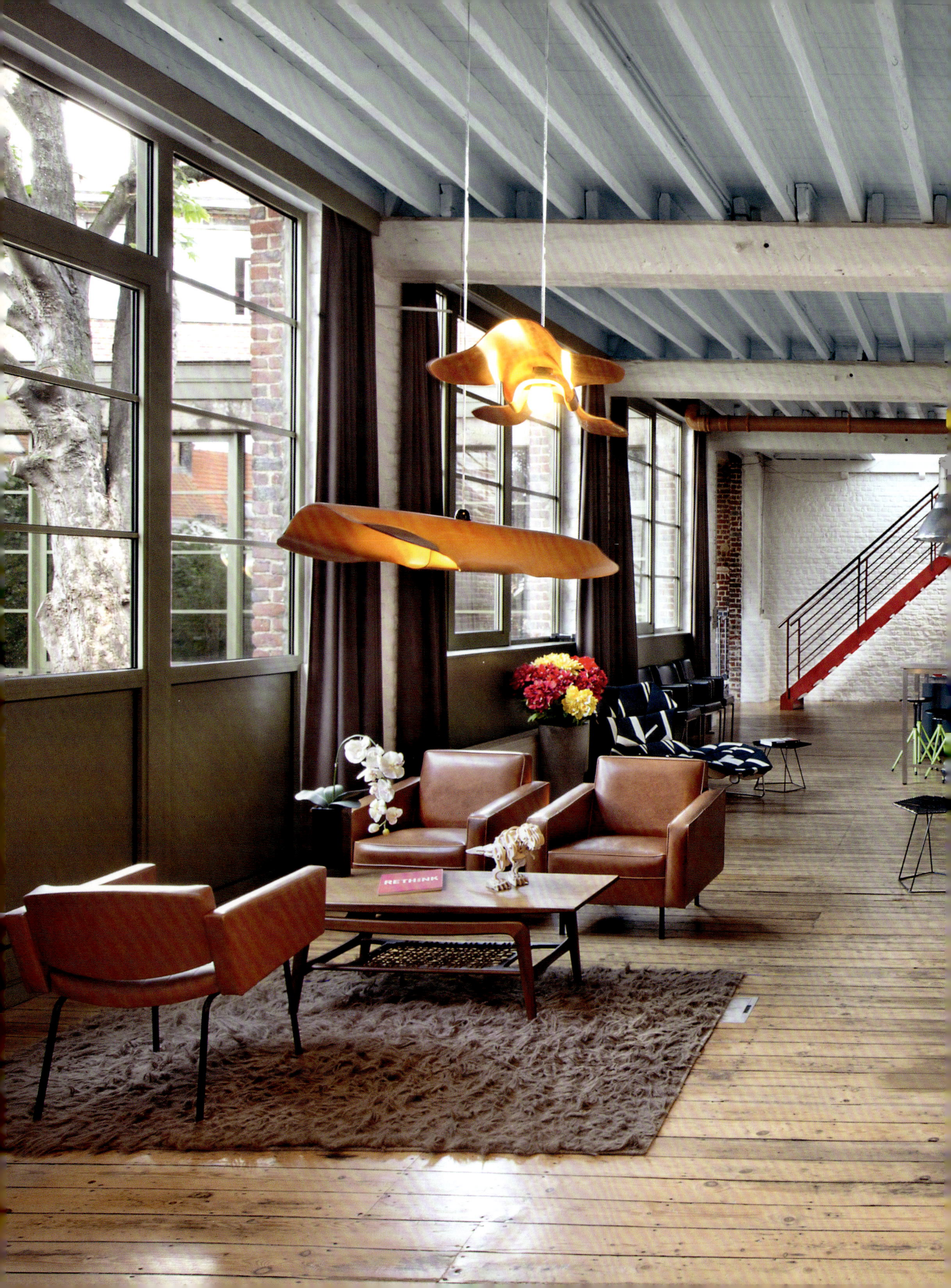
RETHINK

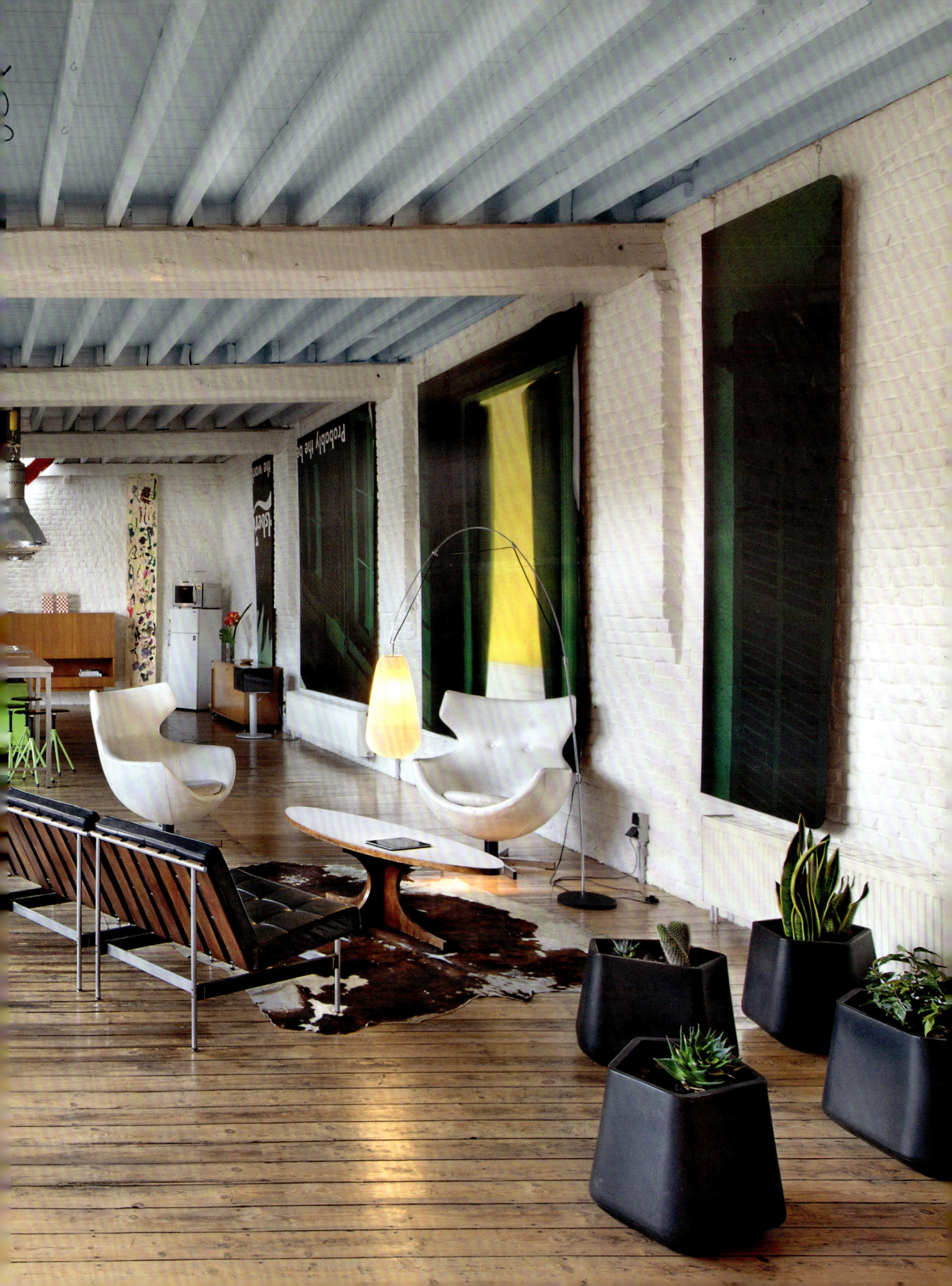

99–101 The huge industrial lights above the stainless steel kitchen island were found at the Brussels flea market. Gilles customized the stools by painting them green; in the vast living room, different seating areas were created to function "like in a hotel lobby." The ceiling was painted blue "as if it were a sky inside the house." • Die Industrie-Leuchten über der Edelstahlküche stammen vom Brüsseler Flohmarkt. Den Hockern gab Gilles mit grünem Lack mehr individuellen Pfiff; im Wohnbereich platzierte er Sitzgruppen „wie in einer Hotellobby"; der hellblaue Anstrich macht die Decke für ihn „zu einem Himmel innerhalb des Hauses". • Les lampes industrielles au-dessus de l'îlot de cuisine viennent du marché aux puces de Bruxelles. Gilles a repeint les tabourets en vert ; dans le spacieux séjour, divers espaces de détente ont été aménagés « comme dans un hall d'hôtel ». Le plafond bleu créé « un ciel dans la maison ».

▼ On the top-floor landing sits Gilles's own *Collage* table. The desk in son Oscar's bedroom was bought for five euros in a Salvation Army store. • Unter der Dachschräge im Obergeschoss steht Gilles' Tisch *Collage*. Den Schreibtisch für Sohn Oscar kaufte er für 5 Euro im Laden der Heilsarmee. • Sur le palier du dernier étage, la table *Collage* de Gilles. Le bureau dans la chambre de son fils Oscar a été acheté pour cinq euros dans un dépôt de l'Armée du Salut.

▶ "I thought it was amusing to put the king and queen in there to mark the fact we're in Belgium:" the former controller's office (with Gilles's *My First Translation* chairs) is now a cloakroom. • „Das Königspaar erinnert uns daran, dass wir in Belgien sind": Aus dem Büro des Vorarbeiters wurde die Garderobe. • « Les portraits du roi et de la reine nous rappellent qu'on est en Belgique » : le bureau du contremaître, transformé en vestiaire, avec deux sièges *My First Translation* de Gilles.

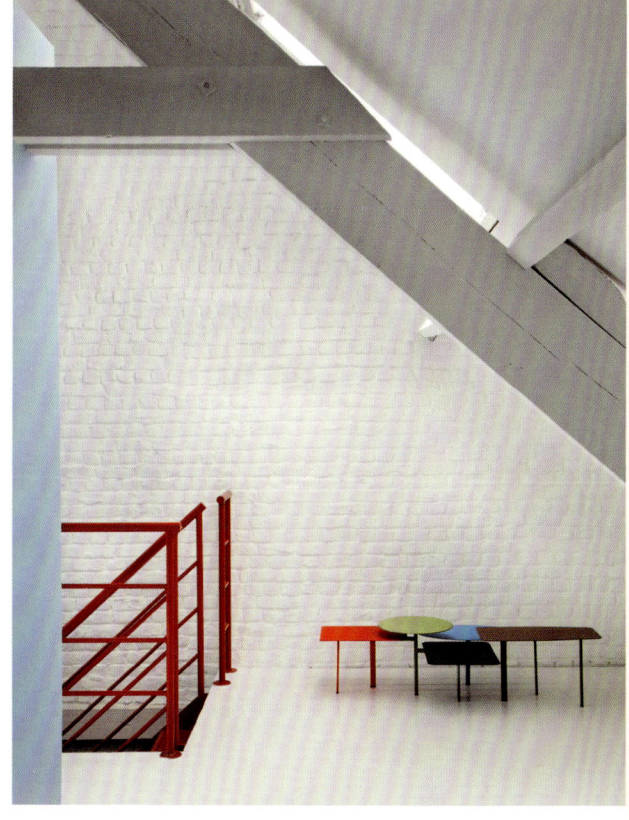

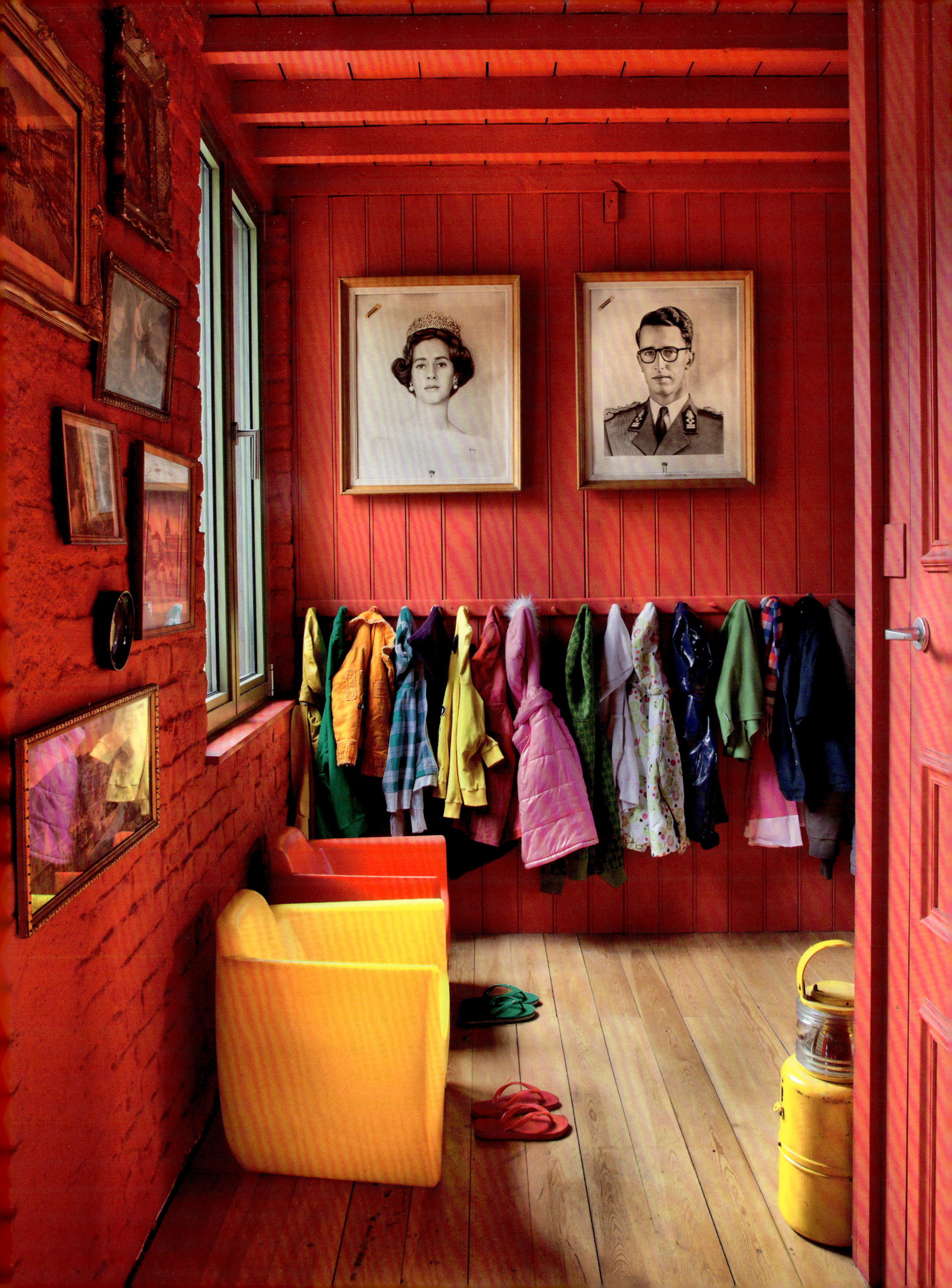

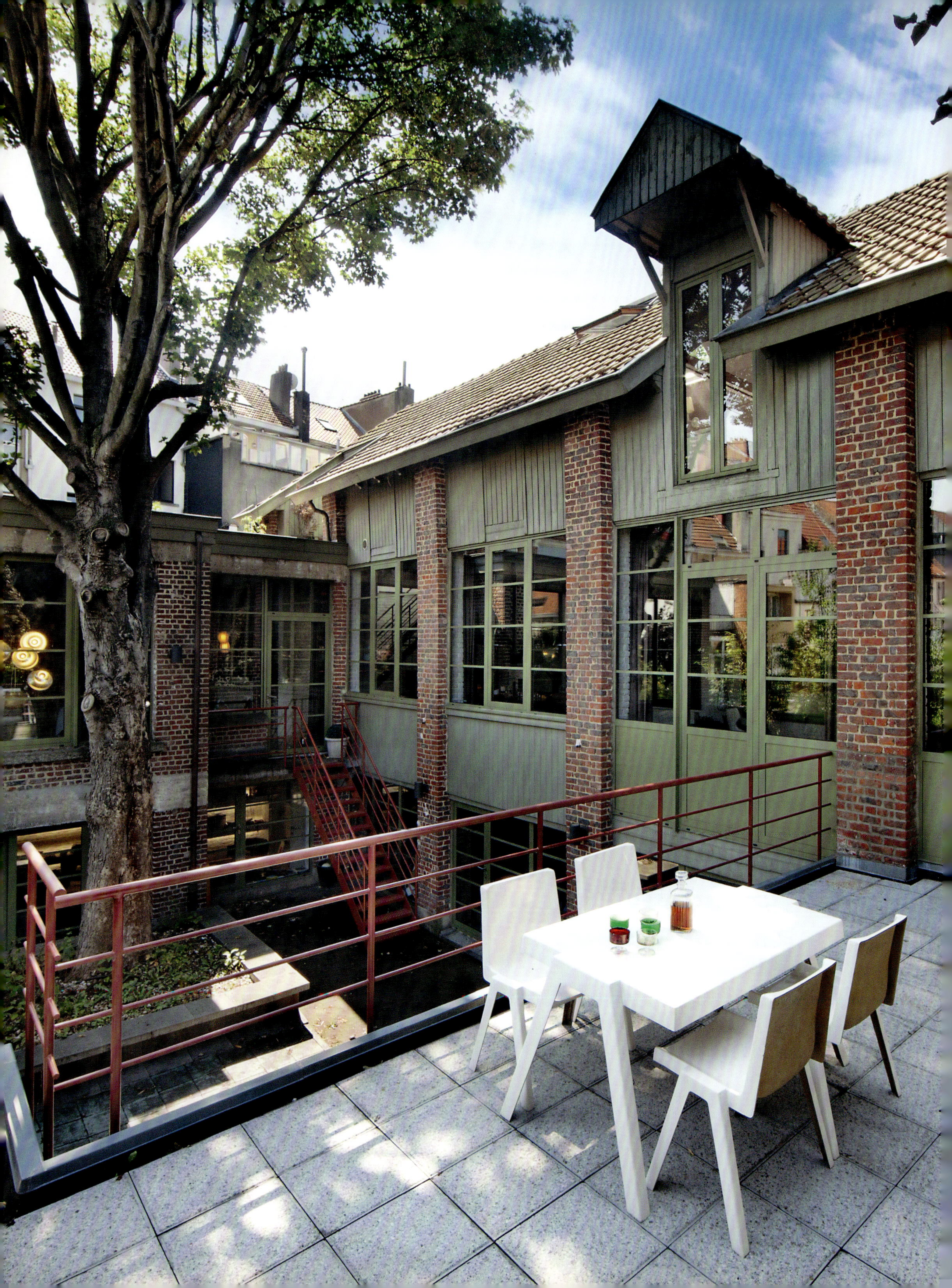

"I was looking for a place with real personality, a place with a history," asserts Alain Gilles. What he found—an old fur-coat workshop—certainly fits the bill. "You could just feel that people had worked there," he adds. His approach was to be as respectful and sympathetic to its past as possible. He decided, for instance, to keep the building's "scars;" nails were left in the walls and used for hanging things, a black mark made on the floor by an old industrial heating system was retained. Gilles then added warmth and whimsy with vintage furnishings and strategically placed bursts of color. The inside of the former controller's office was painted red to resemble a jewel box, and metal stairs were designed to evoke the ladders in a Super Mario Bros. video game. The industrial-style open-plan kitchen, meanwhile, has several modular elements. "I'm always afraid of permanence," explains Gilles. That said, he rarely alters anything. "My wife says, 'You do everything so that things can be modified,' " he laughs, " 'but when I ask, you never want to change them.' "

„ICH WOLLTE EINEN ORT MIT ECHTER PERSÖNLICHKEIT, EINEN ORT MIT EIGENER GESCHICHTE." ALAIN GILLES

Gefunden hat der belgische Designer diesen Ort in einer ehemaligen Kürschnerwerkstatt: „Man konnte einfach spüren, dass hier gearbeitet wurde." Gilles nahm viel Rücksicht auf diese Vergangenheit, ja er beließ sogar die „Narben" des Gebäudes: Vorhandene Nägel in den Wänden wurden als Aufhängung genutzt, und die schwarzen Stellen im Holzboden, die eine alte Heizung verursacht hat, sind noch immer zu sehen. Vintage-Möbel und strategisch gesetzte Farbakzente geben den Räumen eine sympathische Exzentrik. Leuchtend rot ausgemalt wirkt das einstige Vormannsbüro wie ein Schmuckkästchen, und beim Umbau eingezogene Metalltreppen erinnern nicht zufällig an die Leitern in *Super Mario*-Computerspielen. Die offene Küche besteht größtenteils aus mobilen Einzelteilen. „Zuviel Permanenz macht mir generell Angst", erklärt Gilles. Was nicht heißt, dass er ständig umbaut: „Meine Frau sagt immer: ‚Erst strengst du dich fürchterlich an, damit alles veränderbar bleibt. Aber wenn ich tatsächlich mal etwas umstellen will, bist du dagegen.'"

« Je cherchais un endroit avec du caractère et une histoire », explique Alain Gilles. Cet ancien atelier de tourreur avait donc de quoi le combler. Il s'est efforcé de respecter le plus possible le passé des lieux en conservant ses « cicatrices ». Les vieux clous dans les murs ont été reconvertis en patères ; des taches noires sur le sol, réminiscence de l'ancien chauffage industriel, sont restées telles quelles. Le designer a apporté de la chaleur et de la fantaisie avec des meubles vintage et des éclats de couleur placés à des endroits stratégiques. L'ancien bureau du contremaître a été peint en rouge comme une boîte à bijoux et des escaliers métalliques rappelle ceux du jeu vidéo Super Mario Bros. La cuisine industrielle ouverte comporte plusieurs éléments modulables. « J'ai toujours eu peur de l'immobilisme », avoue Gilles. Sa femme lui rappelle toutefois : « Tu conçois tes objets pour qu'ils puissent être modifiés, mais, ensuite, tu ne veux plus jamais y toucher. »

104 Hidden from the street, the former workshop lies behind other houses. "It's a bit like an oasis right in the middle of the city," notes Gilles. The left wing was added in the 1950s. • Die ehemalige Werkstatt ist von der Straße nicht zu sehen – „eine Oase mitten in der Stadt". Links ein Anbau aus den 1950ern. • Invisible depuis la rue, l'atelier se cache derrière d'autres maisons. «C'est une oasis au cœur de la ville», observe Gilles. L'aile gauche date des années 1950.

▼ The master bedroom is separated from the living room simply by a heavy curtain. That patterned painting on the back wall? A sign bearing the logo of German furniture company Musterring. • Nur ein Vorhang trennt das Schlafzimmer vom Wohnraum. Das Gemälde hinter dem Bett? Ein Schild mit dem Logo der Möbelfirma Musterring. • Un épais rideau sépare la chambre principale du séjour. Derrière le lit, une enseigne portant le logo de la compagnie de mobilier allemande Musterring.

▶ The old entrance to the manager's office was emphasized with color. Naturally, Gilles & family live with many of his own creations. Among them are *Tectonic* tables by Bonaldo (front right), and *Rock Garden* planters by Qui est Paul?. The vintage sofa is the *416* by Kho Liang Le for Artifort. • Der Eingang zum früheren Büro wurde farbig hervorgehoben. Familie Gilles lebt mit vielen Designs von Papa, im Hauptraum sind es etwa die *Tectonic*-Tische (re.) von Bonaldo und die Pflanzkübel *Rock Garden* von Qui est Paul?. Das Vintage-Sofa ist das von Kho Liang Le designte Modell *416* von Artifort. • Une couleur contrastante met en valeur l'entrée de l'ancien bureau du contremaître. Le séjour accueille plusieurs créations de Gilles, dont ses cache-pots *Rock Garden* (de Qui est Paul?) et ses tables *Tectonic* (de Bonaldo, au premier plan à droite). Le canapé vintage est le modèle *416* dessiné par Kho Liang Le pour Artifort.

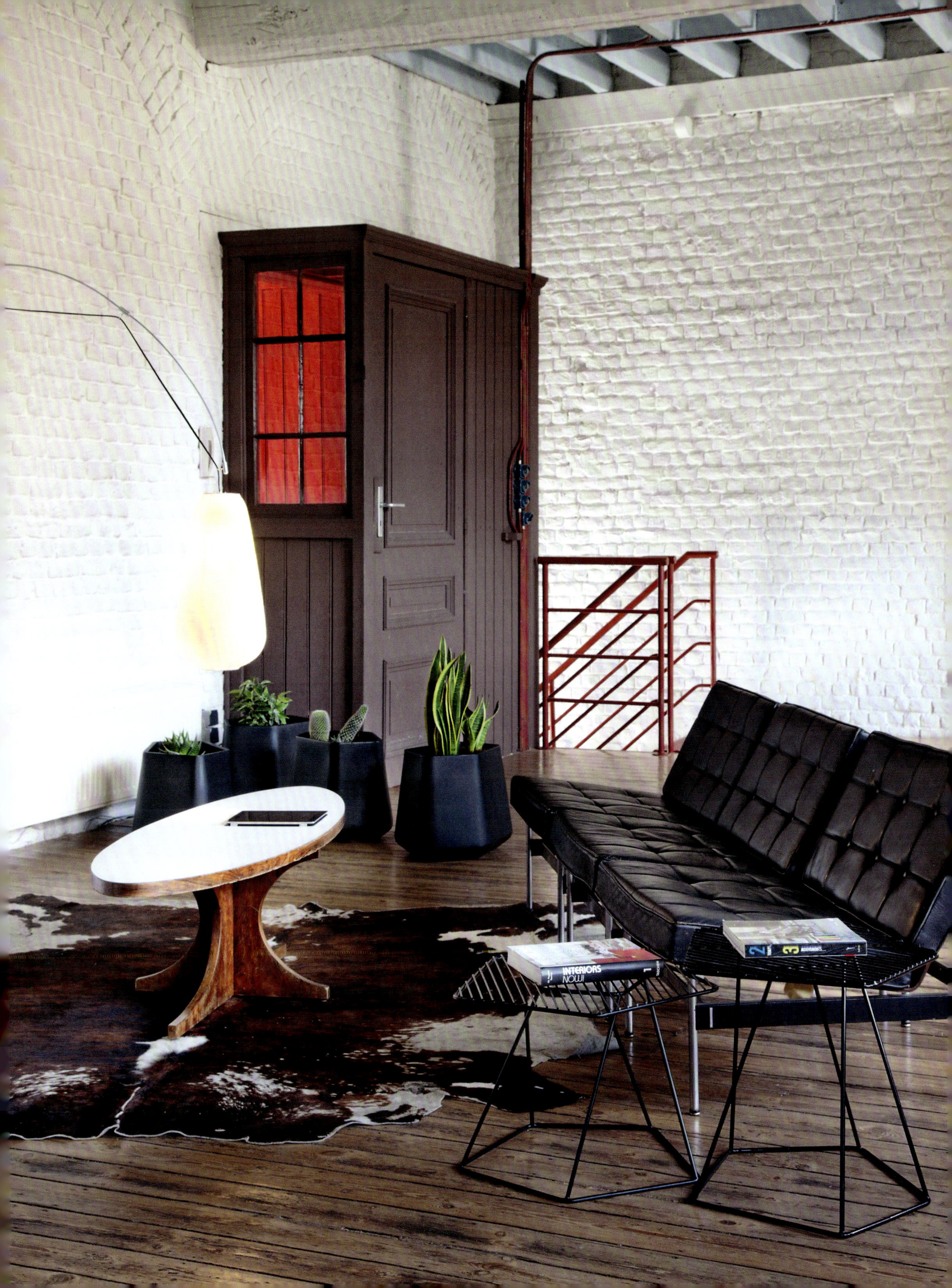
INTERIORS NOW!

PIERRE JORGE GONZALEZ & JUDITH HAASE

AN APARTMENT FOR ART IN BERLIN

WHO Berlin-based architects. Gonzalez hails originally from Paris, Haase from Bremen. **WHAT** A 162 m² (1,744 sq. ft.), one-bedroom flat in an early-20th-century building. **WHERE** Berlin-Charlottenburg. **THE CLIENT** Art consultant Peter Heimer, who has advised, among others, Robert Bosch GmbH and Daimler AG. **FIRST ENCOUNTER** Gonzalez and Haase met while working on Robert Wilson's Water Mill Center. **SPECIALTY** Most of their projects have links to the art world, like the Thomas Schulte and Konrad Fischer galleries in Berlin, a duplex for two artists, and Deutsche Guggenheim's museum shop. **DREAM COMMISSION** Haase: "A museum." Gonzalez: "An art foundation a bit bigger than the one we did"–the 700 m² Jarla Partilager Private Exhibition Space in Berlin. **CULTURE VULTURES** Haase favors classic Minimal Art by the likes of Donald Judd and Dan Flavin; Gonzalez is a fan of the films of Eric Rohmer and Ursula Meier.

PHOTOGRAPHED BY ACHIM HATZIUS   STYLED BY STEPHAN MEYER   PORTRAIT BY MARTIN MAI

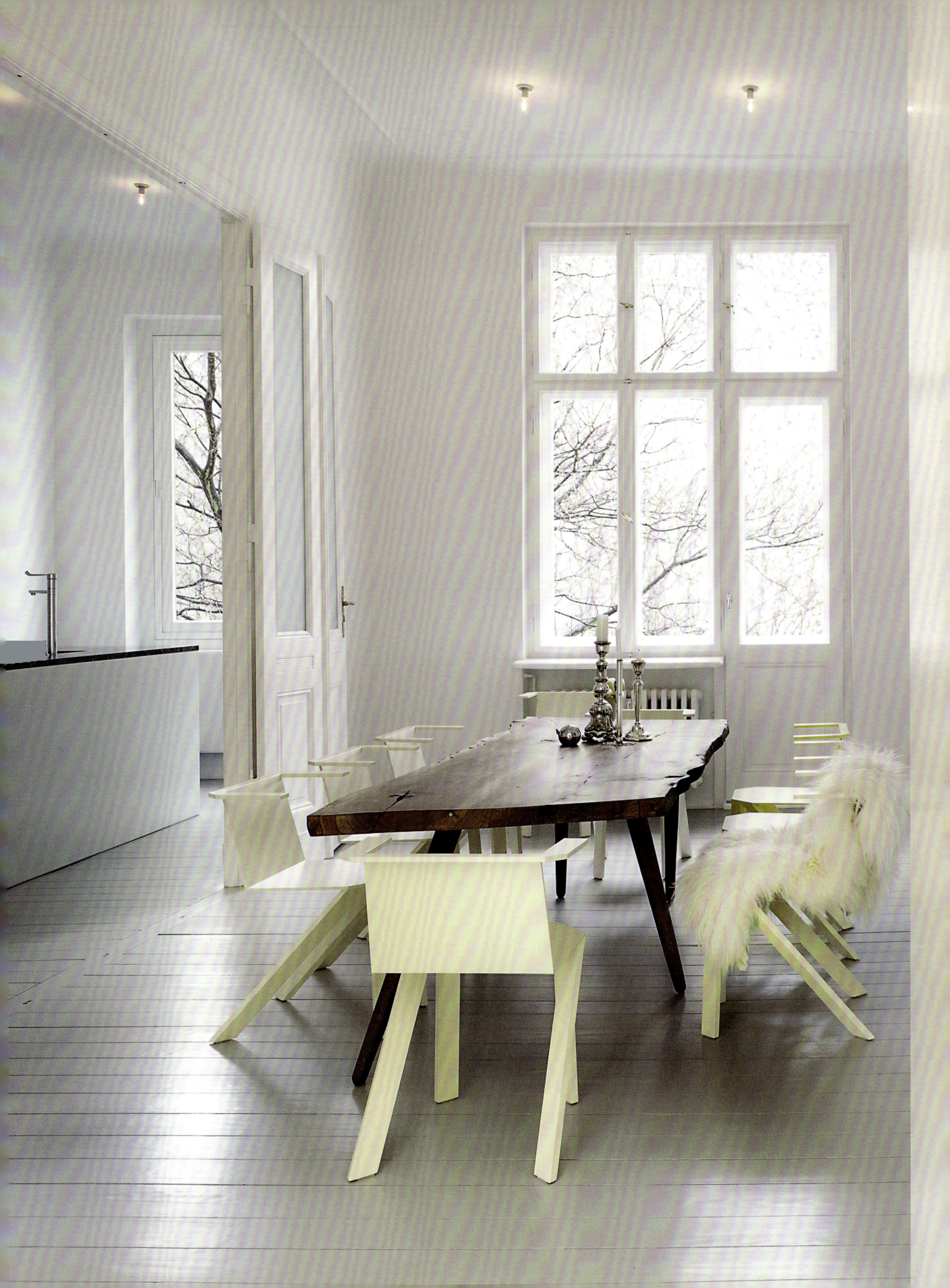

109 Aluminum *Scrap Chairs* by Jerszy Seymour surround a Katja Buchholz oak table in the dining room, which opens directly into the kitchen. • Jerszy Seymours *Scrap Chairs* aus Aluminium umgeben den Eichentisch von Katja Buchholz im Esszimmer, das links in die Küche übergeht. • Dans la salle à manger ouverte sur la cuisine, des *Scrap Chairs* en aluminium de Jerszy Seymour entourent une table en chêne de Katja Buchholz.

▲ A Kirstine Roepstorff collage hangs above a *Conseta* sofa bed by COR in the library-cum-guest room. • Eine Collage von Kirstine Roepstorff hängt in der Bibliothek über dem *Conseta*-Bettsofa von COR für Gäste. • Dans la bibliothèque qui fait également office de chambre d'amis, un collage de Kirstine Roepstorff est accroché au-dessus d'un canapé-lit de COR.

▶▶ Peter Heimer and Vizsla Ludwig in front of a Jeppe Hein sculpture. Carl Strüwe microphotos and a Clemens Tissi lamp in the bedroom. • Peter Heimer mit Vizsla Ludwig vor einer Arbeit von Jeppe Hein. Das Schlafzimmer mit Mikrofotos von Carl Strüwe und Clemens Tissis Lichtkiste. • Peter Heimer et le braque hongrois Ludwig devant une sculpture de Jeppe Hein. Dans la chambre, une lampe de Clemens Tissi et des microphotos de Carl Strüwe.

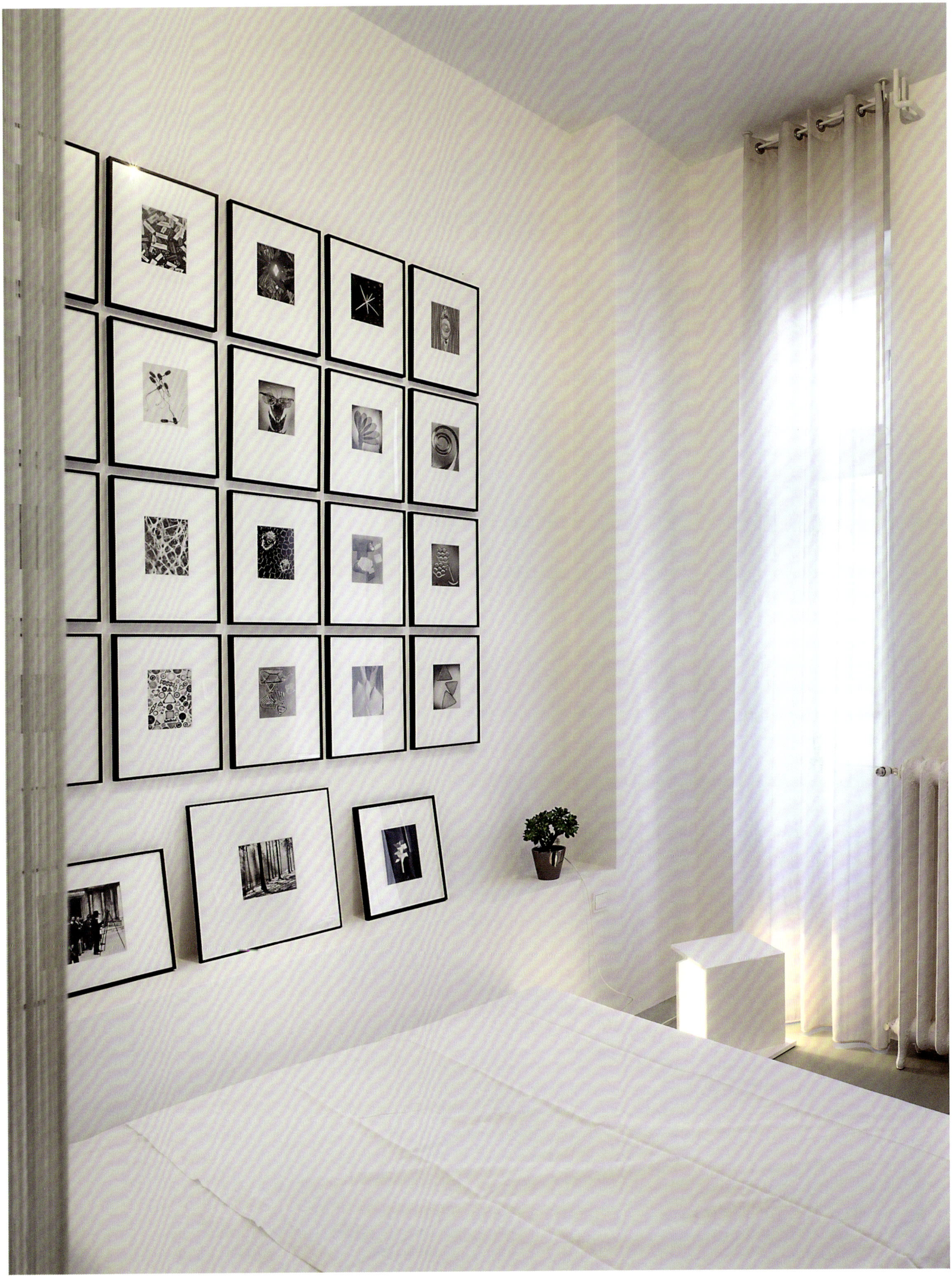

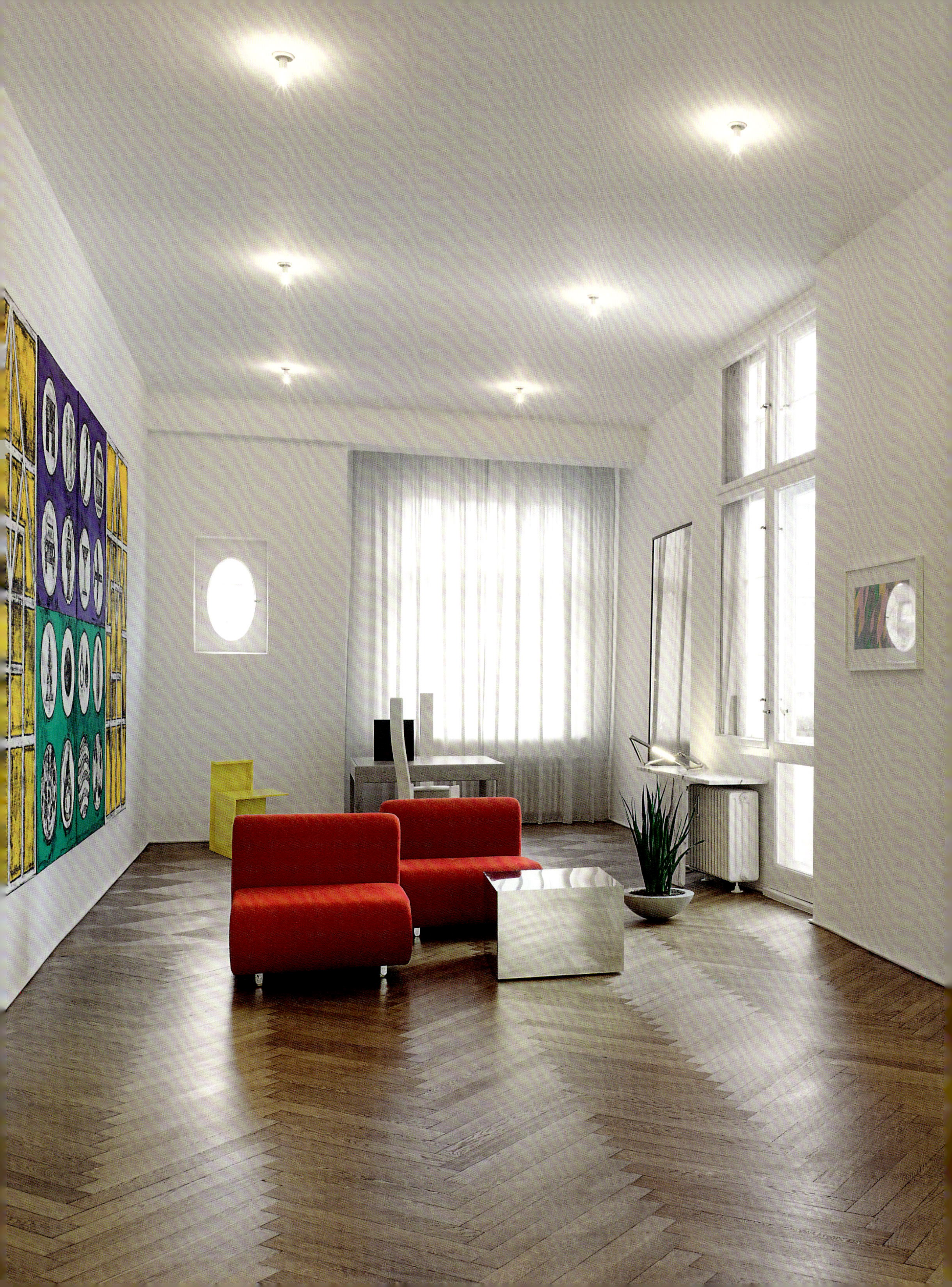

◄ In the gallery-like showroom space, a Katja Buchholz stainless-steel cube is paired with seating from Kazuhide Takahama's *Suzanne* collection for Knoll. • Heimers Showroom möblieren ein Edelstahlquader von Katja Buchholz und Sessel aus Kazuhide Takahamas *Suzanne*-Kollektion von Knoll. • Dans le showroom, une table en inox de Katja Buchholz et deux fauteuils *Suzanne* créés par Kazuhide Takahama pour Knoll.

114 The floor-to-ceiling cupboard unit not only provides a visual link between the two parts of the apartment, but also conceals a number of unsightly chimney vents. • Der breite Einbauschrank verbindet Wohnbereich und Showroom miteinander; außerdem lässt er unansehnliche Lüftungsrohre verschwinden. • Le long placard crée un lien visuel entre les deux parties de l'appartement et permet de dissimuler des conduits de cheminée disgracieux.

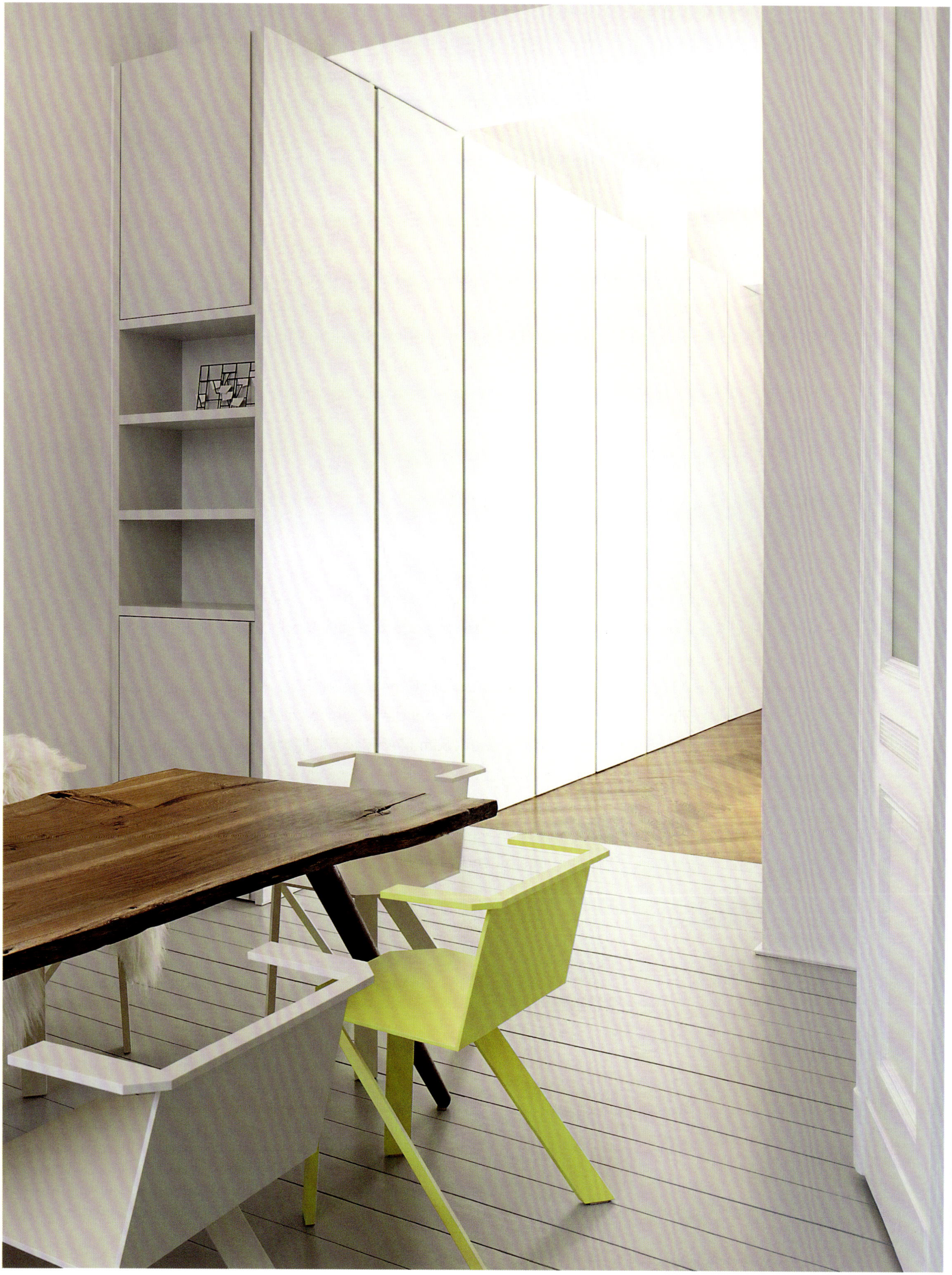

Whatever the project, Gonzalez Haase's approach is always the same. "We free the space of everything that is unnecessary," explains Judith Haase. Over the decades, this L-shaped apartment had suffered from renovation after renovation. "Its essence was lost," notes Pierre Jorge Gonzalez. They removed not only the decorative additions, but also most of the walls to create a public-private hybrid for owner and art consultant Peter Heimer. One section serves as his showroom, the other as his living space. The two are linked by an impressive storage unit (it spans the two zones) but are distinguished by different floor treatments. In the showroom, classical chevron parquet has been left in place. Elsewhere, simpler pine boards were painted light gray. The furnishings are sparse but select, with Clemens Tissi lamps and Katja Buchholz tables. For Heimer, "the flat should be like a stage." To light it, the architects imported tiny but powerful bulbs from Japan, which produce a soft glow in the evening. "When you turn them down," notes Gonzalez, "there's a really warm atmosphere."

„ZUERST BEFREIEN WIR DEN RAUM VON ALLEN ELEMENTEN, DIE EIGENTLICH UNNÖTIG SIND." JUDITH HAASE

So begannen Gonzalez Haase auch dieses Projekt, eine Berliner Wohnung, die über die Dekaden durch eine Renovierung nach der anderen gegangen war. „Ihre Essenz hatte sich verflüchtigt", sagt Pierre Jorge Gonzalez. Die beiden entfernten nicht nur Dekor, sondern auch viele Wände und schufen so eine Wohn-Galerie. Einen Teil nutzt der Kunstberater Peter Heimer als Showroom, den anderen privat. Ein imposantes Staumöbel verbindet die Bereiche, an deren Grenze unterschiedliche Bodenarten aufeinandertreffen: Im Showroom blieb das Fischgrätparkett erhalten, der Rest bekam hellgrau lackierte Kieferndielen. Zur kleinen, feinen Auswahl von Möbeln gehören Tische von Katja Buchholz und Leuchten von Clemens Tissi. „Die Wohnung sollte wie eine Bühne sein", findet Heimer. Umso wichtiger ist die Beleuchtung, für die die Architekten leistungsstarke Mini-Glühlampen aus Japan importierten. „Dimmt man sie", sagt Gonzalez, „entsteht richtig warme Lichtstimmung."

Quel que soit leur projet, la démarche de Gonzalez Haase est la même : « Nous dépouillons l'espace de tout le superflu. » Au fil des décennies, cet appartement en L a subi de nombreuses rénovations. « Il avait perdu son essence », observe Pierre Jorge Gonzalez. Les deux architectes ont ôté les ajouts décoratifs ainsi que la plupart des murs pour créer un hybride entre une galerie et une demeure. Peter Heimer, conseiller en œuvres d'art, vit dans une partie ; l'autre lui sert de showroom. Un grand meuble de rangement relie les deux espaces qui se distinguent par différents traitements au niveau du sol. Dans le showroom, l'ancien parquet en chevrons a été conservé ; ailleurs, un plancher en sapin a été teinté en gris clair. Le mobilier sobre mais sélect comprend des lampes de Clemens Tissi et des tables de Katja Buchholz. Selon Heimer, « l'appartement doit ressembler à une scène de théâtre ». Pour l'éclairer le soir, les architectes ont importé du Japon de minuscules mais puissantes ampoules. « Lorsqu'on baisse leur intensité », note Gonzalez, « cela crée une ambiance très chaleureuse. »

JACQUES GRANGE

A HOTEL FOR FRANCIS FORD COPPOLA IN BERNALDA, ITALY

WHO Legendary French interior designer. **WHAT** Palazzo Margherita–a nine-room hotel in a palace dating from the 1880s. **WHERE** The main street of Coppola's ancestral hometown, Bernalda, in the southern Italian region of Basilicata. **FAMILY PAST** Coppola's grandfather Agostino left for New York in 1904, never to return. **FAMILY PRESENCE** Coppola's great-grandmother's sewing machine can be seen in one of the rooms. Known as "Senza Naso" because she had no nose, she would whip up dresses for the women of Bernalda. **FAMILY CELEBRATION** Coppola's daughter, Sofia, held her wedding there. **MOVIE PICKS** Grange's favorite Coppola films are *The Godfather* series for Francis Ford ("I never tire of watching it") and *Lost in Translation* for Sofia. "It's extremely scholarly and personal," he asserts. **PERFECT MATCH** "It was really easy working with them," states Grange. "They're endearing and artistic and gave me the freedom to express myself."

PHOTOGRAPHED BY MASSIMO LISTRI   PORTRAIT BY ERIC JANSEN

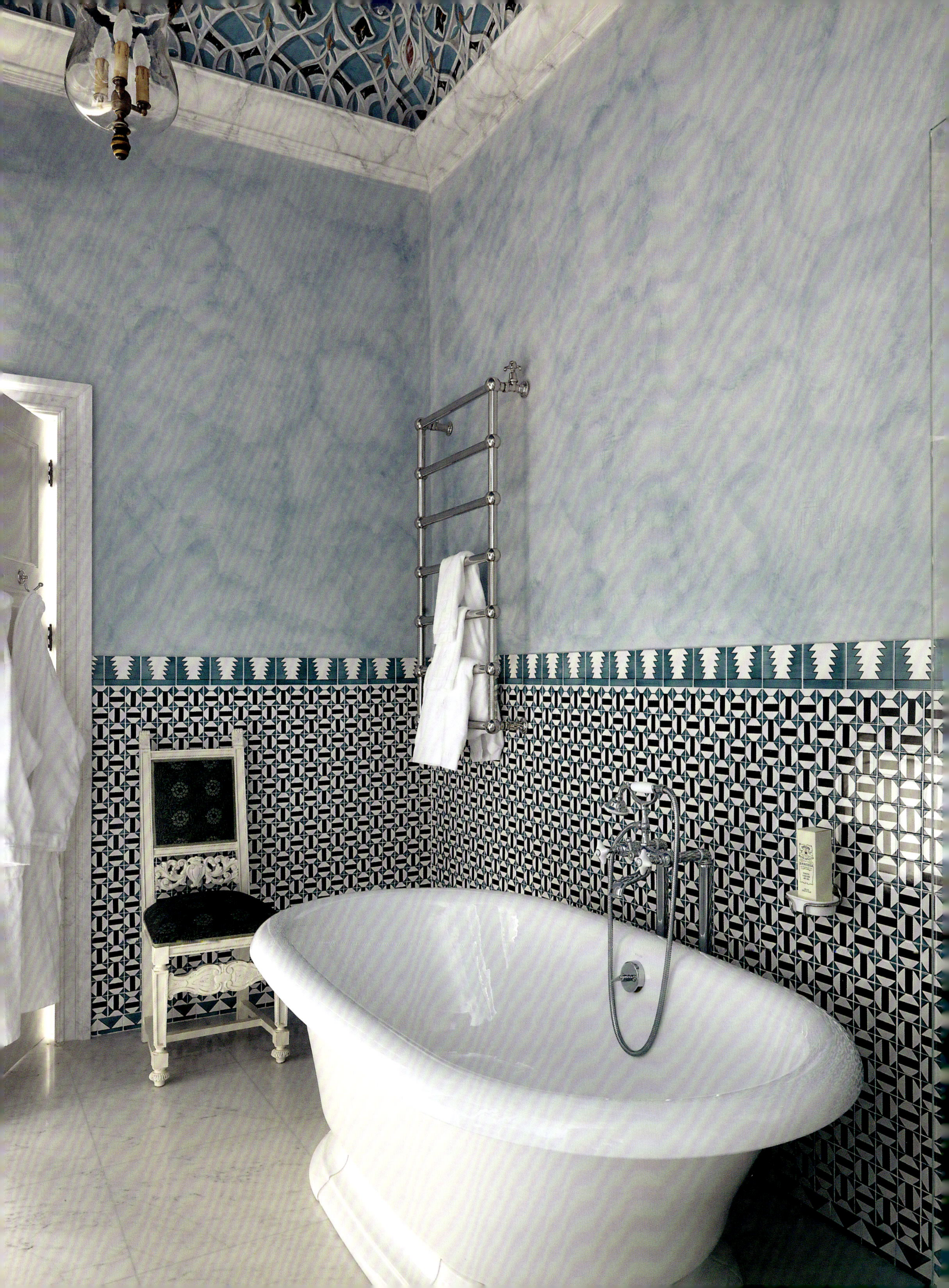

117 Neapolitan tiles were used in the new bathrooms. "The idea," says Grange, "was to give the impression I'd just restored the rooms." • In den neuen Bädern wurden neapolitanische Fliesen verlegt. „Wir wollten den Eindruck erwecken", sagt Grange, „als hätte ich auch diese Räume nur restauriert." • Les nouvelles salles de bains sont décorées de carreaux napolitains. « L'idée était de donner l'impression que le palais venait d'être restauré », explique Grange.

▲ The staircase with its 19th century terrazzo dado was meticulously restored. • Das Treppenhaus mit seiner Terrazzo-Lambrie aus dem 19. Jahrhundert wurde behutsam restauriert. • L'escalier avec son bas lambris du 19ᵉ siècle a été restauré.

▶ Inspired by a Sicilian palazzo, the frescoes in Sofia's room were created by master restorer Roberto Bellantuono and his team of painters. • Die Fresken in Sofias Zimmer stammen von Meisterrestaurator Roberto Bellantuono und seinem Malerteam. • Les fresques de la chambre de Sofia ont été créées par le maître de la restauration Roberto Bellantuono et son équipe d'artisans.

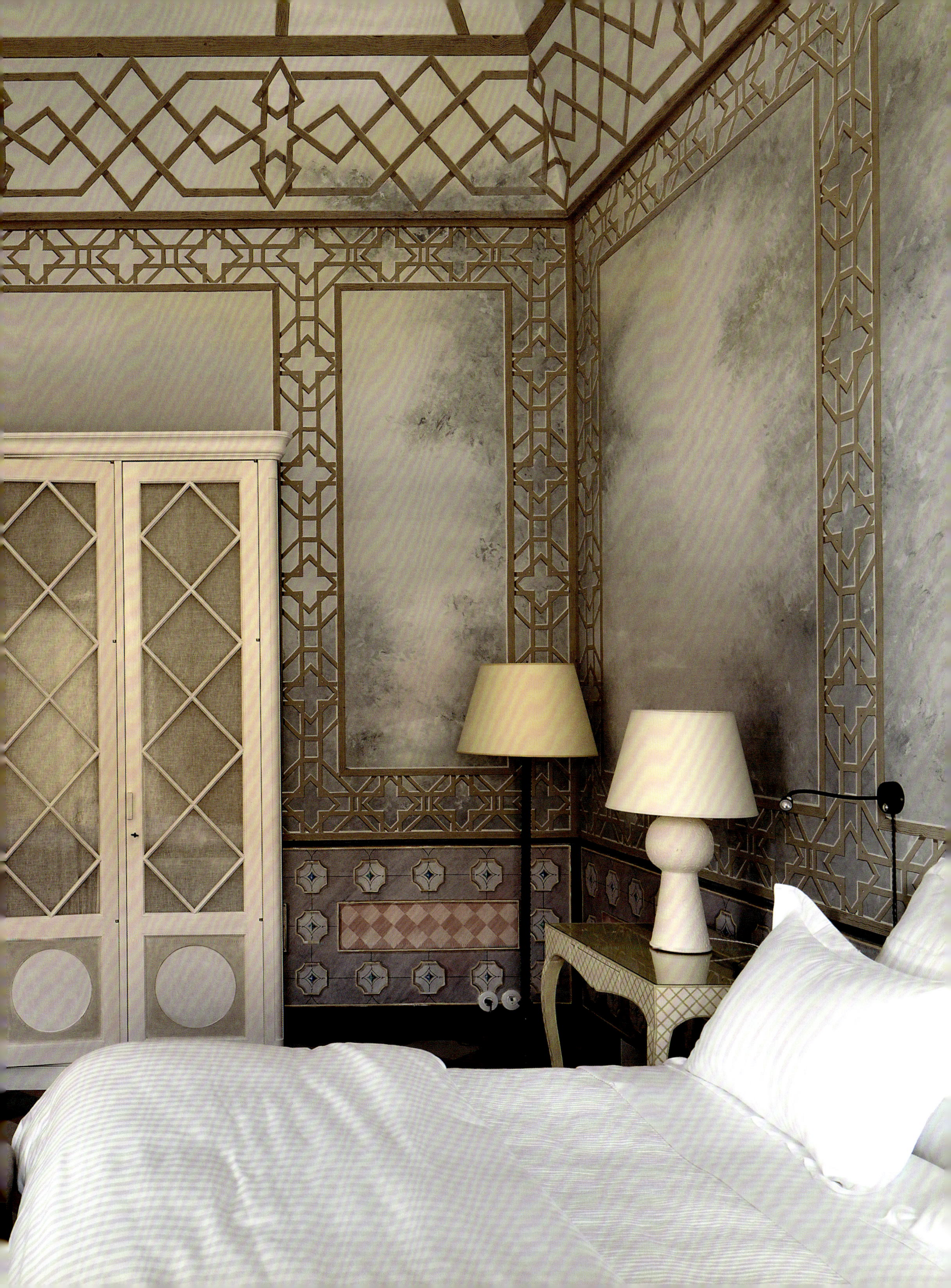

"It was a beast that needed to be awakened and given a face-lift," says Jacques Grange of the Palazzo Margherita. When he first set eyes on the building, it was rundown and abandoned, its frescoed ceilings barely intact. The brief given to him by owner Francis Ford Coppola was to turn it into a hotel that would be like a family home. Three of the suites were conceived for the film director and his two children, Sofia and Roman. That way, each has their own room when they come to visit. For his suite, Coppola senior requested an Orientalist decor reminiscent of his grandmother's childhood in Tunisia. For Sofia's, Grange took inspiration from the frescoes at the Palazzina Cinese in Palermo. "She told me, 'I want to feel like I'm opening a copy of The World of Interiors,' " he recalls. "She wanted an old-world charm." For him, the word that best sums up the project is "lightness." To this end, he painted furniture white and insisted nothing be hung on the already ornate walls. "It was not to be a reconstitution," Grange insists. "I reinterpreted things with my own personal touch."

„Eine schlafende Bestie, die man wecken und etwas auffrischen musste", so beschreibt Jacques Grange den Palazzo Margherita. Als er das Gebäude erstmals in Augenschein nahm, war es heruntergekommen, seine Deckenfresken am Rande des Wegbröckelns. Eigentümer Francis Ford Coppola hatte ihn beauftragt, daraus ein Hotel zu machen, das wie ein Familiensitz sein sollte. Drei der Suiten wurden auf den Filmregisseur und seine Kinder Sofia und Roman zugeschnitten – so hat jeder sein eigenes Zimmer, wann immer er hierherkommt. Für seine Suite wünschte sich Coppola orientalistisches Dekor, als Erinnerung an die Kindheit seiner Großmutter in Tunesien. Für Sofias Zimmer nahm Grange Fresken der Palazzina Cinese in Palermo zum Vorbild. „Sie sagte zu mir: ‚Ich möchte mich fühlen, als ob ich The World of Interiors aufschlage'", erinnert er sich. „Sie wollte den Charme der Alten Welt." Als Leitwort des Projekts wählte der Interiorstar „Leichtigkeit": Viele der Möbel ließ er weiß lackieren und er bestand darauf, die ja bereits geschmückten Wänden ohne Bilder zu belassen. „Es sollte nicht bloß eine Rekonstruktion sein", betont Grange. „Vielmehr habe ich alles mit meinem persönlichen Touch reinterpretiert."

«C'ÉTAIT UNE BÊTE QUI ATTENDAIT D'ÊTRE RÉVEILLÉE ET RELIFTÉE.» JACQUES GRANGE

La première fois que le décorateur star a visité le Palazzo Margherita, ce dernier était délabré et abandonné ; les fresques des plafonds tombaient en ruine. Le client de Grange, Francis Ford Coppola, voulait en faire un hôtel dans l'esprit d'une maison de famille. Trois des suites ont été conçues spécialement pour le cinéaste et ses deux enfants, Sofia et Roman, afin qu'ils y jouissent d'un pied-à-terre. Coppola souhaitait une chambre au décor orientaliste qui lui rappelle l'enfance tunisienne de sa grand-mère. Sofia, elle, aspirait au «charme de l'ancien monde» et voulait se sentir «comme dans un numéro de The World of Interiors». Pour sa suite, Grange s'est inspiré des fresques de la Palazzina Cinese à Palerme. À ses yeux, un mot résume le mieux son projet : «légèreté». À cette fin, il a peint des meubles en blanc et insisté pour que rien ne soit accroché sur les murs déjà ornés. «Ce n'est pas une reconstitution», insiste-t-il. «J'ai réinterprété les lieux avec ma propre patte.»

◀ ▲ In the main salon, Grange restored the original 19th-century wall decoration. The custom sofa is upholstered in a silk damask and flanked by painted-wood tables from John Rosselli in New York. The space doubles as a screening room, thanks to a roll-down screen hidden behind the cornice. "Only Italian movies are shown," the designer notes. • Im Hauptsalon stellte Grange die Wanddekoration aus dem 19. Jahrhundert wieder her. Das Maßsofa mit Bezug aus Seidendamast flankieren lackierte Holztische von John Rosselli in New York. Der Raum ist zugleich Kinosaal: Hinter dem Gesims verbirgt sich eine aufgerollte Leinwand. „Hier werden nur italienische Filme gezeigt", bemerkt der Designer. • Dans le salon principal, Grange a restauré le décor mural du 19ᵉ siècle. Le canapé est tapissé d'une soie damassée et flanqué de tables d'appoint en bois peint de chez John Rosselli à New York. La pièce se transforme en salle de projection grâce à un écran dissimulé sous la corniche. « On ne passe que des films italiens », assure le décorateur.

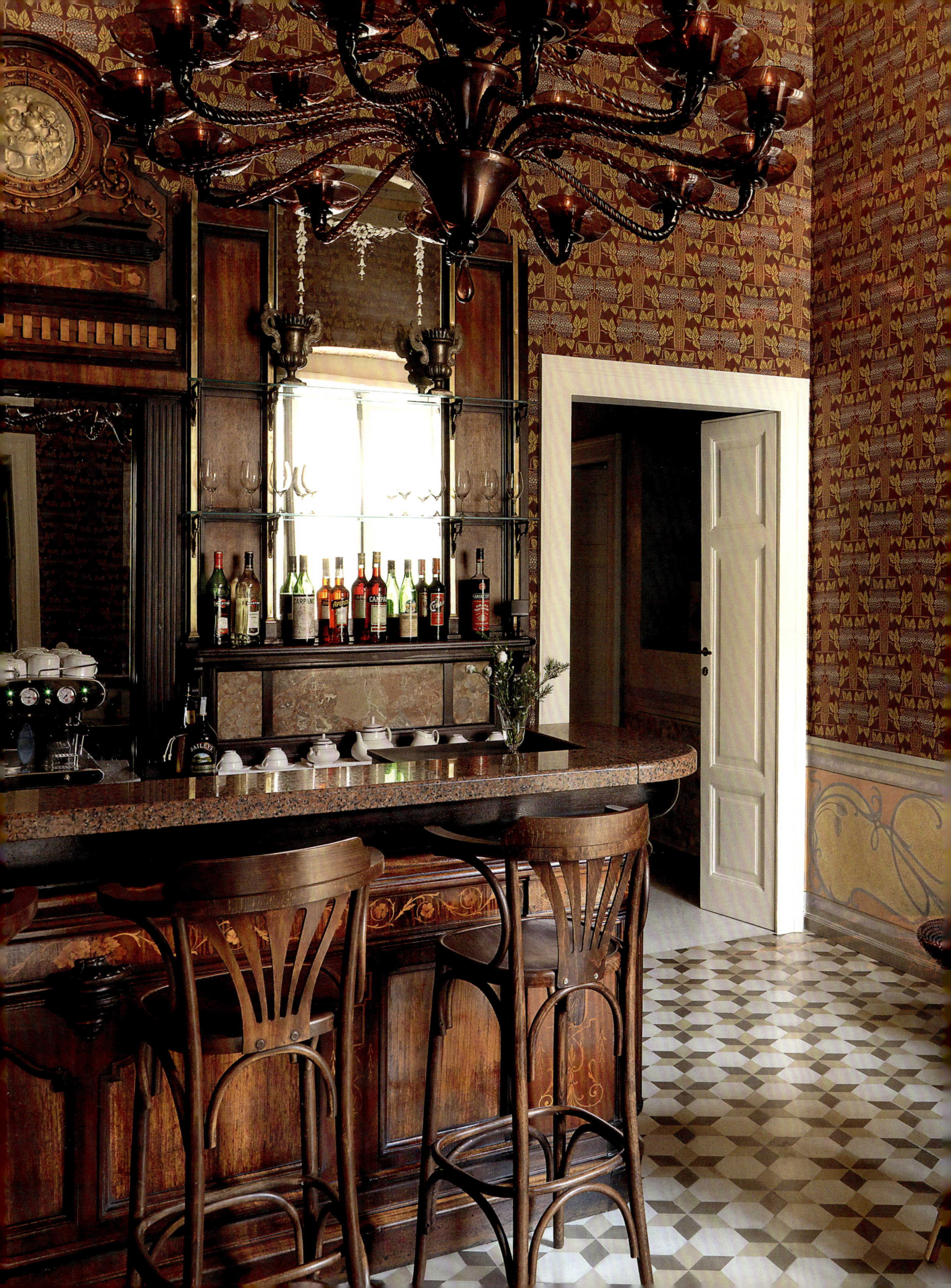

▲ A view toward the garden, which is planted with palm, olive, fig, and lemon trees. The vivid blue lantern is original to the palazzo. • Ein Blick hinein in den Garten, in dem Palmen, Oliven-, Feigen- und Zitronenbäume wachsen. Die blaue Laterne hängt hier seit der Erbauung des Palazzos. • Une vue vers le jardin planté de palmiers, d'oliviers, de figuiers et de citronniers. La lanterne en verre bleu est une pièce d'origine.

◄ The walls of the hotel's private bar are clad in a reproduction of a Le Manach cotton from 1925, chosen for its Arts & Crafts motif. • Die private Hotelbar kleidet die Reproduktion eines Le-Manach-Baumwollstoffs von 1925 aus, den Grange wegen seines Arts-and-Crafts-Dessins auswählte. • Les murs du bar privé de l'hôtel sont tapissés d'une cotonnade de Le Manach de 1925, choisie pour son motif Art & Crafts.

▲ The Palazzo Margherita is one of three palaces on Bernalda's main street, Corso Umberto. • Der Palazzo Margherita ist einer von drei Palazzi am Corso Umberto, Bernaldas Hauptstraße. • Le Palazzo Margherita est l'un des trois palais bordant le Corso Umberto, l'artère principale de Bernalda.

▶ Francis Ford Coppola's room (Suite no. 9) was previously a covered terrace. Its Orientalist decor incorporates *bejmat* floor tiles laid by a local craftsman. • Francis Ford Coppolas Zimmer (Suite 9) war früher eine Loggia. Zum orientalistischen Dekor zählt das Fischgrätmuster am Boden, das ein lokaler Handwerker aus Bejmat-Fliesen legte. • La chambre de Francis Ford Coppola (la suite n° 9) était autrefois une terrasse couverte. Son décor orientaliste comprend un sol avec un motif à chevrons conçu avec des briquettes de céramique émaillées et naturelles posées par un artisan local.

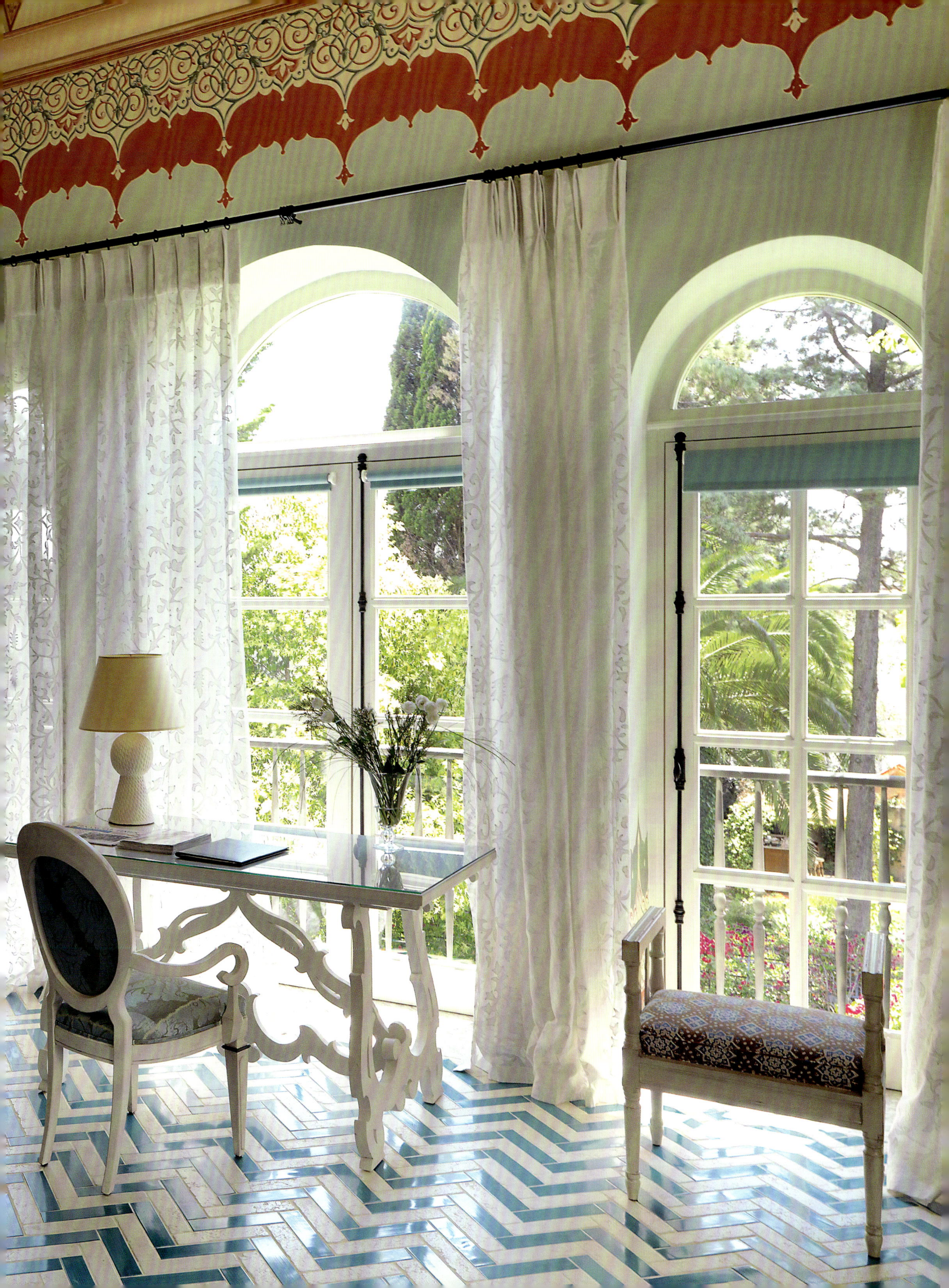

BIJOY JAIN

A WEEKEND RESIDENCE IN HARMONY WITH INDIA'S HERITAGE

WHO Indian architect who founded Studio Mumbai Architects in 2005. **WHAT** Belavali House, a 400 m² (4,306 sq. ft.), four-bedroom new home. **WHERE** Among paddy fields in the district of Alibaug, a 40-minute boat ride from Mumbai. **THE CLIENTS** They are in the garment business and requested a living space for three generations. **BACKGROUND** Jain was brought up in a family of doctors in Mumbai, but "that was the last thing I wanted to be," he says. Between 1989 and 1991, he worked at Richard Meier + Partners. **BACK TO ROOTS** When he returned to India in the mid-1990s, he was determined to set up his practice in a rural setting. "India is fundamentally agrarian as a culture. I wanted to physically and emotionally put myself in a place where I could experience that," he explains. Consequently, Studio Mumbai Architects' workshop in Alibaug consists of simple metal sheds arranged around a grove of trees. **NEW HORIZONS** Recent commissions include a weaver's studio in Dehradun, a house outside Barcelona, and two towers in Zhengdou, China.

PHOTOGRAPHED BY CHRISTIAN SCHAULIN   PRODUCED BY KERSTIN ROSE   PORTRAIT BY STUDIO MUMBAI ARCHITECTS

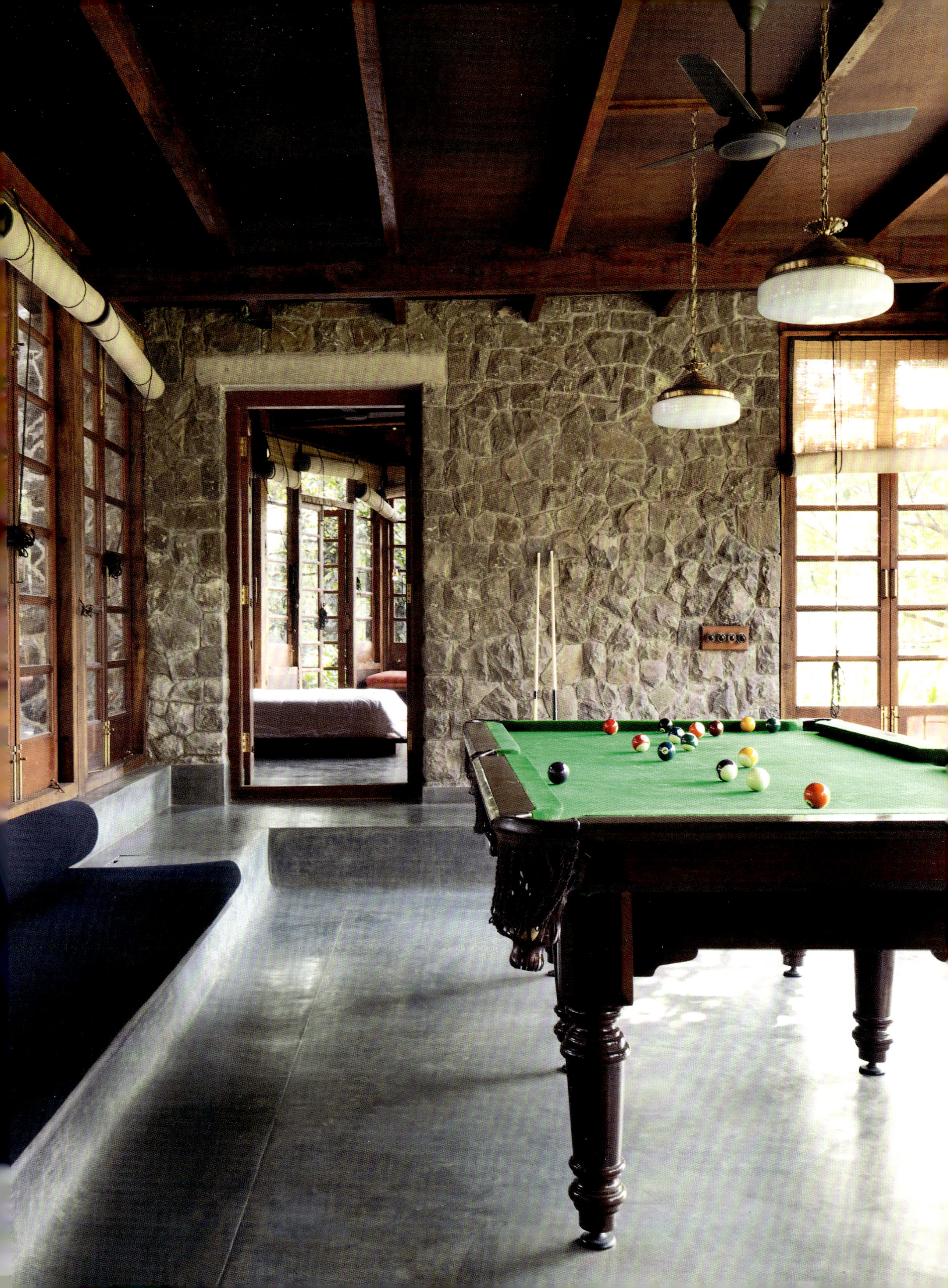

127 Adjacent to the living room, the billiard room features walls made from locally quarried stone and pendants bought at Mumbai's Chor Bazaar. • Im Billardraum neben dem Wohnzimmer hängen Pendelleuchten vom Chor Bazaar in Mumbai. Der Bruchstein der Wände stammt aus der Umgebung des Hauses. • Attenante au séjour, la salle de billard a des murs en pierres provenant d'une carrière locale et des plafonniers achetés au Chor Bazaar de Mumbai.

▼ Custom fittings include the brass-and-aluminum light switches. For Jain, the Kaare Klint chairs "add a certain dignity" to the dining room. • Die Lichtschalter aus Messing und Aluminium sind maßgefertigt. Stühle von Kaare Klint geben dem Esszimmer „eine spezielle Würde", findet Jain. • Les interrupteurs en laiton et aluminium ont été réalisés sur mesure. Selon Jain, les chaises de Kaare Klint « confèrent une certaine dignité » à la salle à manger.

◄ A teak bench wraps around the son's bedroom. Jain gave the lamp, another Chor Bazaar find, a custom MDF base in his shop. • Das Zimmer des Sohns rahmt eine Fensterbank aus Teak. Die Leuchte, ebenfalls ein Fundstück vom Chor Bazaar, erhielt in Jains Werkstatt eine MDF-Basis. • La chambre du fils est flanquée d'une banquette en teck. La lampe dénichée au Chor Bazaar a été montée sur un socle en panneau MDF dans l'atelier de Jain.

▲ The narrow house is discreet. "It occupies the minimum footprint," notes Jain. "For me, that was fundamental." • Ganz selbstverständlich sitzt das schmale Haus in der Landschaft. „Es macht sich nicht unnötig breit in der Natur, das war mir wichtig", erklärt Jain. • La maison étroite se fond dans le paysage. « Elle occupe le minimum de surface », observe Jain. « Pour moi, cela était fondamental. »

▶ Michael Anastassiades's gold-plated *Ball Lights* hang above a custom concrete table in the living room. The staircase leads to the study and master bedroom. • Über dem aus Beton gegossenen Coffeetable im Wohnzimmer hängen Michael Anastassiades' vergoldete *Ball Lights*. Die Treppe führt zu Lese- und Schlafzimmer. • Dans le séjour, *Ball Lights* dorées de Michael Anastassiades et table basse en béton. L'escalier mène au bureau et à la chambre principale.

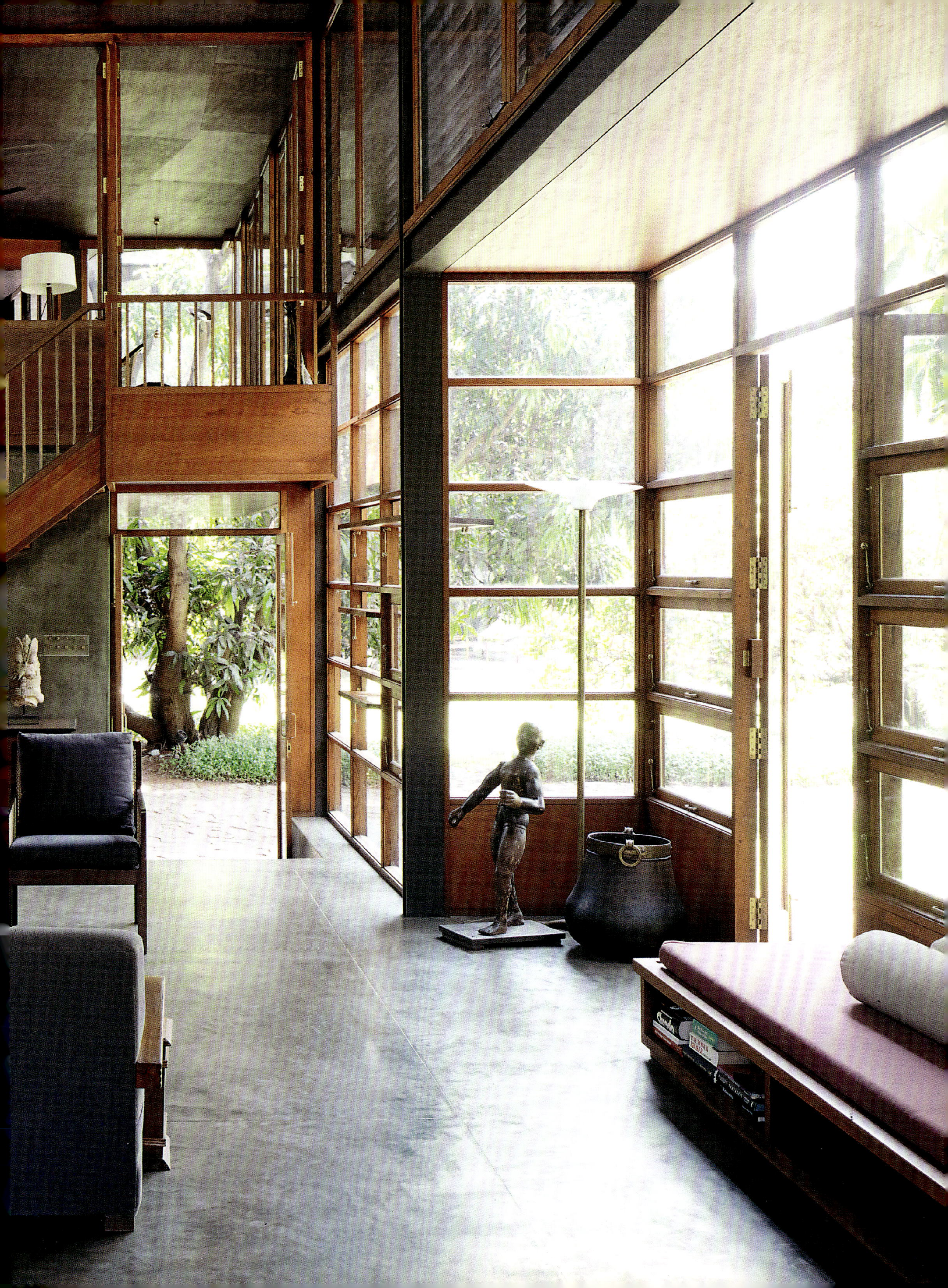

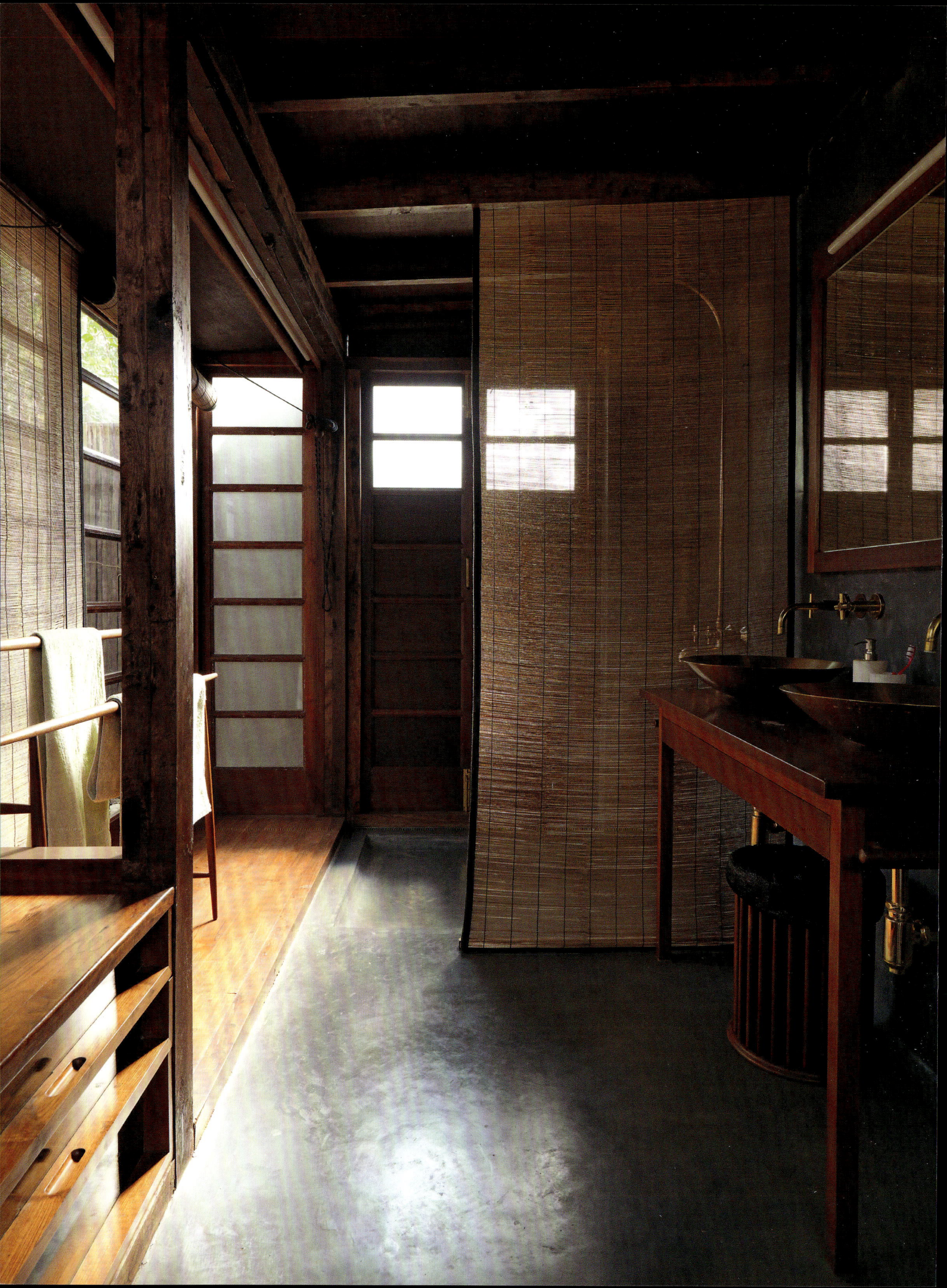

"THE HOUSE SITS LIKE A PAVILION IN AN AGRICULTURAL GARDEN." BIJOY JAIN

Bijoy Jain's projects have a number of common denominators. Among them are the use of traditional building techniques (his practice, Studio Mumbai Architects, works with its own team of craftsmen) and a respect for nature. Nowhere is this more evident than at Belavali House, which lies among paddy fields. At only five meters (16 feet) deep, its narrowness was determined by the surrounding vegetation. "We slipped it into the space between the mango trees," he notes. Those trees not only act as natural sunscreens and rain barriers, but the shadows between them also inspired the dark green of the cement strips used in parts of the house. "We tried to mimic the quality of that light," he adds. "There's a sense of camouflage." Jain describes the interiors as "comfortable and restful." Locally made custom furniture, which he deems "practical, efficient, and robust," is juxtaposed with Kaare Klint's sophisticated *Faaborg chairs* by Rud. Rasmussen. The "umbrella-like" cantilevered roof perfectly expresses the architect's concept for this groundbreaking residence: a house like a pavilion.

Alle Projekte von Bijoy Jain zeichnet zweierlei aus: der Einsatz traditioneller Bauweisen (sein Büro, Studio Mumbai Architects, beschäftigt ein eigenes Handwerkerteam) und Respekt vor der Natur. Bestes Beispiel ist das zwischen Reisfeldern gelegene Belavali House. Sein schmales Volumen – es ist nur 5 m breit –, ist der Vegetation geschuldet. „Wir haben es genau zwischen die Mangobäume eingepasst", erklärt Jain. Diese sind nicht nur natürlicher Sonnen- und Regenschutz, ihre Schatten waren auch Vorbild für den graugrünen Zement-Estrich. „Wir haben versucht, dieses besondere Licht nachzuahmen", fügt Jain hinzu. „Die Landschaft hier ist von Camouflage-Effekten geprägt." Das Interieur beschreibt er als „komfortabel und beruhigend". In der Umgebung gefertigte Maßmöbel – „praktisch, funktional, robust" – finden ein raffiniertes Gegengewicht in Kaare Klints *Faaborg*-Stühlen von Rud. Rasmussen. Und dass das Dach „wie ein Regenschirm" übersteht, passt aufs Schönste zu Jains Grundidee: „Ein Haus wie ein Pavillon in einem Bauerngarten."

Tous les projets de Bijoy Jain ont en commun le recours à des méthodes de construction traditionnelles (son cabinet, Studio Mumbai Architects, dispose de sa propre équipe d'artisans) et un profond respect de la nature. Cachée au milieu de rizières, la Belavali House ne fait que cinq mètres de large, ses modestes dimensions étant dues à la végétation environnante. « Nous nous sommes faufilés entre les manguiers », explique-t-il. Ces arbres la protègent du soleil et de la pluie. Leur ombre a également inspiré le vert sombre du ciment utilisé dans certaines parties de la maison. « Nous avons tenté de reproduire la qualité de cette lumière. La structure semble ainsi se fondre dans le paysage. » Jain qualifie l'intérieur de « confortable et reposant ». Des meubles « pratiques, efficaces et robustes » de fabrication locale côtoient des pièces sophistiquées comme les chaises *Faaborg* de Kaare Klint pour Rud. Rasmussen. Déployé tel un parasol, le toit en porte-à-faux illustre à merveille le concept de l'architecte appliqué à cette demeure innovante : « Une maison tel un pavillon dans un jardin paysan. »

132 Solid luxury: the son's sleek bathroom is clad in Burmese teak, with curtain screens in bamboo. • Robuster Luxus: Im Bad des Sohns dominiert Teak aus Burma, dazu Stores aus Bambusgewebe. • Du luxe robuste : dans la salle de bains épurée du fils, équipée de stores en bambou, c'est le teck birman qui prédomine.

▲ The faucets were purchased at a local market and dechromed to show the brass; the house steps down several terraces, with a pool located on the lowest one. • Um das Messing sichtbar zu machen, wurde die Armatur entchromt; das Anwesen ist über mehrere Levels gestuft, ganz unten liegt der Pool. • Les robinets ont été déchromés pour révéler le laiton. Le niveau en rez-de-jardin de la maison construite en terrasses donne sur une piscine.

◄ Belavali House was slipped in between the sinuous mango trees already on the site. "I try to build in harmony with nature," says Jain. • Das Belavali House wurde zwischen ausladende Mangobäume gefügt, die auf dem Grundstück standen. „Ich versuche, im Einklang mit der Natur zu bauen", sagt Jain. • La Belavali House se glisse entre les manguiers sinueux qui se trouvaient déjà sur le terrain. « Je m'efforce de construire en harmonie avec la nature », explique Jain.

► The kitchen is located on a courtyard tucked behind the house's main pavilion. Here, stainless steel countertops contrast with yet more Burmese teak. • Die Küche grenzt an einen Hof hinter dem Hauptpavillon. Auch hier findet sich reichlich Burma-Teak, einen kühlen Kontrast bilden Arbeitsflächen aus Edelstahl. • La cuisine jouxte une cour cachée derrière le pavillon principal. Ici, le plan de travail en inox contrastent avec le teck birman.

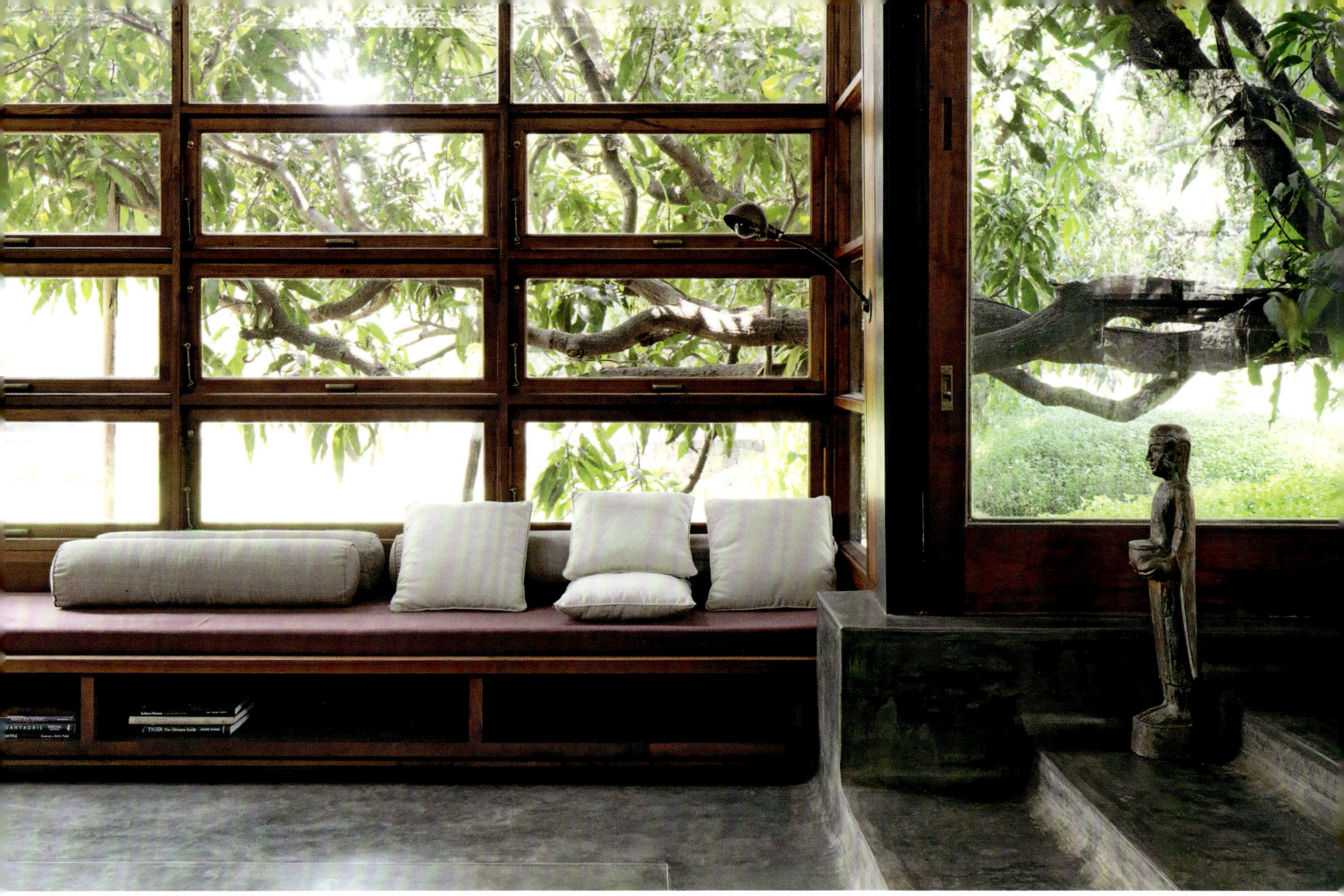
TIGER The Ultimate Guide

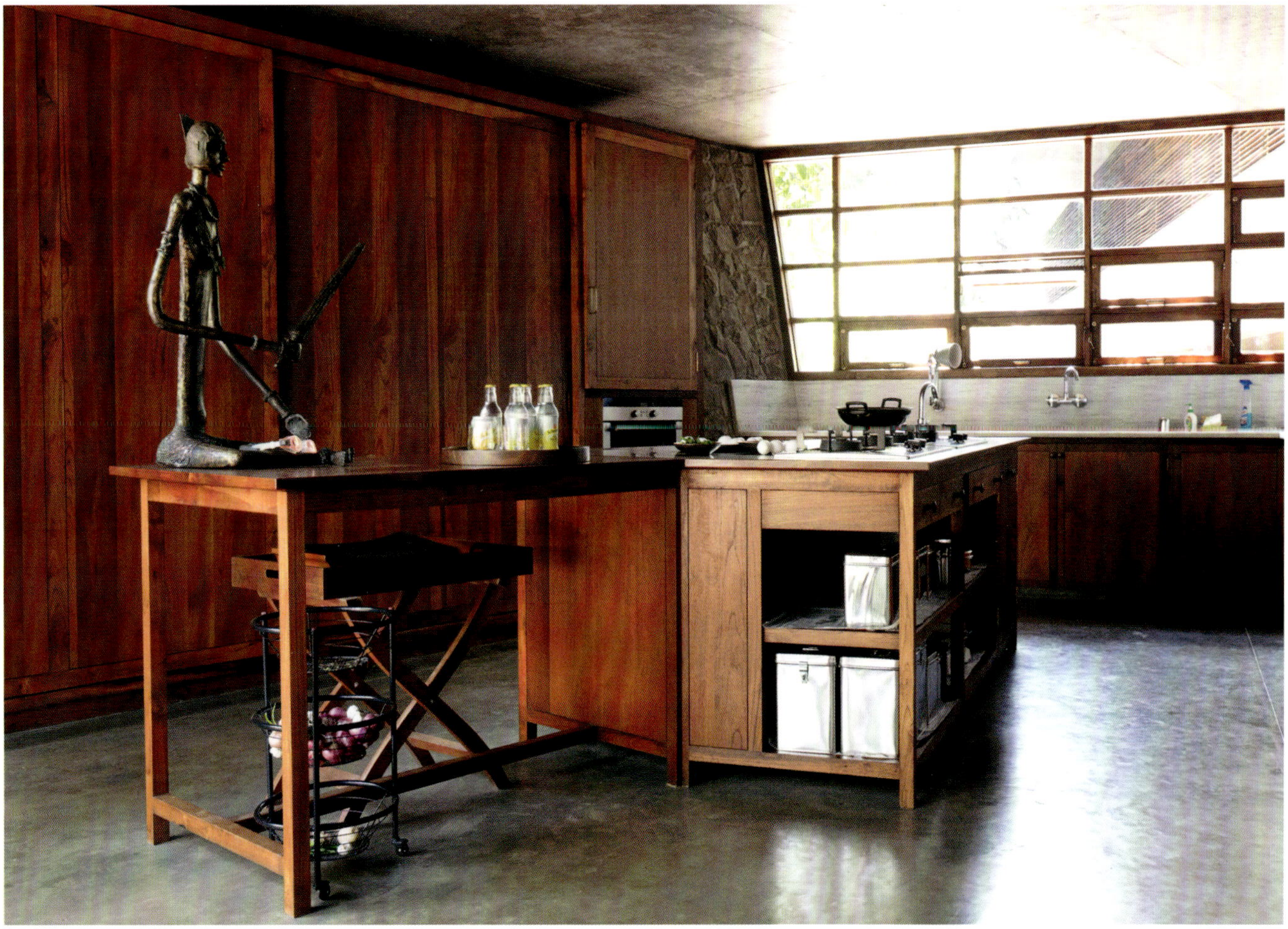

MATHIAS KISS

AN ARTISTIC APARTMENT IN PARIS

WHO Paris-based designer and artist who employs traditional interior crafts with a contemporary edge. **WHAT** A 120m² (1,292 sq.ft.) flat in an 1850s building that used to house a meat market. **WHERE** Next to the Church of Saint-Eustache. **THE OWNER** A sexagenarian who made his career in various artistic fields. Among other things, he designed costumes and record covers. **BOND CONNECTION** Kiss's Hungary-born father was an inventor and designed cars for *007* films. **GOLDFINGER?** At the age of 14, Kiss joined the Compagnons guild of craftsmen. In his 12 years with them, he helped to restore the gilding at the Louvre, Opéra Garnier, and Comédie Française. **CLAIM TO FAME** With Olivier Piel, he runs a decorative arts studio called Attilalou. They have painted skyscapes for Catherine Deneuve and a woodland fresco for fashion designer Stefano Pilati. **BRANCHING OUT** Kiss's recent commissions have included fabric designs for Kenzo and the NYC boutique of jeweler Marie-Hélène de Taillac. His creations are available at the Armel Soyer Gallery in the Marais.

PHOTOGRAPHED BY RICHARD POWERS©THE WORLD OF INTERIORS   PORTRAIT BY ALEXANDRE GUIRKINGER

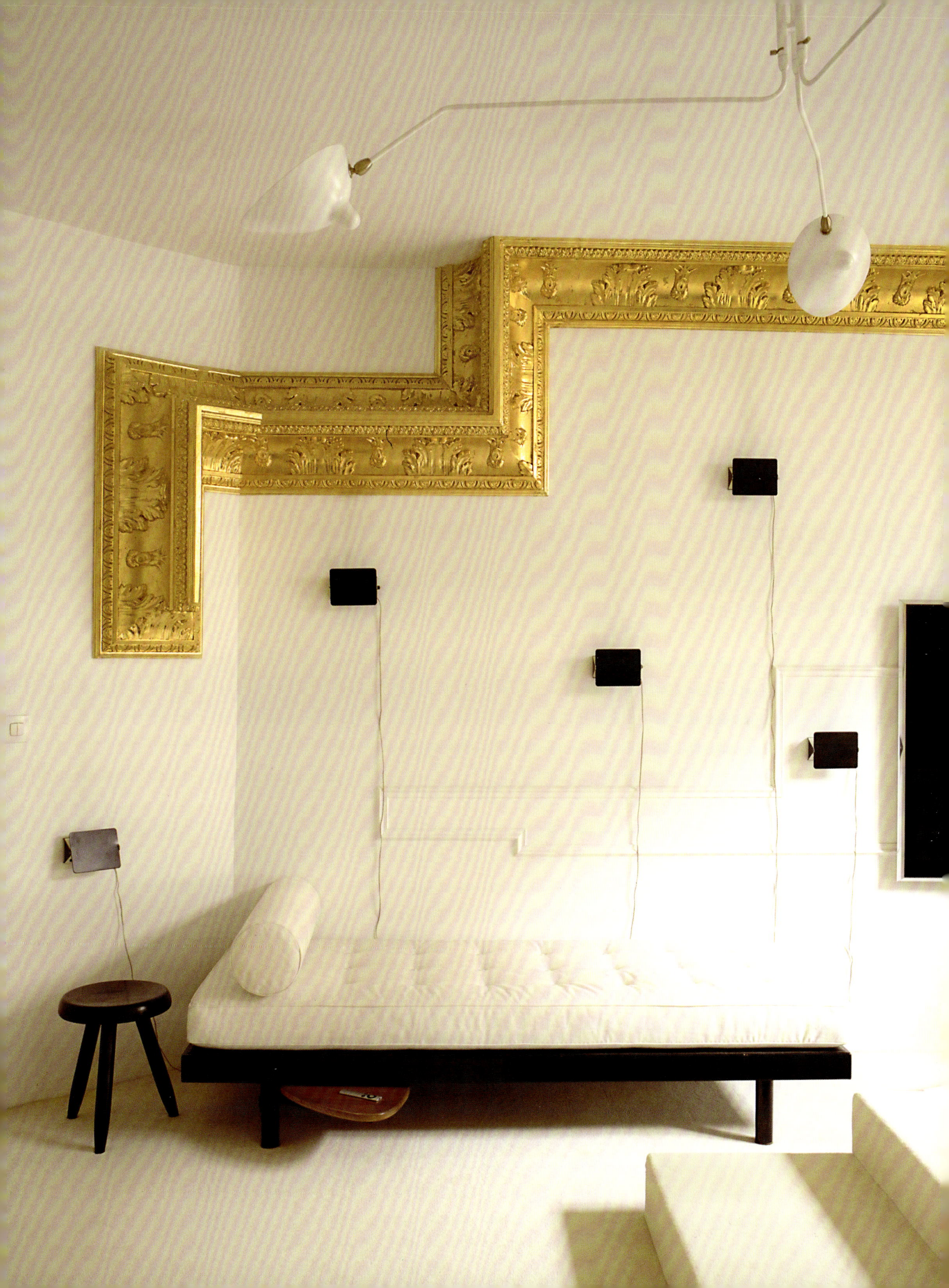

240505 120886 220870

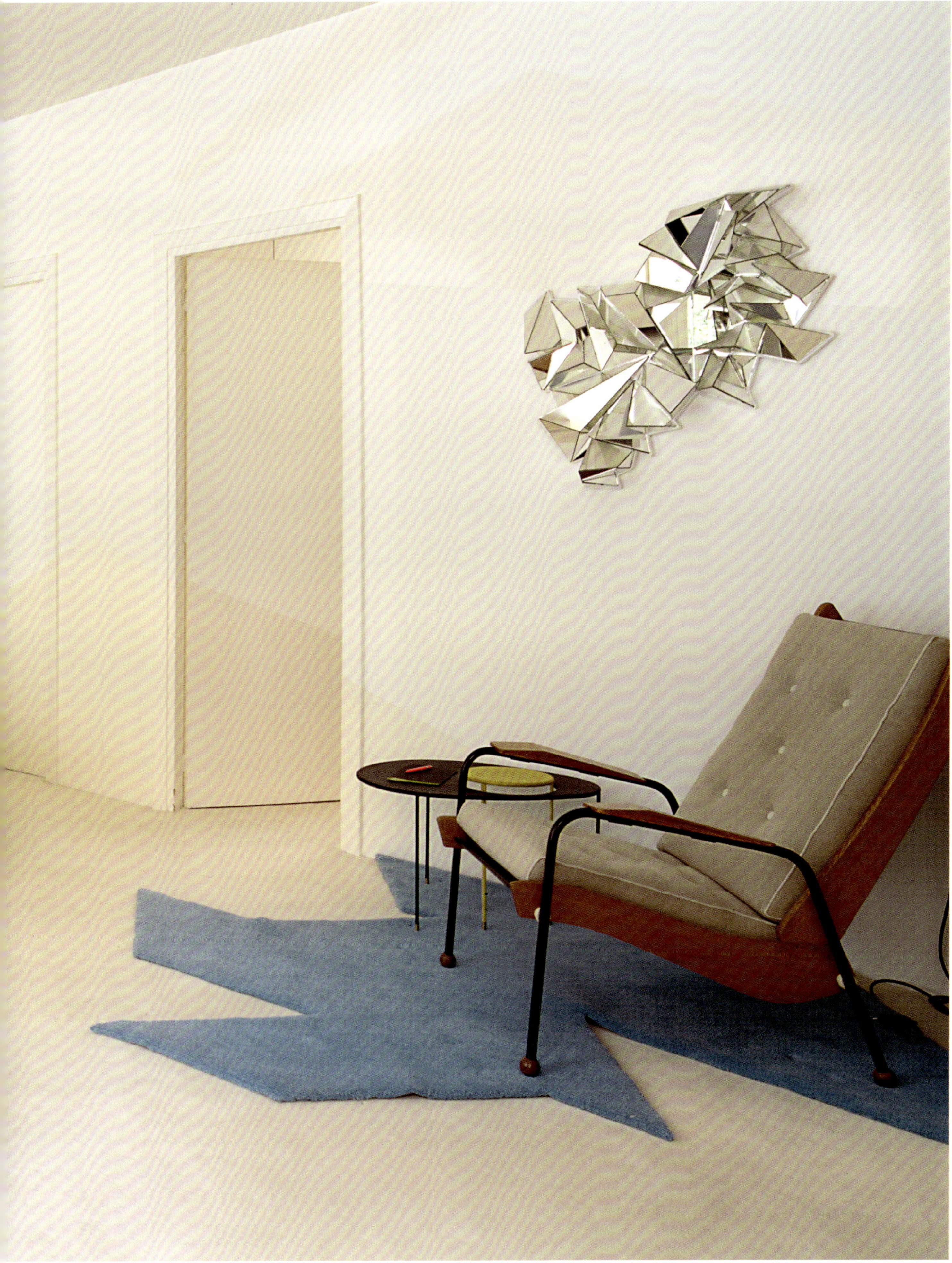

137 The mold for the stepped cornice in the bedroom was taken from a grand Paris townhouse. It is deliberately disproportionate to give it surrealistic prominence. • Der getreppte Stuck ist der Abguss eines Vorbilds in einem Pariser Stadtpalais. Bewusst absurde Proportionen erzeugen einen surrealistischen Effekt. • La corniche de la chambre reproduit celle d'un noble hôtel particulier parisien. Elle est délibérément démesurée pour obtenir un effet surréaliste.

138–139 Vintage furnishings by Prouvé and Perriand in the living room are offset by Kiss's own creations like his *Igloo* sofa and *Froissé* mirrored sculpture. • Vintage-Möbel von Prouvé und Perriand kontrastieren im Wohnzimmer mit Kiss-Designs wie dem *Igloo*-Sofa und der Spiegelskulptur *Froissé*. • Dans le séjour, le côté vintage des meubles de Prouvé et de Perriand est compensé par des créations de Kiss tels que le canapé *Igloo* et la sculpture miroir *Froissé*.

▲◄ Kiss painted a geometric pattern on the walls and ceiling of the entry hall to distract from its awkward shape; the terrace abuts the church of St-Eustache. • Kiss legte ein dunkles Vieleck über Wände und Decke des Vorraums, um dessen unregelmäßigen Schnitt zu überspielen; die Terrasse grenzt an St. Eustache. • Kiss a peint un motif géométrique sur les murs du vestibule pour masquer ses proportions ingrates ; la terrasse jouxte l'église Saint-Eustache.

► The platform in the master bedroom is clad in carpet. All the re-edition Serge Mouille lights are white to make them as inconspicuous as possible. • Das Bettpodest ist mit Auslegeware überzogen. Alle reedierten Serge-Mouille-Leuchten sind weiß, damit sie möglichst wenig herausstechen. • Dans la chambre, l'estrade est recouverte de moquette. Toutes les rééditions de luminaires de Serge Mouille ont été traitées en blanc pour une discrétion optimale.

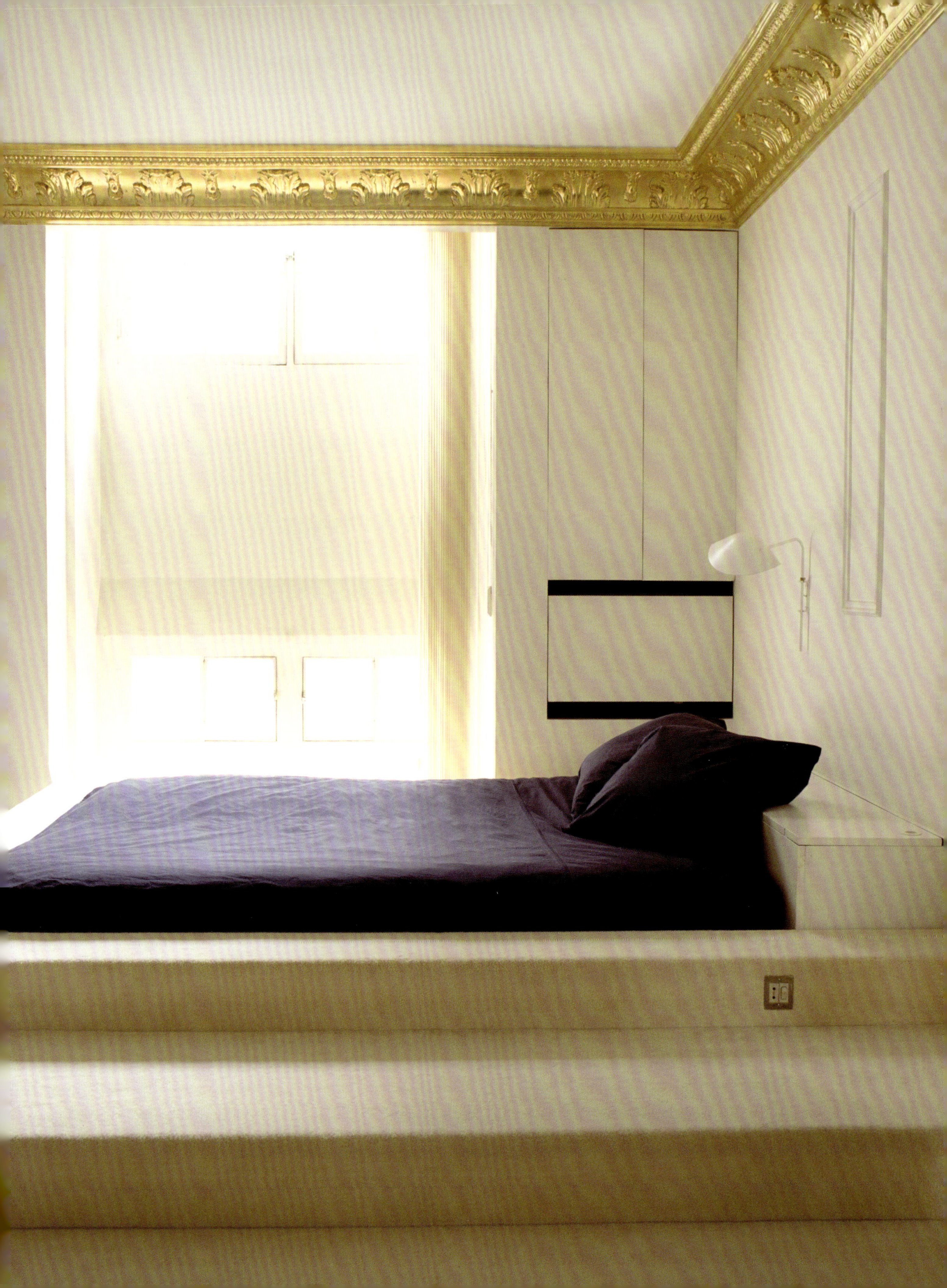

▲ Among the owner's collection of vintage Jean Prouvé pieces are the 1933 *Cité* desk and the 1952 *Métropole* chair, tucked away in one corner of the master bedroom. Kiss acknowledges a certain irreverence in his approach to them. "They are not at all highlighted," he asserts. "For me, they are in their place." • Zur Prouvé-Sammlung des Hausherrn gehören das *Cité*-Pult von 1933 und der *Métropole*-Stuhl von 1952. Kiss ignorierte ihre respektheischende Signatur und platzierte sie in einer Ecke des Schlafzimmers: „Sie stehen hier überhaupt nicht im Mittelpunkt", sagt er. „Ich finde, das passt zu ihnen." • La collection de pièces originales de Jean Prouvé comprend le bureau *Cité* de 1933 et la chaise *Métropole* de 1952, relégués dans un coin de la chambre principale. Kiss reconnaît les traiter avec une certaine irrévérence : « Ils ne sont pas mis en valeur. Pour moi, ils sont à leur place. »

"THE FURNITURE OF JEAN PROUVÉ IS VERY BASIC. WHY PLACE IT ON A PEDESTAL LIKE SOME PRECIOUS ANTIQUE?" MATHIAS KISS

"Prouvé's industrial style doesn't do anything for me," Kiss continues. He also laments that midcentury design is often housed in gallery-like apartments with white walls and concrete floors. So, when asked to decorate this flat for a collector of original pieces by both Prouvé and Charlotte Perriand, Kiss was determined to do something a little different. First he gave the room warmth by adding a carpet. "It lends a touch of glamour and sensuality," he opines. He also played down the vintage factor by bringing in visually striking creations of his own. In the living room, the focal point is a Day-Glo yellow-and-olive-green angular sofa. In the master bedroom, a 23-karat "golden snake" cornice slithers down from the ceiling across the walls. The Charles and Ray Eames coatrack in the entrance hall, meanwhile, was painted white to make it disappear against the faux-marble background. With characteristic irreverence, the sole Prouvé piece Kiss highlighted is one of the few that is not an original here. He painted the legs of Vitra's re-edition *EM* dining table bright red.

„Jean Prouvés Möbel sind sehr *basic*. Warum sollte man sie auf ein Podest stellen wie eine wertvolle Antiquität?", fragt Mathias Kiss. Midcentury-Design auf Betonboden zu präsentieren, wie man es so oft sieht, ist ebenfalls nicht seine Sache. Als es darum ging, dieses Apartment für einen Sammler von Prouvé- und Perriand-Originalen einzurichten, wählte er einen anderen Weg. Er ließ Teppich verlegen – „das bringt Glamour und Sinnlichkeit" – und dimmte den Vintage-Faktor mit auffälligen eigenen Entwürfen. Im Wohnzimmer zieht ein asymmetrisches Sofa in Neongelb und Oliv die Blicke auf sich, und eine Stuckleiste gleitet als 23-karätige „Goldschlange" die Schlafzimmerwand hinab. Die Eames-Garderobe im Vorraum dagegen wurde weiß lackiert, um nicht aufzufallen. Mit der gleichen Nonchalance entschied sich Kiss, ausgerechnet eines der wenigen Prouvé-Stücke zu betonen, die nicht original sind: Er lackierte die Beine des von Vitra neu aufgelegten *EM*-Tischs leuchtend rot.

« Le mobilier de Jean Prouvé est très basique ; alors pourquoi le placer sur un piédestal comme une antiquité précieuse ? En outre, son style industriel ne me convainc pas », déclare Kiss. Il regrette aussi de voir trop souvent le design des années 1950 dans des appartements galeries aux murs blancs et aux sols en ciment. Aussi, lorsqu'un collectionneur de pièces originales de Prouvé et de Perriand lui a demandé de décorer son appartement, il était résolu à faire autre chose. Il a réchauffé l'ambiance à l'aide d'une moquette « qui ajoute du glamour et de la sensualité » et atténué le côté vintage en introduisant quelques-unes de ses créations saisissantes. Le séjour est dominé par un canapé jaune fluo et vert olive. Dans une chambre, une corniche « serpent » à la feuille d'or 23 carats glisse le long des murs. Un portemanteau des Eames a été peint en blanc pour se fondre dans le faux marbre de l'entrée. Toujours aussi irrévérencieux, il a mis en valeur la seule pièce de Prouvé qui ne soit pas un original en peignant en rouge vif les pieds de sa table *EM* rééditée par Vitra.

TIINA LAAKKONEN & JON ROSEN

THEIR HOUSE IN AMAGANSETT, LONG ISLAND

WHO Laakkonen is a Finnish fashion stylist and design guru. Rosen is the owner of the digital postproduction company Nucleus Imaging. **WHAT** A 465 m² (5,000 sq. ft.), five-bedroom, newly built house. **WHERE** On a 1.6-hectare (four-acre) plot surrounded largely by working farms. **COLLABORATION** The couple worked on the project with architects Nandini Bagchee and Tim Furzer. **FANS OF FINLAND** Rosen and Laakkonen visit several times a year. **FINNISH FINDS** Laakkonen's favorite is the Paavo Tynell floor lampin the sitting room. "That's my trophy," she says. **TIINA THE STORE** Her eponymous Amagansett boutique sells the best of contemporary and vintage Nordic design. She particularly recommends the work of Ilmari Tapiovaara and Klaus Haapaniemi. **NEW DIRECTION** The buzz around their own house quickly led to two decorating commissions nearby.

PHOTOGRAPHED BY FRANÇOIS HALARD/TRUNK ARCHIVE PORTRAIT BY JON ROSEN

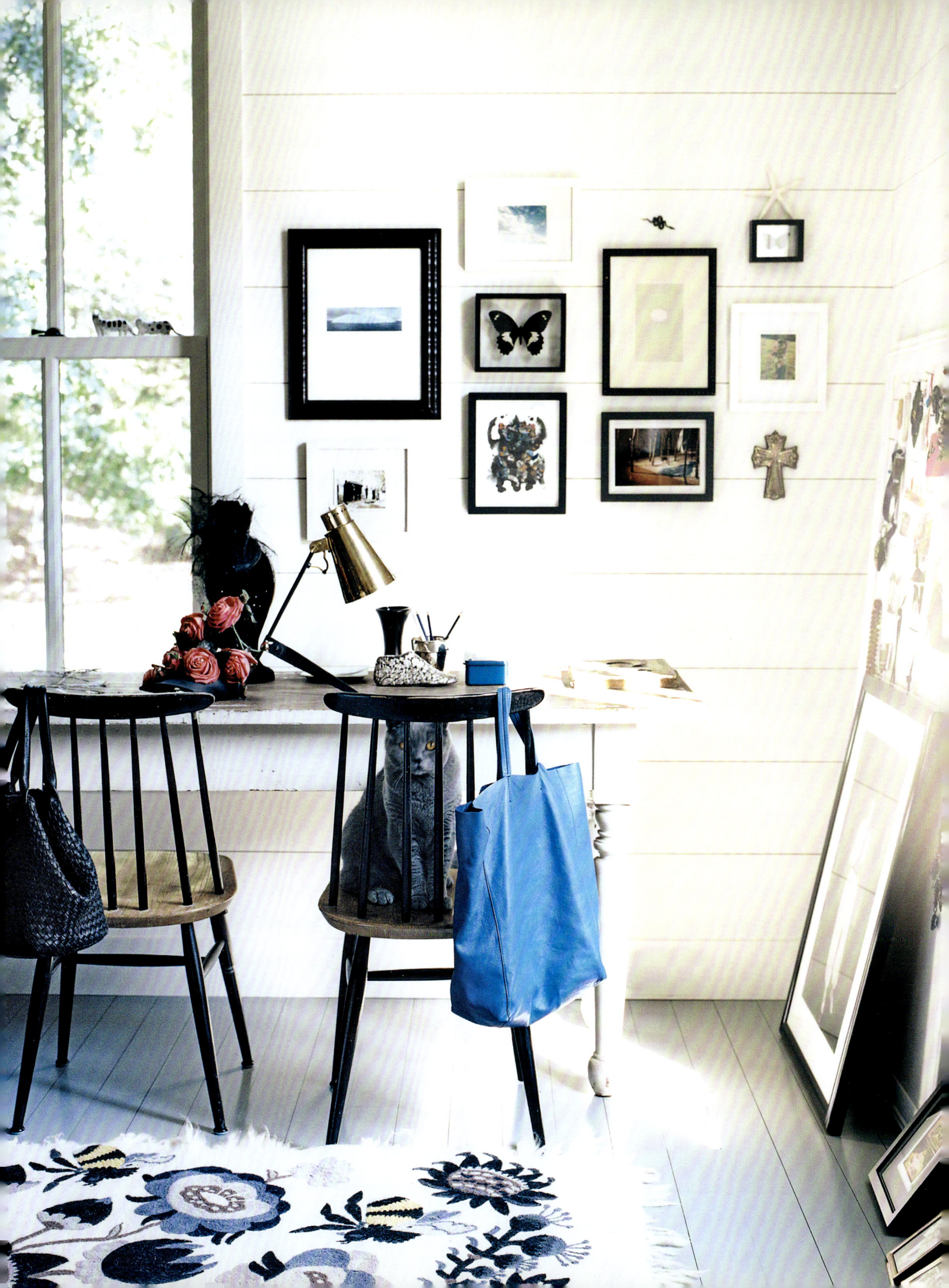

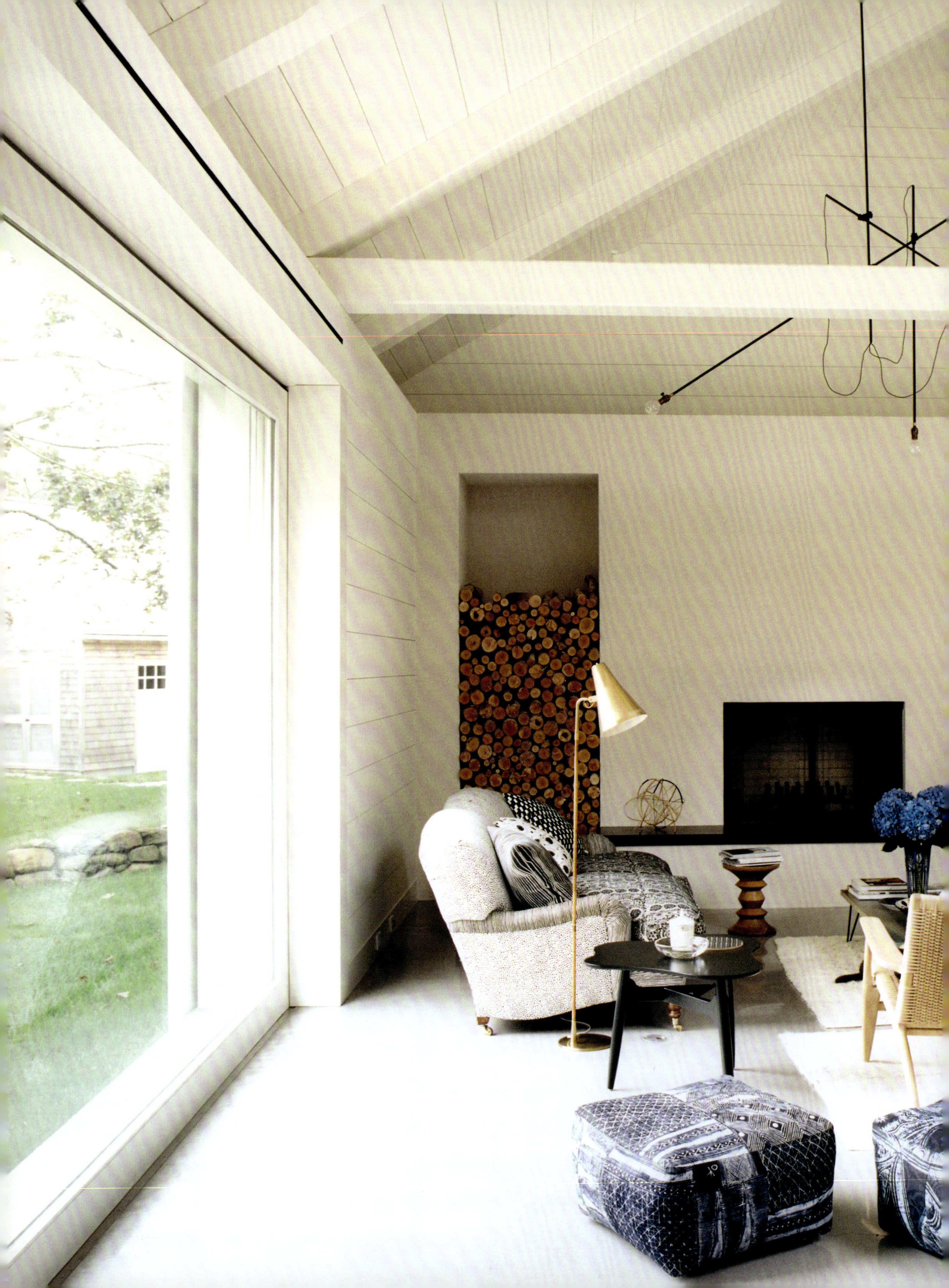

145 Laakkonen's office features pieces by her two favorite Finnish designers—Ilmari Tapiovaara chairs (one with British Shorthair Blue, Monkey) and a Klaus Haapaniemi rug. Artwork includes Christmas cards by photographer Juergen Teller. • In Laakkonens Büro finden sich Stücke ihrer finnischen Lieblingsdesigner – Stühle von Ilmari Tapiovaara (darauf Britisch Kurzhaar Monkey) und ein Teppich von Klaus Haapaniemi. An der Wand unter anderem Weihnachtskarten von Juergen Teller. • Dans le bureau, des œuvres de ses designers finlandais préférés : chaises d'Ilmari Tapiovaara (dont une avec Monkey, le chat British Shorthair), tapis de Klaus Haapaniemi. Au mur, des cartes de vœux encadrées de Juergen Teller.

▲ The main house consists of a central barn-like structure linked to two shingle-clad wings. • Ein scheunenartiger Bau bildet das Haupthaus, das mit modernen Glasfluren an zwei schindelverkleidete Seitenhäuser andockt. • La maison est constituée d'un corps principal rappelant une grange relié par des sas vitrés à deux ailes recouvertes de bardeaux.

◄ A Workstead chandelier above a Paavo Tynell floor lamp and George Sherlock sofas covered in Marimekko prints. • Ein Lüster von Workstead hängt über einer Stehleuchte von Paavo Tynell und George-Sherlock-Sofas mit Marimekko-Bezügen. • Un lustre de Workstead au-dessus d'un lampadaire de Paavo Tynell et de canapés de George Sherlock tapissés de tissus Marimekko.

▲ A path leads down from the main house to the pool. Hydrangea and vines were planted by the fence so it will eventually be concealed • Ein Pfad führt vom Haupthaus zum Pool. Hortensien und Klettergewächse wurden vor dem Zaun gepflanzt, sodass er bald hinter Ranken und Blättern verschwinden wird. • Un chemin mène de la maison principale à la piscine. Avec le temps, les hortensias et plantes grimpantes dissimuleront la clôture.

▶ Patience pays: It took Rosen several years to persuade a dealer in Finland to part with the 19th-century painted-wood storage unit on the guesthouse landing. • Geduld zahlt sich aus: Es dauerte mehrere Jahre, bis Rosen einen Händler in Finnland überredet hatte, das Staumöbel aus lackiertem Holz abzugeben, das nun im oberen Flur des Gästehauses steht. • Il a fallu plusieurs années de patience à Rosen pour convaincre un marchand finlandais de lui céder ce meuble de rangement en bois peint du 19ᵉ siècle, désormais sur le palier de la maison d'amis.

"IN THE HAMPTONS, LOTS OF HOUSES LOOK LIKE FANCY MANSIONS. I CALL IT 'POTTERY BARN DELUXE.'" TIINA LAAKKONEN

"But we wanted a more honest style," says Laakkonen. Her husband, Jon Rosen, was particularly inspired by the former De Menil property in nearby East Hampton, which featured a collection of 18th- and 19th-century barns. "It was always more interesting for me to have a compound of buildings," he explains. The home they constructed consists of five structures—a garage, a pool house, and a main house made up of three linked structures. The outer two are inspired by regional Dutch-influenced architecture of the 1700s, while the central one resembles a basic barn. No one could blame the couple for lack of digital footwork: Jon assembled 500 (!) images of doors and researched chairs for six months. Many furnishings come from Tiina's native Finland. Each bedroom has two wallpapers designed by artists in the 1950s and '60s, while sofas are covered in Marimekko fabrics. "Finnish design has a quirkiness, a bit of folklore and fantasy," she declares. "And that really speaks to me."

„In den Hamptons sehen viele Häuser aus wie extravagante Landgüter – ich nenne es ‚Pottery Barn deluxe'", sagt Tiina Laakkonen. Ihr eigenes Haus wünschte sie sich anders: „Es sollte regional geprägt sein, ehrlicher." Ihren Ehemann Jon Rosen inspirierte besonders das ehemalige De-Menil-Anwesen in East Hampton, das aus verschiedenen historischen Scheunen bestand: „Ich fand es schon immer interessanter, eine Ansammlung mehrerer Gebäude zu haben." Im Fall seines neuen Zuhauses sind es fünf: Garage, Poolhaus und ein Haupthaus, das aus drei Teilen besteht – die beiden äußeren greifen die holländisch beeinflusste Architektur des 18. Jahrhunderts aus der Gegend auf, während das mittlere eine schlichte Scheune sein könnte. Für die Ausstattung leistete das Paar digitale Grundlagenarbeit: Jon sammelte 500 (!) Bilder von Türen und sichtete sechs Monate lang Stühle. Die Möbel stammen größtenteils aus Tiinas Heimat Finnland. Jedes Schlafzimmer bekam zwei Künstlertapeten aus den 1950er- und 1960er-Jahren, die Sofas sind mit Marimekko-Stoffen bezogen. „Finnisches Design hat etwas Schräges, eine Prise Folklore und Fantasie", erklärt sie. „Das spricht mich einfach an."

« Dans les Hamptons, beaucoup de maisons ont des allures de manoirs. Nous voulions un style plus authentique », explique Tiina Laakkonen. Séduit par l'ancienne collection De Menil à East Hampton, qui regroupait un ensemble de granges des 18ᵉ et 19ᵉ siècles, son mari Jon Rosen ajoute : « Il m'a toujours paru plus intéressant d'avoir un groupe de bâtiments. » Leur demeure en compte cinq : un garage, un poolhouse et une maison principale constituée de trois structures distinctes. Les corps latéraux reflètent l'architecture locale du 18ᵉ siècle, d'inspiration hollandaise, tandis que le corps central rappelle une grange classique. On ne peut reprocher au couple d'être mal informé : Jon a rassemblé 500 (!) images de portes et fait des recherches sur des chaises durant six mois. Le mobilier vient en grande partie de la Finlande natale de Tiina. Chaque chambre compte deux papiers peints d'artistes des années 1950 et 1960 tandis que les canapés sont tapissés de tissus Marimekko. « Le design finlandais a un côté excentrique et folklorique qui me parle », déclare Tiina.

▲ Feeling blue: a painting Rosen inherited from his grandmother hangs above a Restoration Hardware sofa in one of the guest rooms. *Tablo* tray table designed by Magnus Löfgren. • Ein Gemälde, das Rosen von seiner Großmutter geerbt hat, hängt über dem Sofa von Restoration Hardware in einem der Gästezimmer. Tablett-Tisch *Tablo* von Magnus Löfgren. • Un tableau ayant appartenu à la grand-mère de Rosen est accroché au-dessus d'un canapé Restoration Hardware dans l'une des chambres d'amis. Table-plateau *Tablo* dessinée par Magnus Löfgren.

▶ "Jon has a really good eye for old light fixtures," declares Laakkonen. The industrial pendants in the kitchen are an eBay find. Dining table by Piet Hein Eek. • „Jon hat einen exzellenten Blick für alte Leuchten", sagt Laakkonen. Die Industrielampen in der Küche sind eBay-Funde. Esstisch von Piet Hein Eek. • « Jon a le coup d'œil pour les luminaires anciens », déclare Laakkonen. Les suspensions industrielles dans la cuisine ont été trouvées sur eBay. Table de Piet Hein Eek.

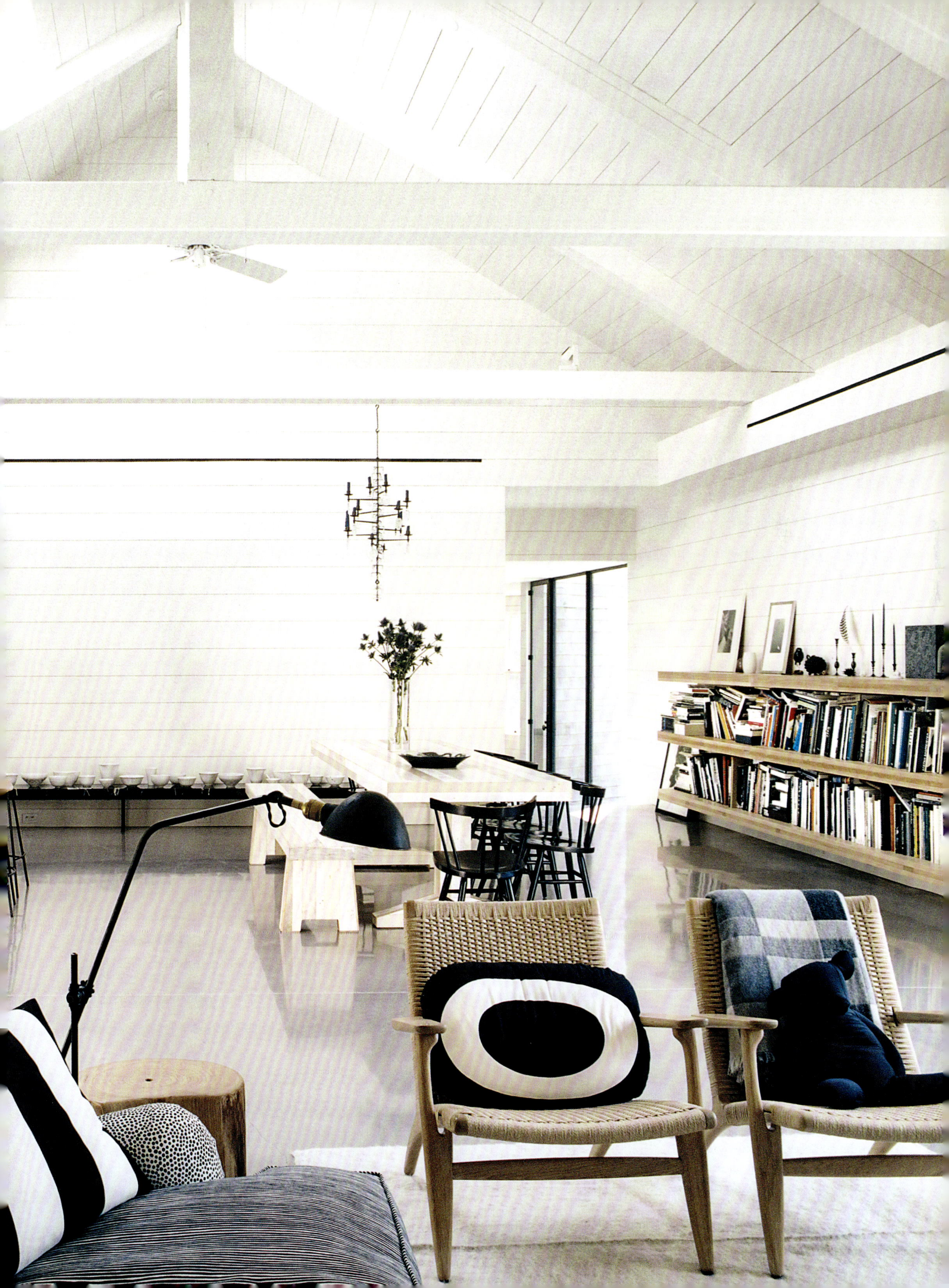

INEZ VAN LAMSWEERDE & VINOODH MATADIN

THEIR COCOON OF COOL IN NEW YORK

WHO Dutch-born photographers. **WHAT** Two lofts combined into one 316 m² (3,400 sq. ft.) apartment for themselves and their son, Charles. **WHERE** A turn-of-the-century ice factory in Nolita. **COLLABORATORS** The couple teamed up on the project with architect Simrel Achenbach of Descience Laboratories and interior designer Daniel Sachs. **WORK** They contribute regularly to *Vogue Paris, V Magazine,* and *W Magazine* and have shot striking campaigns for stylish labels including Saint Laurent and Balenciaga. **HOME WORK** Ideas for their abode came from a Charlotte Perriand ski chalet and Truman Capote's Hamptons house. **SHOOTING STAR** This is Achenbach's first full interiors project. He was previously best known as a woodworker and furniture-maker for hotel moguls André Balazs and Ian Schrager. **SHOOTING THE STARS** Van Lamsweerde and Matadin particularly like portrait sessions. Memorable subjects include Alexander McQueen, Javier Bardem, and Lady Gaga.

PHOTOGRAPHED BY INEZ & VINOODH

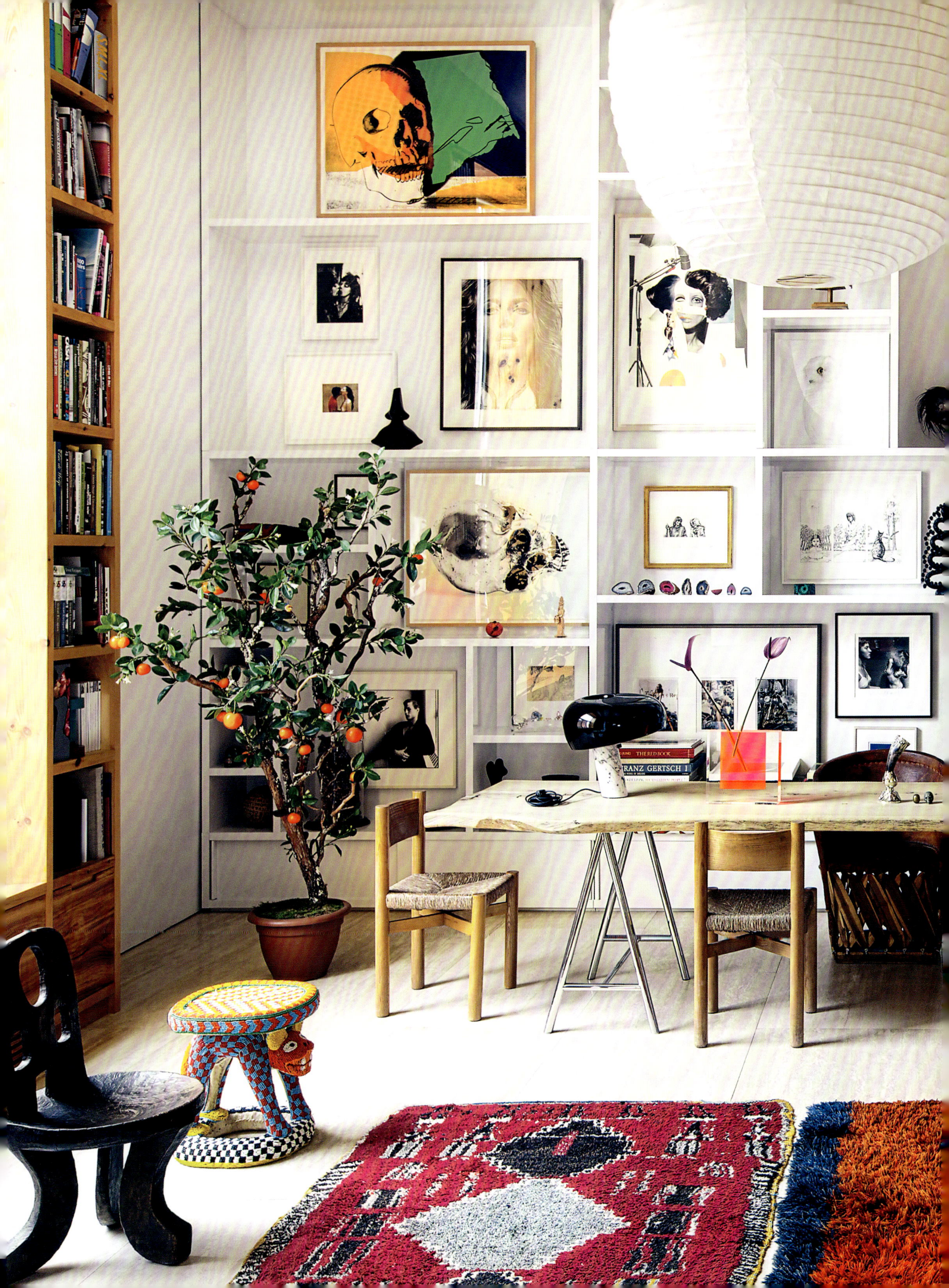
THE RED BOOK
RANZ GERTSCH 1

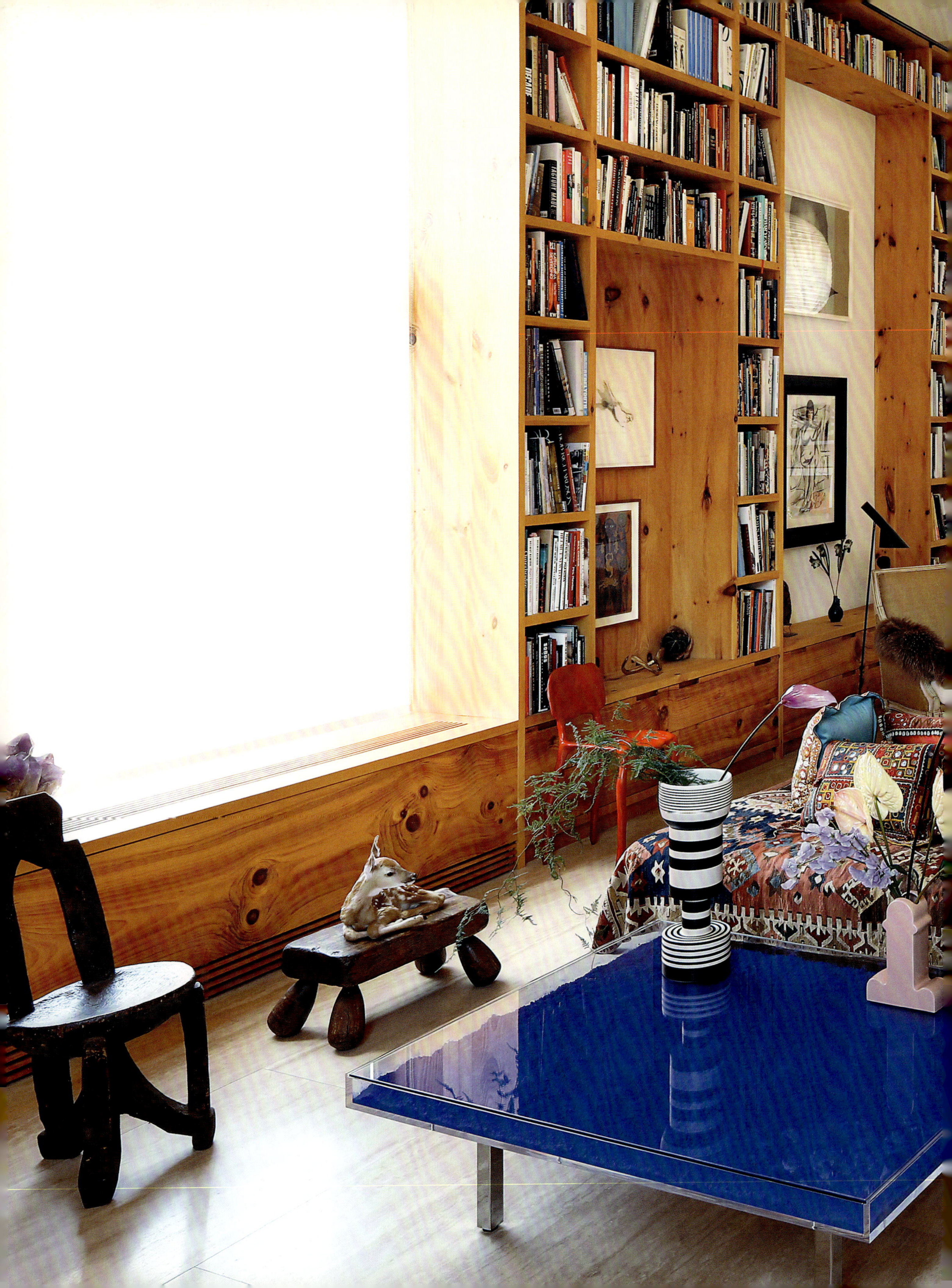

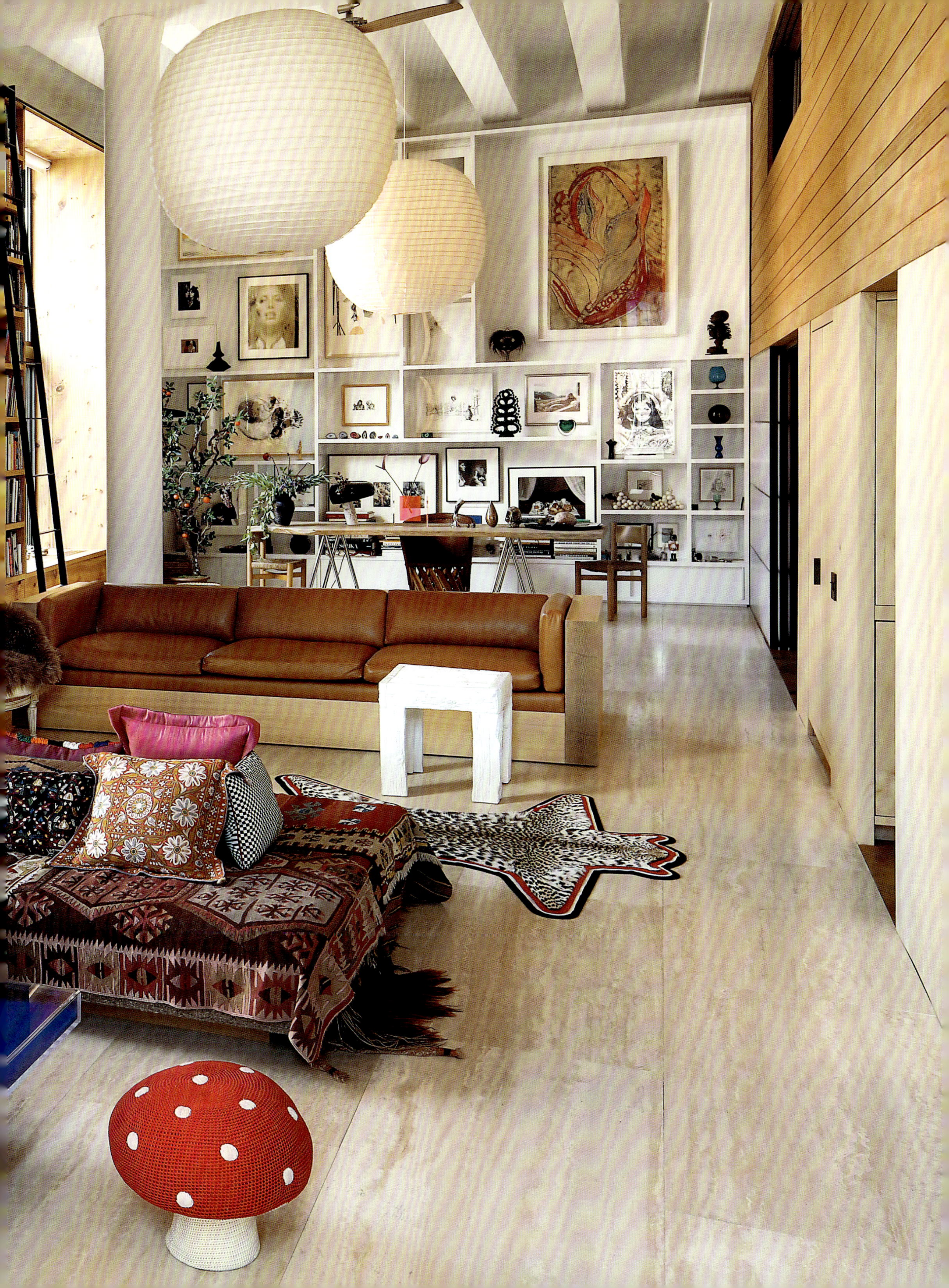

153–155 The wall behind the living room desk is a "mini-exhibition space" with works by Warhol, Louise Bourgeois, and Richard Phillips. *Snoopy* lamp by Flos. The high pine shelves and felt-bordered leopard rug were inspired by Truman Capote's weekend house. Mushroom stool from Anne-Claire Petit. • Die Wand hinter dem langen Tisch im Hauptraum ist als „Mini-Galerie" angelegt, mit Werken von Warhol, Louise Bourgeois und Richard Phillips. *Snoopy*-Lampe von Flos. Die hohen Regale und das filzgesäumte Leopardenfell sind von Truman Capotes Wochenendhaus inspiriert. Pilzhocker von Anne-Claire Petit. • Dans le séjour, le mur du fond sert de « mini galerie », avec des œuvres d'Andy Warhol, de Louise Bourgeois et de Richard Phillips. La bibliothèque en pin et la peau de léopard bordée de feutre s'inspirent d'une maison de Truman Capote. Lampe *Snoopy* de Flos et tabouret Champignon d'Anne-Claire Petit.

▼ In the playroom of the couple's son, Charles, a red Jonathan Adler table sits on a Moroccan carpet. The closets are made from bleached alder. • Im Spielzimmer von Sohn Charles steht ein roter Tisch von Jonathan Adler auf einem marokkanischen Teppich. Die Wandschränke sind aus gebleichter Erle. • Dans la salle de jeux de Charles, le fils du couple, une table rouge de Jonathan Adler est posée sur un tapis marocain. Les placards sont en aulne blanchi.

▶ The playroom's iron-framed partition resembles Japanese shoji screens, with Lucite replacing the paper. • Die Wände des Spielzimmers erinnern an japanische Shoji-Screens; statt Papier füllt Acrylglas die Metallrahmen. • Avec leurs cadres métalliques, les cloisons de la salle de jeux rappellent les *shoji* japonais, le Plexiglas ayant remplacé le papier.

▼ The loft's primary element is wood. While the living room shelves are pine, bleached alder was used for the kitchen cabinetry and walnut for Simrel Achenbach's custom dining table. • Holz ist omnipräsent: Die Regale im Wohnraum sind aus Kiefer, die Küche besteht aus gebleichter Erle und der von Simrel Achenbach entworfene Esstisch aus Nussbaum. • Partout, le bois prime. Les placards de la cuisine sont en aulne blanchi et la table créée par Simrel Achenbach est en noyer.

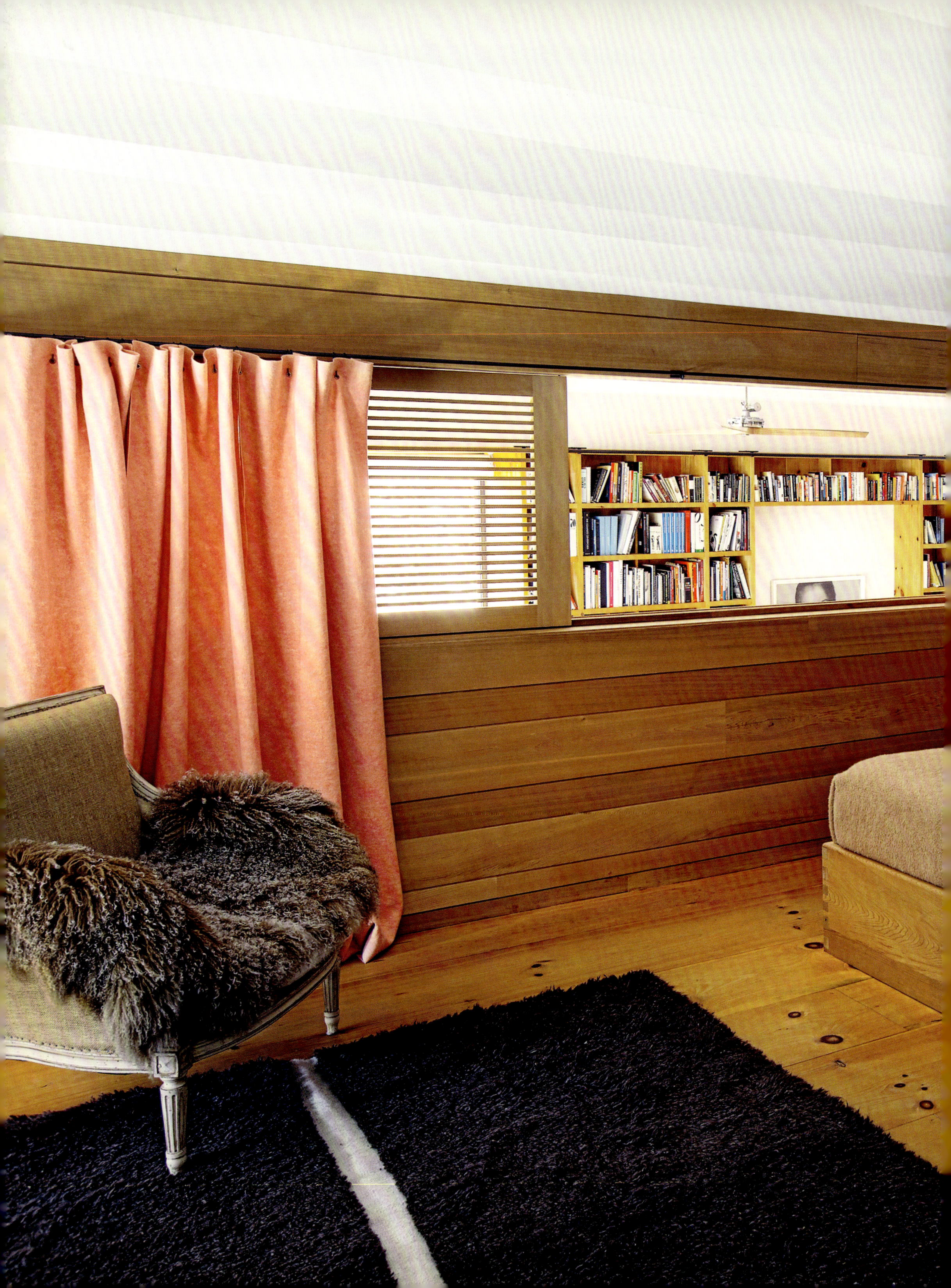

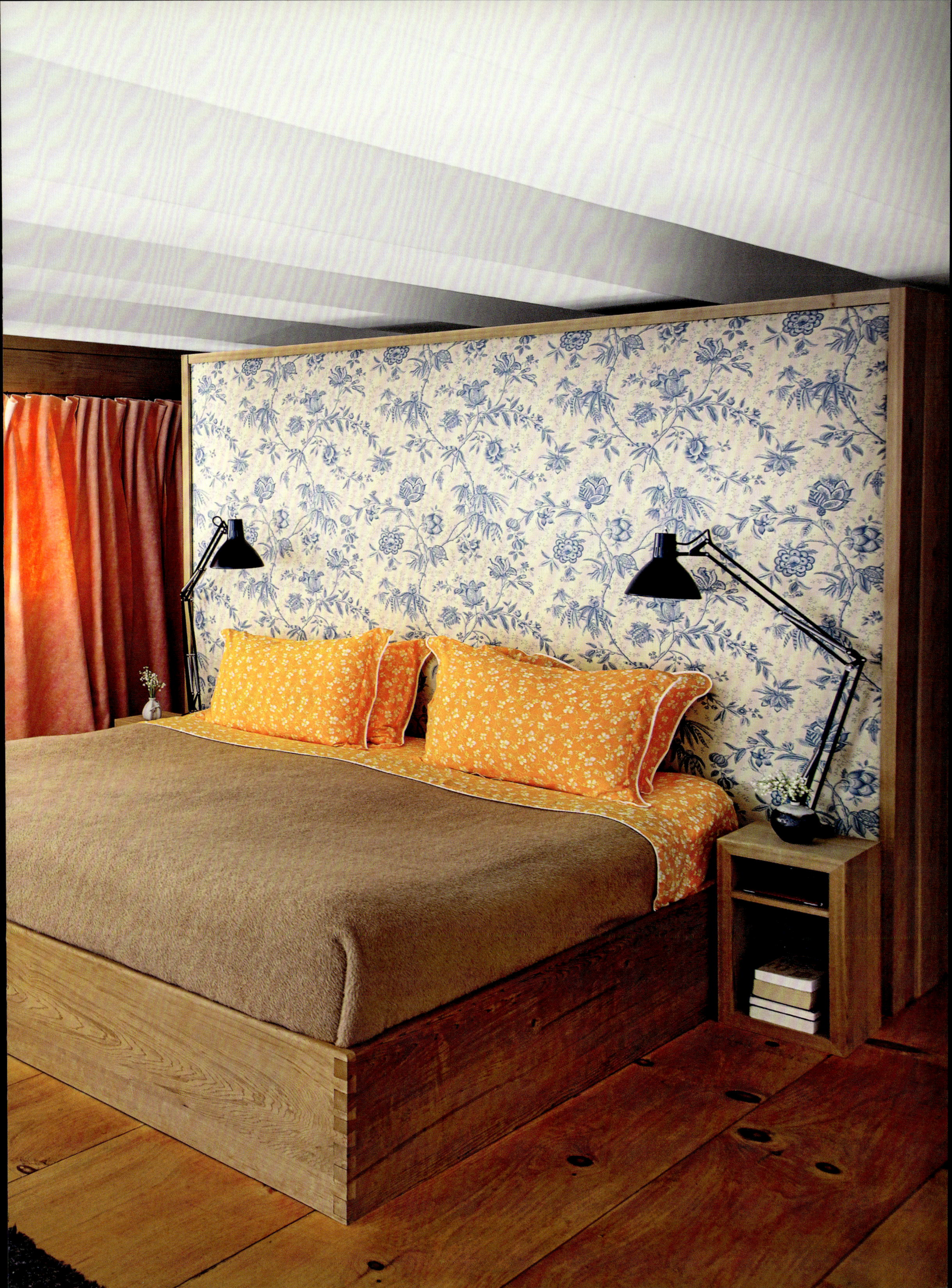

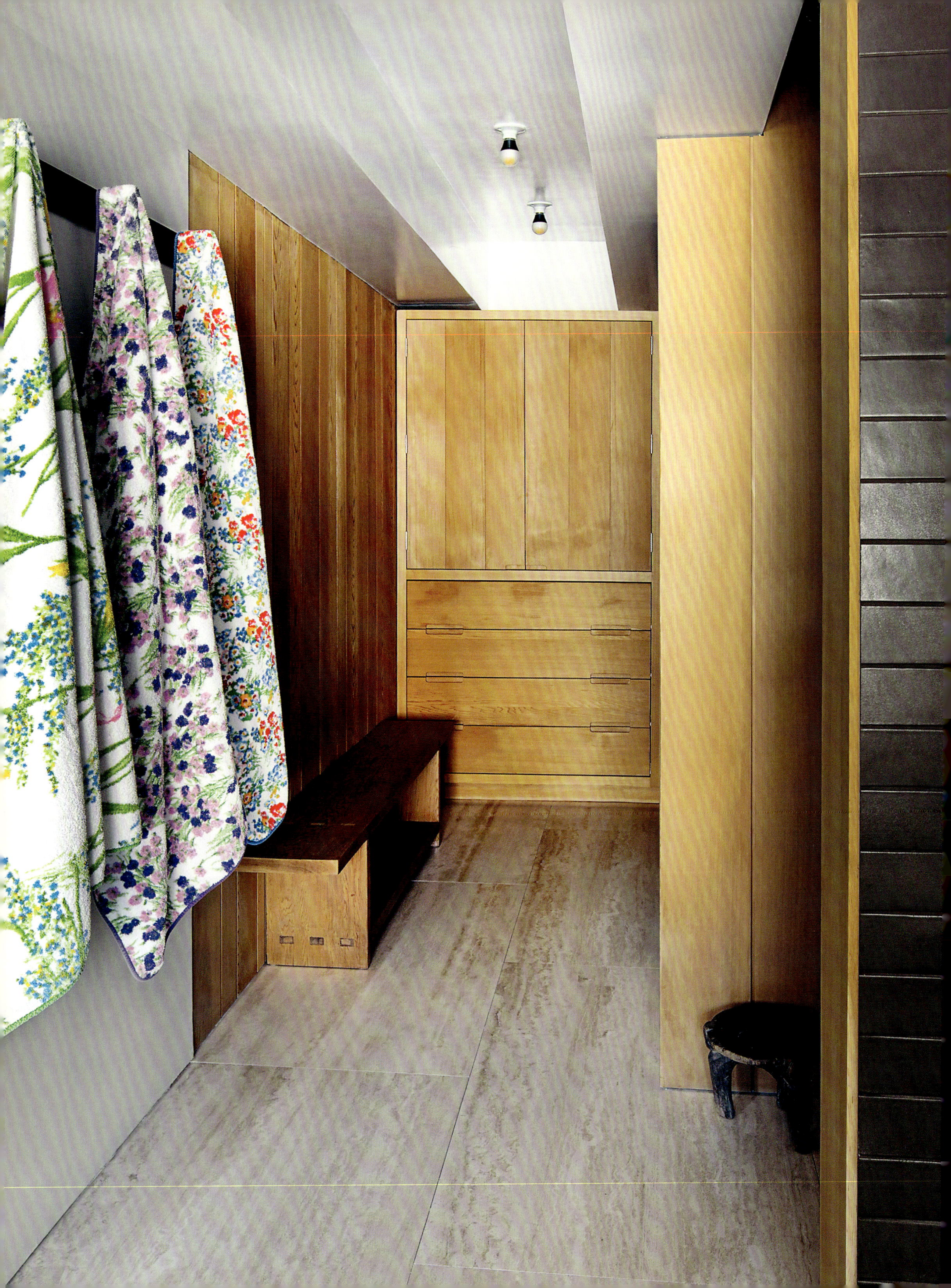

158–159 The headboard in the mezzanine-level master bedroom is covered in a Colefax & Fowler fabric. The lights are Lloytron's Studio Poise desk lamp. • Im Schlafzimmer des Mezzaningeschosses ist das Betthaupt mit Stoff von Colefax & Fowler bezogen. Auf den Nachttischen stehen Büroleuchten von Lloytron. • La chambre principale est perchée sur une mezzanine. En tête de lit, un tissu de Colefax & Fowler. Sur les tables de chevet, des lampes Studio Poise de Lloytron.

◂ Inspiration for the dressing area in the master bath came from Swedish saunas. Handprinted cotton terry towels by D. Porthault. • Vorbild für den Ankleidebereich im Masterbad war eine schwedische Sauna. Handbedruckte Frottee-Handtücher von D. Porthault. • Le coin dressing de la salle de bains principale s'inspire des saunas suédois. Les serviettes en coton imprimées à la main viennent de chez D. Porthault.

▾ Maarten Baas's *Clay* chair stands near one of the couple's images, "A rendition of a head, shoulders, and neck pushed around with Photoshop" from 2008. • Maarten Baas' *Clay*-Stuhl steht vor einer Arbeit des Paars: „Eine Darstellung von Kopf, Hals und Schultern, mit Photoshop verfremdet" von 2008. • La chaise *Clay* de Maarten Baas est posée près d'une photographie du couple : « Une tête, un cou et des épaules malmenés par Photoshop » de 2008.

163 The dining area features Charlotte Perriand chairs and a Georges Jouve glazed-stoneware mirror. The cozy niche to the left is used for watching TV. • Im Essbereich finden sich Perriand-Stühle und ein Spiegel aus glasiertem Steinzeug von Georges Jouve. In der Nische links lässt es sich entspannt fernsehen. • Des chaises de Charlotte Perriand et un miroir de Georges Jouve en grès cérame. Au fond de la pièce, un recoin douillet pour regarder la télé.

"IN A WAY, THIS PLACE IS LIKE A COLLECTION OF OUR JOINT MEMORIES OF THE PAST." INEZ VAN LAMSWEERDE

Inez van Lamsweerde and Vinoodh Matadin used to live in a sparse environment. It was totally white and furnished with just a bed, table, and chairs. "People would come in and say, 'Oh, you just moved in,' and we would be like, 'No, we've lived here for five years already,'" says van Lamsweerde with a laugh. When they decided to combine it with the unit next door, they opted for a radical change of style. The assignment they gave their architect, Simrel Achenbach, was intriguing. "We said we wanted a mix between a Japanese teahouse and a Swedish sauna," she recounts. "That the place should look like as if we'd been living here since the 1970s." The result is a loft that looks like anything but a loft. Mainly furnished in wood, its pieces mix icons like Yves Klein's *Table bleue* or Charlotte Perriand stools with ethnic touches in the form of Moroccan and Uzbek carpets, or Philippe Starck's beaded African chairs. "A lot of it has to do with our childhood, the houses of our parents' friends, things we looked at in magazines," asserts van Lamsweerde.

Früher wohnten Inez van Lamsweerde und Vinoodh Matadin spartanisch. Weiße Wände, ein Bett, ein Tisch und ein paar Stühle. „Wir wurden oft gefragt, ob wir gerade erst eingezogen seien", lacht van Lamsweerde. Als sie beschlossen, ihre Räume mit dem Nachbar-Apartment zu verbinden, wagten sie einen radikalen Stilwechsel. Ihr Architekt Simrel Achenbach bekam ein spannendes Briefing: „Wir wünschten uns einen Mix aus japanischem Teehaus und schwedischer Sauna", berichtet sie. „Und es sollte aussehen, als ob wir hier schon seit den Siebzigern leben." So entstand ein Loft, das kein bisschen nach Loft aussieht. Dominierendes Material ist Holz, kombiniert werden Ikonen wie Yves Kleins *Table bleue* oder Perriand-Hocker mit Folklore-Akzenten, etwa marokkanischen und usbekischen Teppichen oder Philippe Starcks perlenbesetzten afrikanischen Hockern. „Vieles davon geht auf unsere Kindheit zurück oder auf Abbildungen in Magazinen", erklärt van Lamsweerde. „Dieser Ort ist eine Sammlung von Erinnerungen, die wir beide zusammengetragen haben."

Inez van Lamsweerde et Vinoodh Matadin vivaient autrefois dans un environnement tout blanc : il n'y avait qu'un lit, une table et des chaises. « Les gens croyaient qu'on venait d'emménager. Ils faisaient une drôle de tête en apprenant qu'on y vivait depuis cinq ans », se souvient Lamsweerde. Lorsqu'ils ont réuni leur appartement avec celui d'à côté, ils voulaient un changement radical. Leur architecte, Simrel Achenbach, reçut des consignes déroutantes : « Nous voulions un mélange entre une maison de thé japonaise et un sauna suédois. En un sens, ce lieu est un assemblage de tous nos souvenirs communs, comme si nous y habitions depuis les années 1970. » Le bois domine et le mobilier mêle des pièces emblématiques tels que la *Table bleue* d'Yves Klein ou des tabourets de Perriand à des touches ethniques : tapis ouzbeks et marocains, ou encore chaises africaines de Philippe Stark. « Nous nous sommes inspirés de notre enfance, des maisons des amis de nos parents et de magazines. »

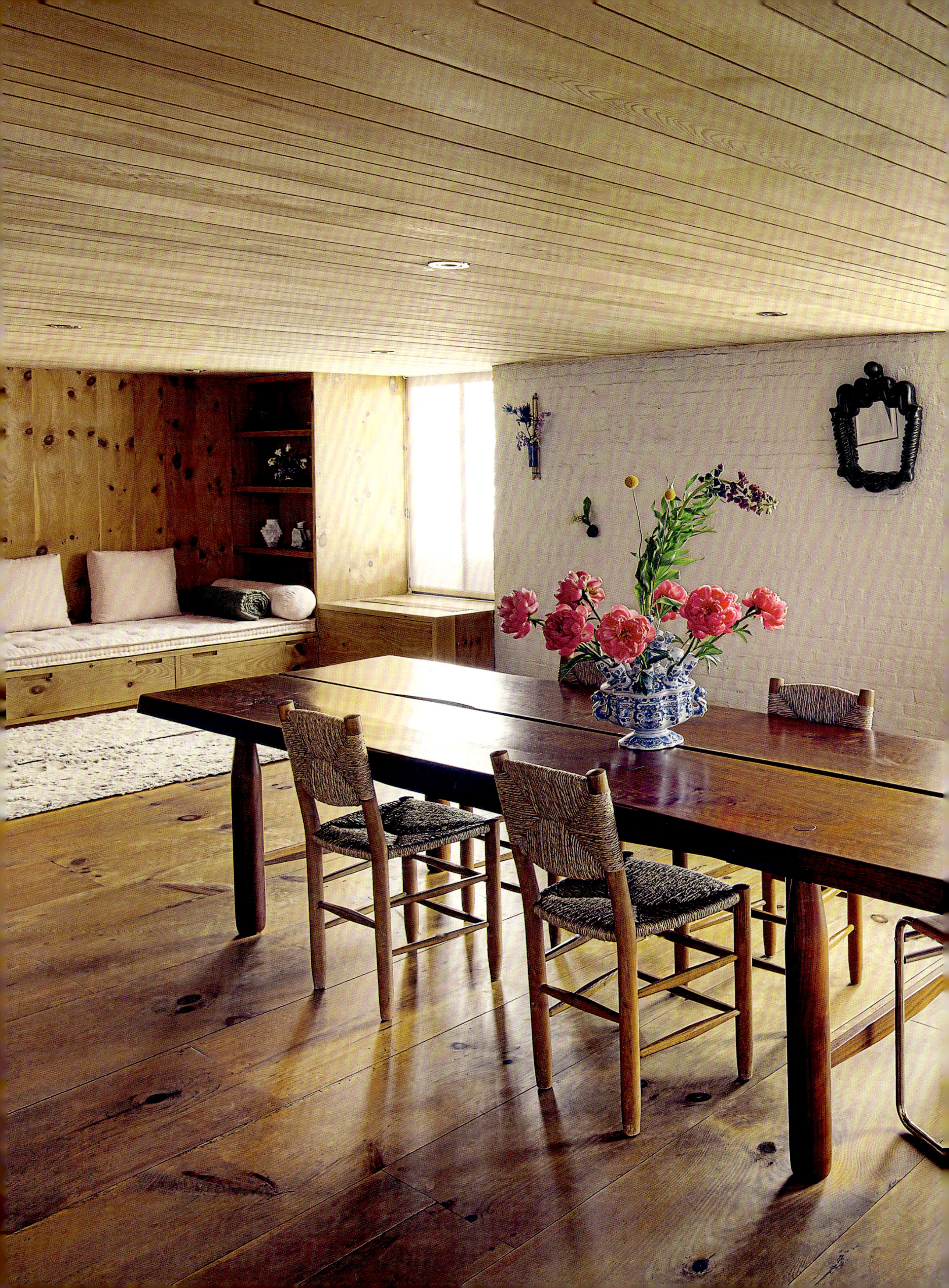

JOHN LOECKE & JASON OLIVER NIXON

THEIR MADCAP HOME IN BROOKLYN

WHO Partners in the New York-based decorating firm, Madcap Cottage. **WHAT** Their 297 m² (3,200 sq. ft.) mock-Tudor row house dating from c. 1910. **WHERE** Brooklyn's Prospect Lefferts Gardens. **EARLY INFLUENCE** Nixon, *above right,* has been hooked on design ever since he went on a family vacation at age 12 to the Dorothy Draper-decorated Greenbrier resort in West Virginia. **CRAZY BUT TRUE** "We like to embellish our wallpaper with Indian wedding rhinestones in candy-colored hues that we purchase by the bucketful at bazaars in Jaipur and Delhi." **CRAZY BUT MAYBE NOT TRUE** "We fell asleep once in our soup at the Connaught Hotel in London after we forgot that pairing an Ambien sleeping pill with a martini might not be advisable." **DREAM DESTINATIONS** Loecke and Nixon spend half the year traveling. Their favorite places include India, the Caribbean island of St. Barts, and Iowa. **DREAM PROJECTS** "A vest pocket-size" hotel and a palace for a sheika ("the feminine of a sheikh") modeled on the Brighton Pavilion.

PHOTOGRAPHED BY JOHN BESSLER

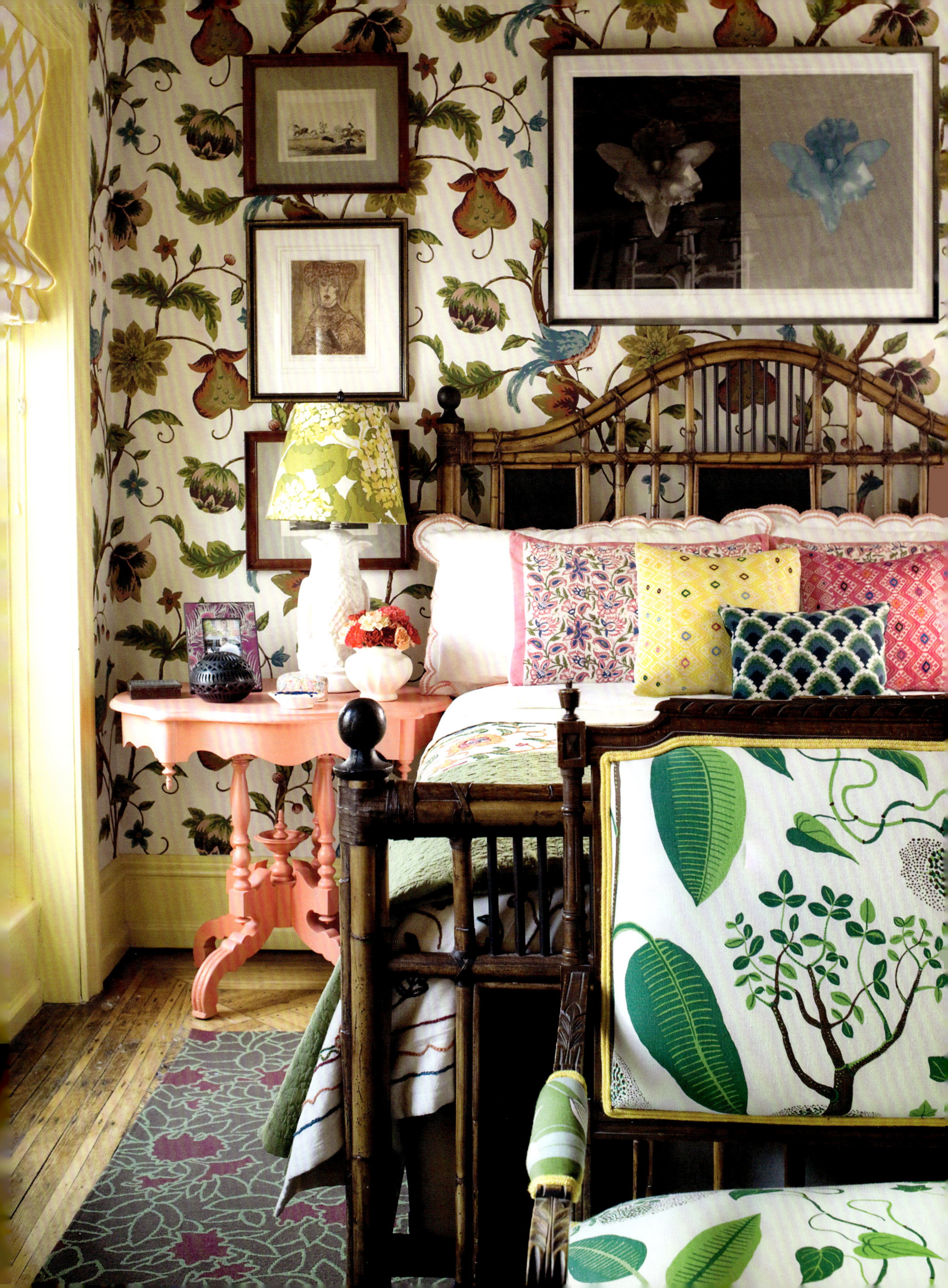

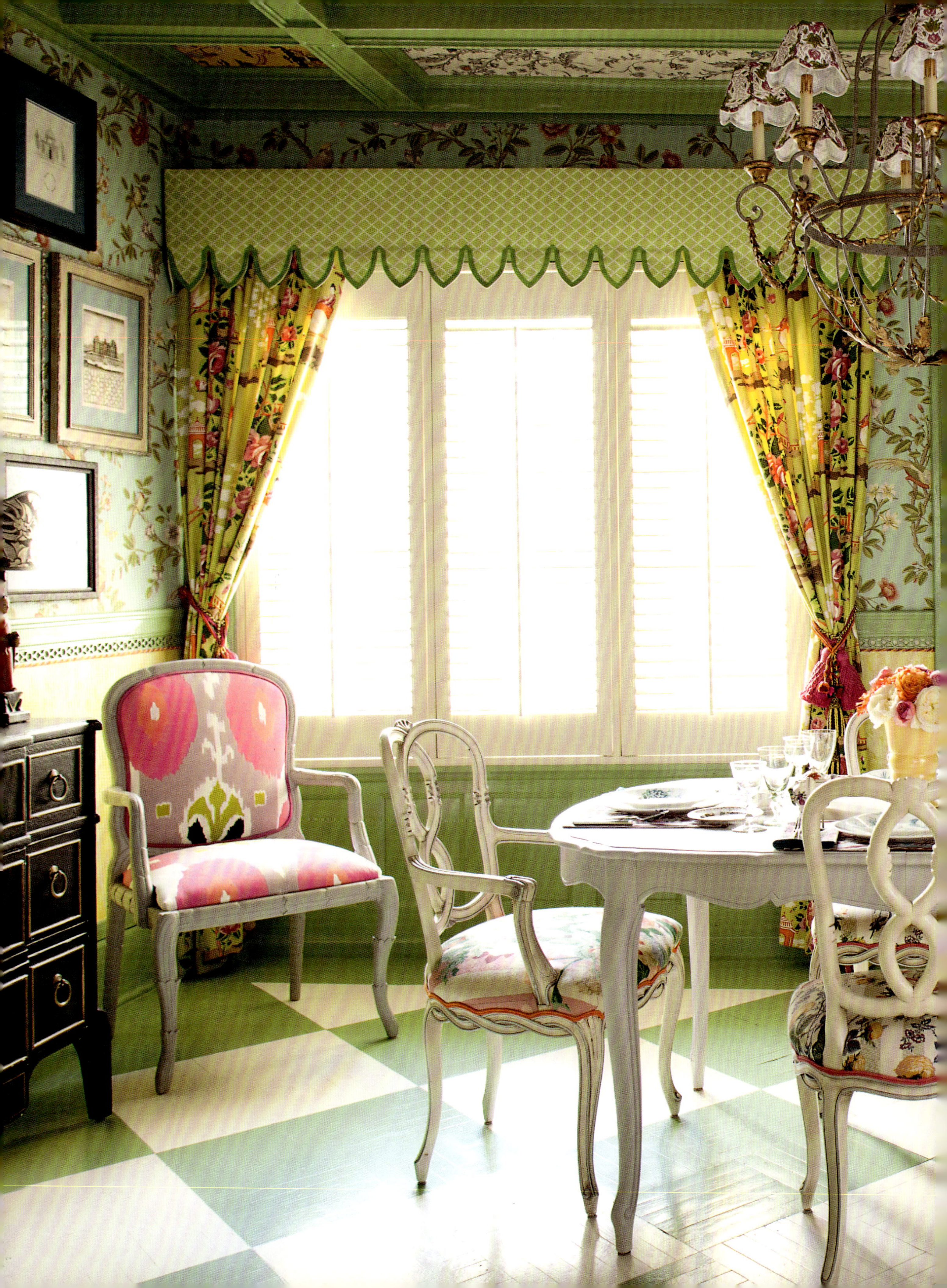

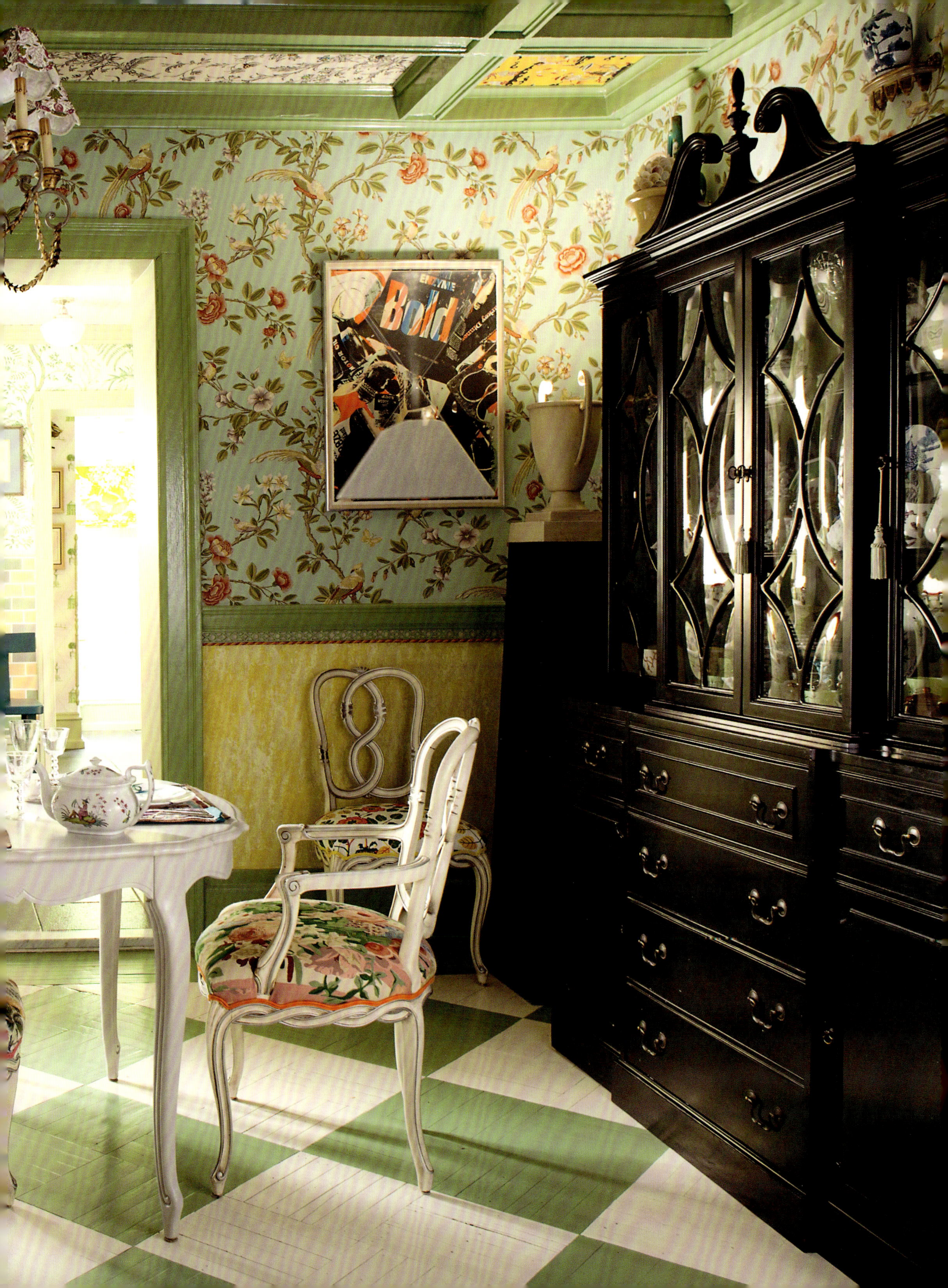

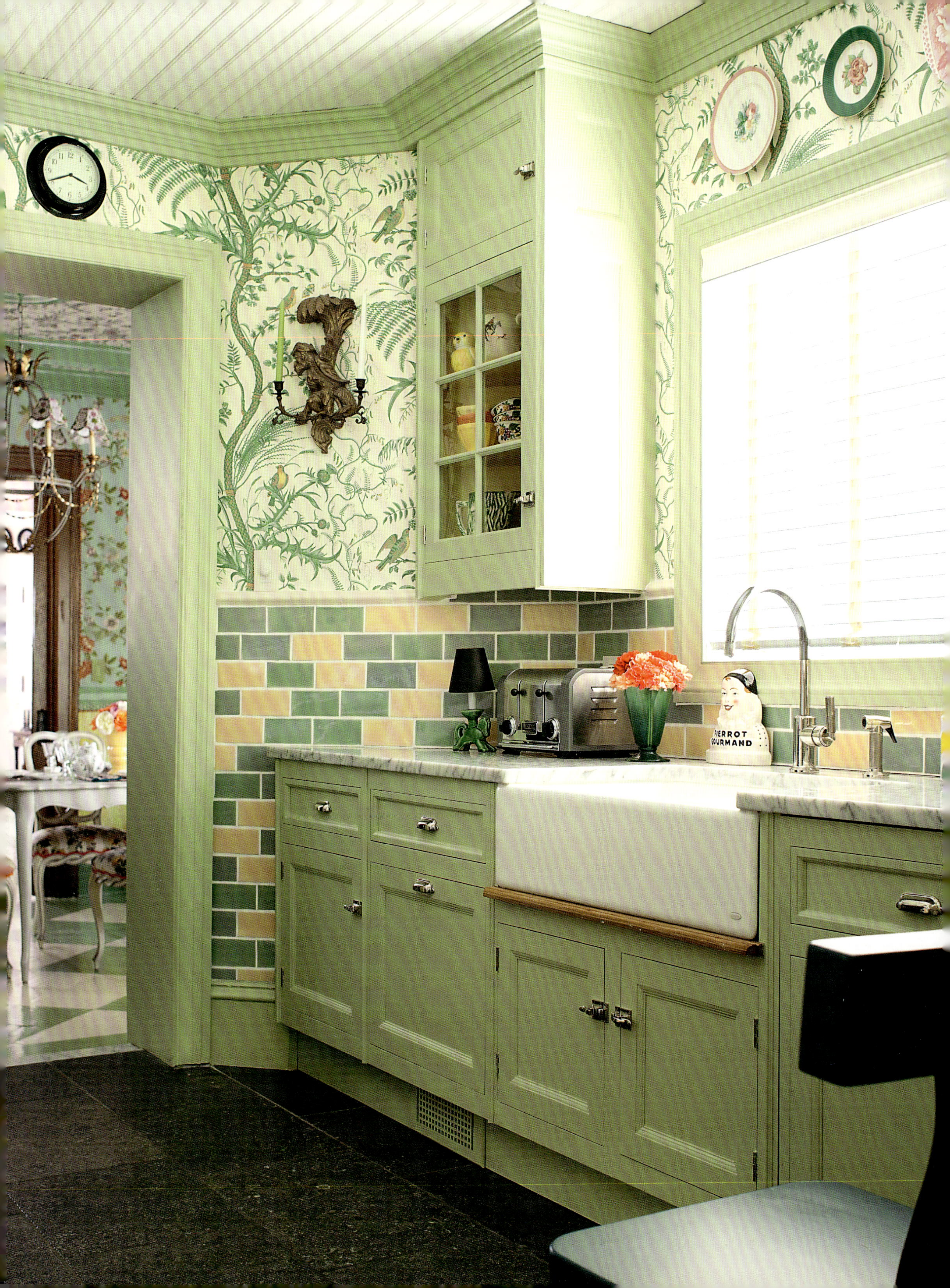
PIERROT
GOURMAND

165 The spare room is "a tad *Little Shop of Horrors* thanks to the floral wallpaper that seems to purr, 'Feed me, Seymour!' " The side table was found in Des Moines and painted pink. • Das Gästezimmer hat „einen Hauch von *Der kleine Horrorladen,* die florale Tapete scheint zu wispern: ‚Seymour, gib uns zu essen!'" Der Beistelltisch aus Des Moines wurde rosa gestrichen. • Avec son papier peint fleuri, la chambre d'amis a un petit côté « Petite boutique des horreurs ». Trouvée à Des Moines, la table de chevet a été peinte en rose.

166-167 Inspired by The Gritti Palace hotel, the dining room features wallpaper on the ceiling. "Why not?" ask Loecke and Nixon. • Inspiriert vom Hotel Gritti Palace: die tapezierte Decke im Esszimmer. „Warum nicht?", finden Loecke und Nixon. • Inspirée de l'hôtel The Gritti Palace, la salle à manger est tapissée de papier peint même au le plafond. « Pourquoi pas ? » demandent Loecke et Nixon.

◀ The kitchen is an homage to Fortnum & Mason in London. "We are just crazy for Eau de Nil, their signature hue," say the Madcap boys. • Die Küche ist eine Hommage an Fortnum & Mason in London. „Wir sind einfach verrückt nach ‚Eau de Nil', ihrer Signatur-Farbe", verkünden die Madcap-Boys. • La cuisine est un hommage au magasin londonien Fortnum & Mason. « Nous adorons leur couleur emblématique, Eau de Nil », déclare le couple excentrique.

▲ "We firmly believe that bathrooms should have rugs and furniture in them," they assert. The shower is clad in blue-and-white penny tile from Ann Sacks. • „Wir glauben fest daran, dass Bäder Teppiche und Möbel brauchen", erklären sie. Die Dusche ist mit blau-weißem Knopfmosaik von Ann Sacks ausgekleidet. • « Nous croyons qu'une salle de bains doit avoir ses meubles et ses tapis », affirment-ils. La douche est tapissée de pastilles de céramique d'Ann Sacks.

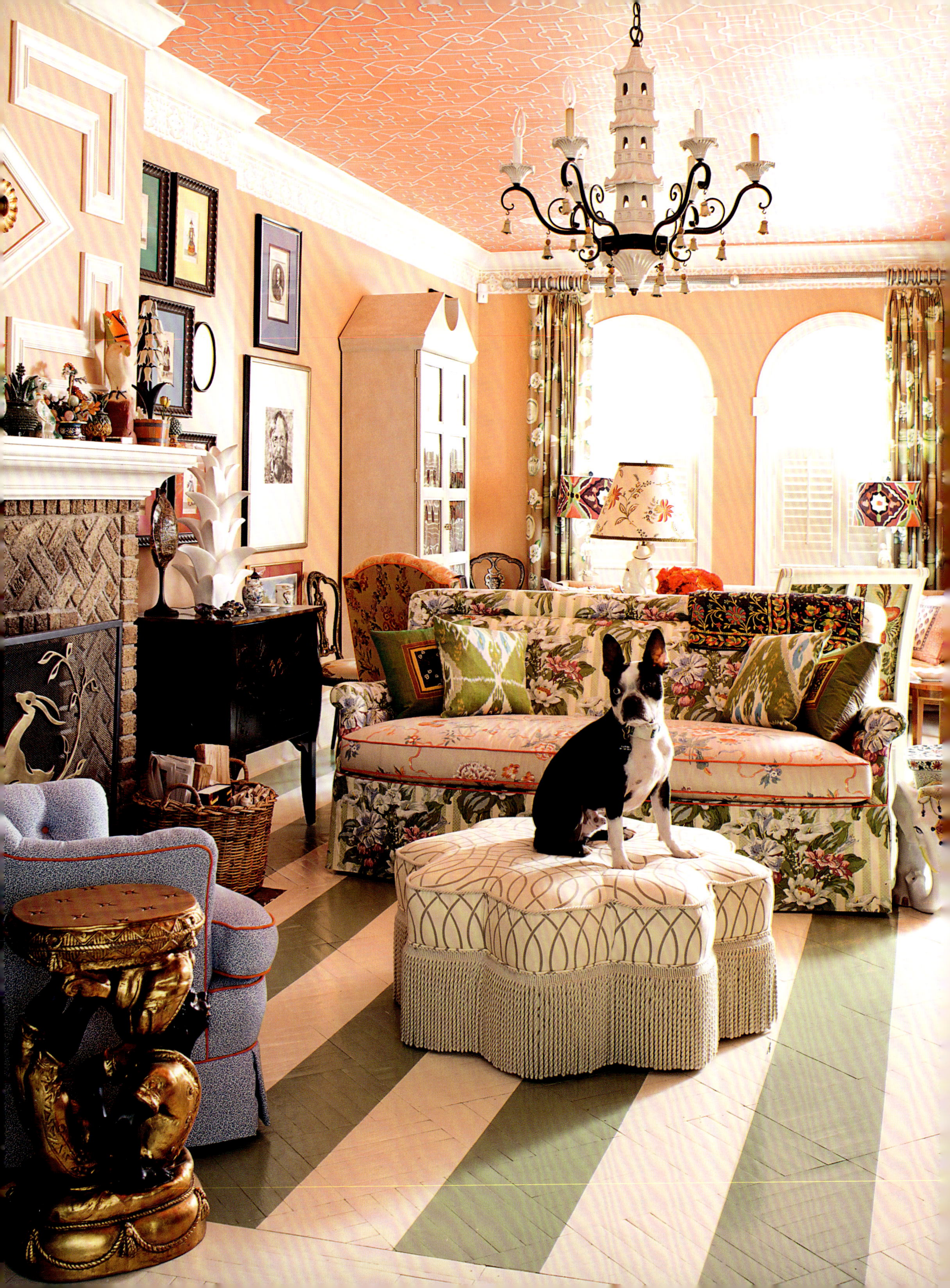

"We would rather fall off the roof of a thatched cottage and right into the prickly briar patch than own a home that is anything but maximalist and marvelous," declare John Loecke and Jason Oliver Nixon. There is certainly no denying their own home has a lot going on. The den is festooned with a dizzying array of patterns, the dining room is modeled after the bar of The Gritti Palace in Venice, and the spare bathroom has a frondy wallpaper inspired by the famous banana leaves in the Fountain Coffee Room at the Beverly Hills Hotel. Furnishings run the gamut from vintage Turkish textiles to a bar found on a roadside in Los Angeles. They describe their guest quarters as "a garden in hell"—"it is a place for your mother-in-law to shack up with wallpaper that just might eat her once the sun goes down." Sounds scary? Maybe, but it's also great fun. More than anything, their abode is an ever-evolving design lab for their discoveries and ideas. "Nothing ever remains static," they assert. "It's always in constant overhaul. That's how we roll. It makes us happy, and that's all that matters."

„WIR WÜRDEN LIEBER VOM DACH IN DORNENGESTRÜPP FALLEN, ALS EIN ZUHAUSE ZU HABEN, DAS NICHT MAXIMALISTISCH IST." MOTTO VON MADCAP

Kein Zweifel, im trauten Heim von John Loecke und Jason Oliver Nixon, dem Duo hinter Madcap Cottage, hat das Auge ganz schön zu tun. Der kleine Salon ist mit einer schwindelerregenden Vielfalt von Mustern ausgeschmückt, das Esszimmer empfindet die Bar des Gritti Palace in Venedig nach, und das Bad hat eine Tapete, die von den berühmten Bananenblättern im Coffee Room des Beverly Hills Hotel inspiriert ist. Die Einrichtung spannt einen weiten Bogen von türkischen Vintage-Textilien bis hin zu einem Barwagen, der in L.A. am Straßenrand stand. Ihre Gästezimmer bezeichnen sie als „einen Garten in der Hölle" – „es ist ein Ort, um die Schwiegermutter einzuquartieren – mit einer Tapete, die sie nach Sonnenuntergang womöglich verschlingen wird". Klingt leicht bedrohlich? Mag sein, aber es ist auch sehr witzig. Vor allem aber ist das Haus ein sich stetig weiterentwickelndes Designlabor für ihre Entdeckungen und Ideen. „Nichts hier bleibt statisch", versichern sie. „Alles wird ständig überarbeitet. So läuft das bei uns. Das macht uns glücklich, und nur das zählt."

« Plutôt tomber du toit d'une chaumière directement dans des buissons de ronces que de vivre dans un décor qui ne soit pas maximaliste et merveilleux », déclarent John Loecke et Jason Oliver Nixon. Le fait est qu'on ne s'ennuie pas chez eux. Leur repaire est un étourdissant pot-pourri de styles. La salle à manger s'inspire du bar de l'hôtel The Gritti Palace à Venise et le feuillage qui tapisse l'une des salles de bains rappelle les feuilles de bananier au Fountain Coffee Room du Beverly Hills Hotel. Le mobilier comprend des étoffes turques et un bar trouvé sur le bord de la route à Los Angeles. Leur chambre d'amis, qualifiée de « jardin en enfer », est un lieu où « votre belle-mère pourrait se faire dévorer par le papier peint une fois la nuit tombée ». Effrayant ? Certes, mais aussi très drôle. Avant tout, leur maison est un laboratoire d'idées en perpétuelle évolution. « Nous changeons constamment. C'est notre manière de vivre et cela nous rend heureux. Et ça, c'est tout ce qui compte. »

170 Jasper the Boston terrier-boxer mix sits on an ottoman in the living room. When a leak caused damage to the parquet floor, it was painted to disguise the stains. The porcelain chinoiserie-style chandelier was bought in the Hamptons. • Mischling Jasper (halb Boxer, halb Boston-Terrier) sitzt auf einem Pouf im Wohnzimmer. Der Parkettboden wurde nach einem Wasserschaden bemalt, um die Flecken zu kaschieren. Der Porzellanlüster im Chinoiserie-Stil ist ein Fundstück aus den Hamptons. • Jasper, moitié terrier, moitié boxer, pose sur un pouf du salon. Suite à un dégât des eaux, le parquet a été peint pour masquer les taches. Le lustre en porcelaine a été acheté dans les Hamptons.

▲ The mock-Tudor row house is tucked away on a quiet cul-de-sac. • Das Reihenhaus im Mock-Tudor-Stil liegt versteckt in einer stillen Sackgasse. • La maison en faux style Tudor se trouve dans une impasse tranquille.

◀ Among the objects on a library table is a Daum crystal turtle christened "Skipperdee". • Unter den Objekten auf einem Bibliothekstisch ist eine Kristallschildkröte von Daum, die *Skipperdee* getauft wurde. • Sur une table de la bibliothèque, une tortue en cristal de Daum baptisée *Skipperdee*.

▶ The den has been outfitted with a Tom Dixon wallpaper for Cole & Son, a Neisha Crosland rug, a chaise covered in a Cowtan & Tout fabric, and a lithograph by James Rosenquist. • Im kleinen Salon finden sich eine Tom-Dixon-Tapete von Cole & Son, ein Teppich von Neisha Crosland und eine mit Stoff von Cowtan & Tout bezogene Chaiselongue. Lithografie von James Rosenquist. • Dans le petit salon, un papier peint de Tom Dixon pour Cole & Son, un tapis de Neisha Crosland, une chaise longue tapissée d'un tissu de Cowtan & Tout et une lithographie de James Rosenquist.

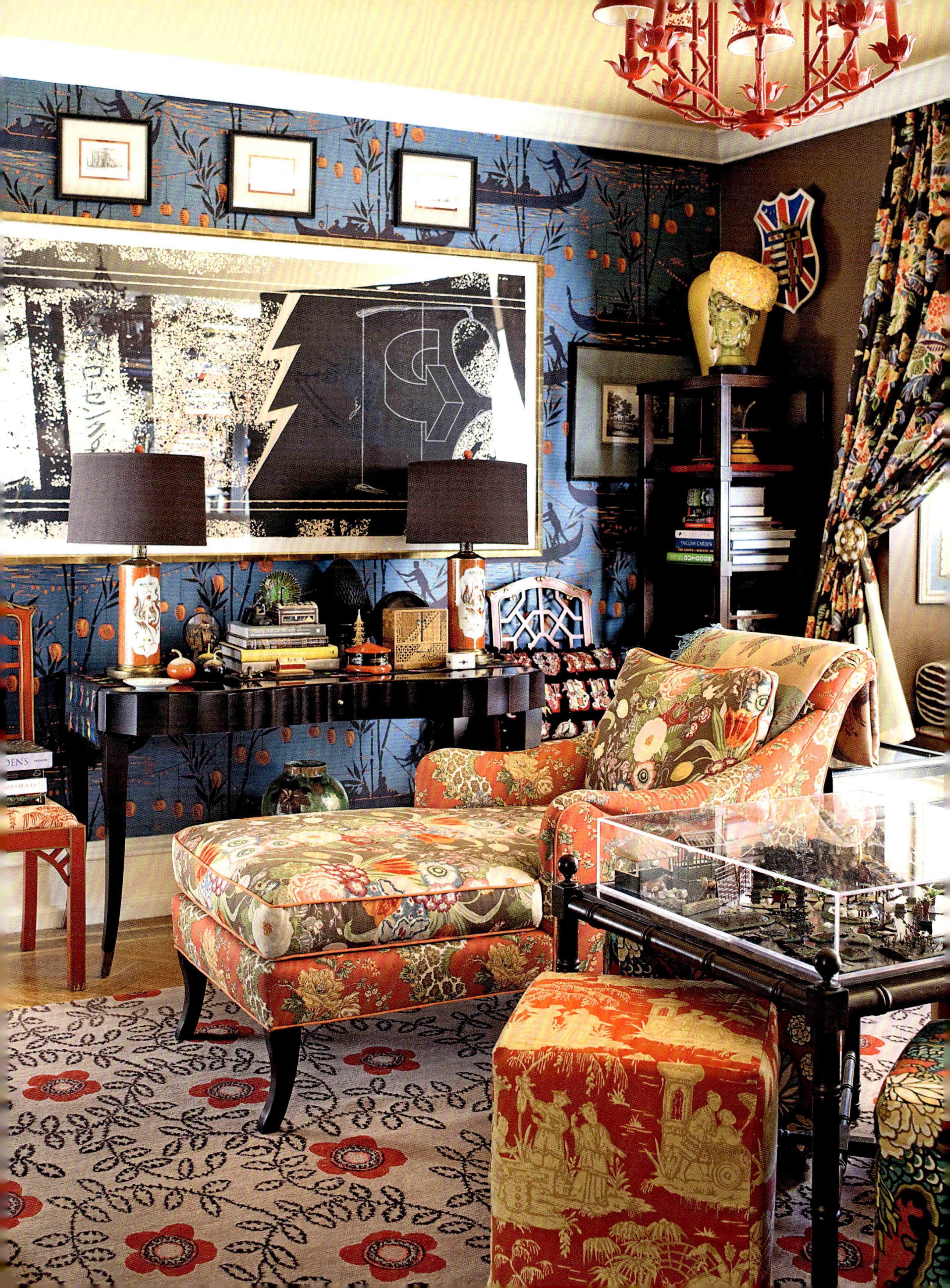

QUEEN ELIZABETH II
JUNE 2nd 1953
EIIR
"God Bless Our
Gracious Queen,
Long Live Our
Noble Queen,
God Save Our
Queen."

◄ "John and I are fatal Anglophiles. Anything vintage with a portrait of an English king or queen—we take it," states Nixon. On the wall of the second-floor landing is a framed tea towel commemorating the coronation of George V. • „John und ich sind in fatalem Maße anglophil. Sobald etwas Vintage ist und das Porträt eines englischen Königs oder einer Königin trägt, können wir nicht widerstehen", gibt Nixon zu. Das gerahmte Geschirrtuch neben der Treppe im ersten Stock erinnert an die Krönung von George V. • « John et moi sommes anglophiles jusqu'au bout des ongles. Nous adorons tout ce qui porte le portrait d'un roi ou d'une reine britannique », déclare Nixon. Sur le palier du premier étage, une serviette encadrée commémorant le couronnement de George V.

▲ The master bedroom is a testament to the couple's love of traveling. The bed was bought at a bric-à-brac shop in Florida, the quilt comes from India, and the Josef Frank fabric on the faux-bamboo bench was acquired at Svenskt Tenn in Stockholm "on a blustery day in June." • Der Masterbedroom bezeugt die Reiselust der beiden: Das Bett fanden sie bei einem Trödler in Florida, der Quilt ist aus Indien, und den von Josef Frank entworfenen Stoff auf der Faux-Bamboo-Bank kauften sie in Stockholm – „an einem stürmischen Tag im Juni". • La chambre principale témoigne de leur goût du voyage. Le lit vient d'une brocante de Floride, le dessus-de-lit d'Inde. Sur le banc de lit, un tissu de Josef Frank acheté chez Svenskt Tenn à Stockholm « un jour de juin où le vent soufflait en rafales ».

SALLY MACKERETH

A FLAMBOYANT BACHELOR PAD IN LONDON

WHO A partner in the London-based architecture practice, Wells Mackereth. **WHAT** A 330 m² (3,552 sq. ft.), one-bedroom home that stretches over two very different structures—what was probably a Victorian coach house and a soaring, brand-new building. **WHERE** London's Little Venice district. **THE CLIENT** The son of a Sudanese telecoms mogul, Hosh Ibrahim is not only a former actor turned property developer, but also a big fan of contemporary architecture. Handsome and always impeccably dressed, he once paid a small fortune at a charity auction to kiss supermodel Kate Moss. **MODERNIST INSPIRATION** Mackereth admires the bold residences of architect John Lautner, whom she met on a trip to California as a student. **MINIMALIST FAN** John Pawson has called the Little Venice House "magical and inventive." **LIVE WHAT YOU PREACH** For clients, not only does Wells Mackereth aim for "inspirational spaces designed to thrill and empower," but Mackereth and her husband have also transformed a lighthouse in Norfolk into their own weekend home.

PHOTOGRAPHED BY SIMON UPTON©THE WORLD OF INTERIORS   PORTRAIT BY SIMON BEVAN

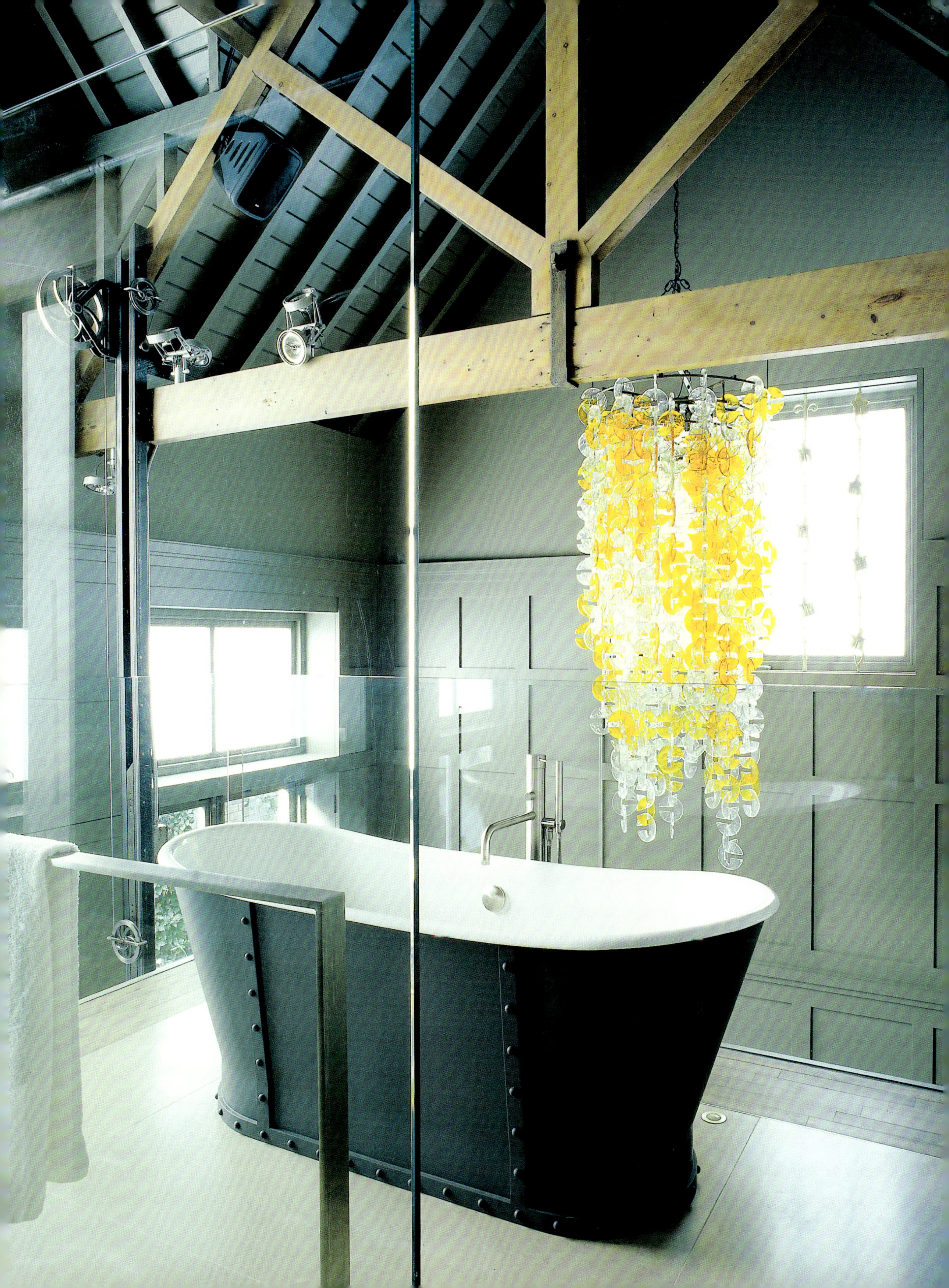

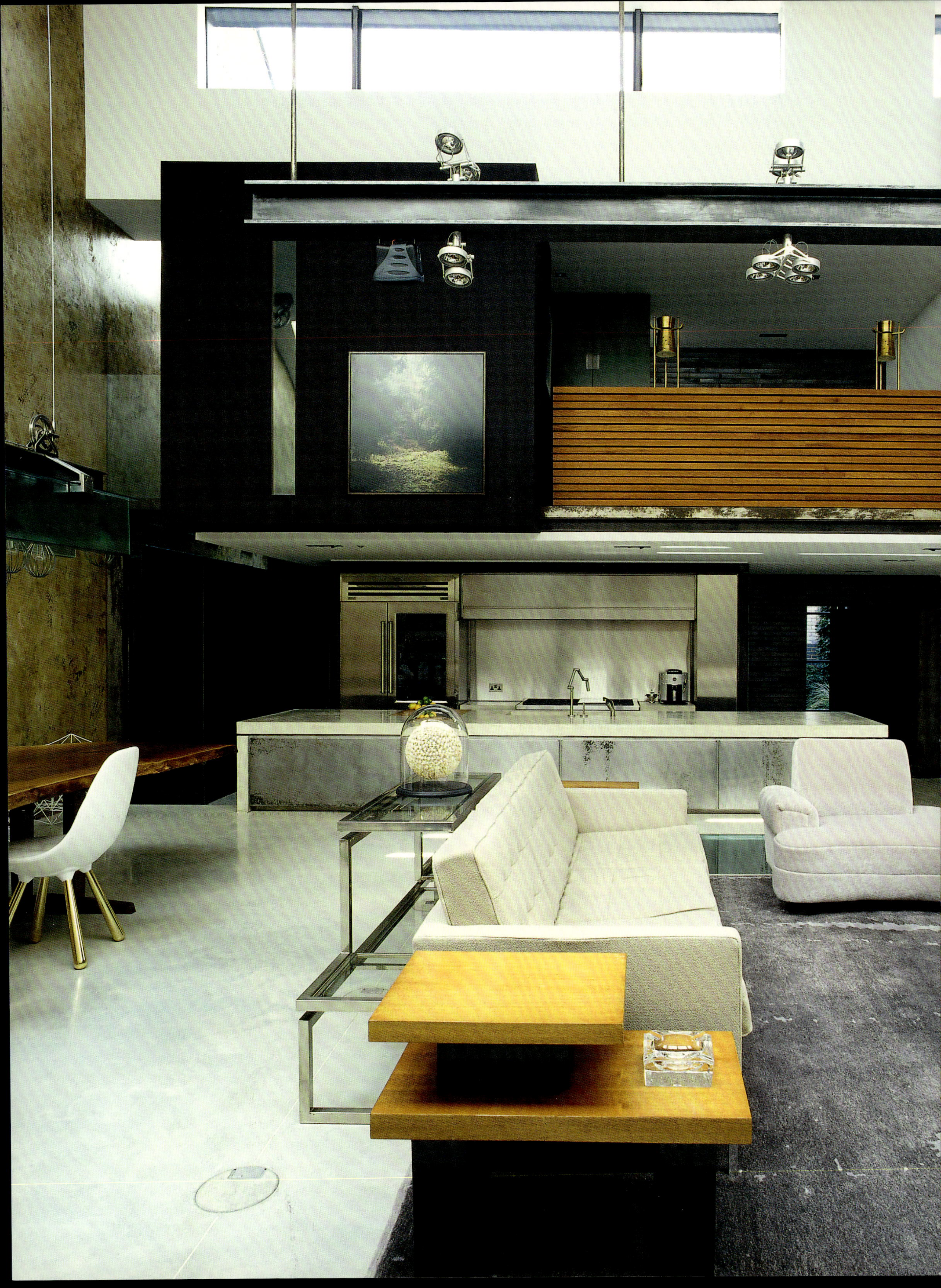

177 Bath as a battleship: a 1960s Venetian chandelier adds glamour to the glass-enclosed platform with Aston Matthews tub. • Bad als Kommandobrücke: Ein venezianischer Lüster aus den 1960ern gibt der Plattform mit Wanne von Aston Matthews noch mehr Glamour. • Une baignoire comme un vaisseau de guerre : sur la mezzanine, un lustre vénitien des années 1960 ajoute une touche glamour à la salle de bains avec baignoire Aston Matthews.

◄ "The idea was to treat the main space like a landscape," says Mackereth of the living room. The end tables are George Nelson, while the round cocktail table is the limited-edition *Iris* by Barber Osgerby. The mezzanine is used as a study. • „Die Idee war, den Wohnbereich wie eine Landschaft zu bestücken", sagt Mackereth. Neben dem Sofa zwei Tische von George Nelson; der Coffeetable *Iris* ist eine Limited Edition von Barber Osgerby. Im Zwischengeschoss liegt das Büro. • « L'idée était de traiter l'espace comme un paysage », explique Mackereth à propos du séjour. Le bout de canapé sont de George Nelson, la table ronde *Iris* est une édition limitée de Barber Osgerby. La mezzanine sert d'espace de travail.

▼ A living room window pivots open at the touch of a button, providing access to a courtyard garden. • Ein Knopfdruck lässt ein Fenster im Wohnbereich aufschwenken und öffnet so den Durchgang zum Innenhof. • Il suffit d'appuyer sur un bouton pour qu'une des fenêtres du séjour pivote, permettant d'accéder à une cour paysagée.

▼ ▶   Housed in the old coach house, the bedroom is "more domestic," yet equally theatrical. Stairs lead to the bathroom on the cantilevered platform. The parquet was salvaged from the workshop that used to stand on the site. Mackereth opted here for historical colors and furniture, such as the Swedish 18th-century Rococo commode, flanked by 1950s Italian Chiavari chairs. The winch is used to raise or lower the TV so it can be watched from either the bed or bath. • Das Schlafzimmer in der ehemaligen Remise ist „heimeliger", doch ebenso theatralisch. Im Hintergrund führt eine Treppe auf die überhängende Bad-Plattform, das Parkett aus der früher hier befindlichen Werkstatt wurde restauriert. Mackereth entschied sich bei diesem Raum für historische Farben und Möbel wie die schwedische Rokoko-Kommode, die Chiavari-Stühle aus den 1950er-Jahren flankieren. Mit dem Handrad lässt sich der Bildschirm heben und senken, sodass man im Bett oder im Bad fernsehen kann. • Située dans l'ancienne remise, la chambre est « plus intime » mais tout aussi théâtrale. Un escalier mène à la salle de bains en mezzanine. L'ancien parquet de l'atelier qui occupait autrefois les lieux a été restauré. Ici, Mackereth a opté pour des couleurs à l'ancienne et des meubles d'époque, comme la commode rococo suédoise du 18ᵉ siècle flanquée de chaises Chiavari des années 1950. La manivelle permet de monter et de descendre la télévision selon qu'on souhaite la regarder depuis le lit ou la baignoire.

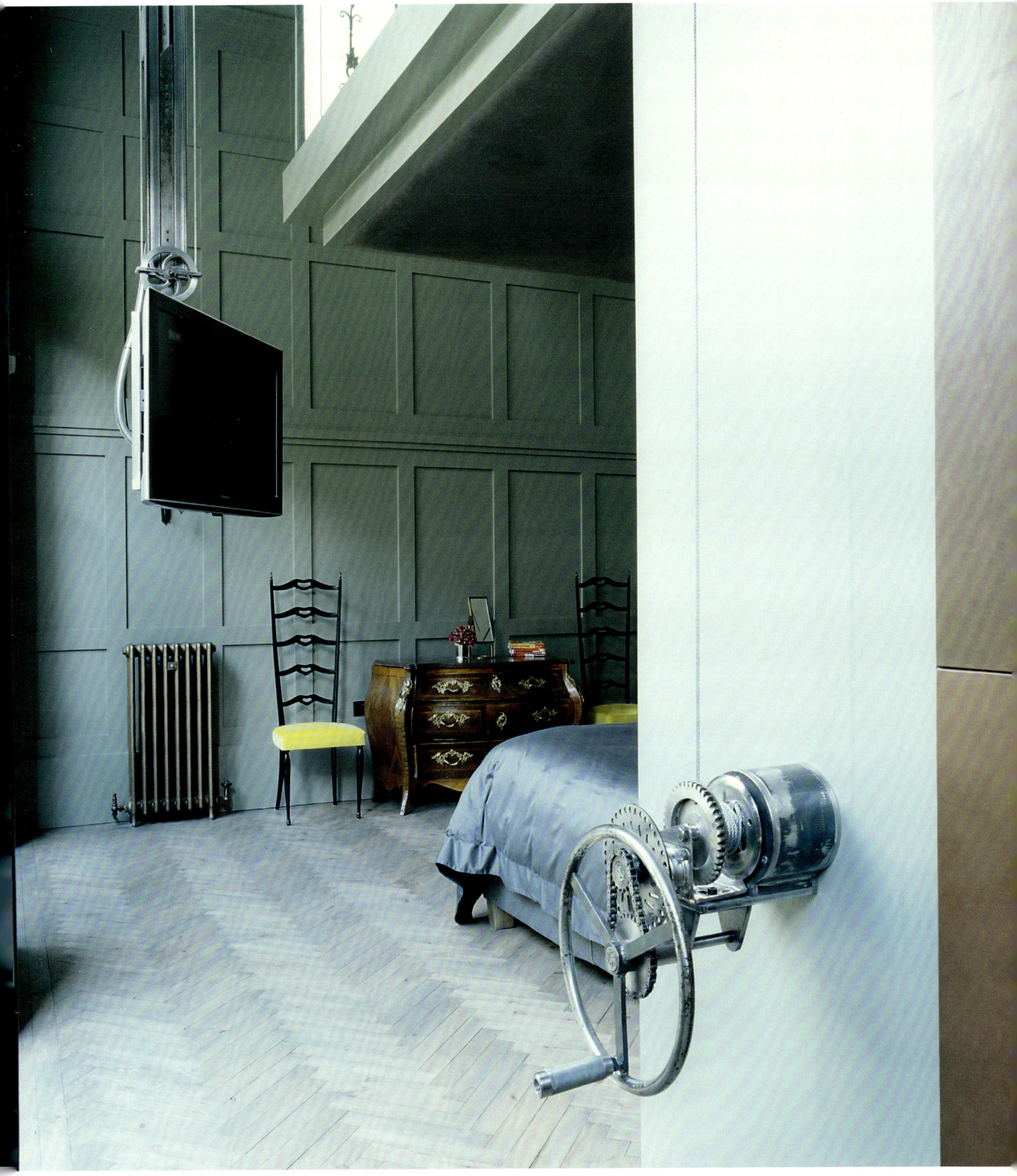

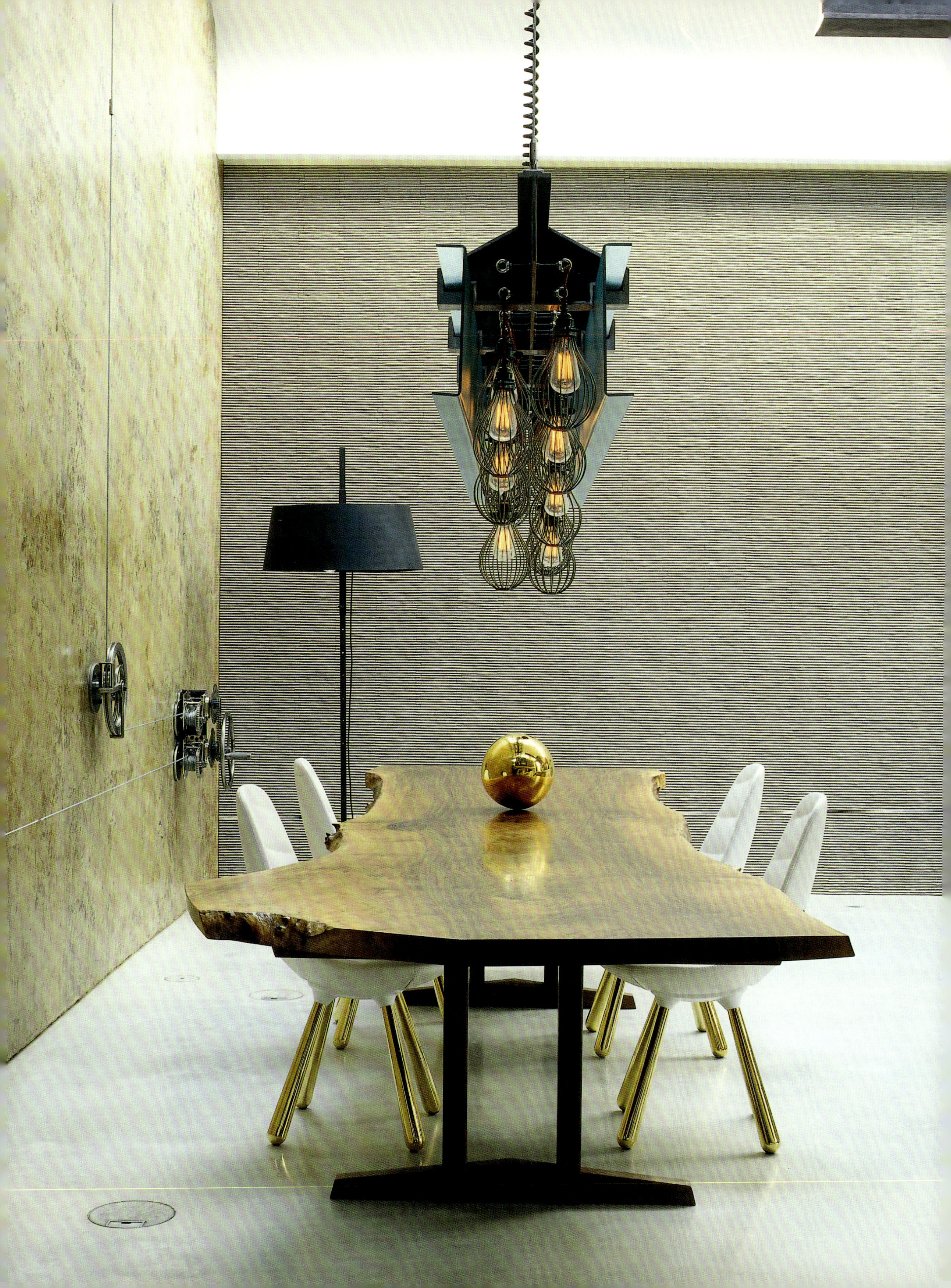

◄ In the dining area, the custom chandelier can also be winched up and down. A playful touch is introduced by Jaime Hayon's *Tudor* chairs from Established & Sons. "They're not so reverent of the Nakashima table," notes Mackereth. • Der maßgefertigte Lüster im Essbereich kann ebenfalls auf- und abbewegt werden. Ein spielerisches Element bringen Jaime Hayons *Tudor*-Stühle von Established & Sons ein. „Ihre Ehrfurcht vor dem Nakashima-Tisch hält sich in Grenzen", bemerkt Mackereth. • Dans le coin repas, une autre manivelle permet de monter ou de descendre le lustre personnalisé. Les chaises *Tudor* de Jaime Hayon pour Established & Sons apportent une touche ludique. « Elles jurent un peu avec la table de Nakashima », observe Mackereth.

▼ The kitchen was modeled after the one at Frank Sinatra's house in Palm Springs. A concealed door leads into the master bedroom. • Die Küche ist derjenigen in Frank Sinatras Haus in Palm Springs nachempfunden. Eine Geheimtür öffnet sich zum Schlafzimmer. • La cuisine s'inspire de celle de la maison de Frank Sinatra à Palm Springs. Une porte secrète mène à la chambre principale.

◄ and **185** The one-foot-thick Scooby-Doo door is equipped with a pivot mechanism set in a metal frame. • Die 30 cm starke Scooby-Doo-Tür ist über einen Drehmechanismus mit ihrem Metallrahmen verbunden. • La porte Scooby-Doo de 30 cm d'épaisseur pivote à l'aide d'un mécanisme inséré dans le chambranle en métal.

"When you do private houses, there has to be a sense of joy," opines architect Sally Mackereth. This one certainly fits the bill. For her, "it's about seduction and surprise, scale and illusion." From the street, it is perfectly discreet. Step inside, however, and you discover a world of drama and whimsy. There are theatrical ceiling lights, a kitchen modeled after Frank Sinatra's in Palm Springs, and a secret "Scooby-Doo" door with brick relief. Patina was added to the new structure with a plaster and paint trompe l'oeil by backdrop artist Harvey Woodward. The old coach house, meanwhile, got an extra dose of character with wall paneling and vintage flooring. There are also lots of industrial winches and winding gear. In the bedroom, for instance, a roller cranks the TV up and down, so you can either watch from the bed or the tub above. "It's absurd," admits Mackereth, "but it's meant to make you smile." Not everyone got the point. She still amusedly recalls the reaction of the quantity surveyor. "Why not just have two TVs?" he asked. "Much cheaper!"

„Bei Privathäusern ist wichtig, dass sie ihren Bewohnern Freude bereiten", betont Architektin Sally Mackereth. In diesem Fall trifft das absolut zu – „es geht um Verführung und Überraschung, Maßstab und Illusion". Von außen fällt nichts Besonderes auf. Doch sobald man durch die Tür tritt, öffnet sich eine Welt zwischen Drama und Screwball Comedy. Es gibt Deckenspots wie im Theater, eine Küche, deren Vorbild bei Frank Sinatra in Palm Springs stand, und eine Geheimtür mit Klinker-Relief. Dem Neubau verhalf Kulissenkünstler Harvey Woodward mit Gips und Farbe zu Trompe-l'œil-Patina, und die alte Remise bekam durch Täfelung und Vintage-Parkett noch mehr Charakter. Auffällig sind die Industrie-Winden. Damit lässt sich etwa ein Bildschirm herauf- und herunterkurbeln, sodass man im Bett oder in der Badewanne fernsehen kann. „Eigentlich absurd", gibt Mackereth zu, „aber es bringt einen zum Schmunzeln." Wenn man den Gag versteht; als ihr Kostenplaner den Mechanismus sah, fragte er jedenfalls: „Warum nicht einfach zwei Fernseher anschaffen? Wäre doch viel billiger!"

« QUAND VOUS CRÉEZ UN INTÉRIEUR POUR DES PARTICULIERS, VOUS DEVEZ LUI INSUFFLER DE LA JOIE. » SALLY MACKERETH

Cette maison en est l'illustration même. Depuis la rue, elle paraît discrète, mais, dès le seuil, on pénètre dans un monde de fantaisie. Pour Mackereth, « tout est question de séduction et d'effet de surprise, d'échelle et d'illusion ». On y trouve des projecteurs de scène, une cuisine inspirée de celle de Frank Sinatra à Palm Springs et une porte « Scooby-Doo » avec un relief en briques. La partie moderne a été vieillie à l'aide de trompe-l'œil réalisés par l'artiste Harvey Woodward. L'ancienne remise a été personnalisée avec des boiseries et des parquets anciens. La maison foisonne de mécanismes industriels. Dans la chambre, une manivelle permet de monter et de descendre la télévision selon qu'on la regarde depuis le lit ou la baignoire située au-dessus. « C'est un détail absurde pour faire sourire », explique Mackereth. Tout le monde n'a pas autant d'humour. Le métreur lui a demandé : « Pourquoi ne pas avoir plutôt deux télés ? Ce serait moins cher. »

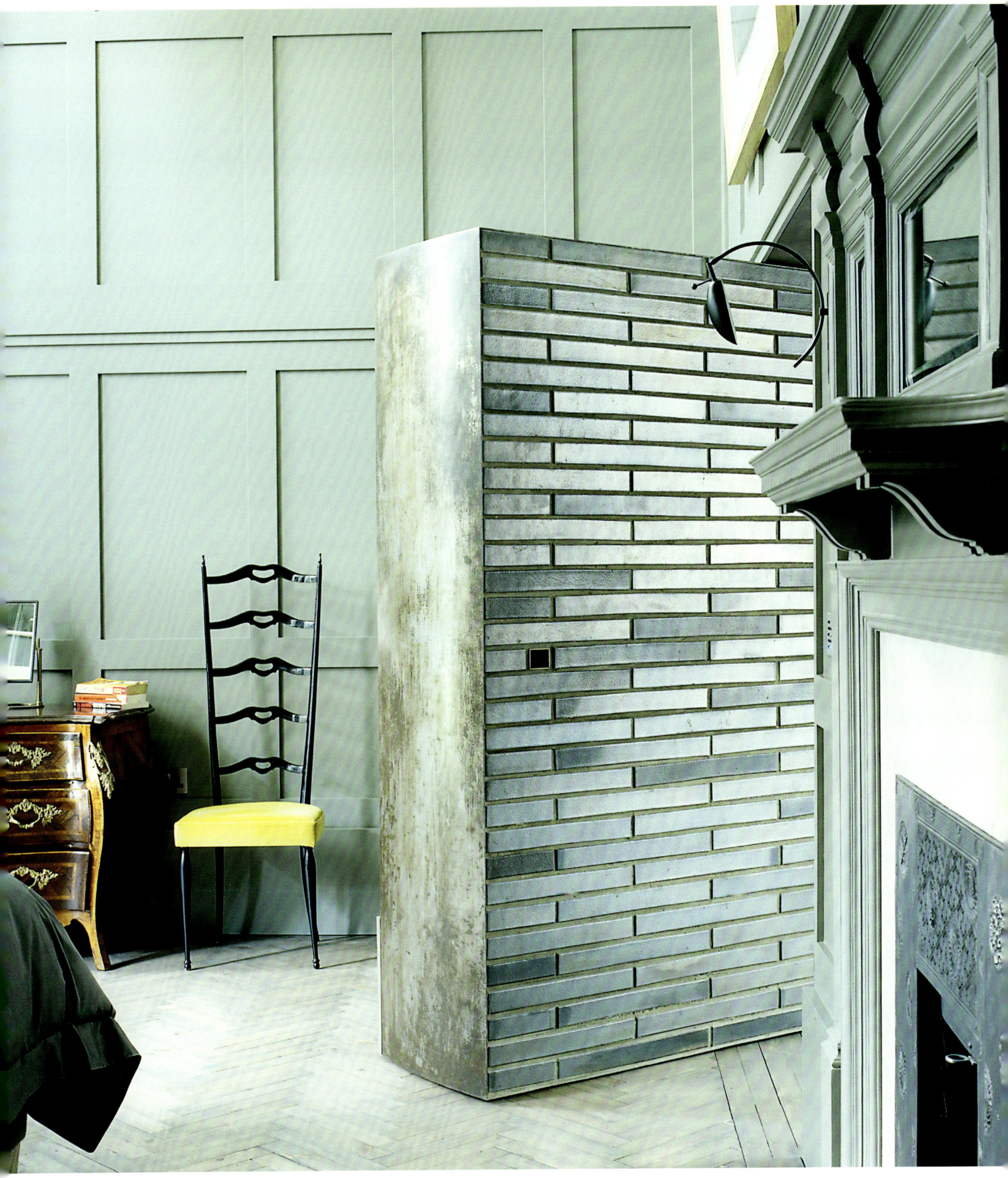

ADAM McCULLOCH & EMMA SLOLEY

THEIR *CASA CÁRDENAS* IN MÉRIDA, MEXICO

WHO Australia-born travel writers now based in New York. **WHAT** A 372 m² (4,000 sq. ft.), Spanish colonial-style house built in the 1880s. **WHERE** On a quiet block in the historic center of Mérida, the capital of Yucatán state. **PAST LIVES** Sloley was part owner of a midcentury design store in Melbourne in the 1990s. McCulloch previously worked in production design on films like *The Matrix*. **VOYAGE OF DISCOVERY** The couple originally came across Mérida when Sloley was assigned to write a story on the Yucatán Peninsula. **BACK TO BASICS** Construction was carried out by a local Mayan crew, who didn't use power tools. "Sometimes they demolish with sledgehammers," explains McCulloch, "but for the most part, they use small hammers you would get for $6 at any hardware store." **TRAVEL TIPS** McCulloch recommends South Africa and Kenya. Being on safari there, he says, "feels like you're on a different planet." Sloley recently visited the Istrian peninsula in Croatia, "a hidden gem of Europe for travellers from other continents".

PHOTOGRAPHED BY BRUCE BUCK FOR THE NEW YORK TIMES

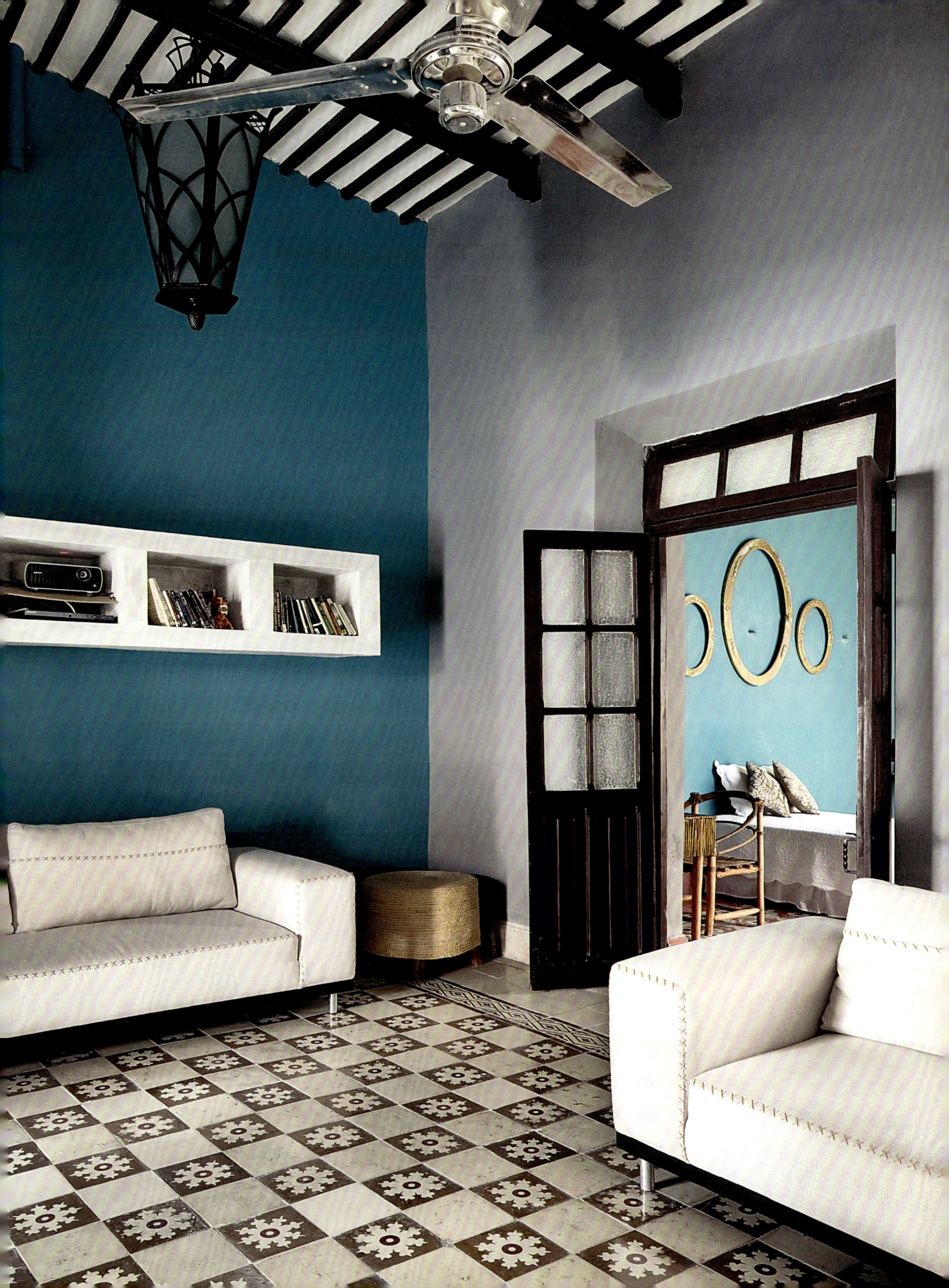

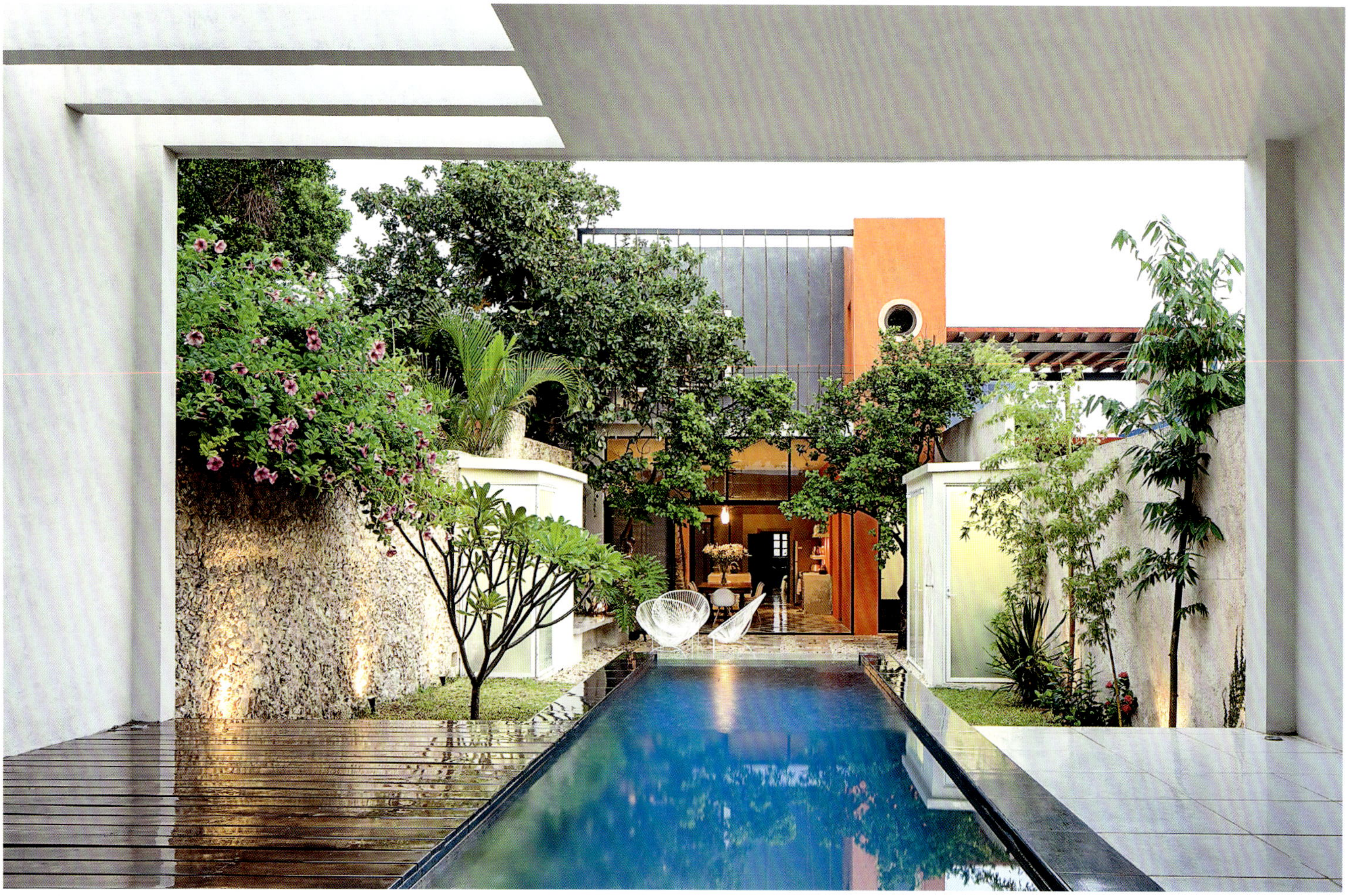

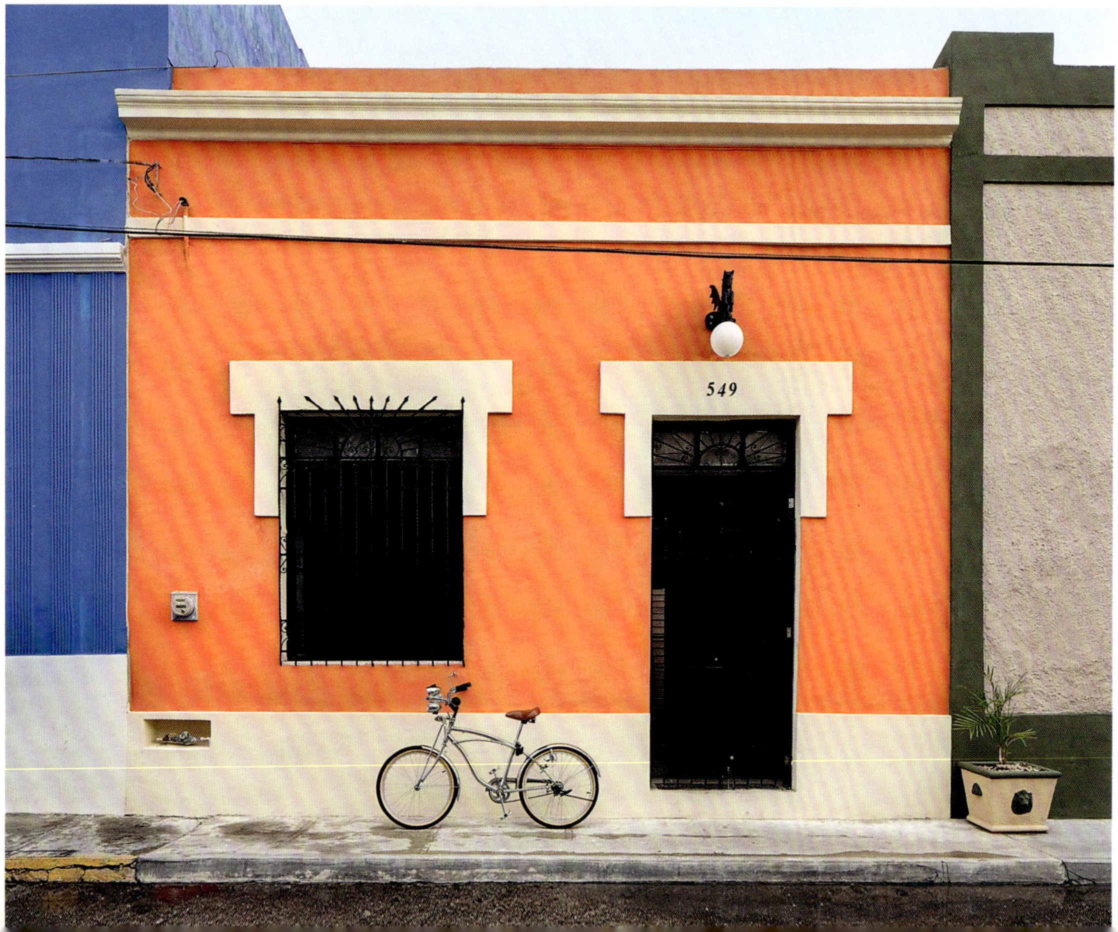
549

187 The floor tiles and ceiling beams in the living room are original. The latter were made from unused railroad tracks in the late 1800s. • Im Wohnzimmer sind sowohl die Bodenfliesen original als auch die Deckenbalken, die Ende des 19. Jahrhunderts aus ausrangierten Eisenbahnschienen gezimmert wurden. • Le carrelage est d'origine, comme les poutres du séjour, récupérées sur des voies ferrées désaffectées à la fin du 19ᵉ siècle.

◄ ► On the long and narrow lot, a 27-foot (8.2-meter) lap pool was inserted between the main house and the newly built casita; measuring just 22 feet (6.7 meters) in width, the front façade is painted in the Yucatán style. • Auf dem langen, schmalen Grundstück wurde ein 8,2 m langer lap pool zwischen dem Haupthaus und der neu gebauten casita eingefügt; die nur 6,7 m breite Fassade ist im Yucatán-Stil gestrichen. • Un bassin de nage de 8,2 m de long a été creusé, entre la maison principale et la nouvelle casita ; la façade de seulement 6,7 m de large a été peinte dans le style du Yucatán.

▼ The 1930s chair with cane seat in Sloley's study is the type that locals still take out onto curbs in the evening to catch up on the daily gossip. • Der Sessel mit Flechtsitz in Sloleys study ist aus den 30er-Jahren. Auf solchen Stühlen setzen sich die Einheimischen noch immer zum abendlichen Plausch vor ihre Häuser. • La chaise cannée des années 1930 dans le bureau de Sloley ressemble à celles que les gens du quartier sortent sur le trottoir le soir pour s'informer des derniers potins.

190-191 Plastic-cord Conch chairs have been made in Mérida since the 1960s. The couple had larger versions custom-made to give their pool patio a modernist slant. • Conch-Stühle aus Kunststoff-Schnüren werden in Mérida seit den 1960ern hergestellt. Das Paar ließ größere maßfertigen, um seinem Pool-Patio einen modernistischen Twist zu geben. • Les sièges Conch à cordes en plastique sont fabriqués à Mérida depuis les années 1960. Ces exemplaires sur mesure, plus grands, apportent une touche chic et moderniste au patio.

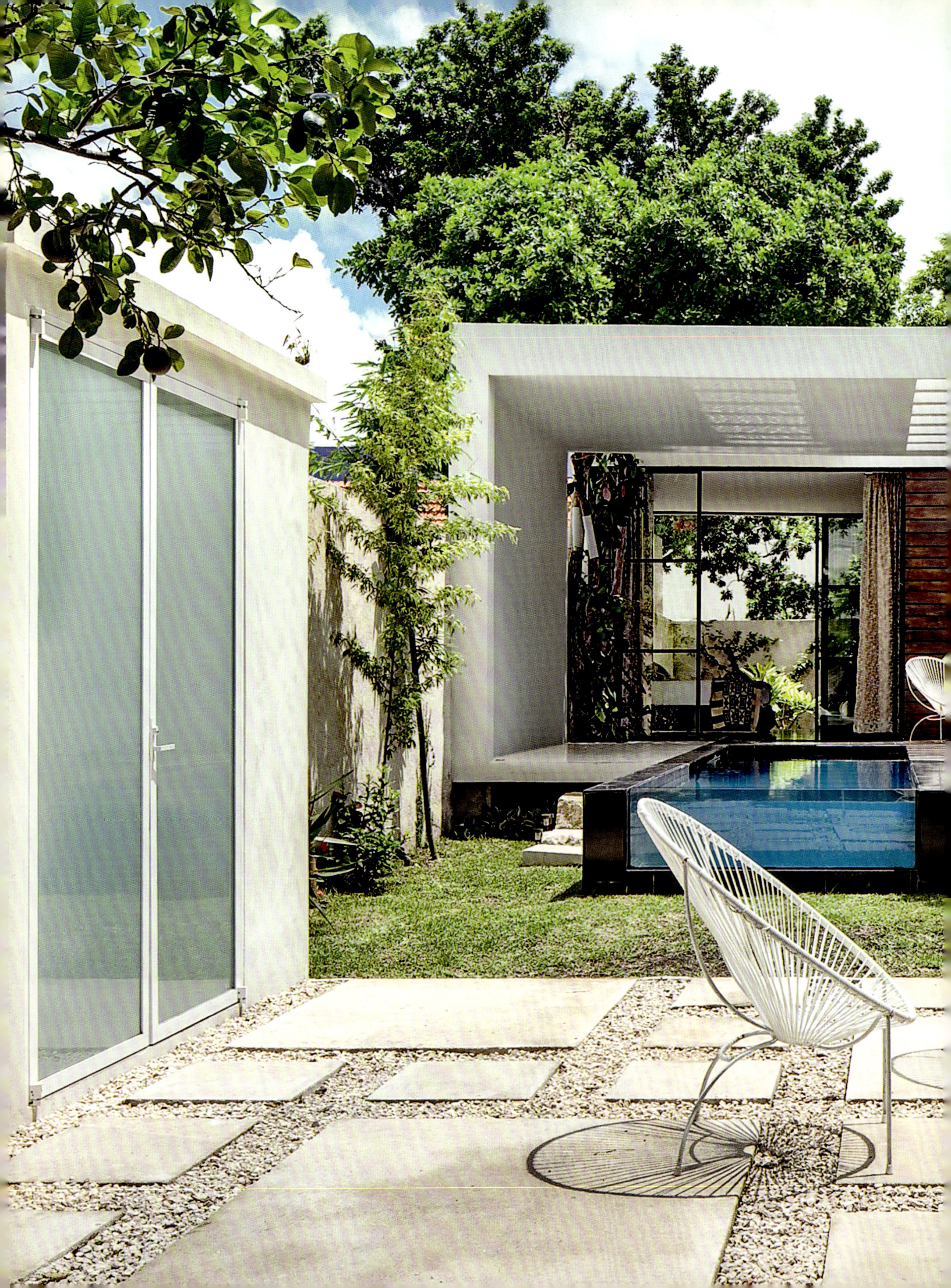

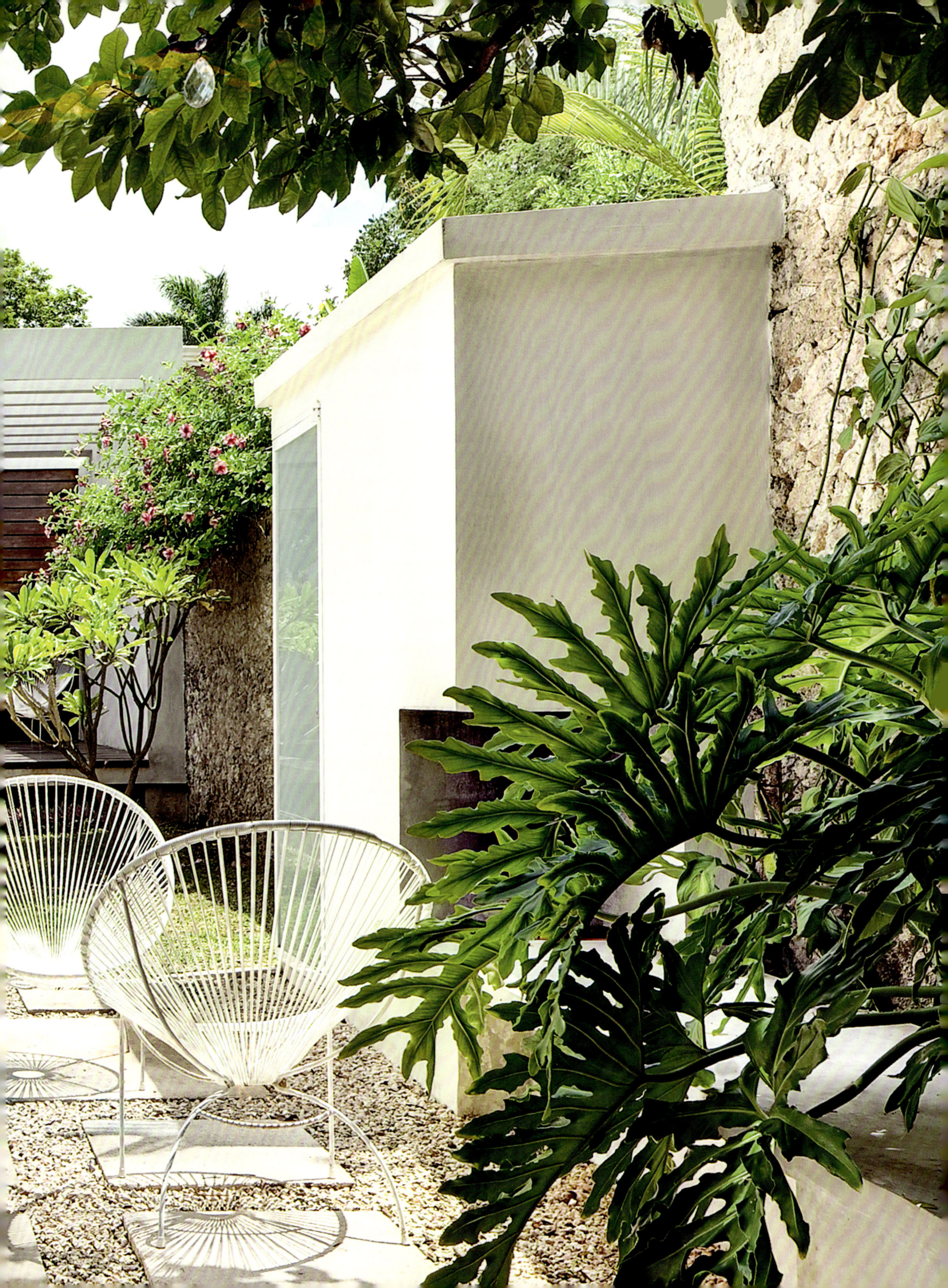

"We stumbled across Mérida and were just enchanted by it," recall Adam McCulloch and Emma Sloley. Located at the heart of the Mexican city, their house had until recently been inhabited by the same family since the late 19th century. The couple were drawn to its tall ceilings, traditional paste-tile floors, and 65-meter-long (213 ft) lot. "One thing I wanted to preserve was that sense of distance," notes McCulloch. He oversaw the construction work and gutted about a third of the main house, adding a second story, a lap pool, and guesthouse (or *casita*). The couple wanted the decor to be "fairly contemporary," but finding furniture locally proved tricky. "Design is a new concept for people here," remarks McCulloch, who transported the Eames chairs by plane from New York by placing the legs in a suitcase and strapping six seats at a time to his backpack. One great find they did make in Mérida is the bust of the 1930s Mexican president, Lázaro Cárdenas, whose term was a time of social reform. As Sloley recounts: "Locals coming to our house pat him on the head and say 'Hi.'"

„Wir stolperten über Mérida, und es hat uns einfach verzaubert", erinnern sich Adam McCulloch und Emma Sloley. Ihr Haus, das zuvor mehr als 100 Jahre von derselben Familie bewohnt worden war, liegt im Herzen der Stadt. Das Paar war begeistert von den hohen Decken, den traditionellen Fliesen und von dem 65 m langen Grundstück. „Dieses Gefühl von Weite wollte ich erhalten", sagt McCulloch, der die Bauarbeiten beaufsichtigte. Etwa ein Drittel des Hauptbaus wurde entkernt, dafür kamen ein weiteres Stockwerk, der Pool und ein Gästehaus (*casita*) dazu. Die Einrichtung wünschte sich das Paar „halbwegs zeitgenössisch", doch passende Möbel vor Ort zu finden erwies sich als schwierig. „Design ist für die Menschen hier ein neues Konzept", bemerkt McCulloch, der die Eames-Stühle im Flugzeug aus New York herbrachte, indem er ihre Beine im Koffer verstaute und je sechs Sitzschalen an seinen Rucksack schnallte. Einen großartigen Fund immerhin machten sie in Mérida: eine Büste von Lázaro Cárdenas, dem reformfreudigen mexikanischen Präsidenten der 1930er-Jahre. „Wenn Einheimische uns besuchen, tätscheln sie ihm gern den Kopf und sagen ‚Hi'", erzählt Sloley.

« NOUS AVONS DÉCOUVERT MÉRIDA PAR HASARD ET SOMMES TOMBÉS SOUS LE CHARME. » ADAM McCULLOCH & EMMA SLOLEY

Située au cœur de la ville, leur maison était habitée par la même famille depuis la fin du 19ᵉ siècle. Ils ont été séduits par ses hauts plafonds, ses sols en carrelage traditionnel et son terrain de 65 m de long. « Je tenais à conserver cette impression de profondeur », explique McCulloch, qui a supervisé les travaux, évidé un tiers de la structure, ajouté un étage, un bassin de nage et une *casita* pour les amis. Le couple, qui souhaitait un décor « plutôt contemporain », a eu du mal à se meubler sur place. « Le design est un concept nouveau ici », observe McCulloch. Il a transporté ses chaises Eames depuis New York en avion en fourrant les pieds dans une valise et en arrimant les six coques sur son sac à dos. Ils ont néanmoins fait une belle trouvaille à Mérida : un buste du président Lázaro Cárdenas qui entreprit de grandes réformes sociales dans les années 1930. Sloley confie : « Quand des Mexicains nous rendent visite, ils lui donnent une tape sur la tête et le saluent. »

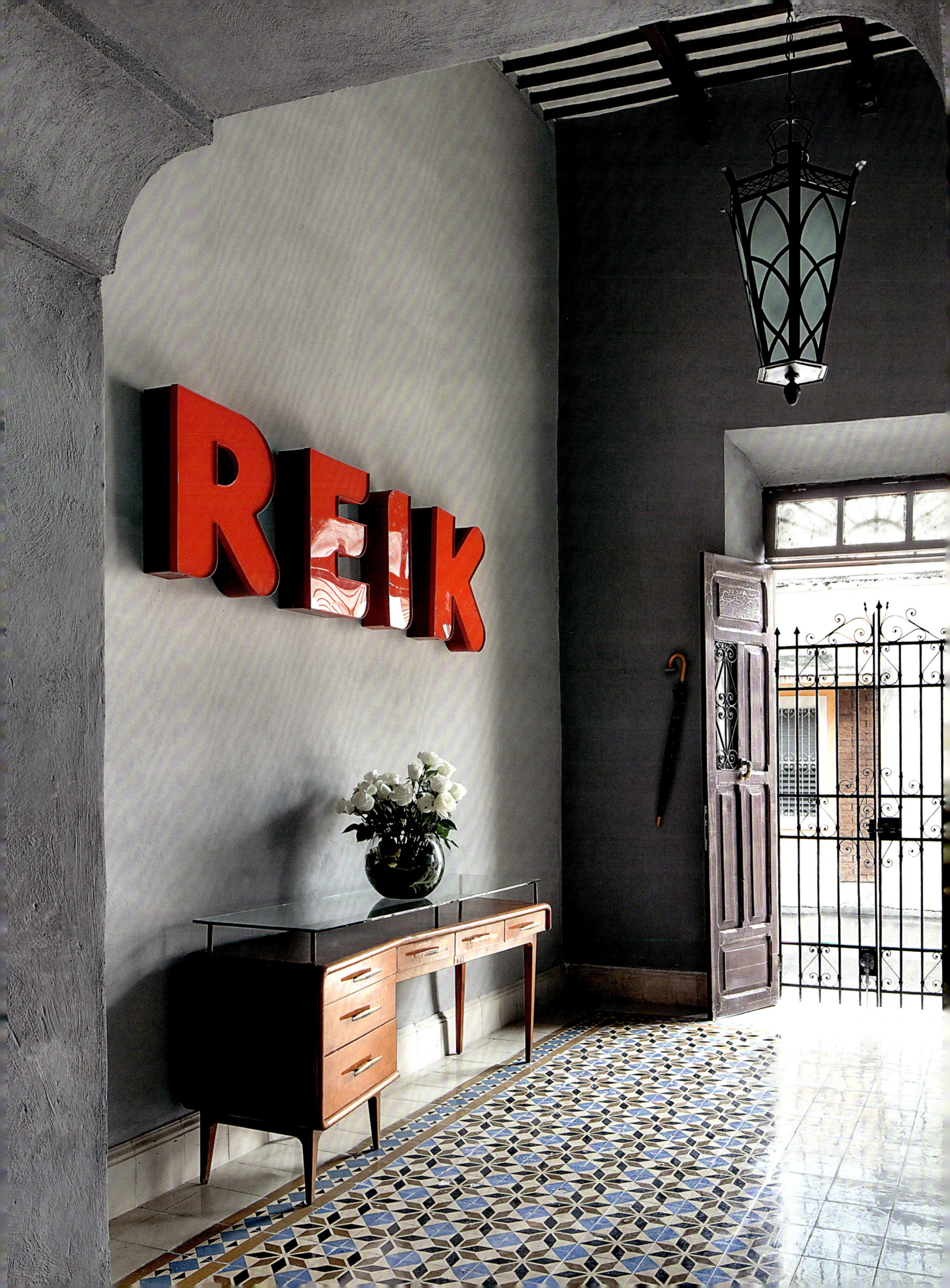
REIK

193 The couple found the plastic letters in a local store and arranged them randomly in the entry hall. Later, they discovered that "Reik" is the name of a Mexican boy band. • Das Paar fand die Plastik-Buchstaben in einem örtlichen Laden und arrangierte sie willkürlich im Vestibül. Dass „Reik" eine mexikanische Boyband ist, erfuhren sie erst später. • Les lettres en plastique disposées au hasard dans l'entrée ont été dénichées dans une boutique locale. Le couple a appris plus tard que Reik était le nom d'un boy's band mexicain.

▼ A vintage hacienda-style table was installed in the eat-in kitchen. The new floor tiles were laid according to the original pattern. • In der Wohnküche steht ein Vintage-Tisch im Hazienda-Stil. Die neuen Fliesen sind nach dem ursprünglichen Muster verlegt worden. • Dans la cuisine, une table ancienne de style hacienda. Le nouveau carrelage reprend les motifs du sol d'origine.

▶ Bull-shaped piggy banks adorn the concrete kitchen shelves. • Spardosen in Gestalt von Rinderbullen defilieren auf den Küchenregalen aus Beton. • Sur les étagères en béton, une collection de taureaux-tirelires.

◀ The master bathroom is clad with tile and polished cement; in the inner courtyard, visitors are greeted by a bronze bust of Lázaro Cárdenas, a legendary Mexican president. The couple named the house "Casa Cárdenas" for him. • Das Hauptbad kleiden Mosaikfliesen und polierter Zement aus; im Innenhof empfängt den Besucher eine Bronzebüste von Lázaro Cárdenas, einem legendären Präsidenten Mexikos. Nach ihm hat das Paar das Haus benannt. • La salle de bains principale, en carrelage et béton poli; dans la cour intérieure, un buste en bronze du légendaire président mexicain Lázaro Cárdenas accueille les visiteurs. La maison a été baptisée « Casa Cárdenas » en son honneur.

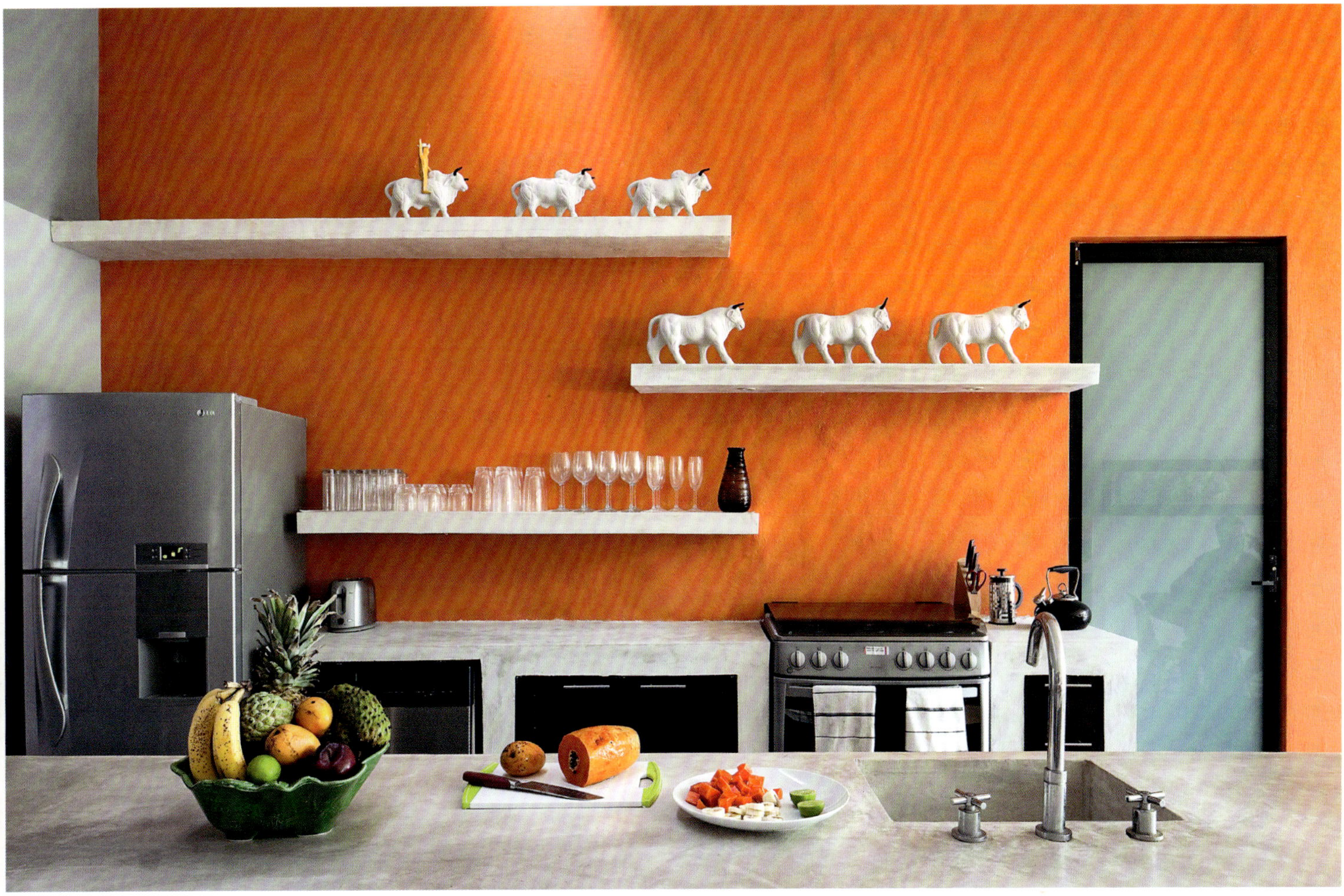

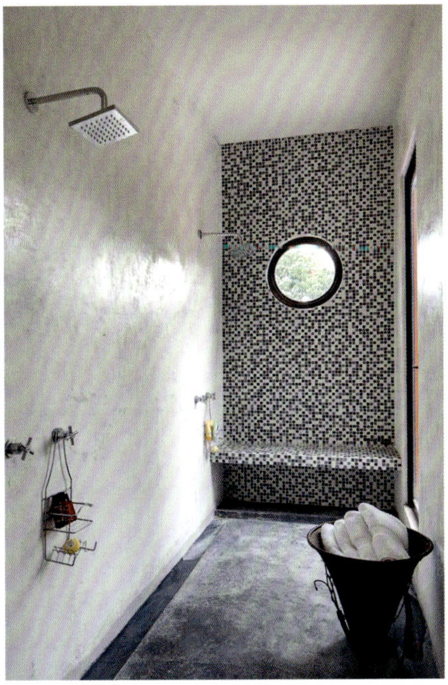

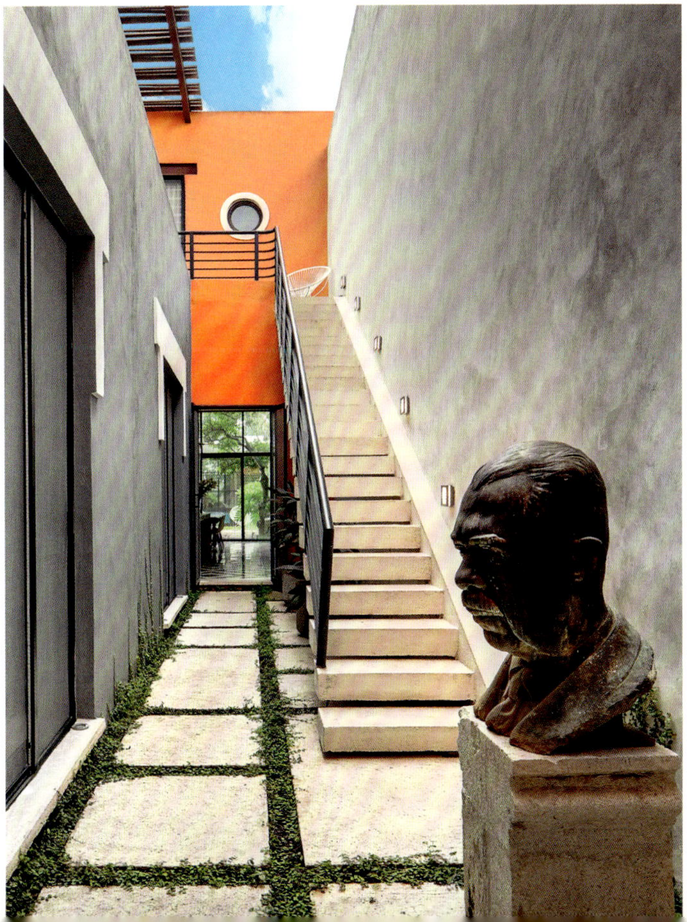

PAULO MENDES DA ROCHA

A CONCRETE HOUSE IN SÃO PAULO

WHO Leading figure of Brazil's Paulista School of architecture and 2006 Pritzker Prize laureat. **WHAT** A 400 m² (4,306 sq. ft.), four-bedroom house originally built in 1969 and renovated from 2008–10. **WHERE** Nestled to a steep slope in the upscale, leafy neighborhood of Pacaembu. **THE CLIENT** Houssein Jarouche, owner of the São Paulo design emporium MiCasa, which spans three buildings—he commissioned one from hip architectural firm Triptych and another from Marcio Kogan. **CLOSE TO HOME** Almost all of Mendes da Rocha's major projects have been in São Paulo. Among them, the Brazilian Sculpture Museum and Saint Peter Chapel. **YOUNG AT HEART** "Paulo is 45 years older than me," says Jarouche, "yet I feel we're the same age because he's so modern." **MENDES ON STYLE** "I think everything superfluous is irritating." **MENDES ON LIFE** "Walking to school, it's the beginning of civic life. If you drive your child, it's a crime."

PHOTOGRAPHED BY PIERO GEMELLI   STYLED BY BEATRICE ROSSETTI   PORTRAIT BY PAULO MENDES DA ROCHA, JR.

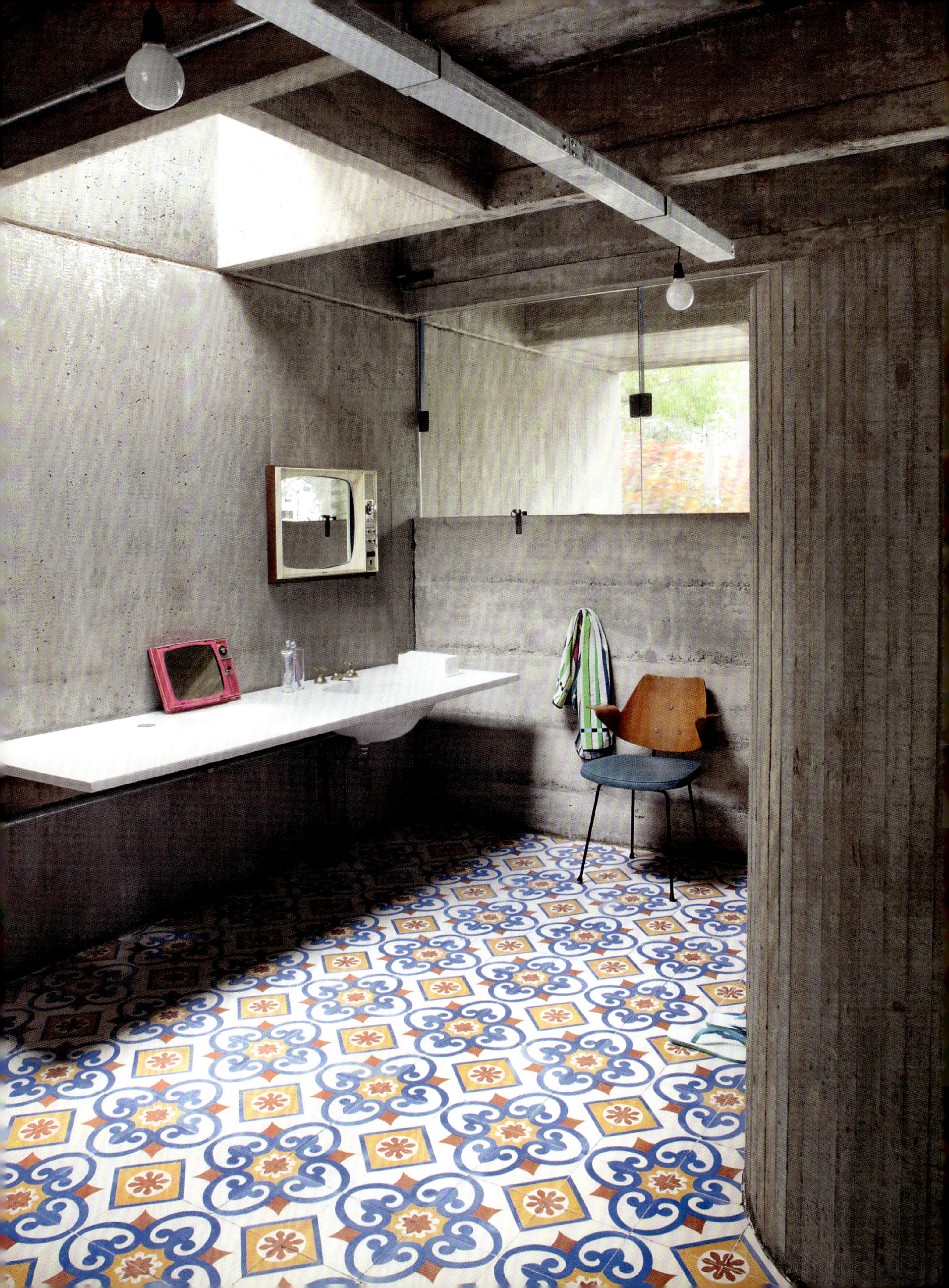

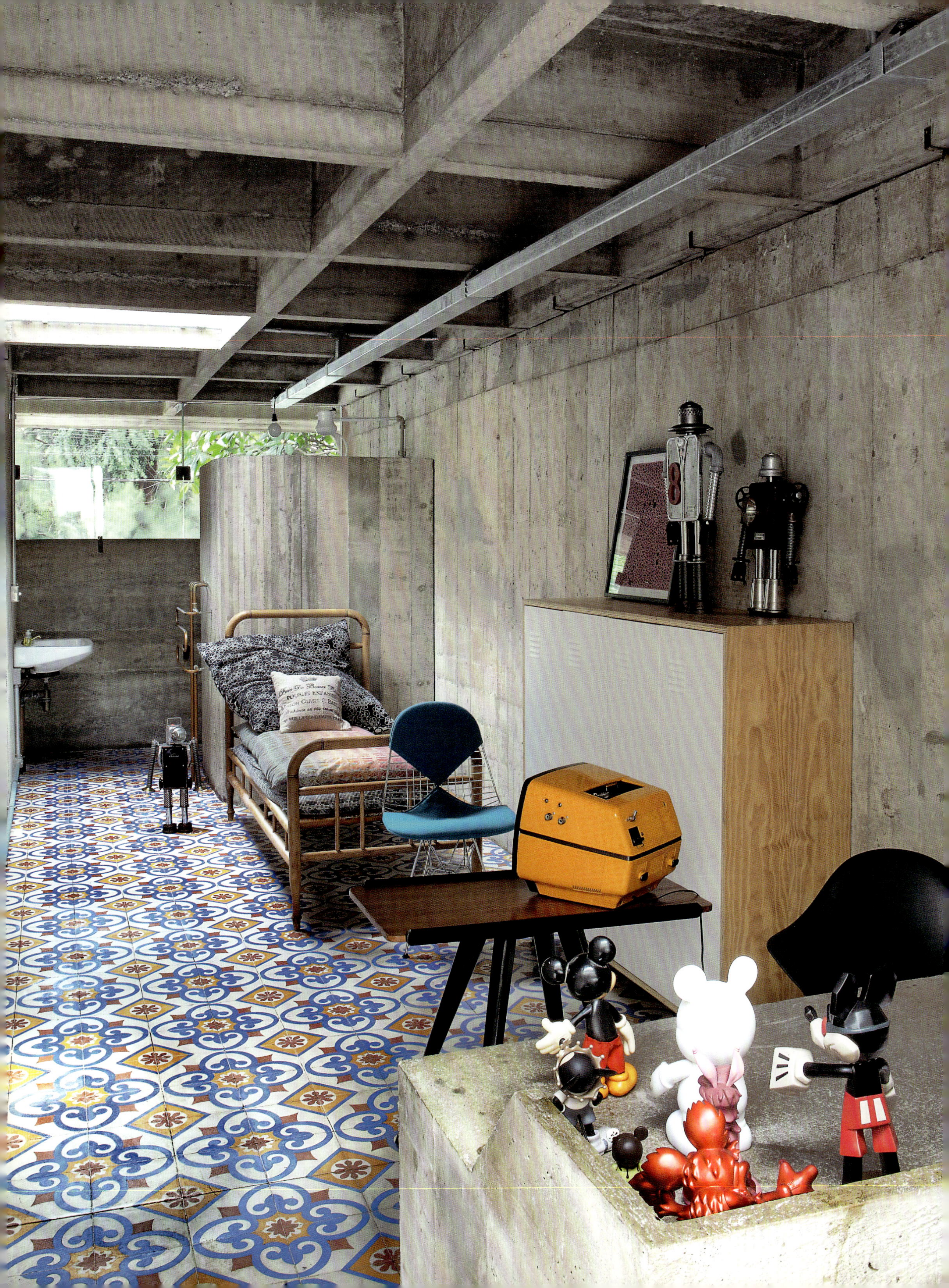

197 Old made new in the master bath: the mirror by Argentinean firm Doméstico consists of a vintage TV frame with a looking glass replacing the screen. • Verjüngungskur für alte Technik: Beim Badezimmer-Objekt der argentinischen Firma Doméstico sitzt der Spiegel im Rahmen eines Vintage-Fernsehers. • Dans la grande salle de bains, un miroir de l'entreprise argentine Doméstico réalisé avec l'ossature d'un vieux poste de télévision.

◄ Mendes's concrete desk and shower in a boy's room. Created by Celso Martinez Carrera in 1915, the bent-wood *Patente* bed is a classic of Brazilian design. • Desk und Dusche in einem Jungszimmer ließ Mendes aus Beton gießen. Celso Martinez Carreras *Patente*-Bugholzbett ist ein brasilianischer Klassiker von 1915. • Une chambre avec un bureau et une douche en béton dessinés par Mendes. Le lit *Patente* en bois a été créé par Celso Martinez Carrera en 1915.

▼ A pair of Willy Guhl fiber-cement *Loop* chairs keep watch by the pool. The sweeping staircase leads up to the main entrance of the house. • Willy Guhls *Loop*-Sessel aus Faserzement halten Wacht am Pool. Die geschwungene Freitreppe führt hinauf zum Haupteingang. • Une paire de sièges *Loop* en fibre de ciment, de Willy Guhl, monte la garde au bord de la piscine. L'escalier mène à l'entrée principale.

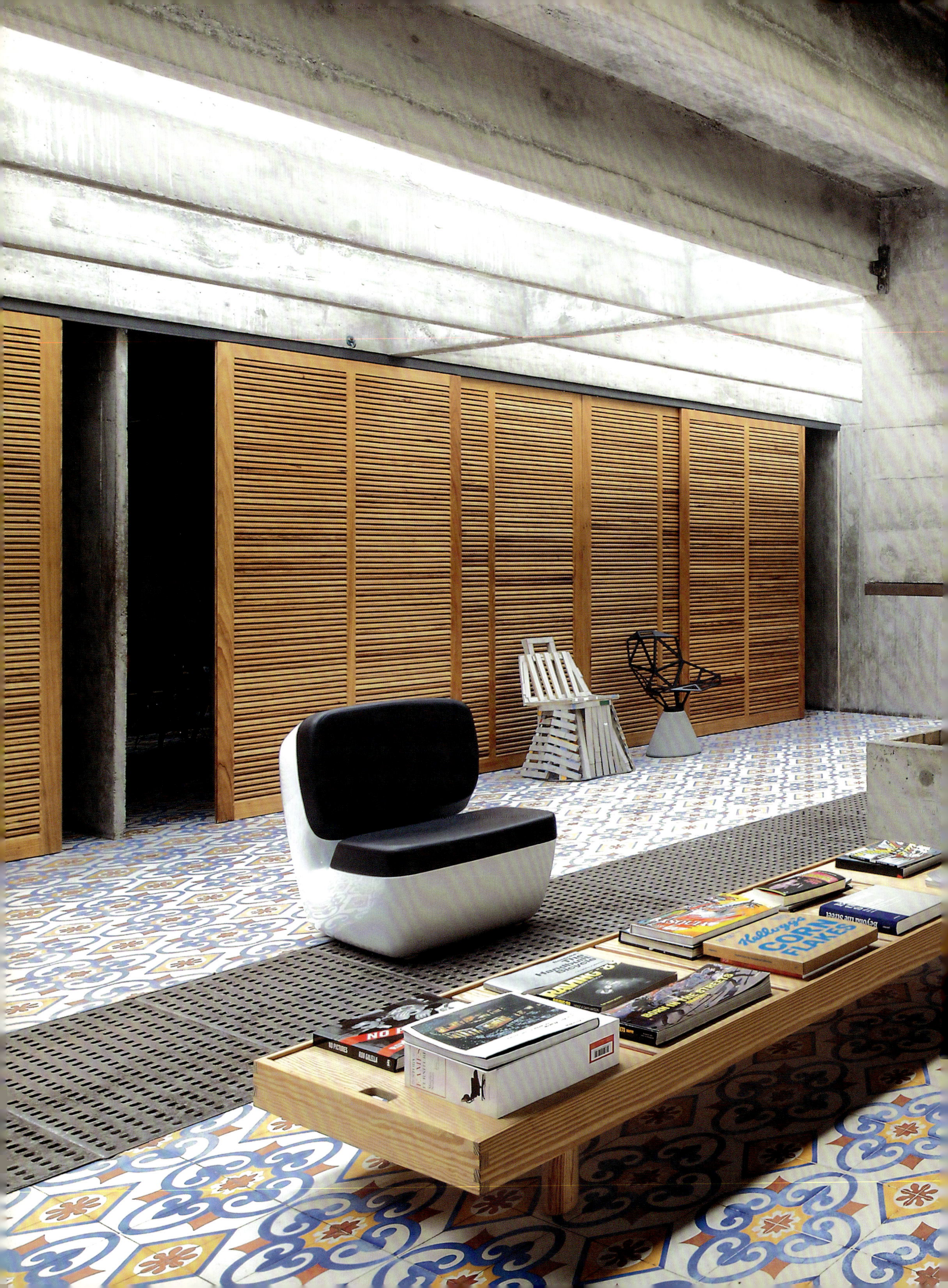
Kellogg's
CORN FLAKES

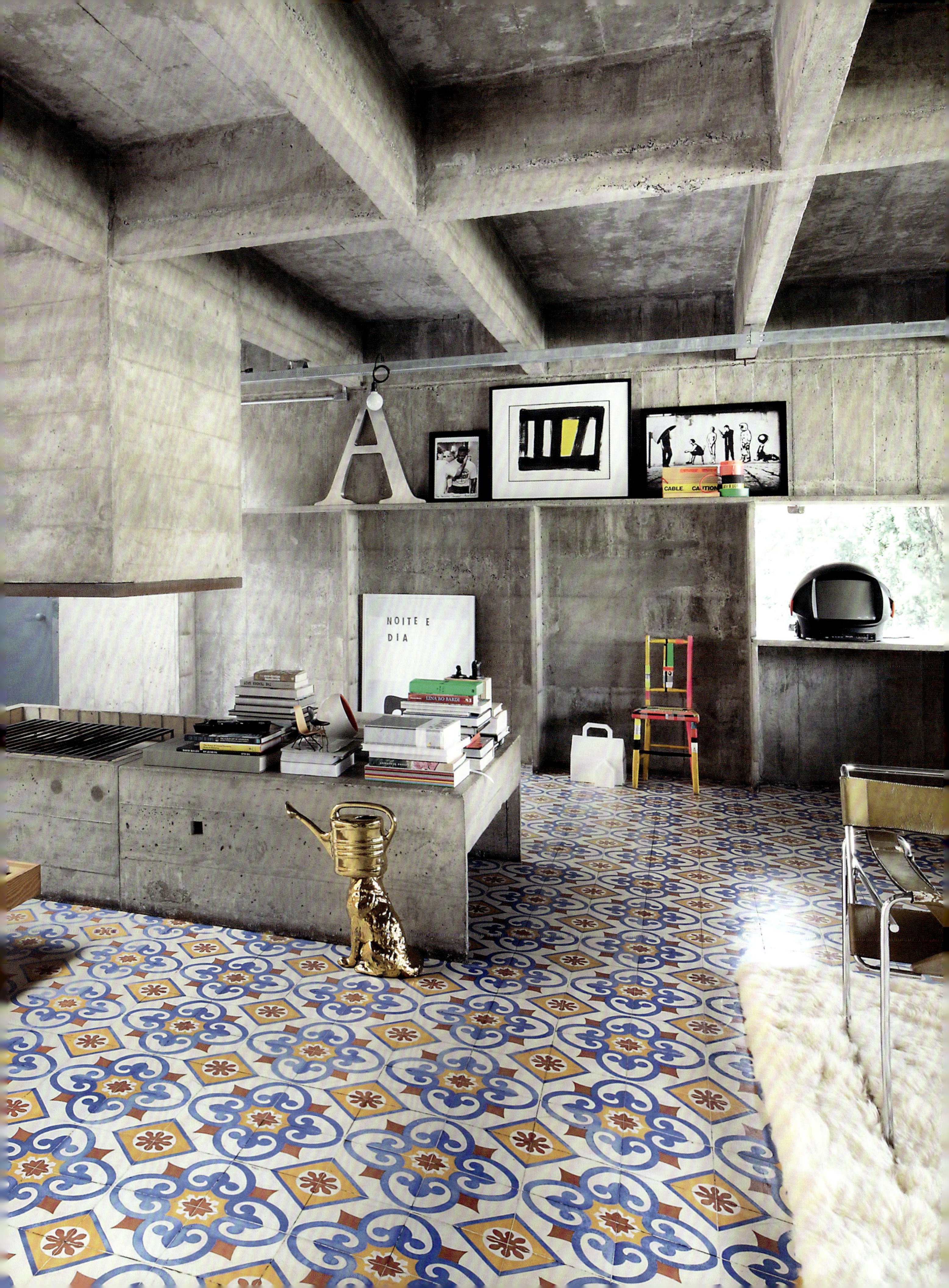
NOITE E
DIA
LINA BO BARDI
CABLE CAUTION

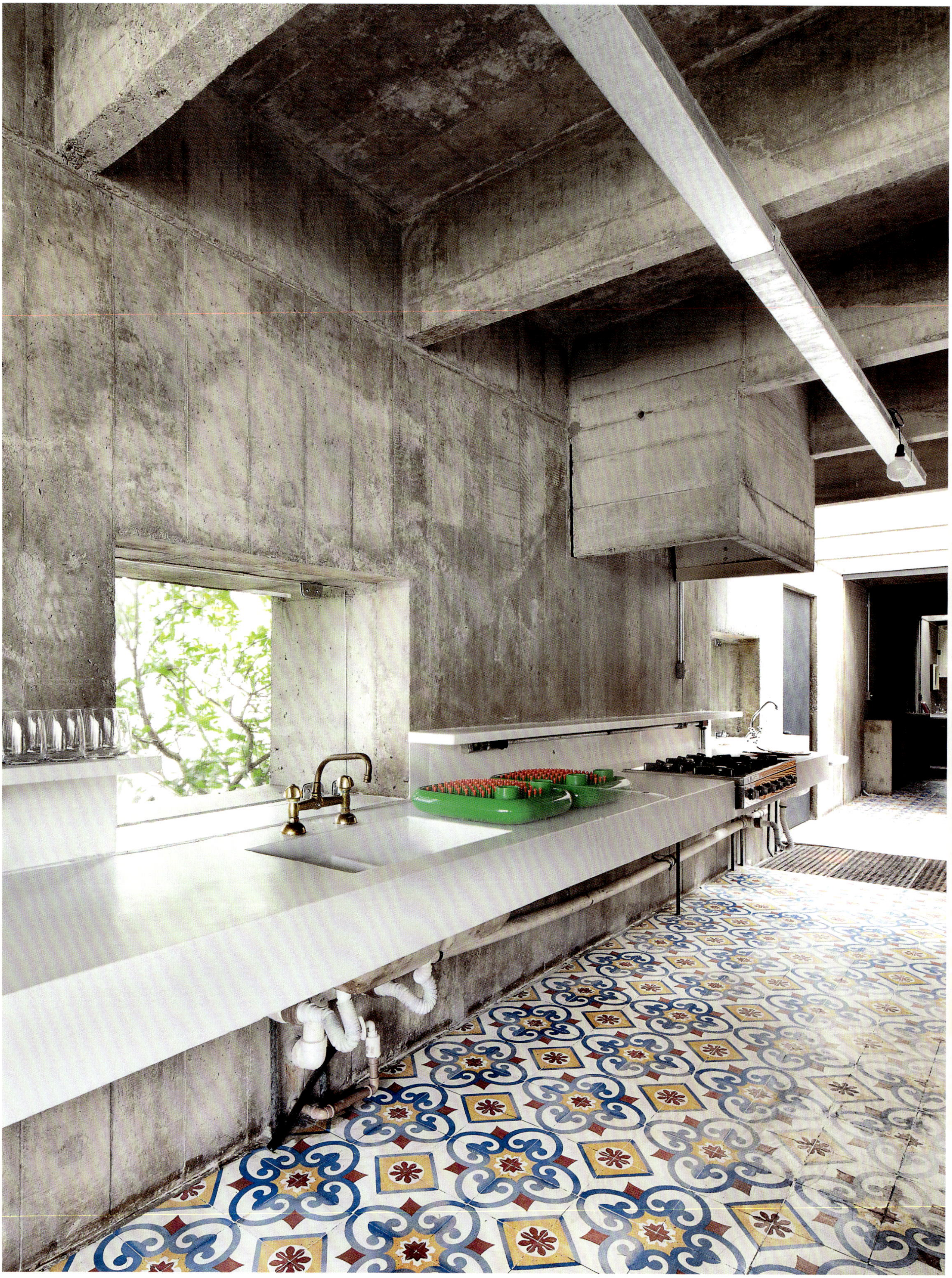

200–201 Mendes's original concrete hearth and brightly patterned floor tiles are still the focus of the living room. *Crate No. 5* by Jasper Morrison for Established & Sons and *Nimrod* chair by Marc Newson. The wooden sliding doors lead into the bedroom wing. • Mendes' originale Beton-Feuerstelle und die leuchtend gemusterten Fliesen prägen das Wohnzimmer bis heute. Vorn *Crate No. 5* von Jasper Morrison für Established & Sons, daneben Sessel *Nimrod* von Marc Newson. Hinter den hölzernen Schiebetüren liegt der Schlafzimmertrakt. • Dans le séjour, la cheminée centrale en béton et le carrelage aux couleurs vives signés Mendes donnent le ton. *Crate N° 5* de Jasper Morrison pour Established & Sons et fauteuil *Nimrod* de Marc Newson. Les portes coulissantes en bois donnent sur les chambres.

◄ Plumbing lines are visible under the epoxy-painted work surface in the kitchen. The brass faucet dates from the construction of the house. • Unter der mit Epoxidharz überzogenen Arbeitsfläche in der Küche sind die Rohre sichtbar. Die Messingarmatur stammt aus der Bauzeit des Hauses. • Dans la cuisine, la tuyauterie est visible sous le plan de travail revêtu d'époxy. Les robinets en laiton sont d'origine.

▼ The owner may refer to it as a beach house, but it still affords spectacular city views through windows that pivot open. *Peacock* chair by Cappellini. • Der Besitzer nennt es „ein Strandhaus", doch die schwenkbaren Fenster bieten spektakulären Stadtausblick. *Peacock*-Stuhl von Cappellini. • Les fenêtres pivotantes offrent des vues spectaculaires sur la ville. Fauteuil *Peacock* de Cappellini.

"I HATE IT WHEN PEOPLE MEDDLE WITH IMPORTANT ARCHITECTURE OR DESIGN." HOUSSEIN JAROUCHE

Thus, when Jarouche decided to renovate this iconic house from 1969, there was only one person to turn to: its original architect, Paolo Mendes da Rocha. "It's always difficult returning to something," admits the living legend, "but we tried to bring everything back to how it was after its completion." The house's concrete fixtures and exposed plumbing stayed in place. New skylights were installed, and the louvered bedroom doors carefully remade in wood according to the initial designs. That said, owner and architect agreed upon a number of changes. Parts of the pool were painted black (something Mendes da Rocha had wanted to do for decades), a spiral staircase connecting the lower levels was replaced, and a gate added to the front of the property. Before, passersby could walk straight into the garden. Jarouche sees his home as "like a beach house in the city." Still, there's no sand underfoot, but rather the original quatrefoil-patterned cement tiles, which had improved with age. "The more you walk on them," notes Mendes da Rocha, "the more lovely they look."

„Ich verabscheue es, wenn an bedeutender Architektur herumgepfuscht wird", erklärt Houssein Jarouche, der Besitzer dieses Hauses. Als die Bauikone von 1969 zu renovieren war, kam für ihn nur einer infrage: Paolo Mendes da Rocha, der ursprüngliche Architekt. „Zu etwas zurückzukehren ist immer schwer", gibt die lebende Legende zu, „doch wir haben versucht, alles wieder in den alten Zustand zu bringen." Beton-Einbauten und sichtbare Rohre blieben erhalten. Die Oberlichter wurden erneuert und die Lamellentüren aus Holz nachgefertigt. Auf ein paar Veränderungen einigte er sich mit dem Eigentümer: Ein Teil des Pools wurde schwarz gestrichen (seit Jahrzehnten ein Wunsch von Mendes da Rocha), eine Wendeltreppe ersetzt und ein Gartentor eingefügt. Jarouche genießt sein Zuhause als „eine Art Strandhaus mitten in der Stadt". Nicht Sand spürt man allerdings hier unter den Füßen, sondern Zementfliesen mit Vierpass-Dekor, denen ihr Alter gut steht: „Je öfter man darüberläuft", erklärt Mendes da Rocha, „desto schöner sehen sie aus."

« Je n'aime pas qu'on fasse n'importe quoi avec la belle architecture », déclare Houssein Jarouche. Pour rénover cette maison construite en 1969, il a donc fait appel à son concepteur, Paolo Mendes da Rocha. « C'est toujours difficile de revenir sur un projet », avoue ce dernier. « Nous nous sommes efforcés de lui rendre son état d'origine. » Ses surfaces en béton et sa tuyauterie apparente n'ont pas été touchées. De nouvelles lucarnes ont été posées et les portes à persiennes des chambres ont été refaites conformément au concept initial. Le propriétaire et l'architecte ont convenu de quelques changements : des parties de la piscine ont été peintes en noir (Mendes da Rocha y songeait depuis longtemps), un escalier a été remplacé et un portail ajouté devant la propriété. Jarouche voit sa demeure comme « une maison de plage en ville ». Au lieu de sable, le sol est tapissé de carreaux en ciment ornés de quadrilobes qui embellissent avec le temps. « Plus vous marchez dessus », note Mendes da Rocha, « plus ils deviennent sublimes. »

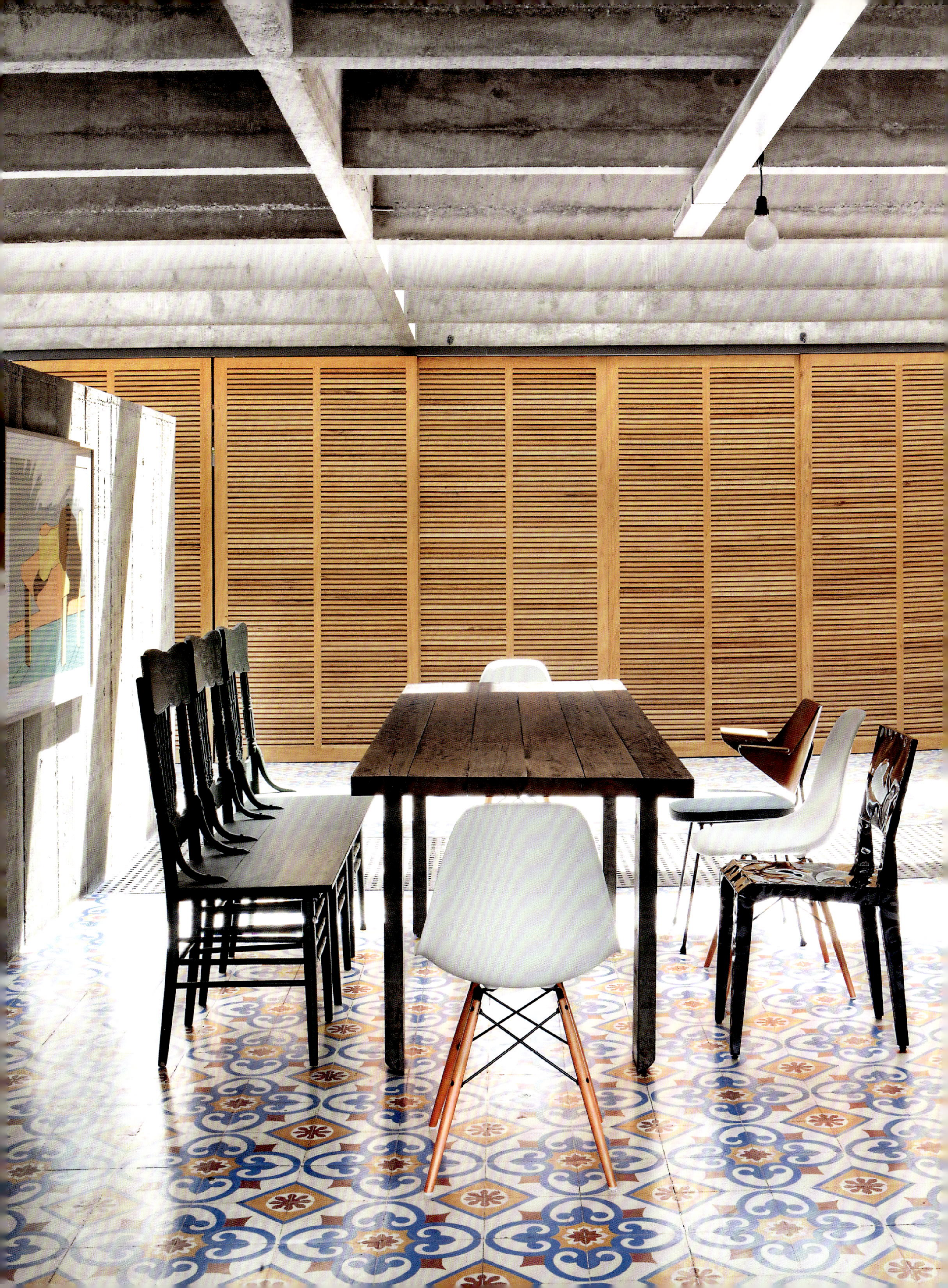

205 An assortment of different chairs, including François Azambourg's *Mr. B* in crumpled metal, surrounds an industrial dining table bought in New York. • Eine bunte Ansammlung von Stühlen, darunter François Azambourgs *Mr. B* aus „zerknittertem" Metall, umgibt einen Werkstatt-Tisch aus New York. • Autour de la table industrielle rapportée de New York, un assortiment de chaises, dont *Mr. B* de François Azambourg en métal froissé.

▼ In the master bedroom, retro-futuristic concrete capsules house a closet and a shower. The bedspread and pillowcases are from Missoni Home. • Im Schlafzimmer bilden retro-futuristische Betonkapseln eine Dusche und einen Schrank. Bettüberwurf und Kissenbezüge von Missoni Home. • Dans la chambre principale, des capsules en béton rétro-futuristes abritent la douche et un placard. Le dessus-de-lit et les taies d'oreiller viennent de chez Missoni Home.

▶ Brutalist architecture at its best: a protruding frame around the living room window helps to shade the interior from the Brazilian sun. • Brutalistische Architektur *at its best*: Der vorspringende Rahmen des Wohnzimmerfensters hält die Strahlen der brasilianischen Sonne ab. • La fine fleur de l'architecture brutaliste : le cadre saillant autour de la fenêtre protège le séjour du soleil brésilien.

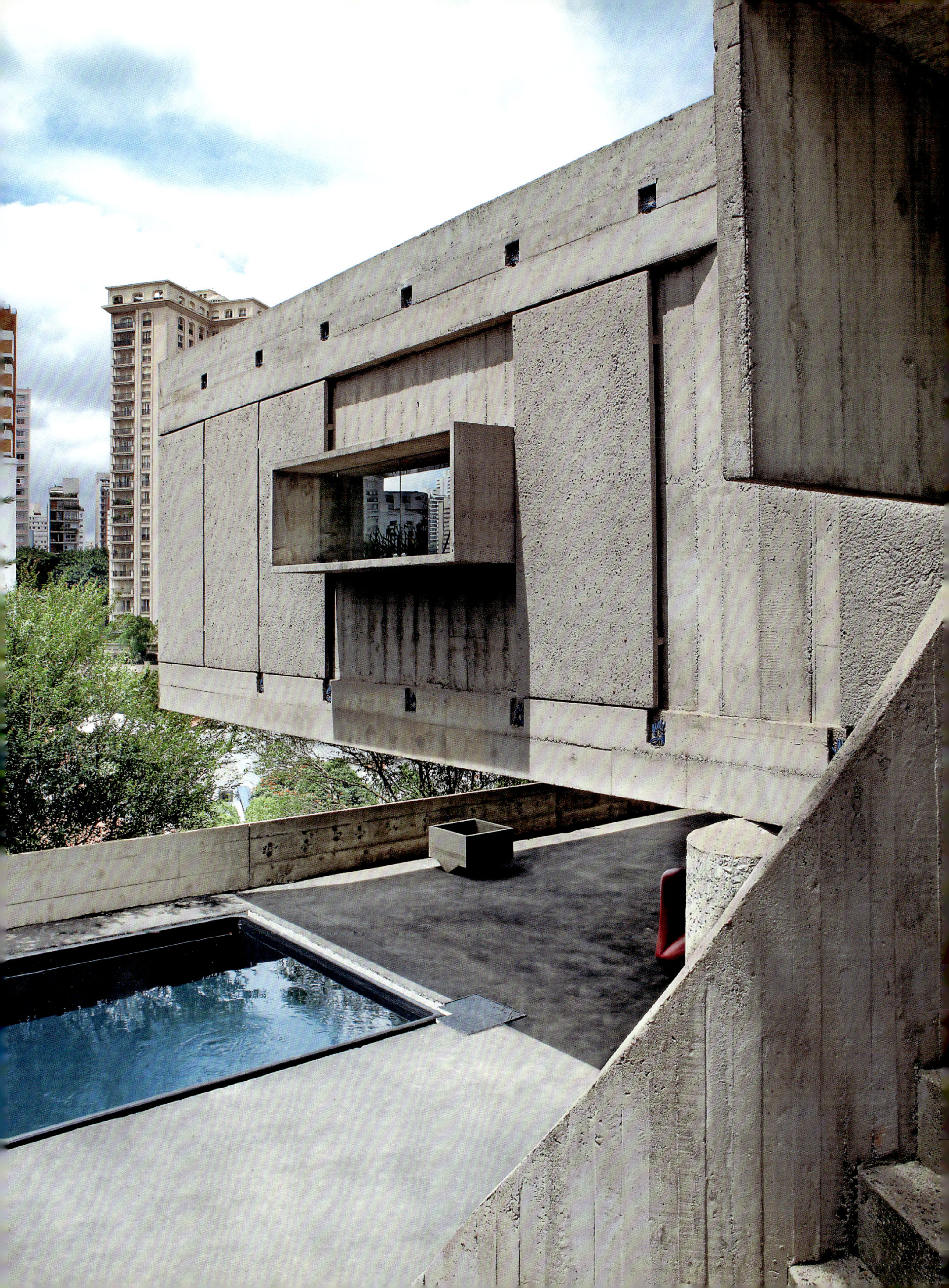

DOUG MEYER

A TRIUMPH OF D.I.Y. DECORATING IN NEW YORK

WHO New York-based decorator. **WHAT** The 167 m² (1,800 sq. ft.) duplex rental of fashion designer Sylvia Heisel and her husband, the sculptor Scott Taylor. **WHERE** In a new Chelsea building. **PARTNERS IN CRIME** Heisel and Taylor create Neo-Dada art installations like the maze of giant white balloons that led to a "cloud room" in a 2012 show at the Pacific Design Center in West Hollywood. **PAST LIFE** During the 1990s, Meyer ran a newsstand in South Beach, Miami. Gianni Versace would regularly pop in for his *Corriere della Sera*. **PRESENT LIFE** With his brother, Gene, he also designs housewares and fashion accessories. **OVER THE POP** In most of his other projects, Doug Meyer favors bright hues. As a child, he asked his mother for an all-pink bedroom. **QUICK-CHANGE ARTIST** He redoes the decor of his own apartment every year. A recent incarnation saw the walls covered with a patchwork of 3,000 colored sheets of paper.

PHOTOGRAPHED BY MARK ROSKAMS/TRIPOD AGENCY

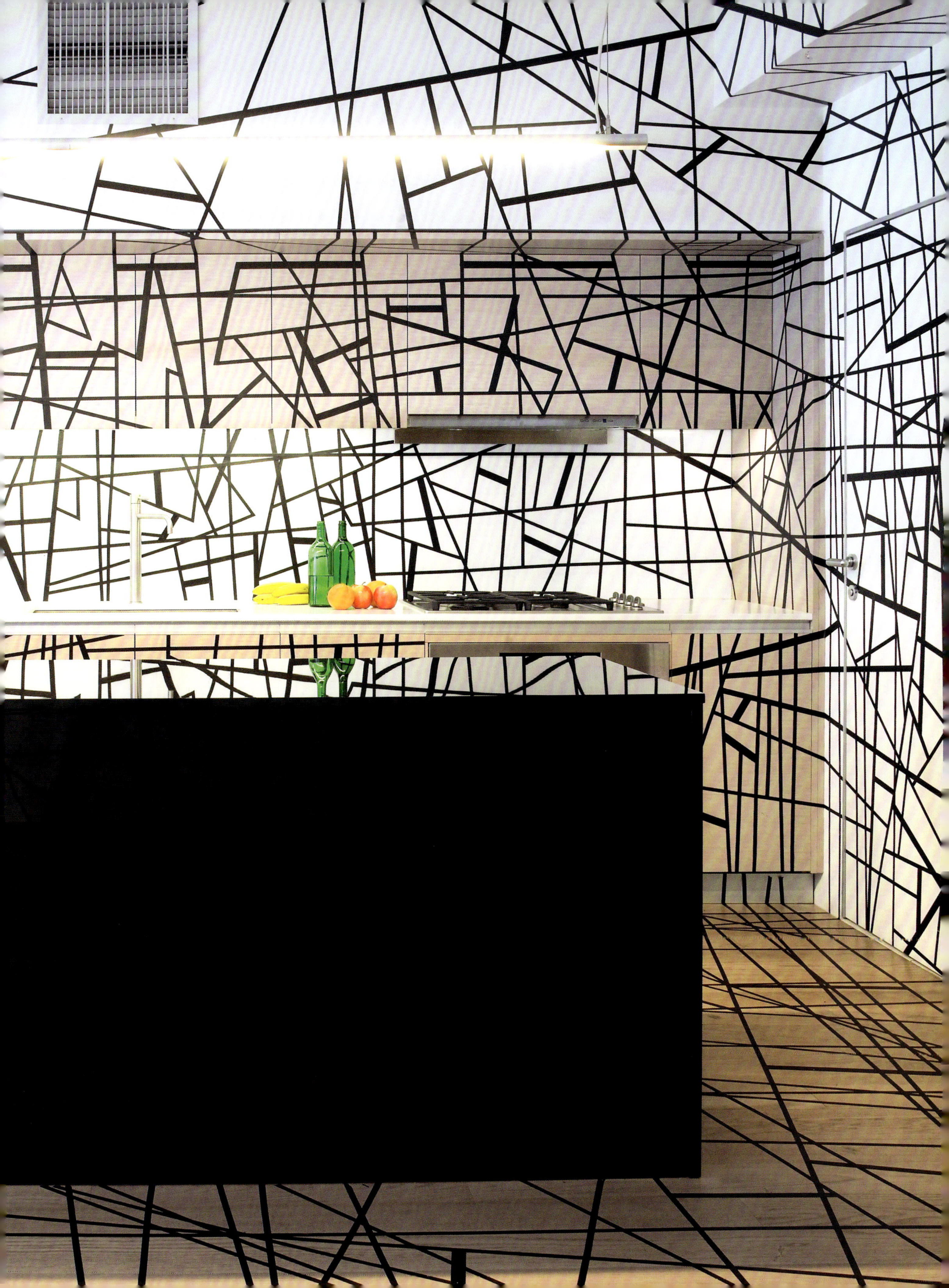

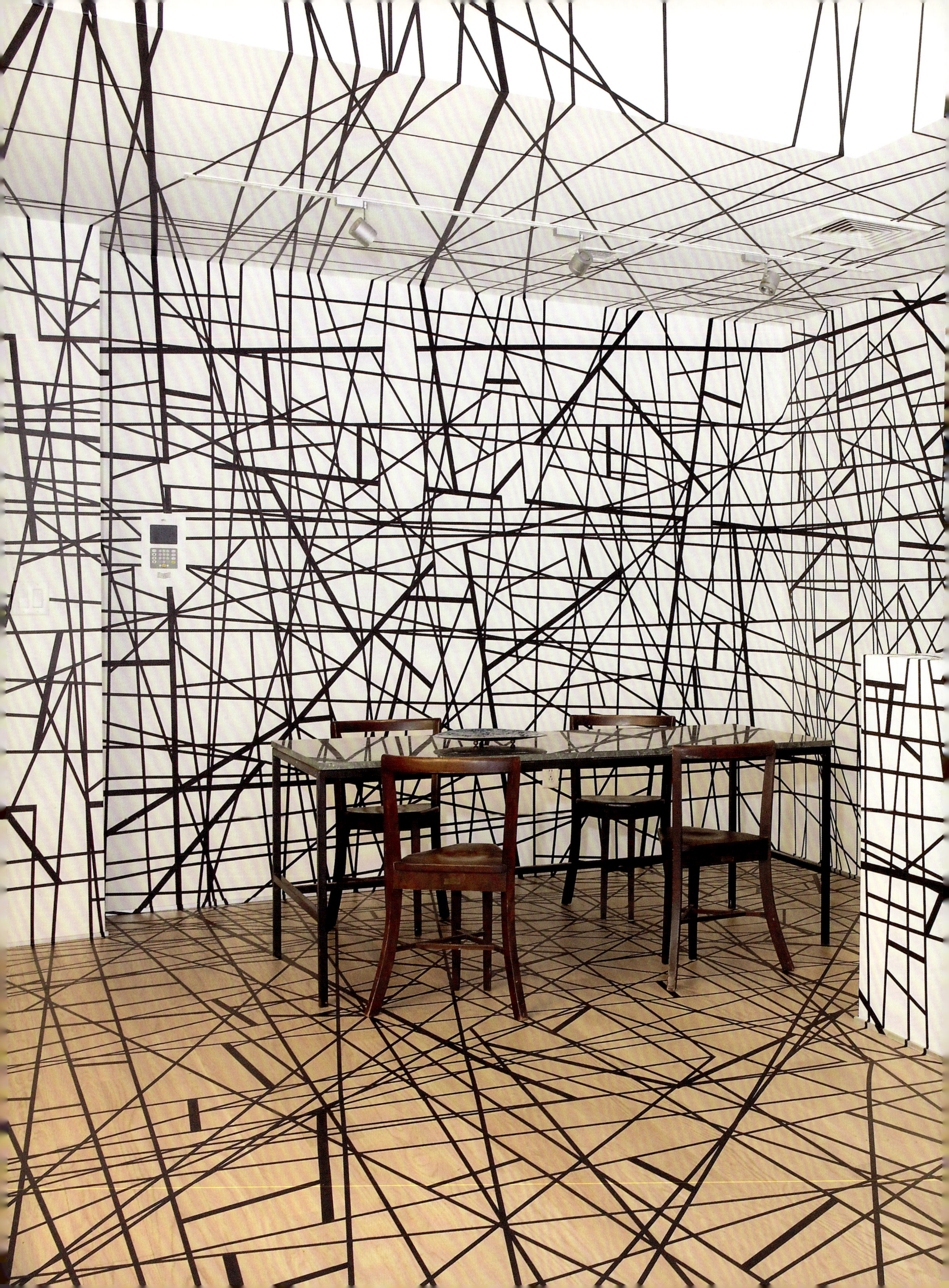

209–211 Different widths of repositioning tape were used for the spiderweb pattern. At right, stairs lead down to the bedroom and office on the lower level. • Das Spinnennetz-Dekor besteht aus unterschiedlich breiten Klebestreifen. Hinter der Brüstung rechts führt eine Treppe zu Schlafzimmer und Büro. • L'effet «toile d'araignée» a été obtenu à l'aide de rubans adhésifs de largeurs différentes. Á droite, l'escalier mène à la chambre et au bureau.

▶ Basement office walls were covered with black-and-white magazine images. The framed drawing is by Joseph Stashkevetch. African stool from Kenya. • Die Wände des Büros im Souterrain bedecken Schwarz-Weiß-Fotos aus Magazinen, davor eine gerahmte Zeichnung von Joseph Stashkevetch. Hocker aus Kenia. • Les murs du bureau sont tapissés d'images en noir et blanc. Le dessin encadré est de Joseph Stashkevetch. Le tabouret est kenyan.

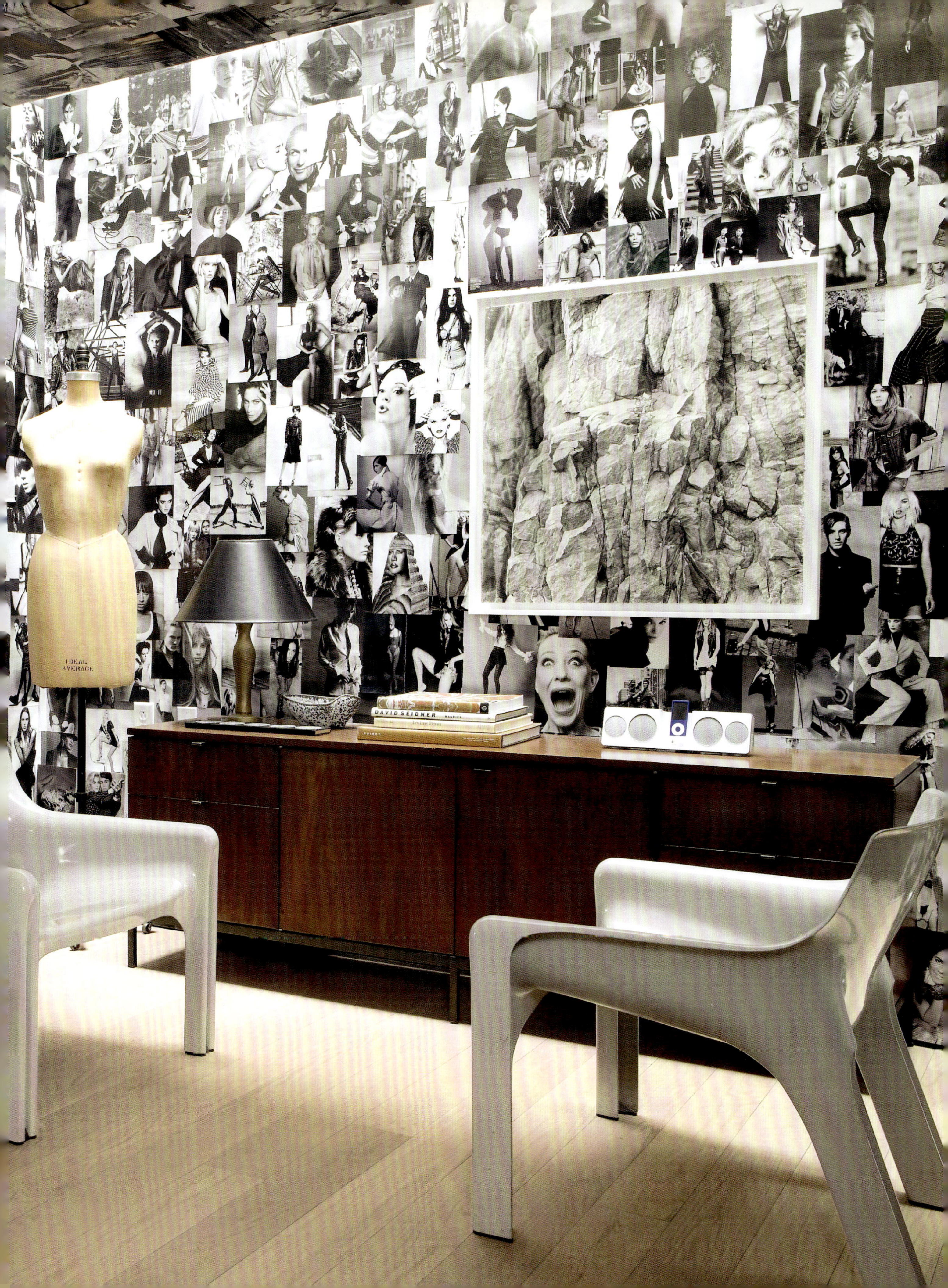
IDEAL
AVERAGE
DAVID SEIDNER

▲ The vestibule was the only space to get a splash of color. Among the artworks is a silk screen print of Joseph Beuys. The dress is Sylvia Heisel Couture. • Das Vestibül ist der einzige Raum in Farbe. An der Wand hängt unter anderem ein Siebdruck-Porträt von Joseph Beuys. Kleid von Sylvia Heisel Couture. • Le seul éclat de couleur se trouve dans le vestibule. Parmi les œuvres d'art, une sérigraphie de Joseph Beuys. La robe est une création Sylvia Heisel Couture.

"We've never had lots of stuff," says Sylvia Heisel. "Everything is on our computers." Still, it is difficult to believe that the Chelsea apartment she and her husband, Scott Taylor, live in was once "boring" and "kind of stark." Initially, however, it was simply a white box. Then they decided to jazz it up and called in their friend and co-conspirator Doug Meyer. In the basement office, they clad one wall with a collage of tear sheets from fashion magazines. In the bedroom, they dribbled tempera paint onto cotton canvas and stapled it to the floor and walls. The most dramatic space, however, is the living room-cum-kitchen, which is covered with a crisscross pattern of black tape (2.2 kilometers or 2,400 yards total). As Heisel and Taylor are renting, it was all devised to be removed without a trace. "It's like a pop-up apartment," opines Meyer. "It has that throwaway luxury sensibility". The result has obviously raised a few eyebrows, especially those of a Chinese-food delivery guy. "When he left, he couldn't find the door," recalls Taylor with a big grin. "The look on his face was just fear."

„VIELE BESITZTÜMER HATTEN WIR NIE. ALLES IST AUF UNSEREN COMPUTERN." SYLVIA HEISEL

Trotzdem möchte man kaum glauben, dass die Wohnung in Chelsea, in der Heisel mit ihrem Ehemann Scott Taylor lebt, einmal „langweilig" und „irgendwie steif" gewesen sein soll. Tatsächlich war das Apartment zunächst bloß eine weiße Box – bis die beiden beschlossen, es aufzupeppen. Mit ihrem Freund und Mitverschwörer Doug Meyer bedeckten sie eine ganze Wand im Untergeschoss mit einer Collage aus Ausrissen verschiedener Modemagazine. Im Schlafzimmer besprtizten sie Segeltuch mit Temperafarbe und tackerten es danach an Boden und Wände. Noch spektakulärer ist das Wohnzimmer mit integrierter Küche: Kreuz und quer überzieht schwarzes Klebeband (insgesamt 2,2 km) den Raum. Da Heisel und Taylor zur Miete wohnen, lässt sich alles wieder entfernen, ohne Spuren zu hinterlassen. „Es ist quasi ein Pop-up-Apartment", erklärt Meyer. „Wegwerf-Luxus, der sich nicht zu ernst nimmt." Einfach nur verwirrend fand es wohl der Lieferant eines China-Imbisses. „Als er gehen wollte, fand er die Tür nicht mehr", erinnert sich Taylor. „In seinen Augen stand die nackte Angst."

« Nous ne possédons pas grand-chose ; tout est dans nos ordinateurs », confie Sylvia Heisel. On a pourtant du mal à croire que l'appartement de Chelsea où elle vit avec son mari Scott Taylor n'était autrefois qu'une boîte blanche « ennuyeuse » et « austère ». Pour l'égayer, ils ont fait appel à leur ami et complice Doug Meyer. Dans le bureau en sous-sol, ils ont revêtu les murs d'un collage de coupures de magazines de mode. Dans la chambre, ils ont projeté de la peinture *a tempera* sur de la toile avant de l'agrafer sur le sol et les murs. La pièce la plus spectaculaire est le séjour cuisine tapissé d'un enchevêtrement de ruban adhésif noir (2,2 km au total). Comme il s'agit d'une location, tout a été conçu pour être enlevé sans laisser de traces. « C'est un appartement pop-up ; comme un objet de luxe jetable », opine Meyer. Le résultat en a surpris plus d'un, notamment le livreur d'un restaurant chinois. Taylor en rit encore : « En repartant, il ne trouvait plus la porte. Il avait l'air terrorisé. »

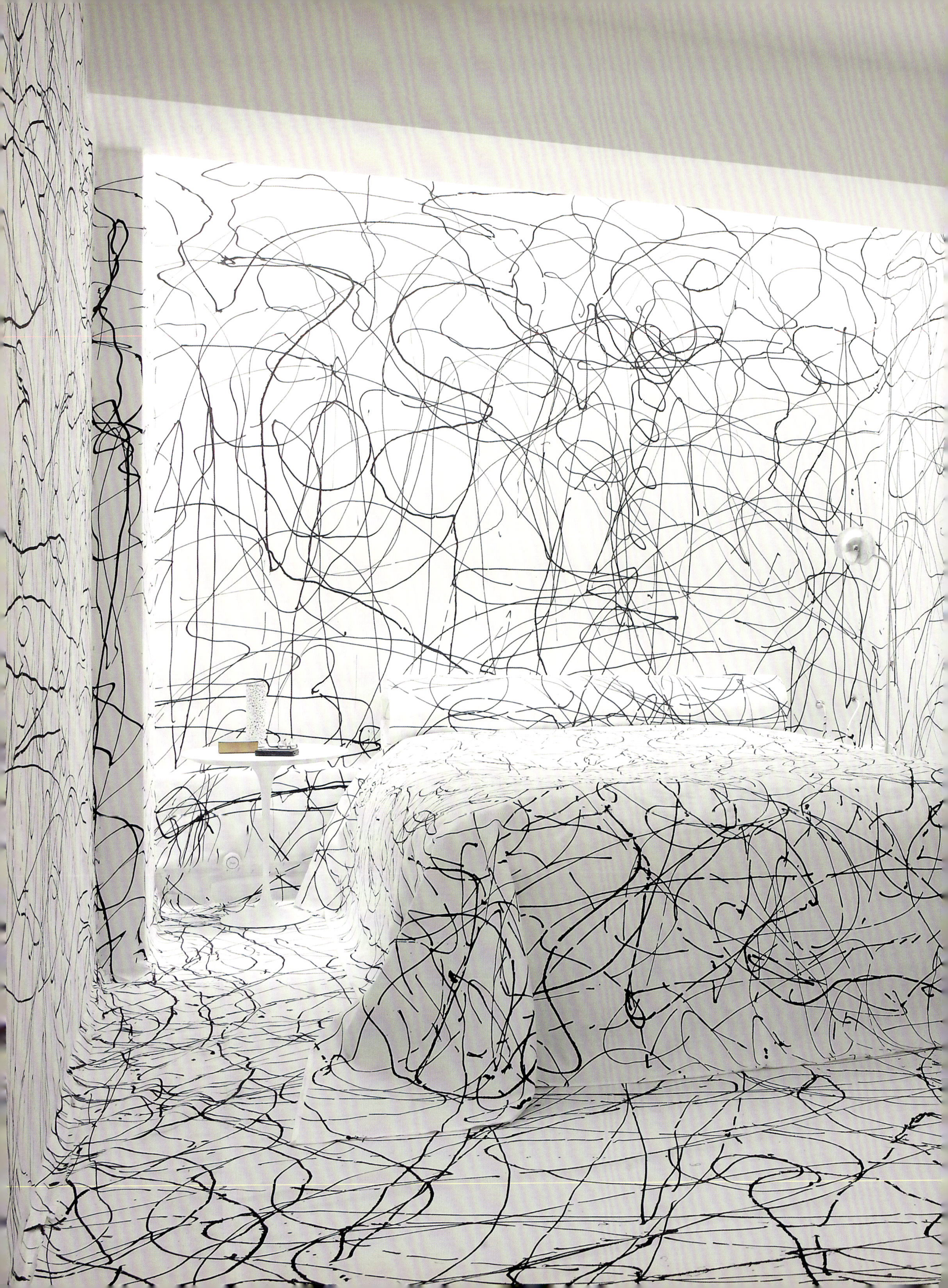

◄ The paint à la Pollock was squirted from plastic salad dressing bottles. Scott Taylor created the chair for a Beverly Hills club he ran in the 1990s. • Die Schlieren à la Pollock wurden mit Salatdressing-Flaschen aufgespritzt. Den Stuhl entwarf Taylor in den 1990ern für seinen Club in Beverly Hills. • La peinture à la Pollock a été projetée avec des bouteilles à vinaigrette en plastique. Taylor a créé la chaise pour son club de danse de Beverly Hills dans les années 1990.

JOHN MINSHAW

A HOUSE IN KENT

WHO English interior designer, famous for his work on historic properties. **WHAT** A 722 m² (7,772 sq. ft.), six-bedroom late-Georgian house. **WHERE** The village of Hever, Kent. Its claim to fame: Hever Castle was the childhood home of Henry VIII's second wife, Anne Boleyn. **THE CLIENTS** A commercial real estate entrepreneur and his research scientist wife. **FAMOUS FRIEND** Minshaw was close to legendary ceramicist Lucie Rie, who taught him at Camberwell School of Art. "I used to have tea with her once a week," he recalls. **FAR AWAY** He is crazy about ancient Egypt: "I just love the elegance of the buildings." **CLOSER TO HOME** His favorite edifice in the U.K. is Queen's House in Greenwich, designed by Inigo Jones in the Palladian style after his travels through Italy. "Imagine the houses around that period—the early 17th century—and suddenly this thing landed," Minshaw says. "It must have been like a space capsule arriving." **HUMBLE GRANDEUR** His own home is a series of buildings in Oxfordshire that were once the barn, stable, and carriage house of a manor.

PHOTOGRAPHED BY JAMES MCDONALD©THE WORLD OF INTERIORS   PORTRAIT BY NEIL BLAKE

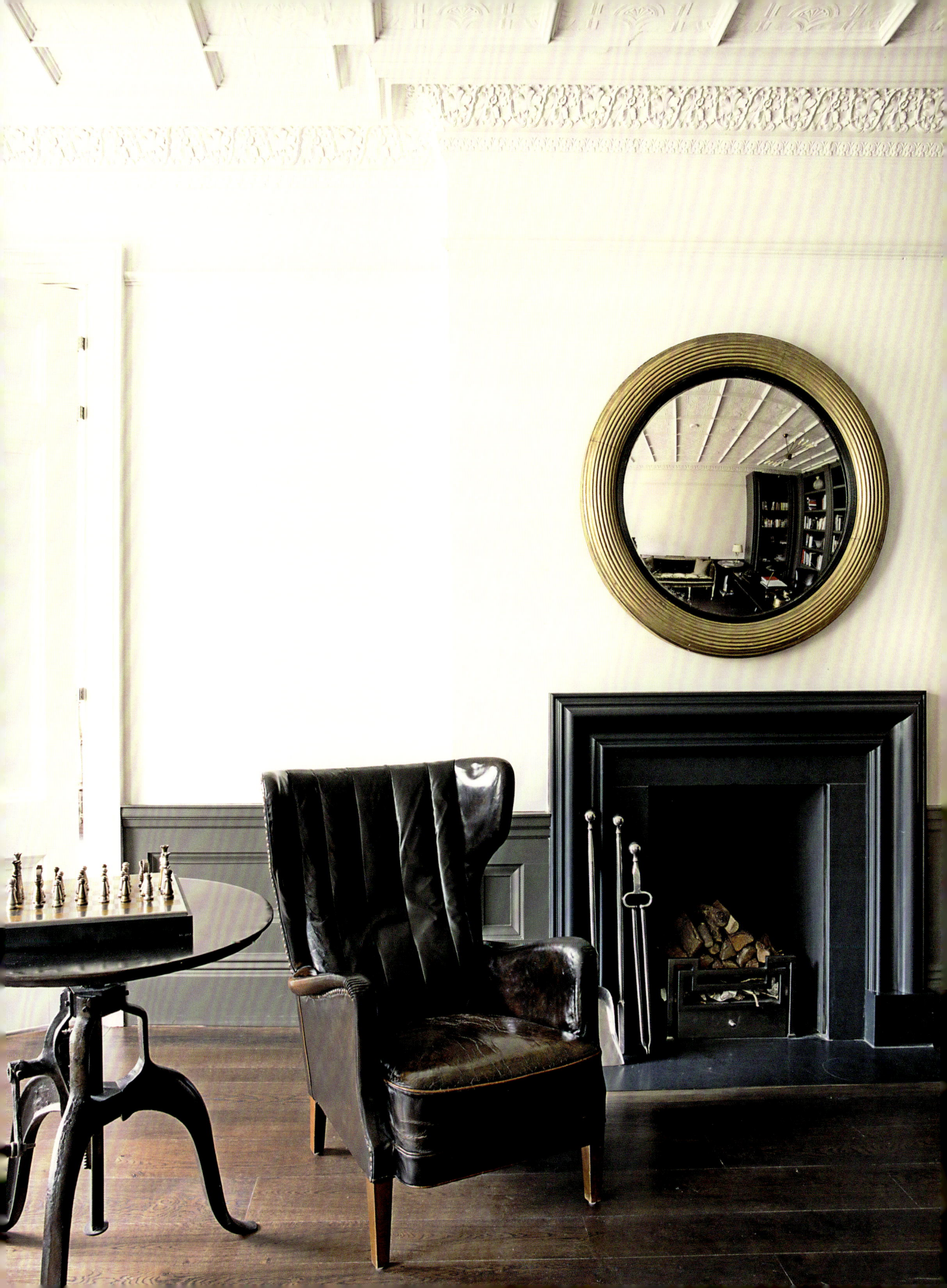

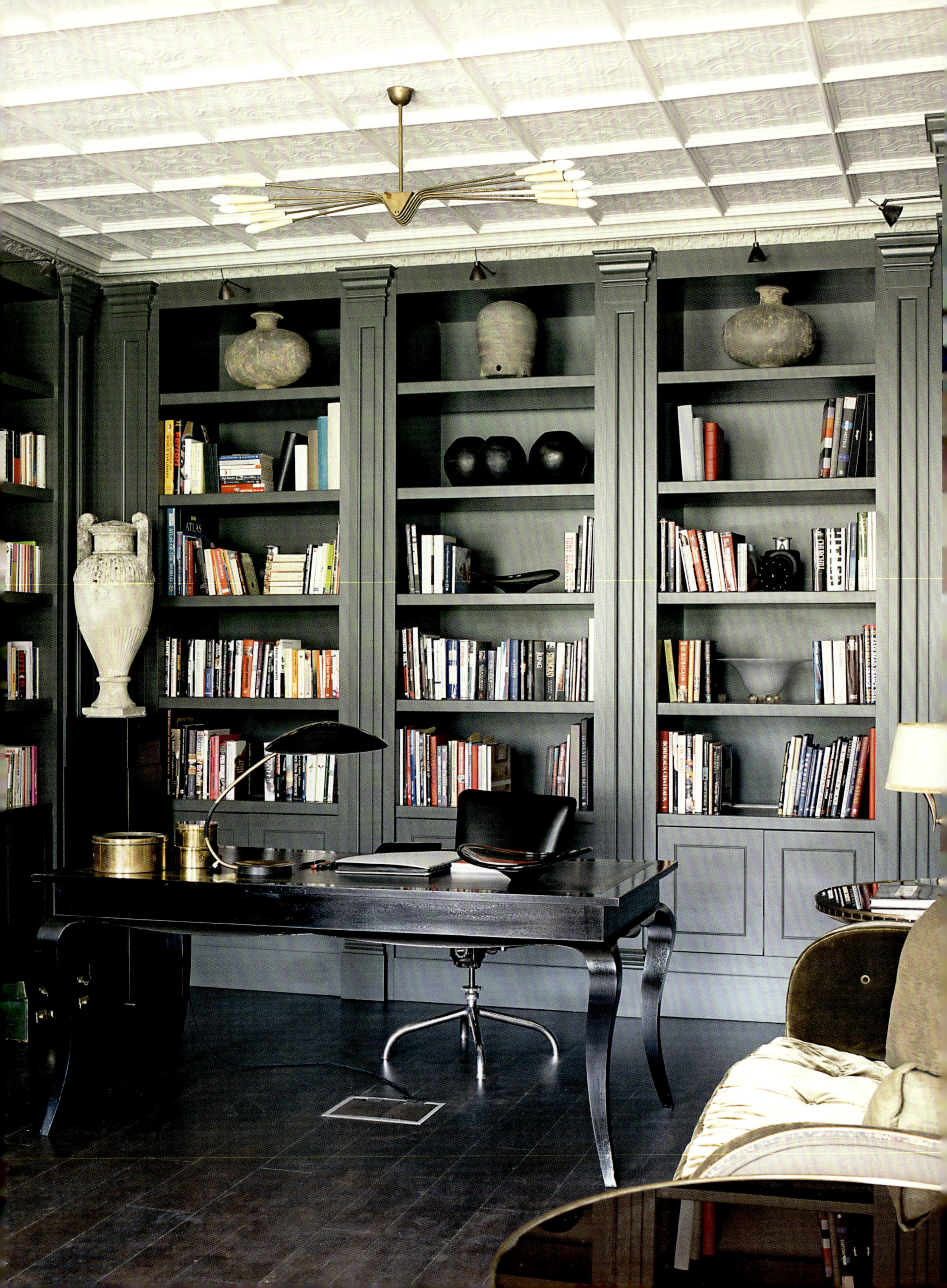
ATLAS
JUNG

219 A 1930s Danish wingback armchair and 19th-century adjustable tripod table stand by the fireplace in the library. The gilt wood mirror dates from the Regency period. • Vor dem Kamin in der Bibliothek stehen ein dänischer Sessel aus den 1930ern und ein verstellbarer Tisch aus dem 19. Jahrhundert. Vergoldeter Holzspiegel aus der Regency-Zeit. • Dans la bibliothèque avec sa cheminée en bois peint, une bergère danoise des années 1930 et un guéridon du 19ᵉ siècle. Miroir en bois doré de l'époque Regency.

◂ In the same room, a 1930s Italian swivel chair, French desk, and Han Dynasty urns are juxtaposed. The bookshelves were painted in Marston & Langinger's "Roman Bronze." • Im selben Raum finden sich ein italienischer Drehstuhl aus den 1930ern, ein französischer Schreibtisch und Urnen der Han-Dynastie. Regale in „Roman Bronze" von Marston & Langinger. • Dans la même pièce, un fauteuil pivotant italien des années 1930, un bureau français et des urnes de la dynastie Han. La bibliothèque a été peinte dans la couleur « Roman Bronze » de chez Marston & Langinger.

▾ A pair of French armchairs provides secluded seating in a niche at one end of the drawing room. The Italian marble fireplace was already in the house. • Auf den französischen Fauteuils in einer Nische des Salons sitzt man wie im Separee. Der Kamin aus italienischem Marmor war bereits vorhanden. • Une paire de fauteuils français crée un petit coin intime dans une alcôve du salon. La cheminée en marbre italien se trouvait déjà dans la maison.

223 Soft sleep: the master suite, with the bed and an antique Chinese chest clad in vellum, soothes with its seafoam coloring. Bedside *Buquet* lamp by Tecnolumen. • Die Mastersuite ist in beruhigenden Gischt-Tönen gehalten, das Bett und die antike chinesische Truhe sind mit Pergament bezogen. *Buquet*-Leuchte von Tecnolumen. • Toute en nuances d'écume de mer, la chambre principale, avec son lit et son coffre chinois du 19ᵉ siècle tendu de vélin, repose le regard. La lampe *Buquet* vient de chez Tecnolumen.

"THE THINGS I WORRY ABOUT FIRST ARE THOSE THAT WOULDN'T FALL OUT IF YOU TURNED THE HOUSE UPSIDE DOWN AND SHOOK IT." JOHN MINSHAW

In other words, on every project, John Minshaw's principal concern is the architecture. When he first saw this property, it was "a basket case." There was fake oak paneling in the drawing room and a warren of small spaces upstairs. On the ground floor, each room could only be accessed via a corridor at the back. He greatly improved the flow by installing a 22-meter (72-foot) enfilade along the front of the house. He also added period-style cornices, paneling, and architraves, and opted for largely 20th-century furniture. "They're a young couple, and I just thought a bit of freshness was right for the house," Minshaw explains. He also steered away from traditional chintz fabrics and chose textured velvets and linens instead. "I've never been a big pattern man," he asserts. "It's like camouflage. I prefer to see the architecture." The clients' only specific request was the gilded kitchen island. "We tried to persuade them not to have it because of the problems of scratching," he says. "But actually, they were right."

„Die meisten Gedanken mache ich mir über die Dinge, die nicht herausfallen würden, wenn man das Haus auf den Kopf stellte", erklärt John Minshaw. Mit anderen Worten: Sein Hauptanliegen ist die Architektur. Als er dieses Anwesen erstmals sah, schien es ein hoffnungsloser Fall – der Salon mit Eiche-Imitat getäfelt, ein Gewirr aus kleinen Zimmern im Obergeschoss, und im Parterre konnte man sämtliche Räume nur über einen rückwärtigen Korridor betreten. Minshaw verbesserte den Raumplan entscheidend, indem er entlang der Front eine 22 m lange Enfilade anlegte. Außerdem fügte er Gesimse, Boiserien und Architrave im Stil der Bauepoche hinzu und wählte überwiegend Mobiliar aus dem 20. Jahrhundert. „Die Besitzer sind ein junges Paar – und ich dachte mir, ein bisschen Frische würde dem Haus guttun." Konventionelle Chintz-Dessins ignorierte er zugunsten von Samt und Leinen. Der einzige ausdrückliche Wunsch der Kunden war die vergoldete Kücheninsel. „Wir versuchten, sie davon abzubringen, wegen der Probleme mit Kratzern", erzählt er. „Aber letzten Endes hatten sie recht."

« Ma première préoccupation, c'est tout ce qui ne tomberait pas si vous retourniez la maison et la secouiez », explique John Minshaw. Lorsqu'il découvrit cette propriété, « c'était n'importe quoi ». Il y avait de fausses boiseries en chêne dans le salon et un dédale de petites pièces à l'étage. Celles du rez-de-chaussée ne communiquaient que par un couloir à l'arrière du bâtiment. Il a amélioré la circulation en créant une enfilade de 22 m à l'avant, a ajouté des corniches, des boiseries, des architraves d'époque et a privilégié le mobilier du 20ᵉ siècle. « Les clients sont un jeune couple ; j'ai pensé que ce serait plus frais. » Il a évité les chintz traditionnels, leur préférant des velours et des lins texturés. « Je n'ai jamais été porté sur les motifs. Ça fait camouflage. Je préfère voir l'architecture. » La seule exigence des clients était l'îlot de cuisine doré. « Nous avons tenté de les dissuader, en raison du problème des éraflures. Mais, en fait, ils avaient raison. »

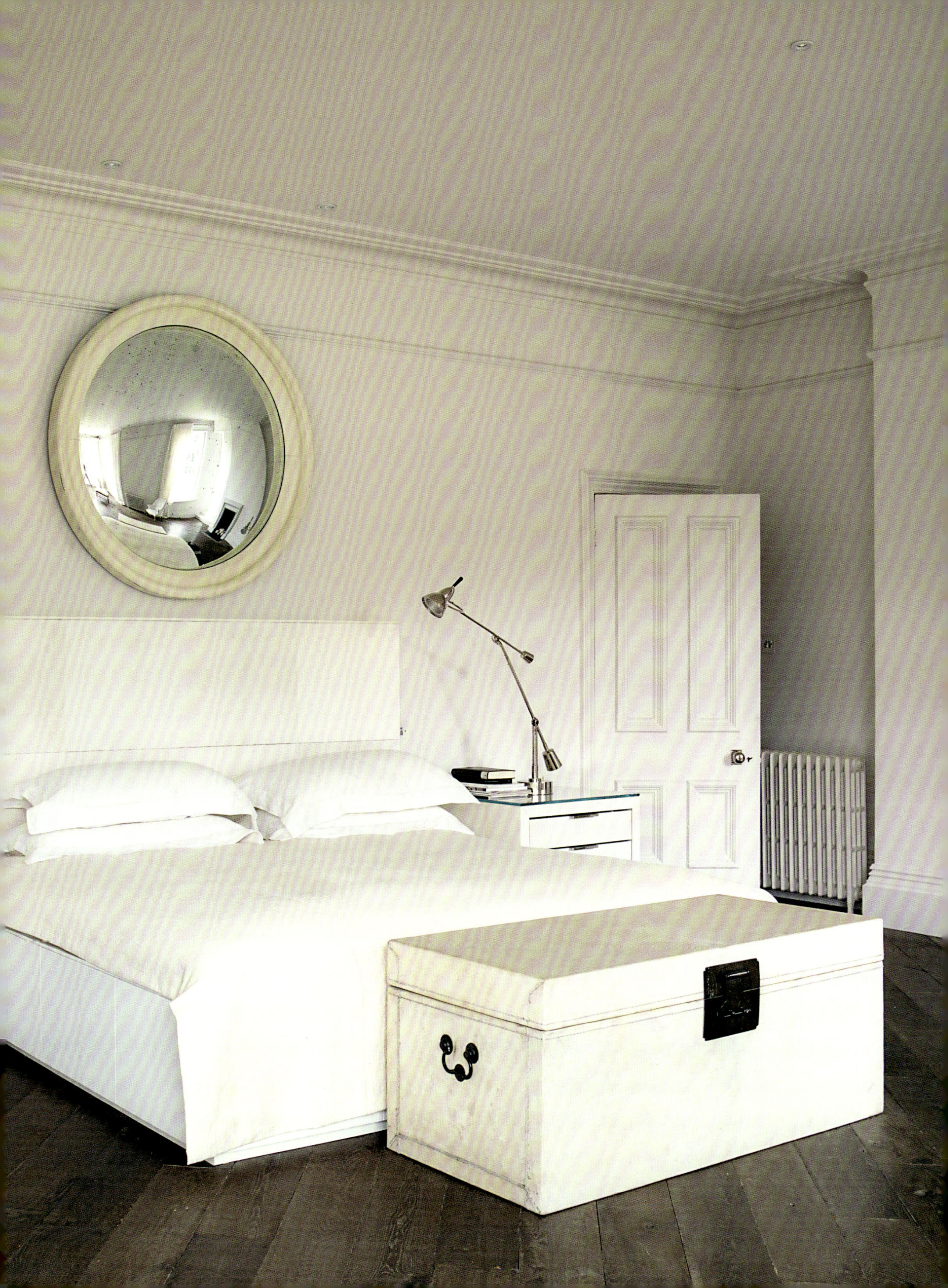

▶ Who needs chintzy patterns if you can have elegant contrast instead? The front door, at left, leads directly into the drawing room, previously decorated with faux-oak paneling. *Brian Junior* sofa by Axel Vervoordt. • Wer braucht Chintz-Muster, wenn man elegante Kontraste haben kann? Die Eingangstür links führt direkt in den Salon, der zuvor mit Eiche-Imitat vertäfelt war. Sofa *Brian Junior* von Axel Vervoordt. • Des contrastes élégants valent mieux que des chintz surchargés. La porte d'entrée donne directement sur le salon, autrefois décoré de boiseries en faux chêne. Le canapé *Brian Junior* est d'Axel Vervoordt.

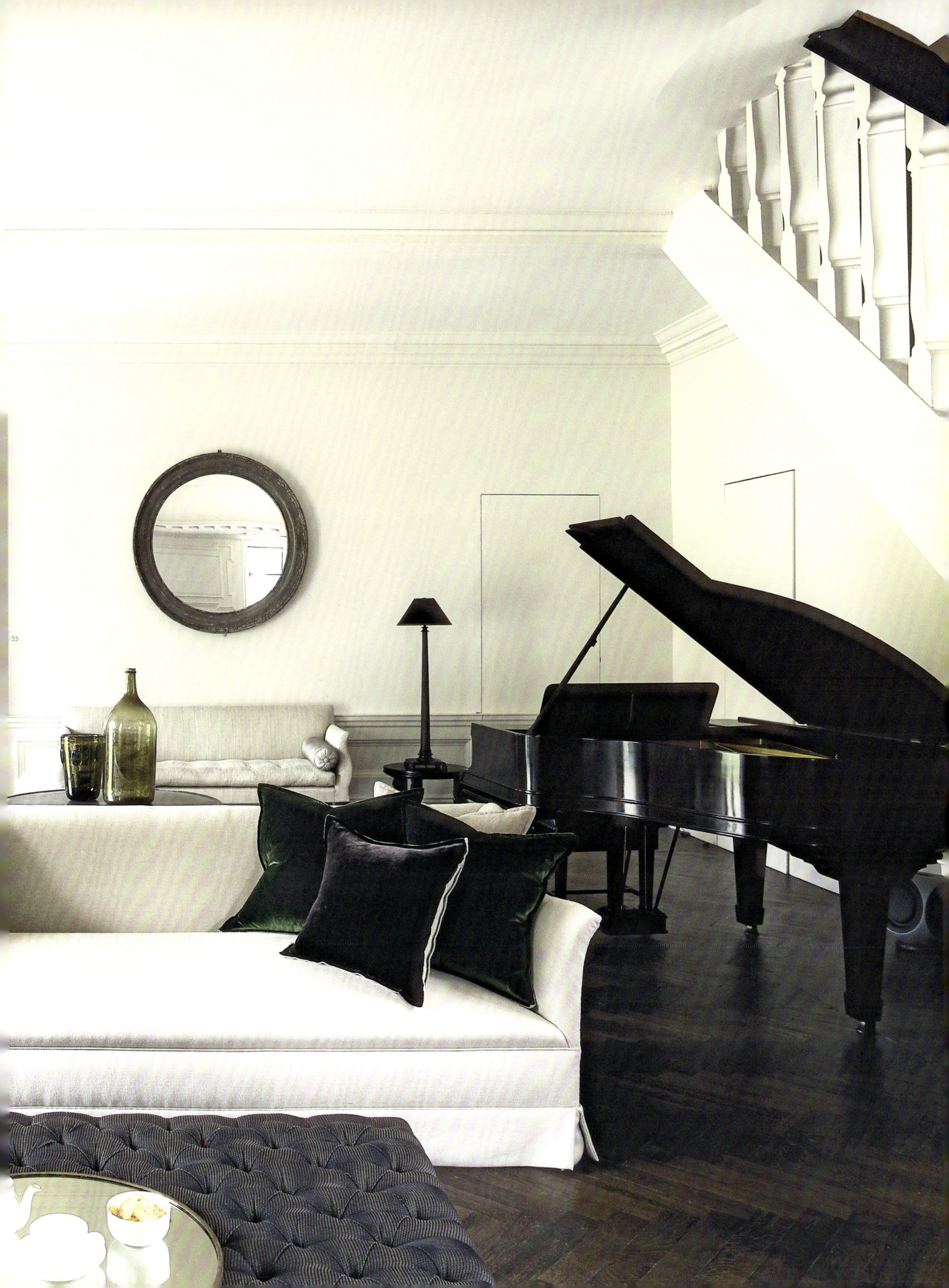

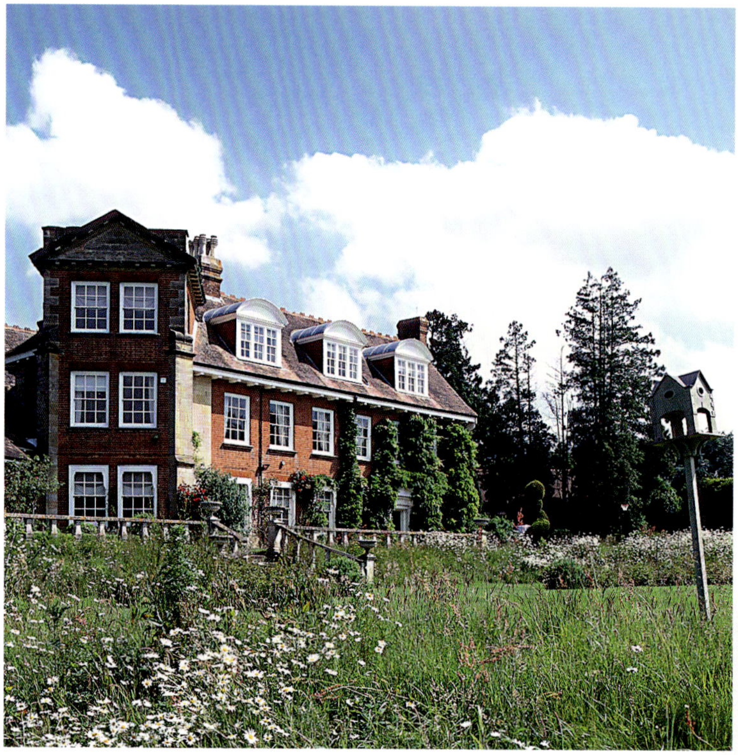

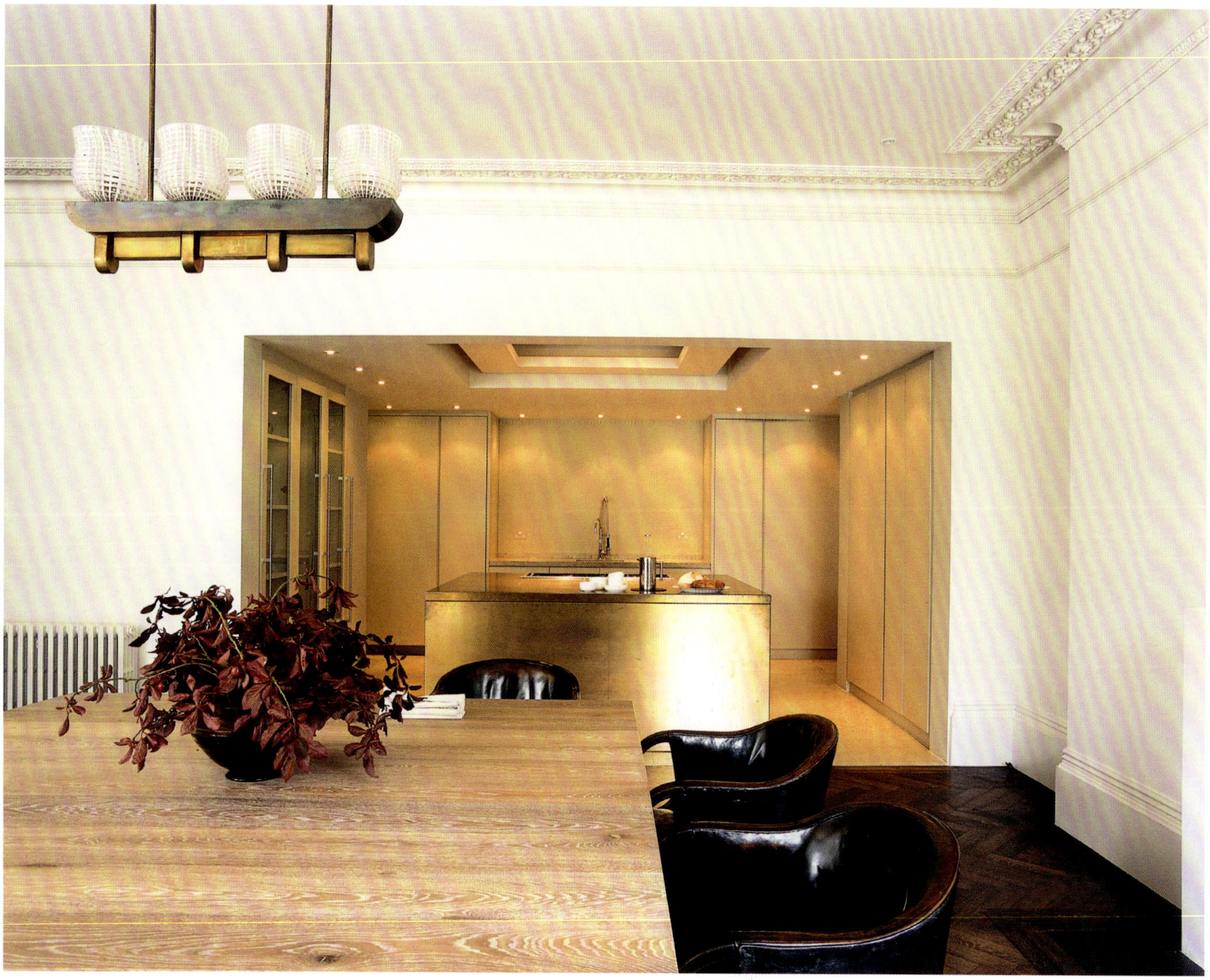

◀ The Georgian structure was not listed, which gave Minshaw greater freedom for the interiors. "Normally what happens is we've got Grade II or starred properties and if you cough, somebody wants to know why you're coughing," he says. The owners plan to restore the garden, including croquet lawn and lake. • Das georgianische Haus aus Klinker und Stein stand nicht unter Denkmalschutz, das gab Minshaw mehr Freiheit: „Normalerweise haben wir es mindestens mit ‚Grade II' zu tun – da braucht man nur zu husten, schon werden Fragen gestellt." Langfristig planen die Besitzer, den Park mit Krocketrasen und See orginalgetreu zu gestalten. • Le bâtiment de style géorgien en brique et pierre n'étant pas classé, Minshaw disposait d'une grande latitude. « Généralement, dans le cas d'un bien inscrit au patrimoine, on ne peut pas tousser sans qu'on vous demande de vous justifier », observe-t-il. Les propriétaires souhaitent restaurer le jardin, avec son terrain de croquet et son lac.

▶ Above the custom English oak table hangs a 1920s Italian chandelier; a gilded-metal island in the kitchen. • Über dem Eichentisch hängt ein italienischer Leuchter aus den 1920ern. Das vergoldete Metall der Kochinsel taucht die Küche in seinen warmen Widerschein. • Un lustre italien des années 1920 au-dessus d'une table anglaise en chêne sur mesure. L'îlot de cuisine doré crée des reflets « incroyablement chaleureux ».

▼ A late-19th-century French chair and a tub made from Quarella marble composite in the contemporary master bath. • Ein französischer Sessel aus dem späten 19. Jahrhundert gibt dem zeitgenössischen Bad einen klassischen Touch. Wanne aus Marmorkomposit von Quarella. • Un fauteuil français de la fin du 19ᵉ siècle apporte une touche de classicisme dans la grande salle de bains résolument moderne. Baignoire en marbre composite de chez Quarella.

CECILIA MORELLI PARIKH

AN APARTMENT FOR HER AND HER HUSBAND IN MUMBAI

WHO The half-Italian co-founder of the Mumbai concept store Le Mill. Her husband, Rohan, runs the hospitality and real estate divisions of his family's business. **WHAT** A 223 m² (2,400 sq. ft.), two-bedroom apartment in an early-1930s building. **WHERE** The city's most select street—Marine Drive. **PATIENCE PAYS** Rohan looked for an apartment there for six years. The couple bought this one without seeing it. "Isn't that crazy?" admits Morelli Parikh. "We were living in America at the time." **PROS AND CONS** They love the expansive sea views, but not the noise from the nearby cricket stadium. "During matches, millions of people stand in line and play Bollywood songs," she smiles. **FASHION BACKGROUND** Morelli Parikh used to be a women's buyer at Bergdorf Goodman, the New York department store. **LE MILL** Located in a 1935 rice mill, her store is a one-stop shop for design, fashion, books, and beauty products, with an emphasis on all things made in India. **IT'S A DOG'S LIFE** On a scouting visit with a potter in Pune, she was greeted by 50 canines he had rescued.

PHOTOGRAPHED BY GAELLE LE BOULICAUT

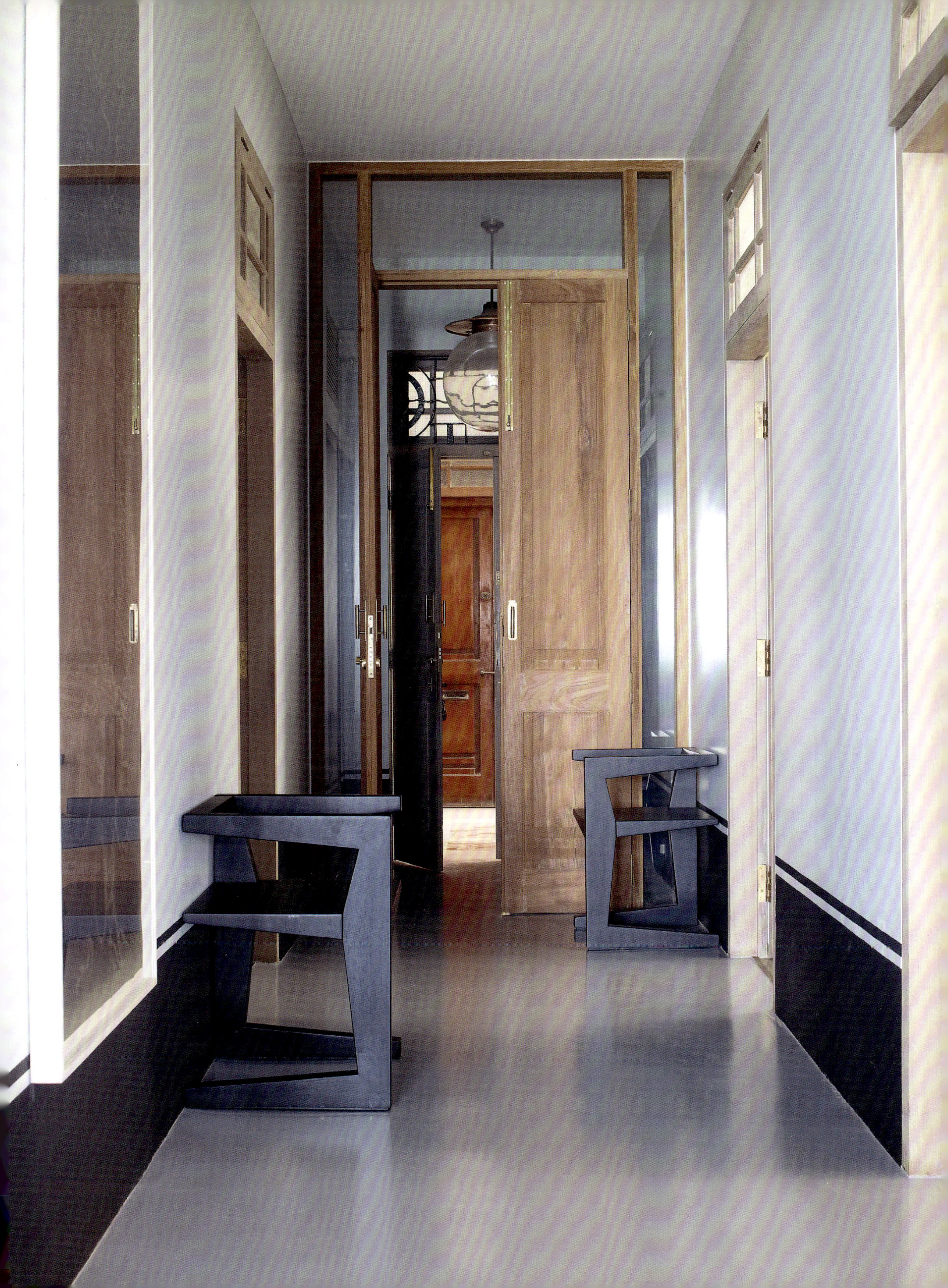

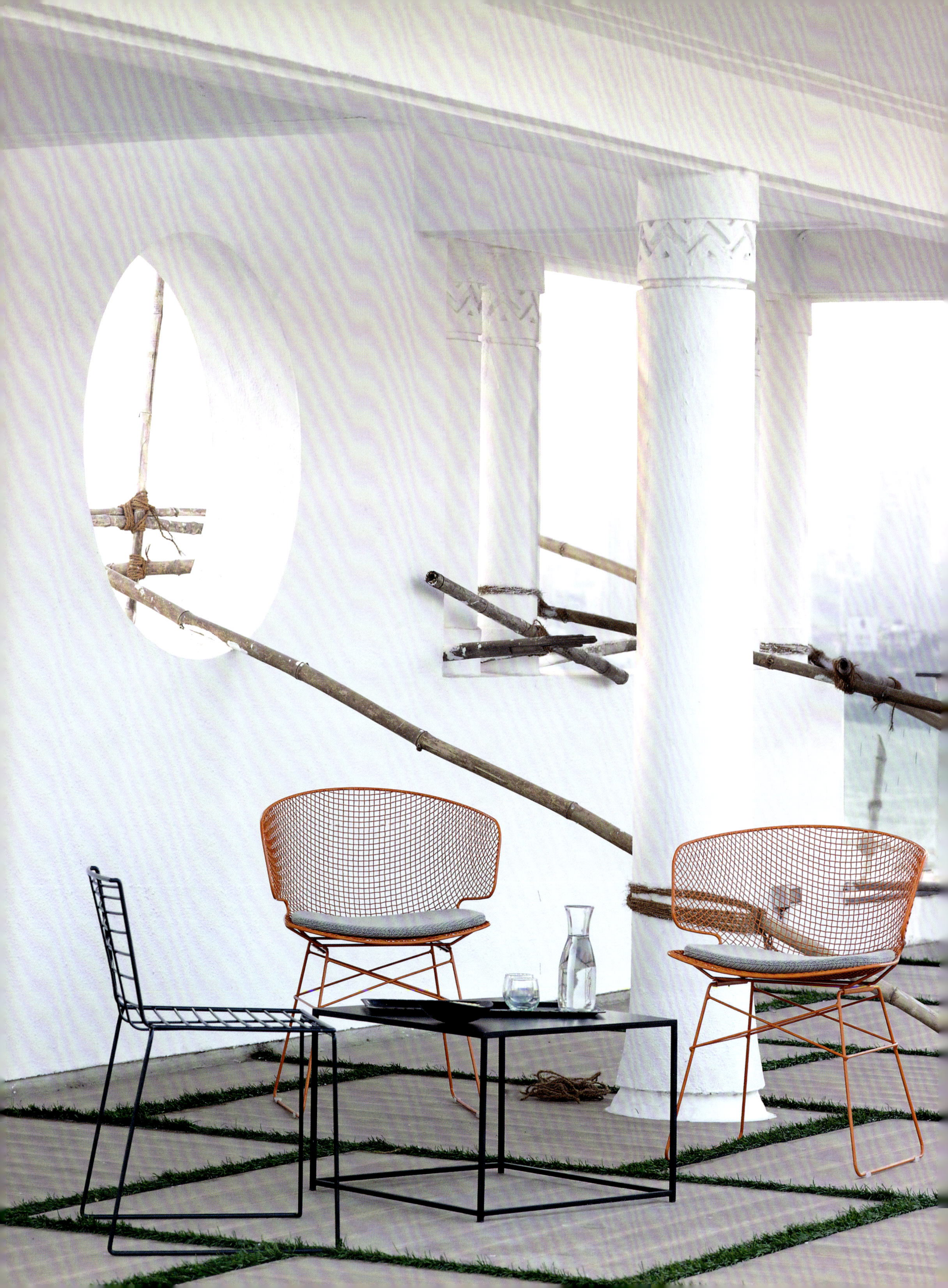

229 Designed by Rooshad Shroff for Morelli Parikh's store, Le Mill, the reclaimed teak chairs in the entry hall are coated in a polyurethane finish. • Die Stühle aus recyceltem Teak mit Polyurethan-Finish im Entree designte Rooshad Shroff für Morelli Parikhs Concept-Store Le Mill. • Dans l'entrée, les fauteuils en teck recyclé avec finition en polyuréthane ont été dessinés par Rooshad Shroff pour Le Mill, la boutique de Morelli Parikh.

◂ The black table and chair on the private roof terrace are also available at Le Mill. The orange chairs are the *Arkys* model created by Jean-Marie Massaud. • Den Tisch und den schwarzen Stuhl auf der Dachterrasse gibt es ebenfalls bei Le Mill. Orange *Arkys*-Sessel von Jean-Marie Massaud. • La table et la chaise noires sur le toit-terrasse se trouvent également chez Le Mill. Les chaises orange *Arkys* ont été créées par Jean-Marie Massaud.

▴ A diptych by Sarnath Banerjee hangs above the sofa with Jennifer Shorto-designed cushions. The yarn of the rug was dyed naturally with plant parts and yogurt. • Ein Diptychon von Sarnath Banerjee über einem Sofa mit Kissen von Jennifer Shorto. Das Garn für den Teppich wurde mit Pflanzen und Joghurt gefärbt. • Un diptyque de Sarnath Banerjee au-dessus d'un canapé avec des coussins de Jennifer Shorto. Les fibres du tapis ont été teintées naturellement à l'aide de yaourt.

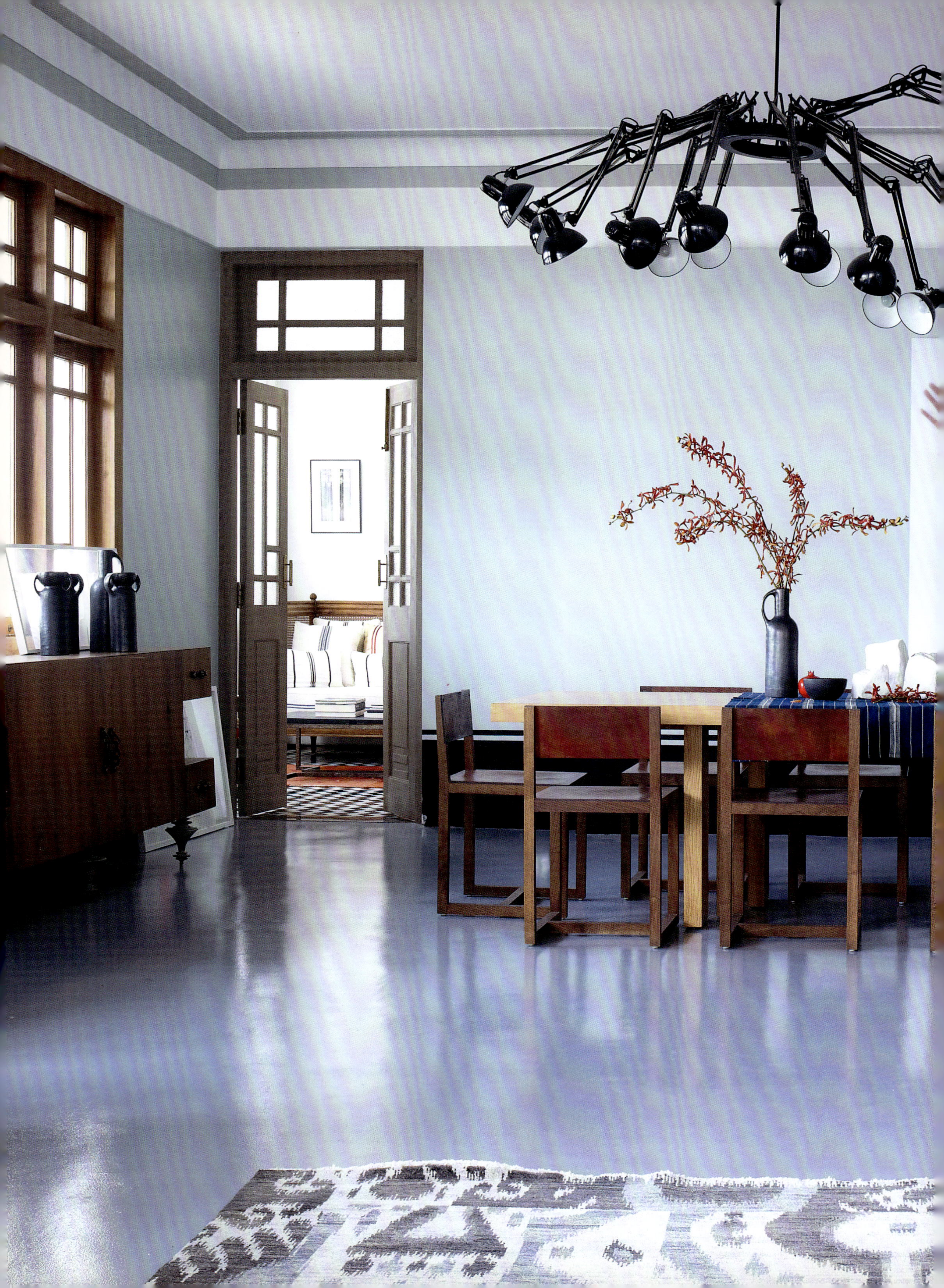

◀ Cleo the collie next to a Poltrona Frau table, BDDW chairs, and Ron Gilad's *Dear Ingo* ceiling light for Moooi. The artwork is a Shilpa Gupta C-print diasec. • Collie Cleo posiert vor dem Poltrona-Frau-Tisch mit Stühlen von BDDW. Lüster *Dear Ingo* von Ron Gilad für Moooi. C-Print als Diasec von Shilpa Gupta. • Une table Poltrona Frau, des chaises de BDDW et le lustre *Dear Ingo* de Ron Gilad pour Moooi ; au mur, un tirage Diasec de Shilpa Gupta.

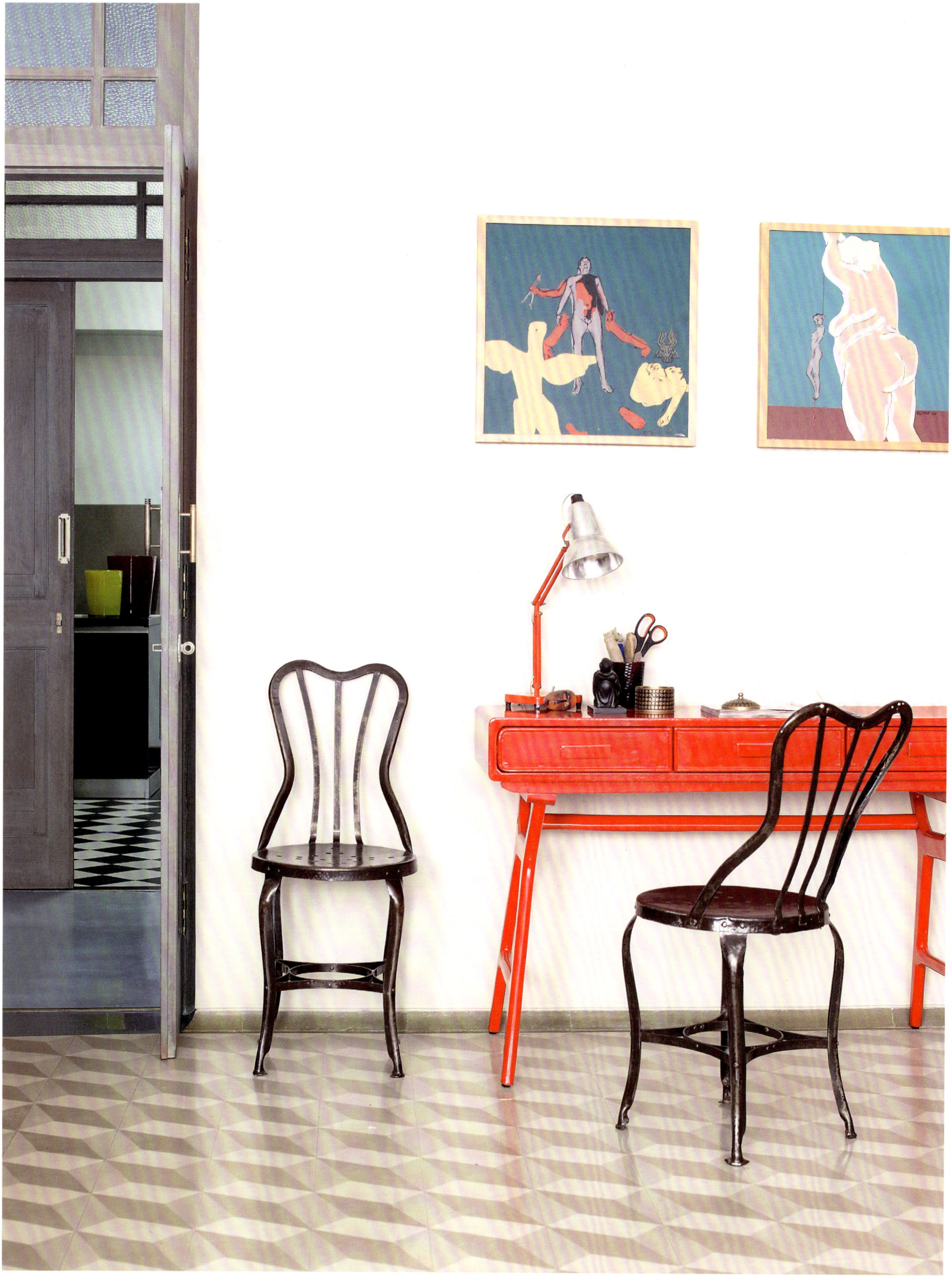

When Cecilia Morelli Parikh and her husband, Rohan, first visited their apartment, it hadn't been updated in 80 years. "It was filthy," she recalls. "The first thing I did was put my scarf over my mouth." Still, they were seduced not only by the select location, but also by the original Art Deco features. "We wanted to pay respect to the heritage of the building," she notes. They moved the living and dining room to the front, and stripped the doors and windows of layers of paint to reveal the Burmese teak underneath. They also replaced the terrazzo floors with geometric designs using local tiles and marble. It took four months for the marble chevron in the master bedroom to be laid "and another six months before that to persuade the tiler to do it." Rohan Parikh describes his wife's tastes as "quite stern, monkish." She herself wanted to keep things simple and import as little as possible. One exception is the set of BDDW dining chairs, which got stuck at customs during the monsoon rains. "They arrived with these incredible stains," she explains. "To me, they are now 100 percent more beautiful."

„ALS WIR DIE WOHNUNG ZUM ERSTEN MAL BETRATEN, ZOG ICH SOFORT MEINEN SCHAL VOR DEN MUND." CECILIA MORELLI PARIKH

Seit 80 Jahren hatte man in den Räumen nichts mehr verändert. „Es war entsetzlich schmutzig", erinnert sich Cecilia Morelli Parikh. Dennoch erlagen sie und ihr Mann Rohan sofort den Reizen des Apartments: exquisite Lage und Art-Déco-Elemente. „Wir wollten der Geschichte des Gebäudes Respekt zollen", sagt die Inhaberin des Concept-Store Le Mill. Das Paar verlegte Wohn- und Esszimmer zur Meeresseite und entfernte mehrere Farbschichten von Türen und Fenstern, um das Burma-Teak freizulegen. Den Terrazzobelag ersetzten sie durch Fliesen und Marmor. Letzteren im Schlafzimmer als Fischgrätmuster zu verlegen, dauerte vier Monate „plus sechs weitere davor, um den Handwerker überhaupt dazu zu bewegen". Morelli Parikh stellte sich einen fast mönchischen Look vor, für den möglichst wenig importiert werden sollte. Eine Ausnahme bilden die BDDW-Stühle um den Esstisch, die ausgerechnet während des Monsuns beim Zoll feststeckten. „Sie kamen mit unfassbaren Regenflecken an", berichtet sie. „Ich finde, das hat sie nur noch schöner gemacht."

La première fois que Cecilia Morelli Parikh et son mari Rohan sont entrés dans l'appartement, il n'avait pas été rénové depuis 80 ans. « C'était immonde. J'ai dû me couvrir le nez avec mon écharpe », se souvient la propriétaire du concept store Le Mill. Toutefois, ils ont été séduits par l'emplacement et l'architecture Art déco. Ils ont déplacé le séjour et la salle à manger côté mer, décapé les portes et les fenêtres en teck birman et remplacé le terrazzo par du carrelage et du marbre. Il a fallu quatre mois pour poser les carreaux en chevrons dans la chambre principale « et six autres mois avant ça pour convaincre le carreleur ». Rohan Parikh qualifie le goût de sa femme d'« austère et monacal ». Voulant conserver le lieu « dans son jus », elle a importé fort peu de meubles, à l'exception de chaises de salle à manger signées BDDW. Coincées à la douane pendant la mousson, « elles sont arrivées couvertes de traces de pluie fascinantes », explique Morelli Parikh. « Je les trouve infiniment plus belles ainsi. »

234 Two Raghava KK oil paintings hang above a lacquered desk from Le Mill in the study. The industrial chairs and lamp were found at Mumbai's Chor Bazaar. • Zwei Ölbilder von Raghava KK hängen über dem Tischchen von Le Mill im Büro. Metallstühle und Lampe kommen vom Chor Bazaar in Mumbai. • Dans le bureau, deux huiles de Raghava KK au-dessus d'un secrétaire laqué de Le Mill. La lampe et les chaises industrielles viennent du Chor Bazaar de Mumbai.

▲ A master bath modeled after washrooms in 1950s New York. The couple kept the red table from a previous rental. • Das Bad ist von Waschräumen im New York der 1950er inspiriert. Der rote Tisch ist eins der wenigen Möbel aus der vorigen Wohnung des Paars. • La salle de bains principale évoque le New York des années 1950. Le guéridon est l'un des rares meubles rescapés du précédent appartement du couple.

▶ An oiled teak bench with a Sri Lankan cotton cushion stands on the master bedroom floor made of marble tiles. Self-portrait by artist Tejal Shah. • Im marmorgefliesten Schlafzimmer steht eine Bettbank aus geöltem Teak mit Kattunpolster aus Sri Lanka. Das große Foto ist ein Selbstporträt von Tejal Shah. • Dans la chambre principale au sol en marbre, un banc en teck huilé avec un coussin en coton du Sri Lanka. Au-dessus, à droite, un autoportrait de Tejal Shah.

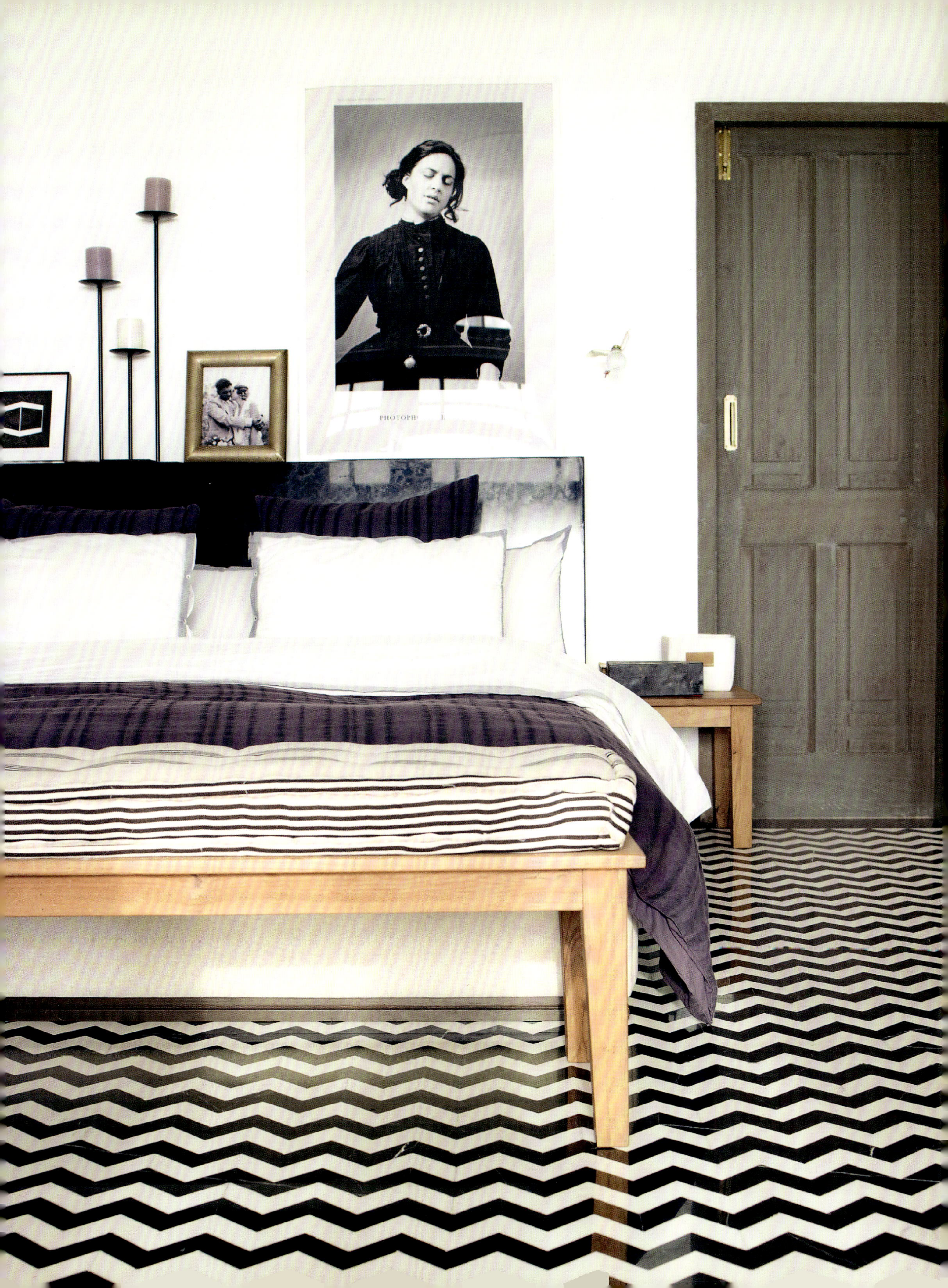

MELINDA RITZ

A MANSION FOR A FAMILY IN BEVERLY HILLS

WHO Los Angeles–based interior and set designer. **WHAT** A mock-Tudor, three-bedroom house built in the 1930s for the son of John Clum, the federal agent who captured Geronimo in 1877. **THE CLIENTS** TV producer Max Mutchnick, who co-created the *Will & Grace* sitcom, his lawyer husband, Erik Hyman, and their twin daughters Evan and Rose. **COLLABORATORS** Ritz worked on the project with architect Tim Campbell and landscape designer Bill Shapiro. **DROLL DAD** Her father Harry was a member of the Ritz Brothers, a comedy trio who starred in films like *The Goldwyn Follies*. **SPORTING PAST** The house's previous owner was Pete Sampras, who installed (you guessed it) a tennis court on the property. **IN THE NICK OF TIME** Mutchnick and Hyman were wed in the garden the last day same-sex marriage was legal in California. In the course of the ceremony, they had to switch off the fountain so the soft-spoken rabbi could be heard.

PHOTOGRAPHED BY STEPHAN JULLIARD/TRIPOD AGENCY   STYLED BY IAN PHILLIPS   PORTRAIT BY ERIK NELDER

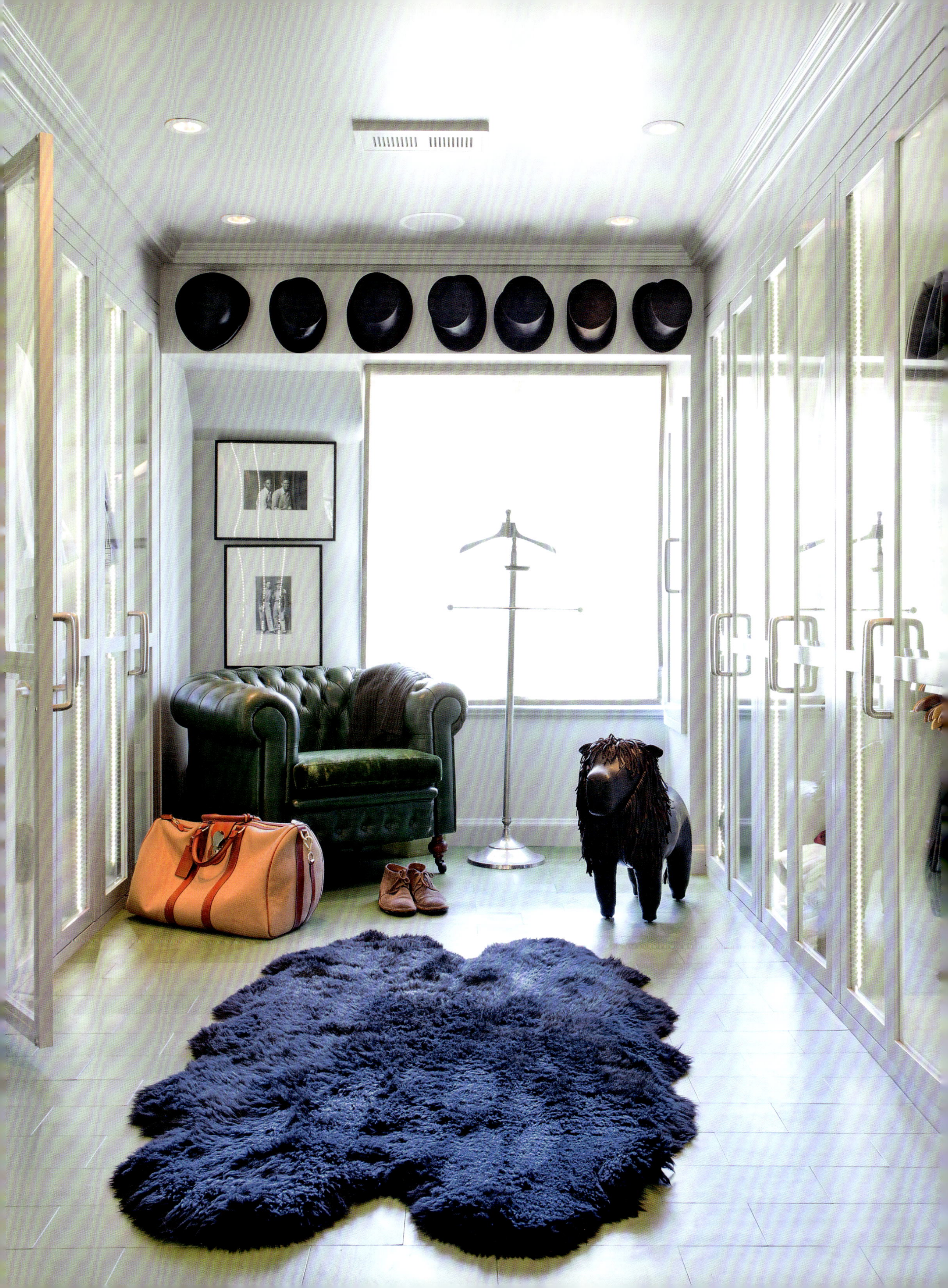

239 A dandy dressing room: glass-fronted doors make it easy to choose outfits. Leather floors by Illuminare are comfortable underfoot. Valet stand by Nicky Haslam. • Ein Dandy-Traum: In der Ankleide erleichtern Glastüren die Auswahl. Lederfliesen von Illuminare schmeicheln den Sohlen. Stummer Diener von Nicky Haslam. • Un vrai dressing de dandy : portes en verre, sol en cuir d'Illuminare, valet de Nicky Haslam.

▼ "Tudors are not that common in Beverly Hills," notes architect Tim Campbell, who oversaw the structural renovation. "It's unique in the neighborhood." The former owner, Pete Sampras, extended the property significantly. Planters from Mecox Gardens flank a teak bench. • Häuser im Tudor-Stil sieht man nicht oft in Beverly Hills", bemerkt Architekt Tim Campbell, der den Umbau leitete. „Hier in der Nachbarschaft ist dieses das einzige." Der vorherige Besitzer Pete Sampras erweiterte das Anwesen deutlich. Pflanzgefäße von Mecox Gardens flankieren eine Teakbank. • « Le style Tudor n'est pas courant à Beverly Hills », observe Tim Campbell, qui a supervisé la rénovation. L'ancien propriétaire Pete Sampras a considérablement agrandi la propriété. Des jardinières de Mecox Gardens flanquent un banc en teck.

▶ *Backflip, Paradise Cove, 1987* is only one of numerous Herb Ritts photos in the house. The runner on the stairs was made from wool kilims. • *Backflip, Paradise Cove, 1987* ist eine von zahllosen Herb-Ritts-Fotografien im Haus. Der Treppenläufer wurde aus Wollkelims zusammengesetzt. • *Backflip, Paradise Cove, 1987* est l'une des nombreuses photos d'Herb Ritts de la maison. Le chemin d'escalier est composé de kilims en laine.

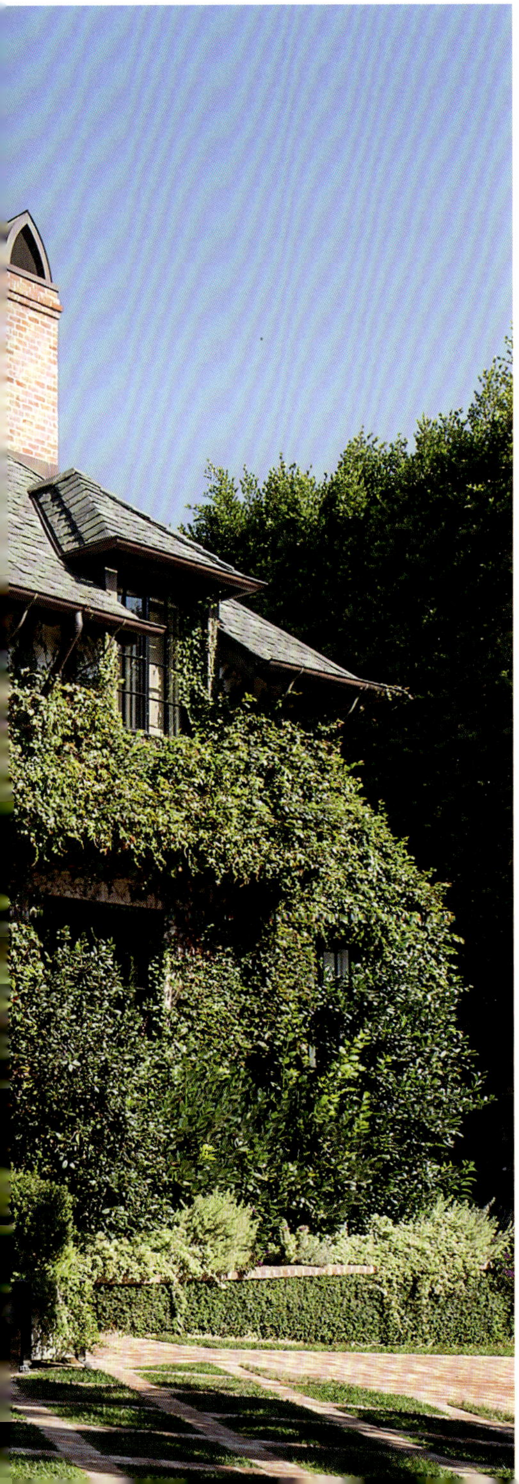

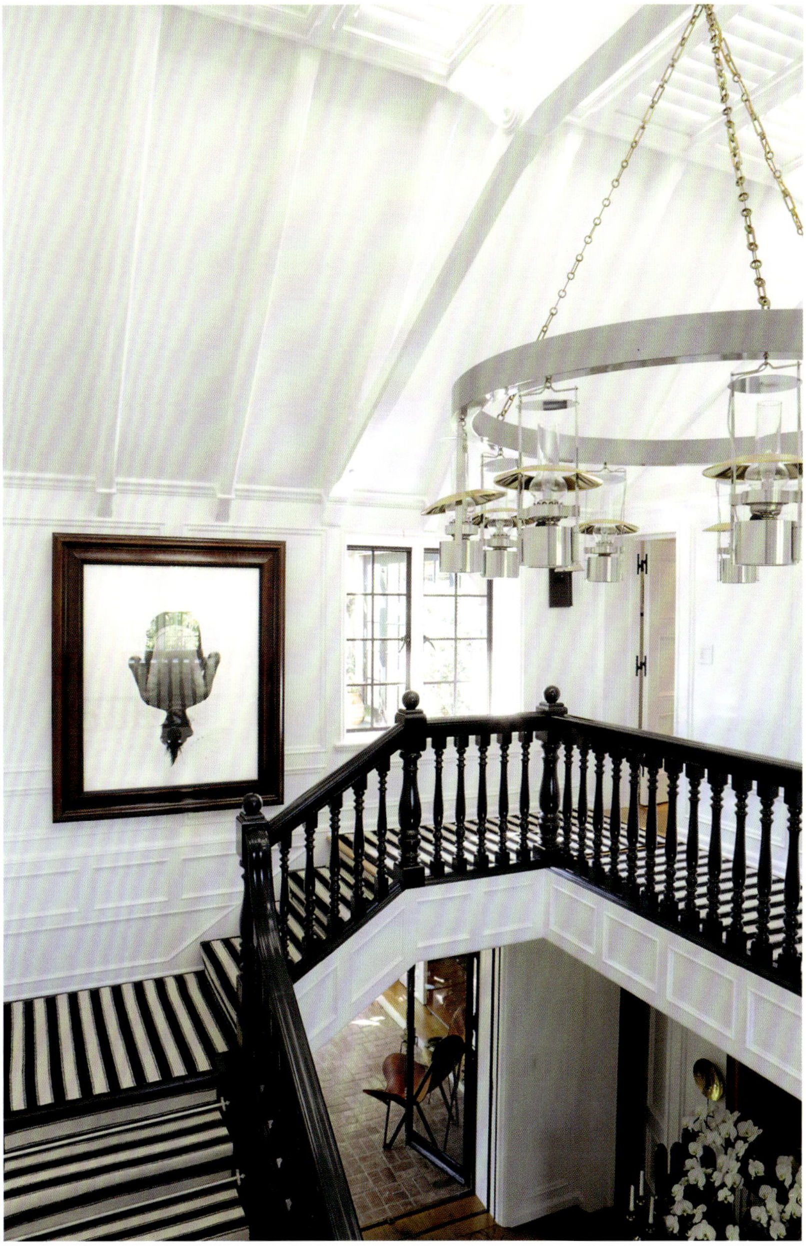

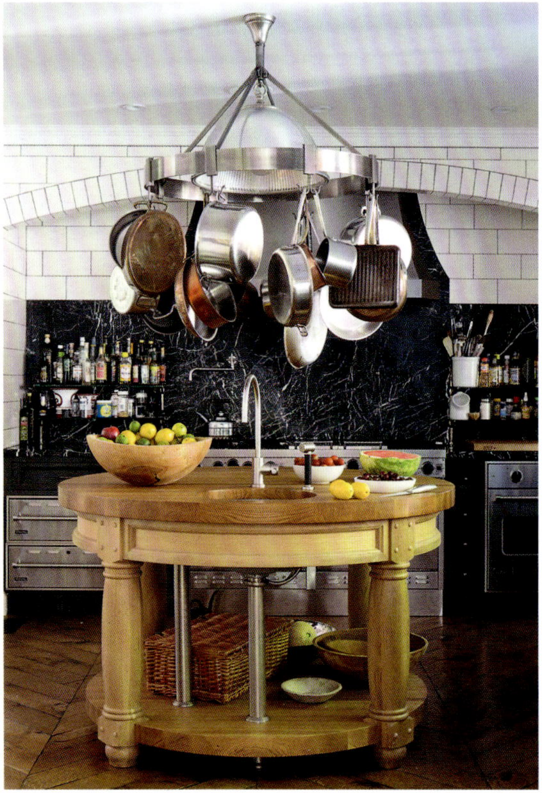
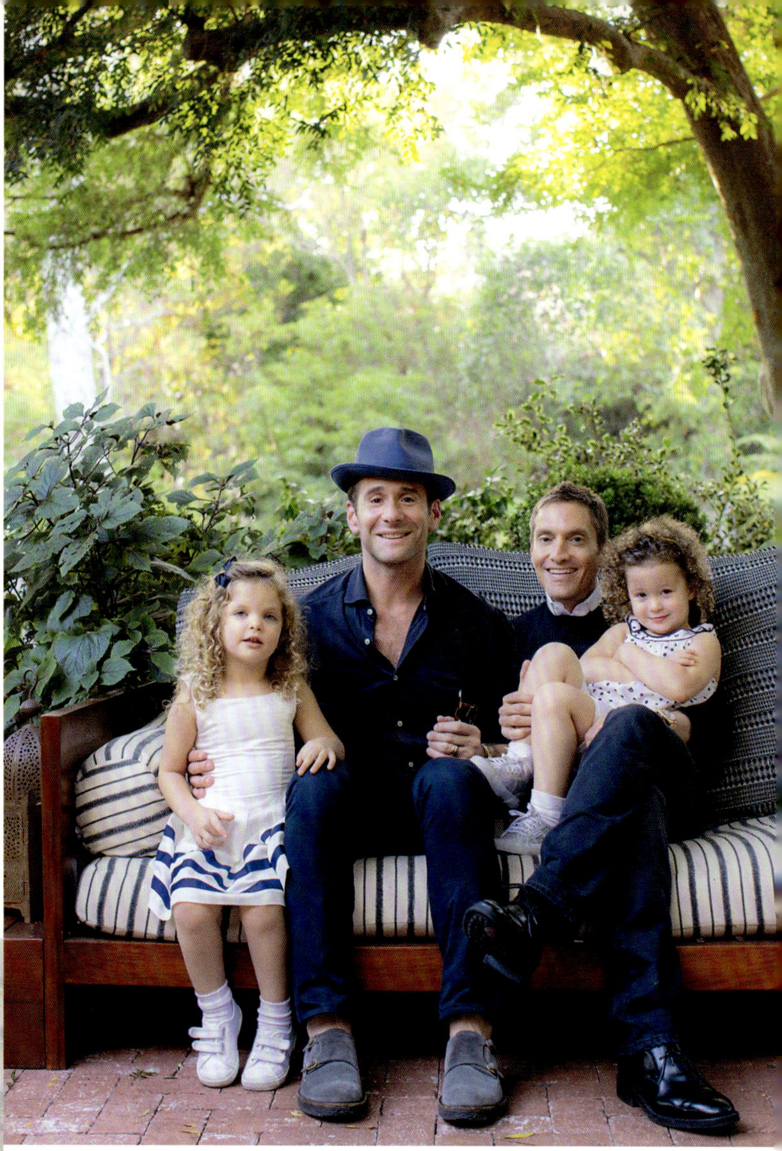
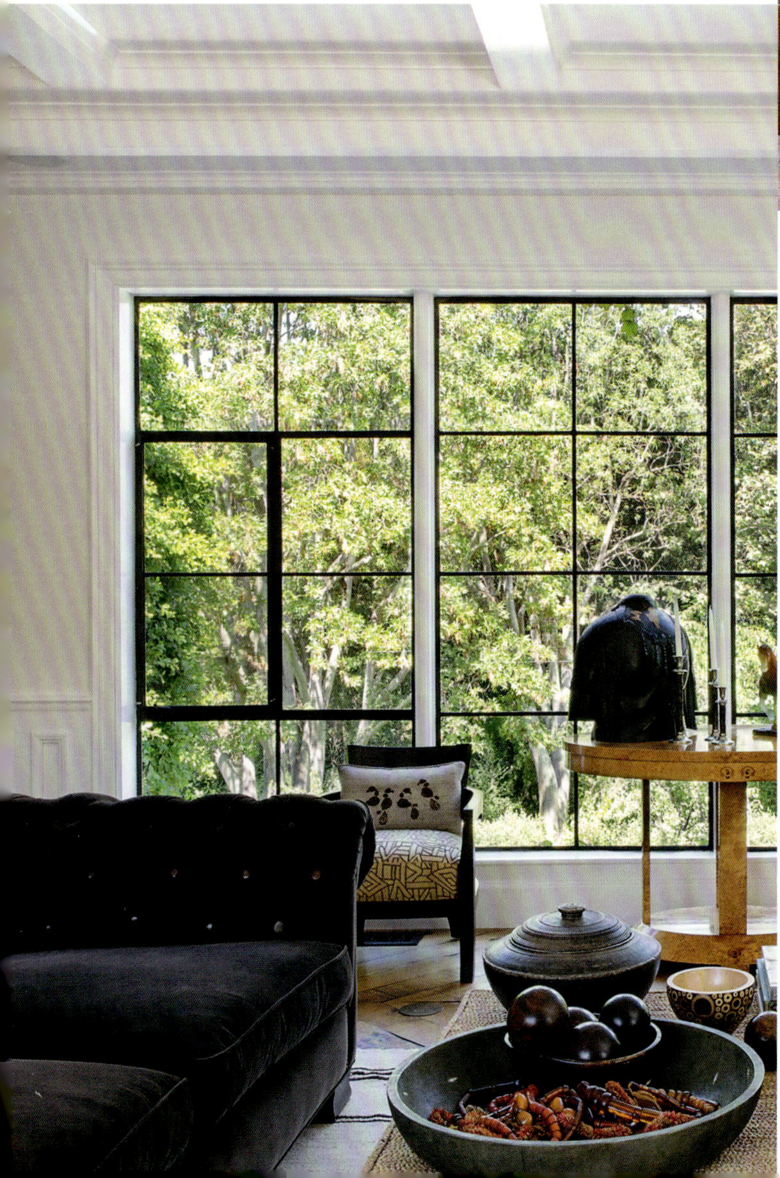
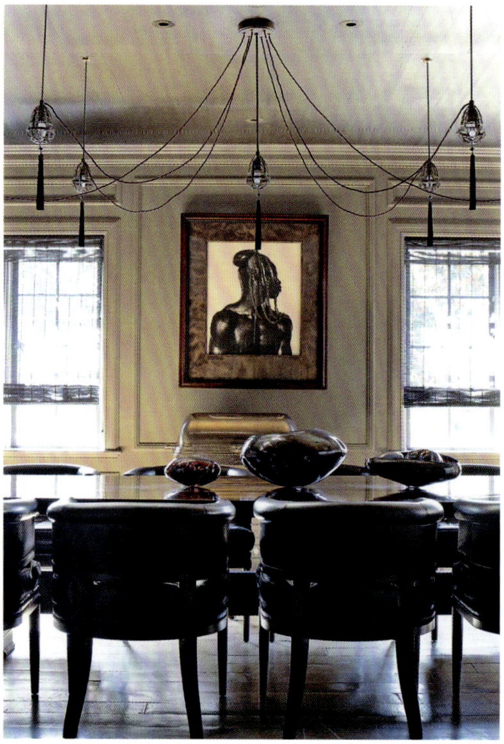

◀ *(clockwise)* In the white-tiled kitchen, pans hooked on a custom pendant hang above an island inspired by an Edwin Lutyens design; a family of four, *from left:* Rose, Max, Erik and Evan; leather-upholstered *Quiver Klismos Chairs* by Soane Britain flank the Indian rosewood dining table. On the wall is *Djimon with Octopus, 1989* by Herb Ritts; a Roman torso stands on a Russian table in the sitting room that opens up to nature.

• *(im Uhrzeigersinn)* In der weiß gefliesten Küche hängt Kochgeschirr an der eigens gefertigten Deckenleuchte, die Insel ist einem Entwurf von Edwin Lutyens nachempfunden; eine moderne Familie, von li.: Rose, Max, Erik und Evan; ledergepolsterte *Quiver Klismos Chairs* von Soane Britain am Esstisch aus Ostindischem Palisander. An der Wand *Djimon with Octopus, 1989* von Herb Ritts; römischer Torso auf einem russischen Tisch im Wohnzimmer, das sich ins Grüne öffnet.

• *(Dans le sens des aiguilles d'une montre)* Les casseroles sont suspendues au-dessus d'un îlot de cuisine inspiré par Edwin Lutyens ; les quatre membres de la famille : Rose, Max, Erik et Evan ; des chaises *Quiver Klismos* en cuir de Soane Britain autour d'une table indienne en palissandre. Au mur, *Djimon with Octopus, 1989* d'Herb Ritts ; dans le salon ouvert sur la verdure, un torse romain sur un guéridon russe.

▼ A portrait of TV chef Julia Child by an unknown artist hangs near the door to the walk-in fridge. Ritz originally bought the Art Deco clock as a prop for *Will & Grace.* • Ein Porträt der Fernsehköchin Julia Childs hängt neben der Tür zur Kühlkammer. Die Art-déco-Uhr kaufte Ritz ursprünglich als Requisit für *Will and Grace.* • Un portrait du chef Julia Child est accroché près de la chambre froide. L'horloge Art déco a servi d'élément décoratif pour la série télévisée *Will and Grace.*

▼ Oriental touches in the guest room include a vintage Chinese rug and Asian metal bedside lamps. The wallpaper is from Fromental's Prunus collection. • Das Gästezimmer gibt sich fernöstlich mit chinesischem Vintage-Teppich, asiatischen Metall-Leuchten und einer Tapete aus Fromentals Prunus-Kollektion. • Un parfum d'Orient dans la chambre d'amis : tapis chinois, lampes de chevet en métal et papier peint de la collection Prunus de la maison Fromental.

▶ "The backyard is essentially a private park," remarks owner Max Mutchnick. It stretches over one acre, features trees more than 38 meters (125 feet) high, plus an elliptically shaped pool. Loungers by The Heveningham Collection upholstered in a Ralph Lauren striped fabric. Concrete table from Mecox Gardens. • „Der Garten ist unser privater Park", sagt Hausherr Max Mutchnick. Auf über 4000 m² wachsen einige fast 40 Meter hohe Bäume. Am ovalen Pool stehen Liegen von The Heveningham Collection, bezogen mit Streifenstoff von Ralph Lauren. Betontisch von Mecox Gardens. • Un parc privé : le jardin s'étire sur un demi-hectare, avec des arbres de plus de 38 m de haut et une piscine elliptique. Chaises longues de The Heveningham Collection tapissées d'une toile rayée Ralph Lauren. Table en béton de Mecox Gardens.

RITZ 245

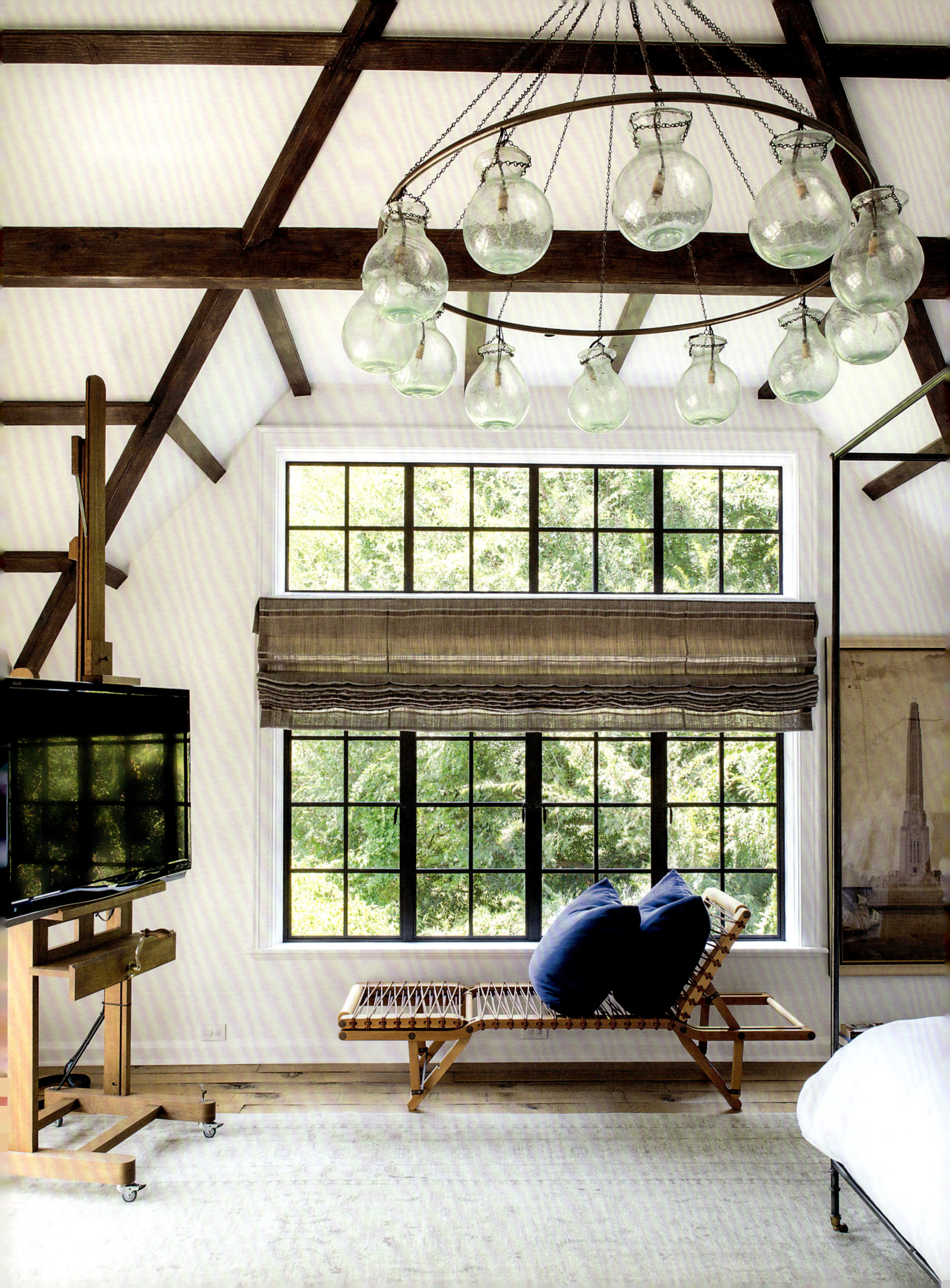

"MY CLIENTS SAID, 'YOU CAN USE ANY COLOR AS LONG AS IT'S GRAY, BLACK, OR BROWN.'" MELINDA RITZ

More than anything, Max Mutchnick and Erik Hyman wanted a "light, crisp home—a little edgy," that would "match the vibe of a couple of gay guys." Taking her inspiration from a traditional British gentlemen's club, Ritz put down oak floors with an antique finish and conceived a spectacular master bathroom modeled on a barber's shop. It features cozy club chairs and a dramatic round tub room with a freestanding bath and walls clad in waterproof plaster. She also mixed in Colonial touches: Turkish kilims were turned into runners, and a collection of African, Hawaiian, and Tahitian beads is displayed in the sitting room. The latter was sourced by Hyman and his late partner, photographer Herb Ritts, a number of whose most iconic images are scattered throughout the house. "I trust Melinda explicitly," enthuses Mutchnick. "She always gets it right." Even when she breaks those color "rules." Just check out the avocado-green dressing room floor or the guest bed upholstered in yellow velvet!

„Meine Auftraggeber sagten: ‚Bei der Einrichtung ist uns jede Farbe recht, solange sie grau, schwarz oder braun ist'", lacht Melinda Ritz. Doch in erster Linie wünschten sich Max Mutchnick und Erik Hyman ein „helles, frisches Zuhause – ein bisschen *edgy*", passend „zum *vibe* eines schwulen Paars". Als ihre Hauptinspiration wählte Ritz britische Gentleman's Clubs: Sie verlegte Eichendielen mit Antik-Finish und entwarf ein spektakuläres Bad mit Clubsesseln und einem runden, wasserfest verputzten Extraraum für die freistehende Wanne. Dazu kam ein Schuss Kolonialstil: Türkische Kelims wurden zu Treppenläufern, und im Wohnzimmer ist eine Sammlung afrikanischer, hawaiianischer und tahitianischer Glasperlen zu bewundern. Hyman hat sie noch mit seinem einstigen Lebensgefährten angelegt, dem 2002 verstorbenen Fotografen Herb Ritts, dessen ikonischen Aufnahmen man hier mehrfach begegnet. „Ich vertraue Melinda absolut", begeistert sich Mutchnick. „Ihr gelingt alles." Wohl gerade, weil sie sich nicht immer an sein „Gesetz der Neutralität" in Sachen Farben hielt – siehe den avocadogrünen Boden der Ankleide oder das mit gelbem Samt bezogene Gästebett.

«Mes clients m'ont dit : ‹Utilisez n'importe quelle couleur, tant que c'est du gris, du noir ou du marron›», s'amuse Melinda Ritz. Surtout, ils voulaient une maison lumineuse, joyeuse et légèrement excentrique à l'image d'un couple gay. S'inspirant des clubs de gentlemen anglais, la décoratrice d'intérieur a posé des parquets en chêne vernis à l'ancienne et créé une salle de bains spectaculaire évoquant une échoppe de barbier avec des fauteuils club et une baignoire dans une pièce ronde aux murs en plâtre imperméables. Elle a ajouté ici et là des touches coloniales : des kilims turcs et, dans le salon, des perles africaines, hawaïennes et tahitiennes collectionnées par Hyman et son ancien compagnon Herb Ritts, dont les œuvres parsèment la demeure. « J'ai une confiance aveugle en Melinda. Elle trouve toujours le ton juste », déclare Mutchnick. Même quand elle rompt avec le code de couleurs, comme dans le cas du sol vert du dressing ou du lit d'ami tapissé de velours jaune.

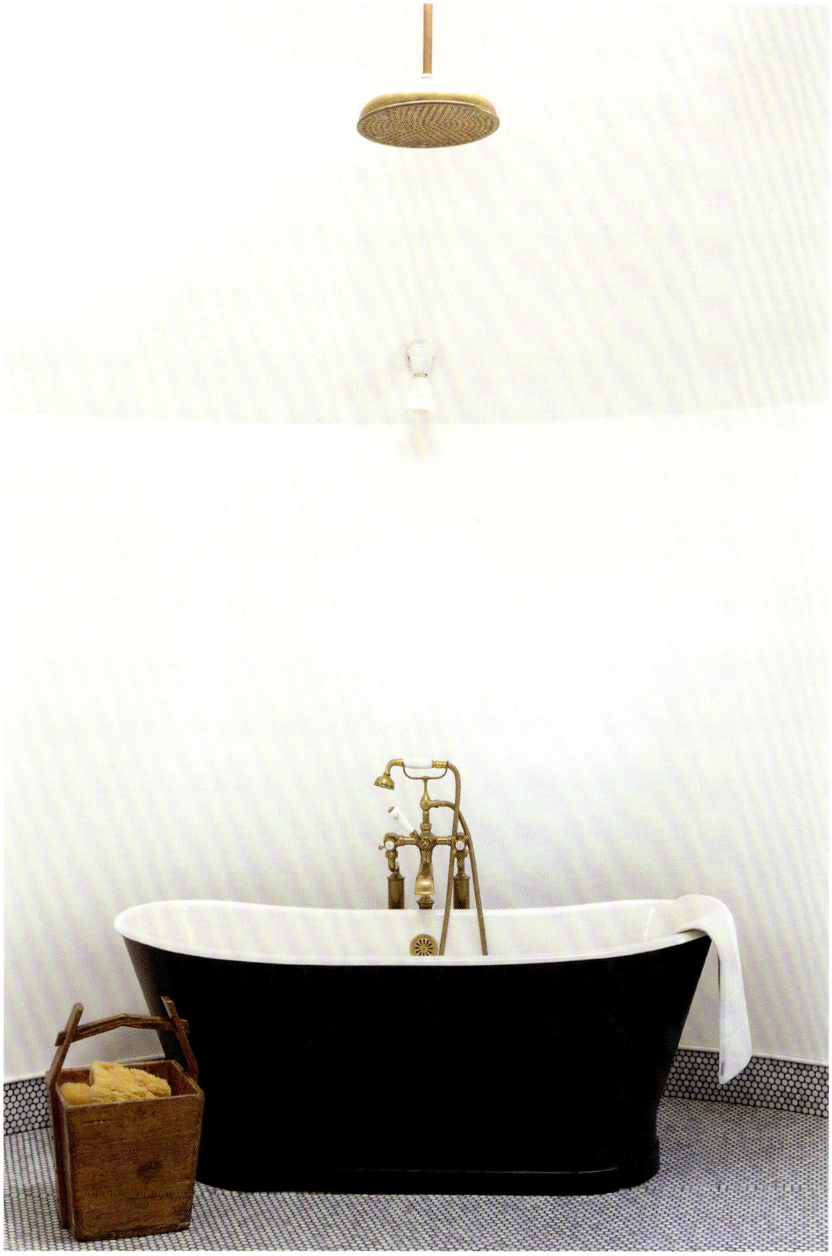

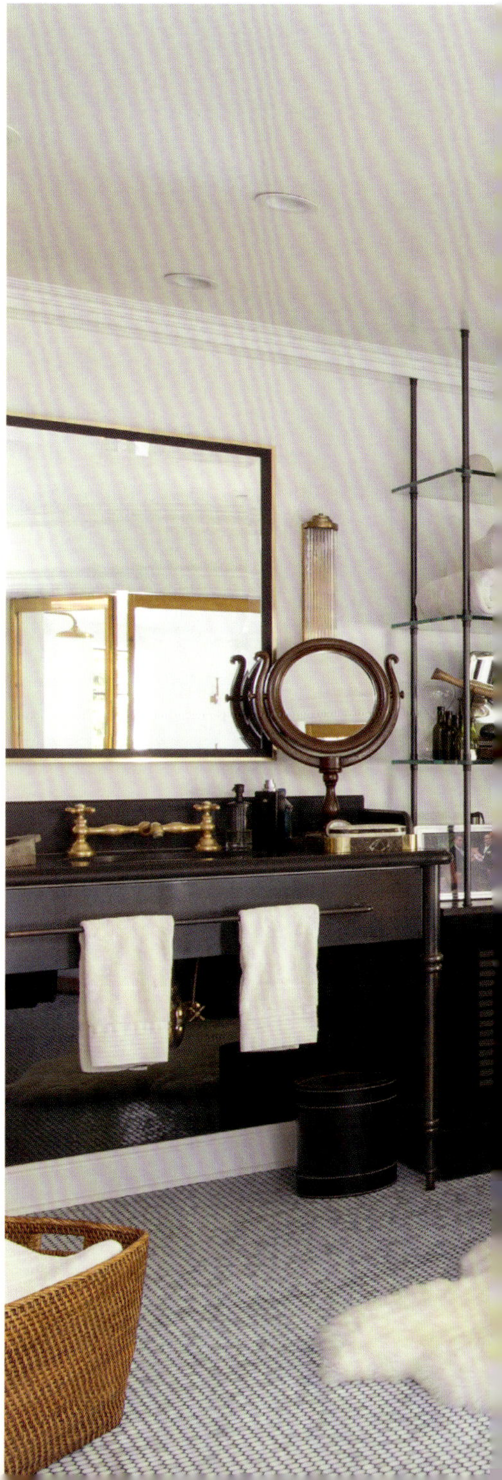

246 Artistic entertainment: the TV rests on an easel in the master bedroom. *Pippa* daybed by Rena Dumas for Hermès and custom chandelier made from Egyptian hand-blown glass. To the right of the window is a 19th-century Italian architectural drawing acquired from the late Amy Perlin. • Kunstvolle Unterhaltung: Der Fernseher steht auf einer Staffelei im Masterbedroom. Liege *Pippa* von Rena Dumas für Hermès, eigens gefertigter Lüster aus mundgeblasenen ägyptischen Gläsern. Neben dem Fenster eine italienische Architekturzeichnung des 19. Jahrhunderts aus dem Besitz der legendären Antikhändlerin Amy Perlin. • Dans la chambre principale, la télévision repose sur un chevalet. Lit de repos *Pippa* de Rena Dumas pour Hermès et lustre improvisé avec des bocaux égyptiens en verre soufflé. À droite de la fenêtre, un dessin d'architecture italien du 19ᵉ siècle acheté à feu Amy Perlin.

◀ ▼ Fit for a barber: French 1930s leather armchairs, glass floor tiles by Waterworks, and a clock that once hung in an Associated Press newsroom add character to the bathroom. The en-suite tub chamber is round, featuring Barber Wilsons plumbing fixtures and walls covered in a waterproof exterior plaster. • Barbiersalon deluxe: Französische Ledersessel aus den 1930ern, gläsernes Bodenmosaik von Waterworks und eine Uhr, die einst in einem Newsroom von Associated Press hing, bringen Charakter ins Bad. Die Wand der anschließenden runden Badekammer wurde mit Außenputz wasserdicht gemacht. Dusche von Barber Wilsons. • Un vrai salon de barbier : fauteuils en cuir français des années 1930, carrelage en pâte de verre de Waterworks, horloge provenant d'un bureau de l'Associated Press. Dans la salle ronde attenante, la robinetterie vient de chez Barber Wilsons et les murs sont enduits de plâtre imperméable.

JOHN ROBSHAW

HIS MULTI-CULTI APARTMENT IN NEW YORK

WHO Globe-trotting American textile designer. **WHAT** A 130 m² (1,400 sq. ft.), two-bedroom apartment in one of Manhattan's earliest co-ops, the Amalgamated Dwellings. **WHERE** The Lower East Side. **COLLABORATOR** Robshaw revamped the flat with his decorator friend, Sara Bengur. **FROM ART TO LIFE** In his early career, he worked as an installer at Gagosian Gallery and as assistant to Julian Schnabel. He also had his own painting studio in the squash court of an abandoned Wall Street men's club. **GIVING BACK** He is busy developing an NGO side to his business, working with weavers in the Philippines and northeast India. **PRESIDENTIAL PRINTS** Decorator Michael S. Smith chose Robshaw's bedding for First Daughters Malia and Sasha Obama's rooms at the White House. **IN PRINT** His first book, *John Robshaw Prints: Textiles, Block Printing, Global Inspiration, and Interiors*, was published in 2012. **DEAD RINGER** In person, he looks uncannily like actor Hugh Grant.

PHOTOGRAPHED BY WILLIAM WALDRON FOR ELLE DECOR STYLED BY ANITA SARSIDI

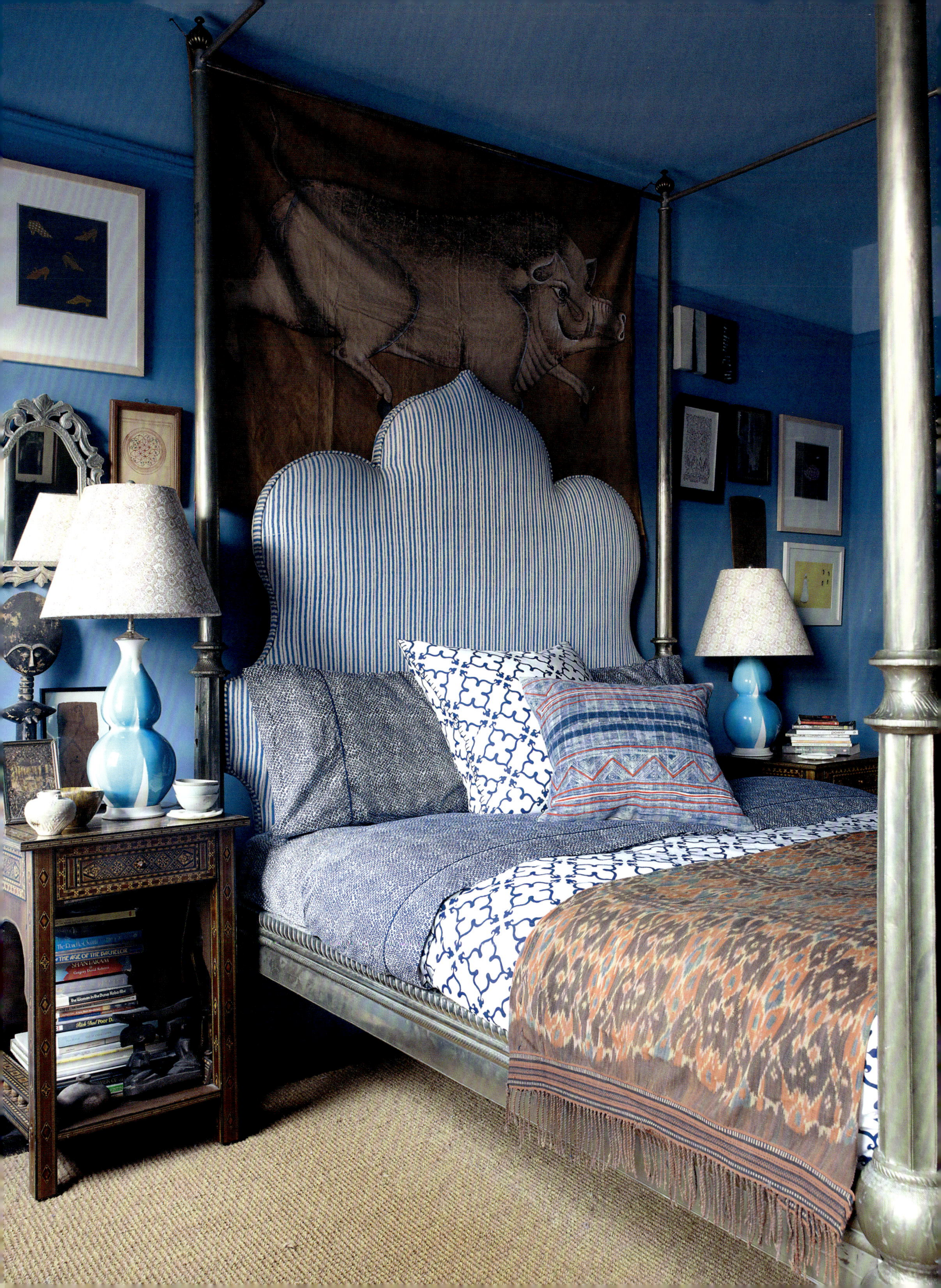

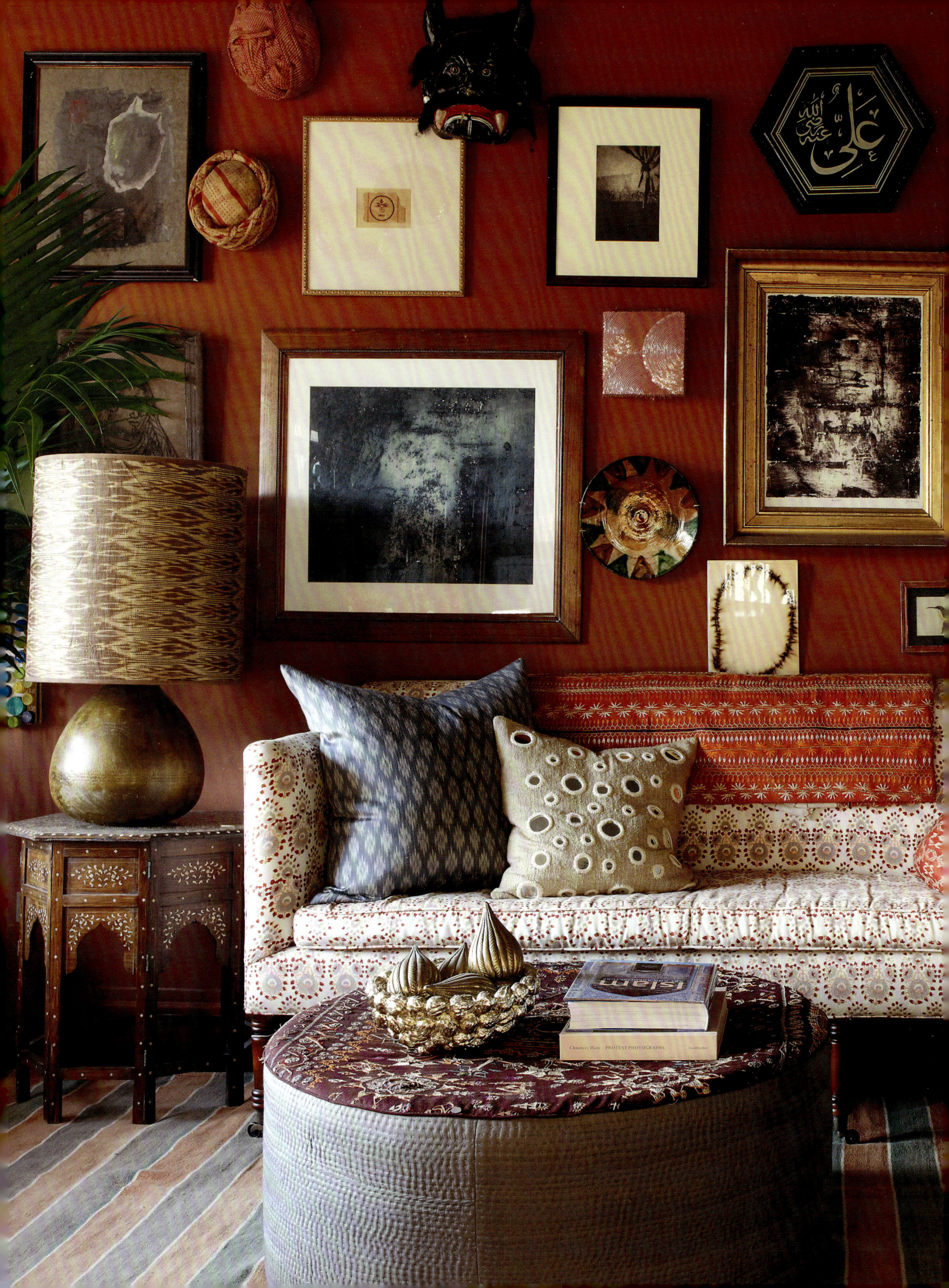
Islam
Chauncey Hare PROTEST PHOTOGRAPHS

251 A painting of a boar from Jaipur and mid-20th-century Indonesian throw in the master bedroom. Bed linen by John Robshaw Textiles. Lamps by Christopher Spitzmiller. • Den Eber über seinem Bett kaufte Robshaw in Jaipur, die Überdecke stammt aus Indonesien. Bettwäsche von John Robshaw Textiles, Lampen von Christopher Spitzmiller. • Dans la chambre principale, une peinture de sanglier, achetée à Jaipur, et un jeté de lit indonésien vintage. Les draps sont de John Robshaw Textiles ; les lampes de Christopher Spitzmiller.

◀ Mango-wood lamps, tables with camel-bone inlay, and a couch upholstered in the cotton-linen blend *Lanka Oyster* by Robshaw. The artworks on the wall include his own etchings. • Leuchten aus Mangoholz auf Tischen mit Kamelknochenintarsien flankieren ein Sofa, das mit Robshaws Baumwoll-Leinen-Mix *Lanka Oyster* bezogen ist. Unter den Bildern sind zwei seiner eigenen Radierungen. • Des lampes en manguier et des tables indiennes incrustées d'os de chameau flanquent un canapé tapissé d'un tissu de Robshaw, *Lanka Oyster,* mélange de coton et de lin. Parmi les œuvres au mur, deux de ses gravures.

▲ Vintage Indian rug and Richard Wrightman desk and chair in the study-cum-guest room. • Ein indischer Vintage-Teppich „erdet" das Arbeits- und Gästezimmer. Tisch und Stuhl von Richard Wrightman. • Dans le bureau-chambre d'amis, un vieux tapis indien. Bureau et fauteuil sont de Richard Wrightman.

▲ A portrait of an Indian filmstar and folk paintings from Bihar hang above antique campaign chests in the master bedroom. The feather headdress is from Zimbabwe. • Über den antiken *campaign chests* im Schlafzimmer hängt das Porträt eines indischen Filmstars zwischen nordindischer Volkskunst. Der Feder-Kopfputz stammt aus Simbabwe. • Le portrait d'une star indienne et des peintures du Bihar sont accrochés au-dessus d'une commode de bateau dans la chambre du maître. La coiffe en plumes vient du Zimbabwe.

▶ In the living room, a John Derian chair covered in a Thai fabric sits in front of an ink-and-gesso painting by Robshaw and spears from Nagaland. • Im Wohnzimmer steht ein Stuhl von John Derian mit Bezug aus Thailand vor einem Robshaw-Gemälde in Gesso und Tinte und zwei Speeren aus Nagaland. • Dans le séjour, un fauteuil de John Derian tapissé d'un tissu thaïlandais se tient devant une œuvre à l'encre et au plâtre de Robshaw et des lances du Nagaland.

"I want all the colors, processes, and designs from each culture to blend." John Robshaw is talking about his fabric designs, but he could just as well be referring to his bohemian-chic apartment, which brings together a heady mix of objects. Among them are Indonesian textiles, a Syrian table, an antique shield from Papua New Guinea, and spears from Nagaland in northeast India. Describing his style with typical understatement as "hodgepodgey" and "cross-bred," Robshaw avows a love of both folk art ("completely fantastic and creative") and the color blue. There is lots of the latter in his home, though decorator friend Sara Bengur suggested warming things up with a terra-cotta "art wall." Needless to say, they used many of his own fabrics and artwork, but also pieces from designer friends. The bedside lamps, for instance, are by Christopher Spitzmiller, whom Robshaw has known since childhood. Nothing is ever fixed. Instead, things evolve with every new find. "The nice thing is adding on," Robshaw enthuses. "You can keep building and building. It's really rather like a puzzle."

„All die Farben, Techniken und Ornamente verschiedener Kulturen sollen verschmelzen." Was John Robshaw über seine Stoffdekore sagt, passt genauso auf sein New Yorker Apartment, dessen Boheme-Chic einen berauschenden Mix umfasst: indonesische Textilien, einen Tisch aus Syrien, einen antiken Schild aus Papua-Neuguinea, Speere aus Nagaland in Nordostindien. Robshaw, der seinen Stil mit typischem Understatement „Mischmasch" oder „hybrid" nennt, begeistert sich besonders für Volkskunst („absolut fantasievoll und kreativ") und für die Farbe Blau. In seiner Wohnung ist sie reichlich vertreten, wobei Interiordesignerin Sara Bengur die terrakottafarbene „Kunstwand" ins Spiel brachte, um alles wärmer wirken zu lassen. Neben Robshaws eigenen Stoffen und Kunstwerken verwendeten die beiden vor allem Stücke von Designer-Freunden wie die Nachttischlampen von Christopher Spitzmiller, den Robshaw seit Kindertagen kennt. Mit jedem neuen Fund entwickelt sich die Einrichtung weiter, nichts bleibt lange, wie es ist. „Es macht Spaß, Dinge hinzuzufügen", freut sich Robshaw. „Man kann das immer weiter fortsetzen. Es ist wirklich wie ein Puzzle."

«JE VEUX QUE LES COULEURS, LES TECHNIQUES ET LES MOTIFS DE TOUTES LES CULTURES FUSIONNENT.» JOHN ROBSHAW

Robshaw parle de ses textiles, mais il pourrait tout autant décrire son appartement au chic bohème où règne un mélange étourdissant d'objets, parmi lesquels des tissus indonésiens, une table syrienne, un bouclier ancien de Papouasie-Nouvelle-Guinée et des lances du Nagaland, dans le Nord de l'Inde. S'il qualifie humblement son style de «fourre-tout» et d'«hybride», Robshaw proclame son amour de l'art populaire («fantastique et créatif») ainsi que du bleu, présent presque partout – bien que son amie décoratrice Sara Bengur lui ait conseillé de réchauffer l'ambiance avec un «mur d'art» dans les tons terre cuite. Ensemble, ils ont utilisé bon nombre de ses œuvres et de ses textiles, conjugués avec des pièces de ses amis designers. Les lampes de chevet, par exemple, sont de Christopher Spitzmiller qu'il connaît depuis l'enfance. Rien n'est jamais établi et le décor évolue en fonction de ses trouvailles. «J'aime additionner. On peut ainsi construire peu à peu, comme un puzzle.»

▲ An antique shield from Papua New Guinea in the study. The cane stool is another Jaipur purchase. • Im Arbeitszimmer gibt ein antiker Schild aus Papua-Neuguinea der Bibliothek von textilem Fachwissen etwas Verwegenes. Korbhocker aus Jaipur. • Un bouclier ancien papou ajoute une touche d'aventure à la bibliothèque dédiée aux arts textiles. Le tabouret en jonc vient lui aussi de Jaipur.

▶ A teak totem from India watches over a Syrian dining table, German-silver chairs, and a replica stone bust from Angkor Wat. Painting in bleach on denim by John Robshaw. • Ein Teak-Totem aus dem nordöstlichen Indien wacht über den syrischen Esstisch, Neusilber-Stühle und die Kopie einer Steinbüste aus Angkor Wat. Für das Kunstwerk im Hintergrund bearbeitete Robshaw Denim mit Bleichmittel. • Un totem en teck du nord-ouest de l'Inde monte la garde sur une table syrienne, des chaises en argentan et la réplique d'un buste en pierre d'Angkor Vat. La toile en denim décoloré est de John Robshaw.

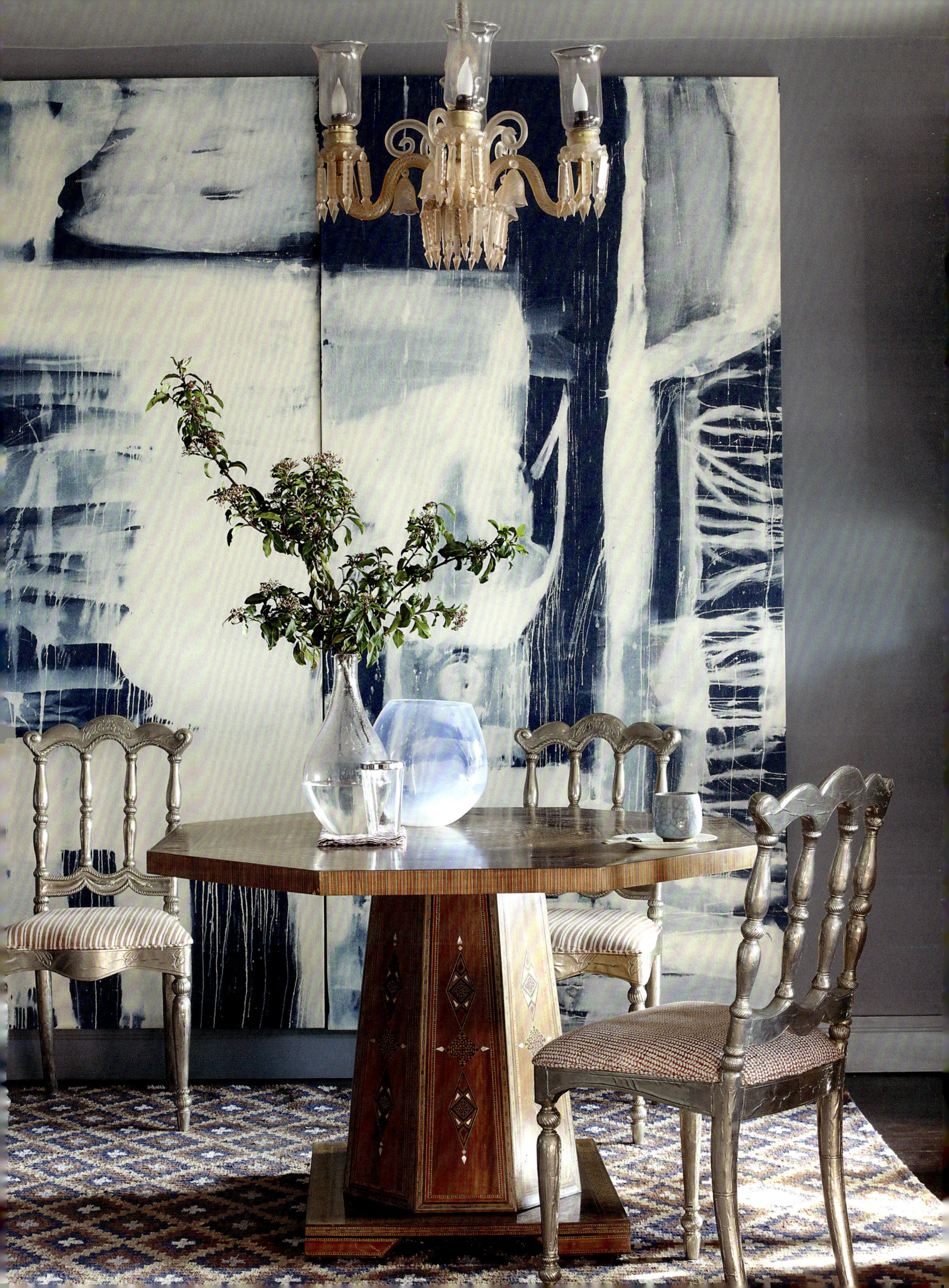

BEATRICE ROSSETTI & PIERO GEMELLI

THEIR PHOTO-STUDIO-CUM-HOME IN MILAN

WHO Gemelli is a highly respected fashion, still life, and portrait photographer who also works as an artist, designer, and architect. Rossetti is an interiors stylist for magazines including *D Casa* and *Elle Decoration China*. **WHAT** A 400 m² (4,306 sq. ft.), two-bedroom loft created by Gemelli himself in a postwar industrial building that once housed a printing press. **WHERE** Adjacent to the Navigli district. **EYE FOR STYLE** Gemelli's first shoot for *Vogue Italia* in the 1980s was of a lipstick. Clients since have included Tiffany & Co., Gucci, and Versace. **EYE FOR STYLE** Rossetti consults for furniture über-brands such as Zanotta, Cassina, and Gervasoni, and recently worked on a bed linen collection for Italian textile label Society. **LIKES AND DISLIKES** She has had a passion for flea markets from an early age and hates "noise and traffic, stupid people and gossip." Gemelli is a fan of Bach, Mozart, and The Rolling Stones, but is averse to singing himself.

PHOTOGRAPHED BY PIERO GEMELLI   PRODUCTION BY ANA CARDINALE

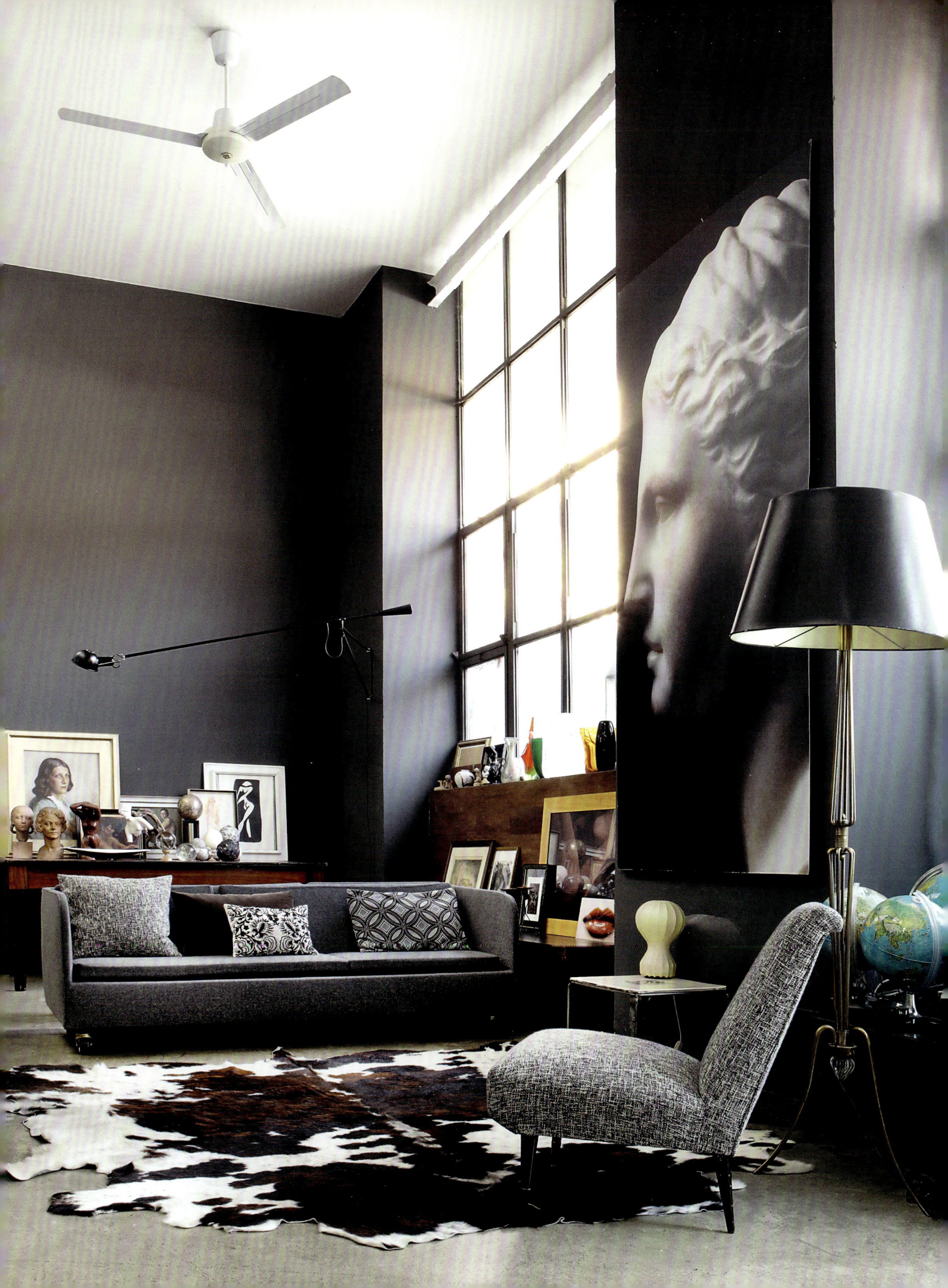

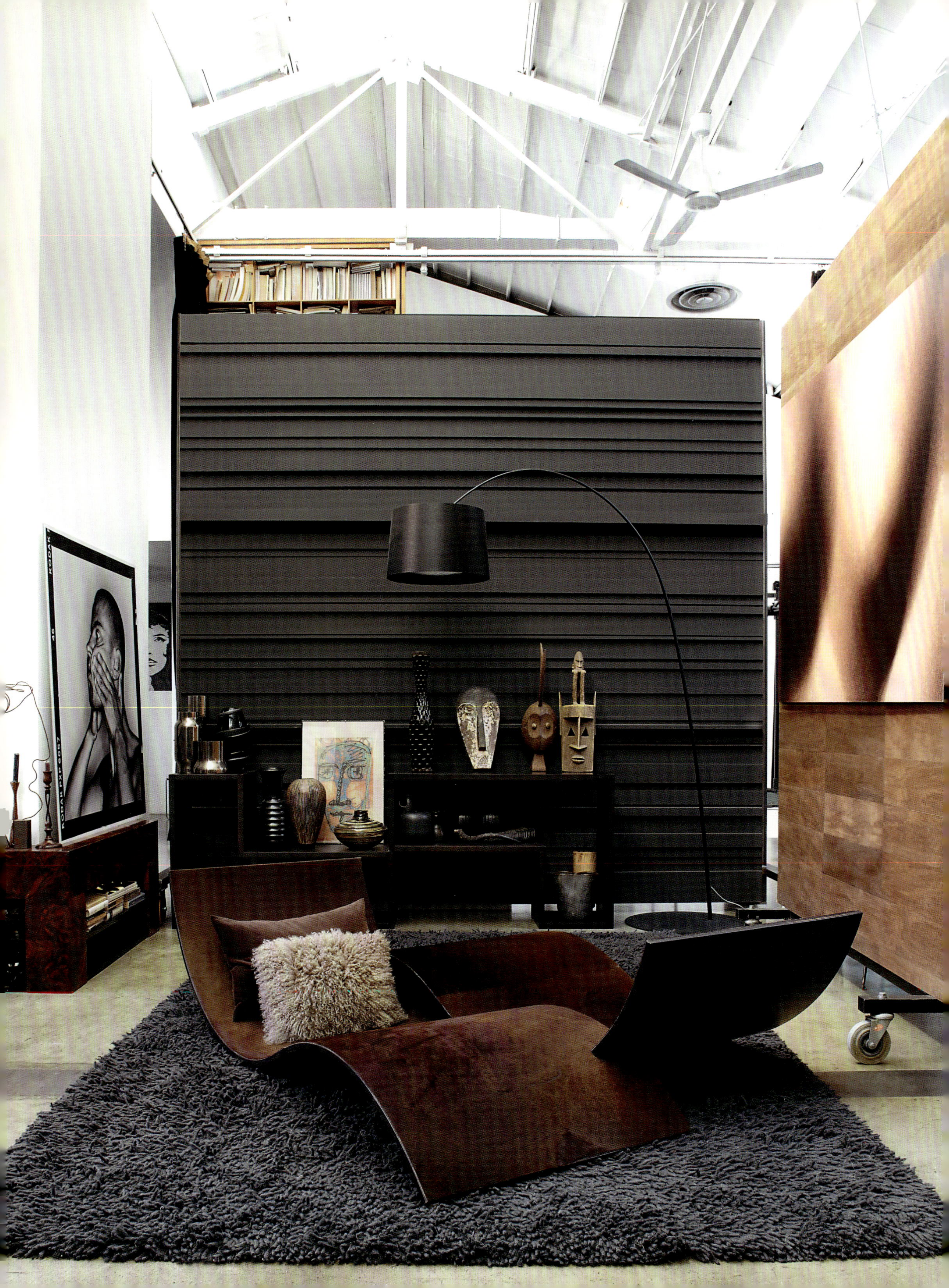
KODAK
46
KODAK PXP 6057

259 Part of the living room is dominated by a photo Gemelli took of a neoclassical bust he found in a New York City antique store. The gray felt sofa is his design. • Eine Sitzecke im Wohnzimmer beherrscht Gemellis Aufnahme einer klassizistischen Büste, die er in New York entdeckte. Das Filzsofa entwarf er selbst. • Une part du séjour est dominée par une photo de Gemelli représentant un buste néoclassique déniché chez un antiquaire à New York. Il a dessiné le canapé en feutre gris.

◀ Gemelli's *Ondina 6.9* loungers were shown at the Milan fair. Rossetti covered screens-on-wheels with painted pine and wood tiles. • Gemellis Doppelliege *Ondina 6.9* wurde auf der Mailänder Möbelmesse gezeigt. Rossetti ließ die Raumteiler auf Rollen mit Holz umkleiden, mal mit und mal ohne Lackierung. • Les chaises longues *Ondina 6.9* de Gemelli ont été montrées au Salon du Meuble de Milan. Les grands écrans à rouleaux en bois sont des créations de Rossetti.

▼ One of Gemelli's wire sculptures enlivens the wall next to the stairs. 1947 Gio Ponti console table. Chair object from S.M.OG Milano. • Eine von Gemellis Drahtskulpturen belebt die Wand hinter der Gio-Ponti-Konsole von 1947. Sesselobjekt von S.M.OG Milano. • Au pied de l'escalier, une sculpture en fil de fer de Gemelli anime le mur. 1947 console de Gio Ponti. La chaise plastifiée vient de S.M.OG Milano.

▲ The industrial-style kitchen features steel units, a raw-metal ceiling, and a concrete floor. • Die Küche ist mit Stahl-Elementen, roher Metalldecke und Betonboden im Industrial Style gehalten. • Dans la cuisine à l'allure industrielle, des meubles en acier, un plafond en métal brut et un sol en béton.

"DARK GRAY WALLS MAKE PIECES PLACED IN FRONT OF THEM LOOK MORE THREE-DIMENSIONAL." BEATRICE ROSSETTI

For a decade, this space served solely as Piero Gemelli's photo studio. He had chosen white or raw concrete for the walls, and the present-day kitchen was little more than a bar. Then, he decided to transform it into a place where he and his partner could also sleep when in town. Their most heated discussions were over color, as Beatrice Rossetti preferred something dark. They settled on a smoky gray for the ground floor and chocolate and beige tones for upstairs. "Piero hated browns," admits Rossetti, "but I wanted some intimacy for the bedrooms." The furnishings include African masks and antiques from Gemelli's parents' home. There are also many of his quirky wire sculptures and a wall covered with his fashion images. For the needs of his job, the couple wanted to keep the lower level flexible, so movable screens were installed as room-dividers. Some are plain, others covered in wood-tiles. "The result," says Beatrice Rossetti, "is the exact reflection of the two of us."

„Vor einer dunkelgrauen Wand erscheint jedes Objekt dreidimensionaler", erklärt Beatrice Rossetti. Sie spricht über das Mailänder Loft, das ihrem Lebensgefährten Piero Gemelli zehn Jahre lang als Fotostudio gedient hatte. Als die beiden beschlossen, es auch zum Wohnen zu nutzen, begann die unvermeidliche Diskussion um die Wandfarben: Rossetti wünschte sich dunkle Töne. Schließlich wurde es ein rauchiges Grau für das Erdgeschoss und Beige bis Schokobraun im oberen Bereich. „Piero hasste Braun", gibt Rossetti zu, „aber ich fand nun mal, die Schlafzimmer sollten intim wirken." Neben afrikanischen Masken und Antiquitäten aus Gemellis Elternhaus gehören viele eigene Werke, so etwa seine amüsant-raffinierten Drahtskulpturen im Calder-Look und eine ganze Wand seiner Modefotografien. Um die untere Ebene für seine Arbeit an der Kamera flexibel zu halten, wurden riesige rollbare Screens als Raumteiler installiert. Manche sind eher geometrisch im Look, andere wurden mit Holzfliesen verkleidet. „Das Ergebnis", sagt Beatrice Rossetti, „spiegelt uns beide exakt wider."

Pendant dix ans, l'espace abritait uniquement le studio de photo de Piero Gemelli. Les murs étaient blancs ou en béton brut, la cuisine actuelle un simple bar. Puis, sa compagne et lui ont décidé d'en faire également un pied-à-terre. Ils ont mis du temps pour s'entendre sur les couleurs, car Beatrice voulait du sombre. « Devant un mur gris foncé, les objets paraissent plus tridimensionnels », déclare-t-elle. Ils ont tranché pour du gris fumé au rez-de-chaussée et des tons chocolat et beige à l'étage. « Piero déteste les bruns, mais je voulais des chambres intimes. » Le décor comprend des masques africains et des antiquités provenant de chez les parents de Gemelli. On y trouve aussi plusieurs de ses œuvres en fil de fer ainsi qu'un mur tapissé de ses photos de mode. Comme le rez-de-chaussée sert encore de studio, des panneaux sur roulettes font office de cloisons. Certains sont stricts et géometriques, d'autres en panneaux de bois plus décoratifs. Pour Beatrice Rossetti, « le résultat est le reflet exact de nos deux personnalités ».

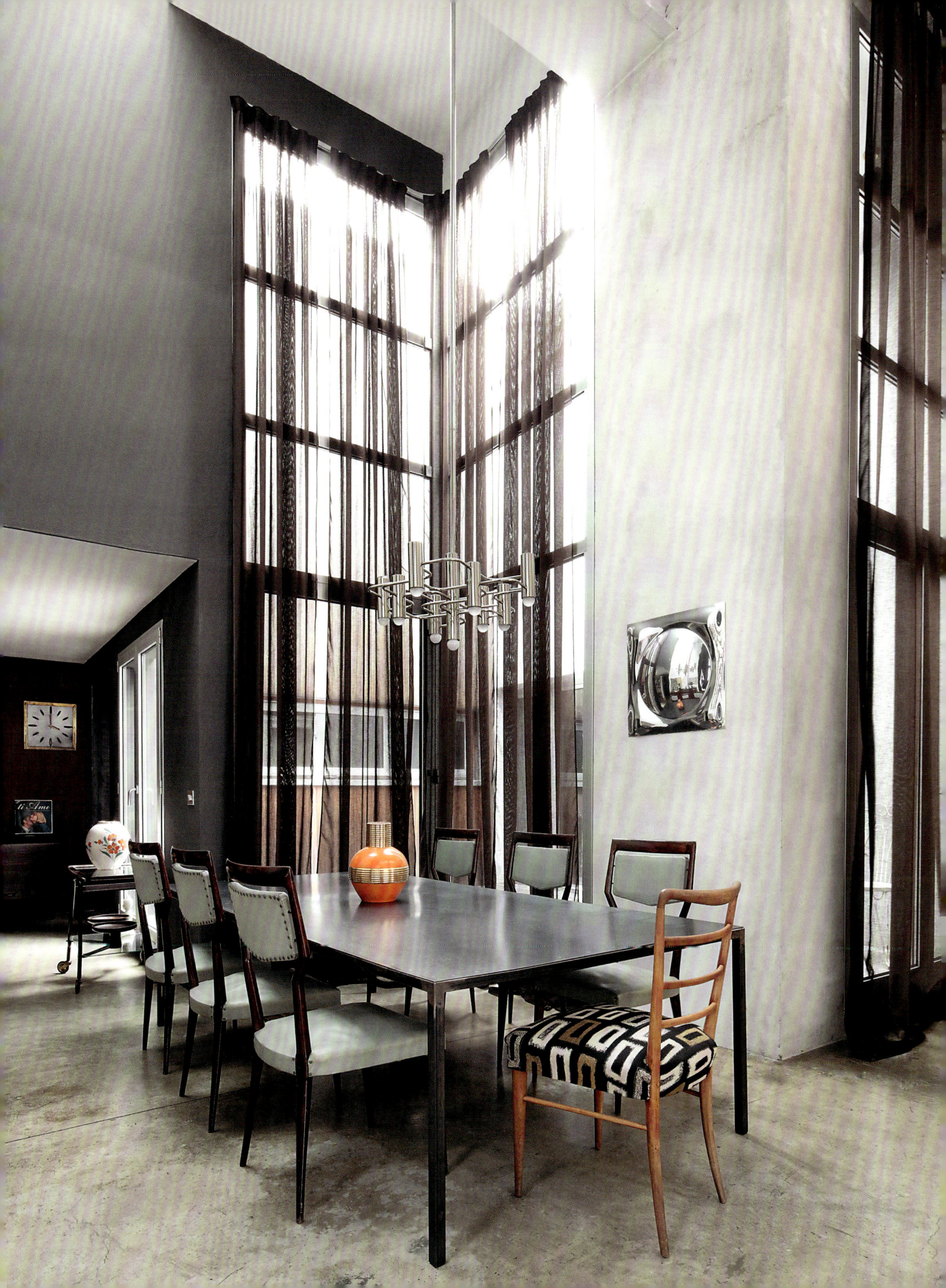
ti Amo

263 The windows in the dining area are five meters [16 ft.] high. A set of vintage 1950s chairs surround a custom table made from iron. • Die Fenster des Essbereichs sind 5 m hoch. Vintage-Stühle aus den 1950ern flankieren den maßgefertigten Eisentisch. • Dans le coin repas, les fenêtres font cinq mètres de haut. Des chaises des années 1950 entourent une table en fer réalisée sur mesure.

▲ Rossetti wanted a "cozy and intimate" atmosphere in the master suite. The bed was designed by Mario Prandina for Plinio il Giovane. • „Behaglich und intim" wünschte sich Rossetti die Mastersuite. Das Bett ist ein Entwurf von Mario Prandina für Plinio il Giovane. • Dans la suite principale, Rossetti voulait une atmosphère «douillette et intime». Le lit a été dessiné par Mario Prandina pour Plinio il Giovane.

◀ In the breakfast space, a 1950s bar stands next to an old floor lamp with a goatskin lampshade found in Corsica. • In der Frühstücksecke steht eine Fifties-Bar neben einer alten Stehleuchte mit Pergament-Schirm, die die beiden auf Korsika entdeckten. • Dans le coin du petit déjeuner, un lampadaire réalisé avec une vieille base et un abat-jour en peau de chèvre trouvé en Corse côtoie un bar des années 1950.

▶ A wall near the dining area is covered with Gemelli images, mostly taken for *Vogue*. The Gio Ponti armchair still boasts its original fabric. • Eine Wand nahe dem Essbereich bedecken Gemelli-Fotos; die meisten davon entstanden für Vogue. Der Ponti-Sessel trägt noch den Originalbezug. • Un mur près du coin repas est tapissé de photos signées Gemelli, la plupart pour *Vogue*. Le fauteuil de Gio Ponti possède encore son tissu d'origine.

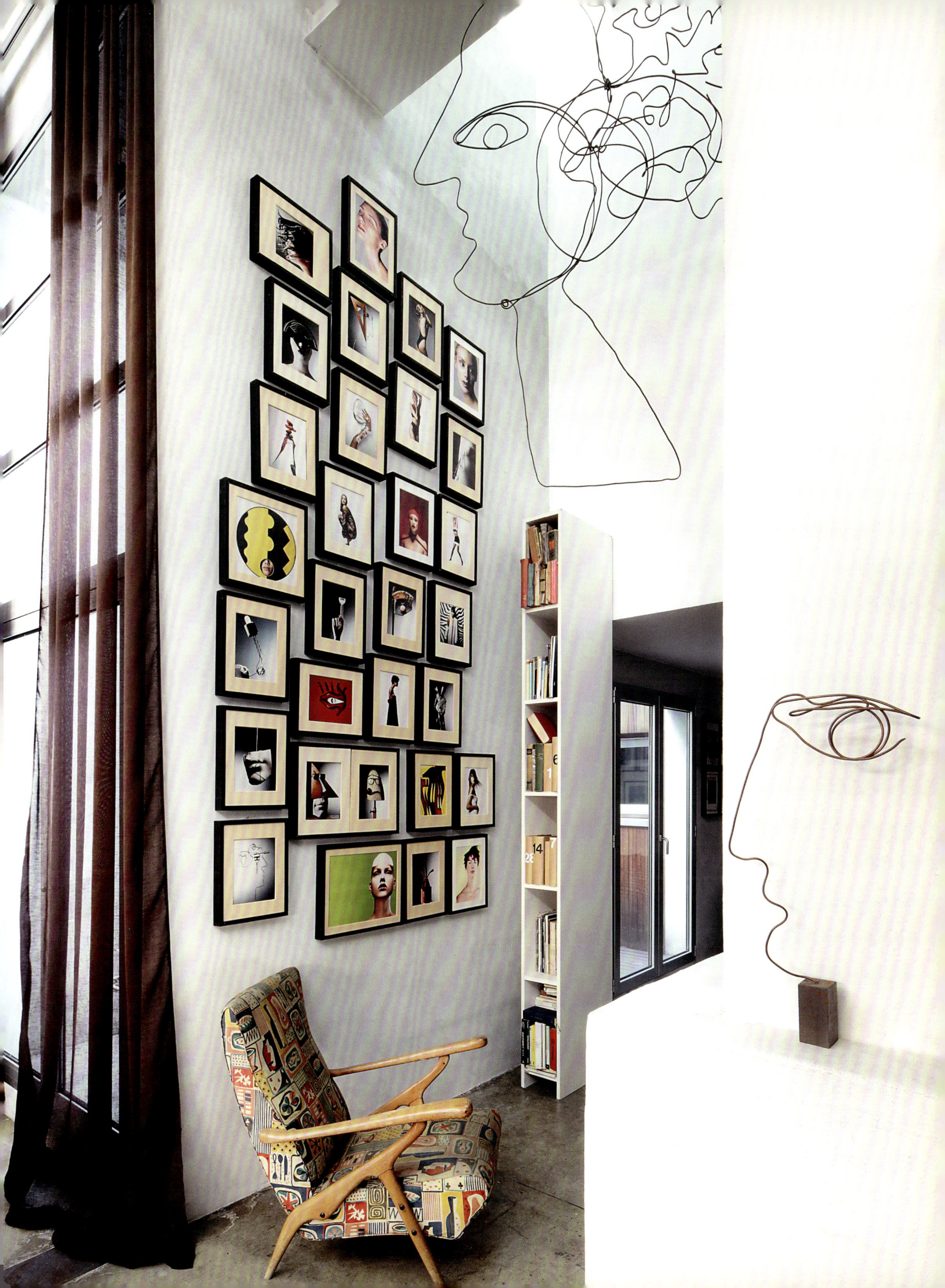

HECTOR RUIZ VELÁZQUEZ

A SMALL WONDER IN MADRID

WHO Madrid-based architect. **WHAT** A 50 m² (538 sq. ft.) concept apartment developed together with the Spanish Association of Tile and Ceramic Flooring Manufacturers. **WHERE** Originally created for the Casa Décor trade show, where the clients fell in love with it and had it adapted for a 1960s building in Madrid's Usera District. **LIMITED SPACE** Ruiz Velázquez recommends putting either your bed or dining table on a pedestal and integrating storage beneath them. The first small apartment he worked on was a penthouse just 2.5 meters (8 ft.) wide. "It was like a train wagon," he says. **THE SKY IS THE LIMIT** Ruiz Velázquez has trained for his pilot's license. **PROJECTS** His multifaceted studio works on everything from graphic design and corporate branding to interiors. Among other things, he has created a restaurant at the Ritz Carlton in Madrid, showrooms for Cadillac, and the prototype for 20 beauty clinics across Spain.

PHOTOGRAPHED BY MANOLO YLLERA/PHOTOFOYER   PORTRAIT BY ALICIA MONEVA

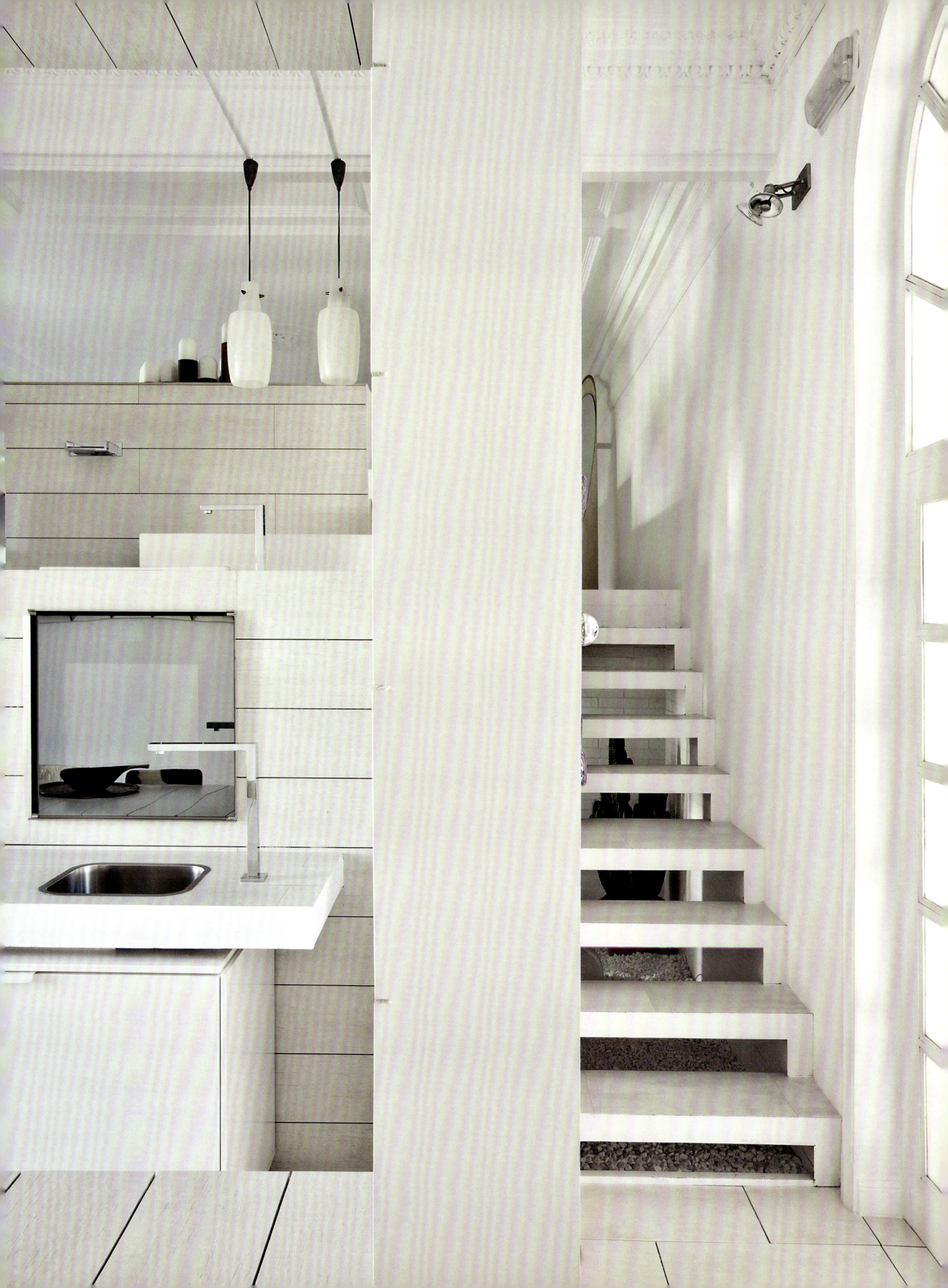

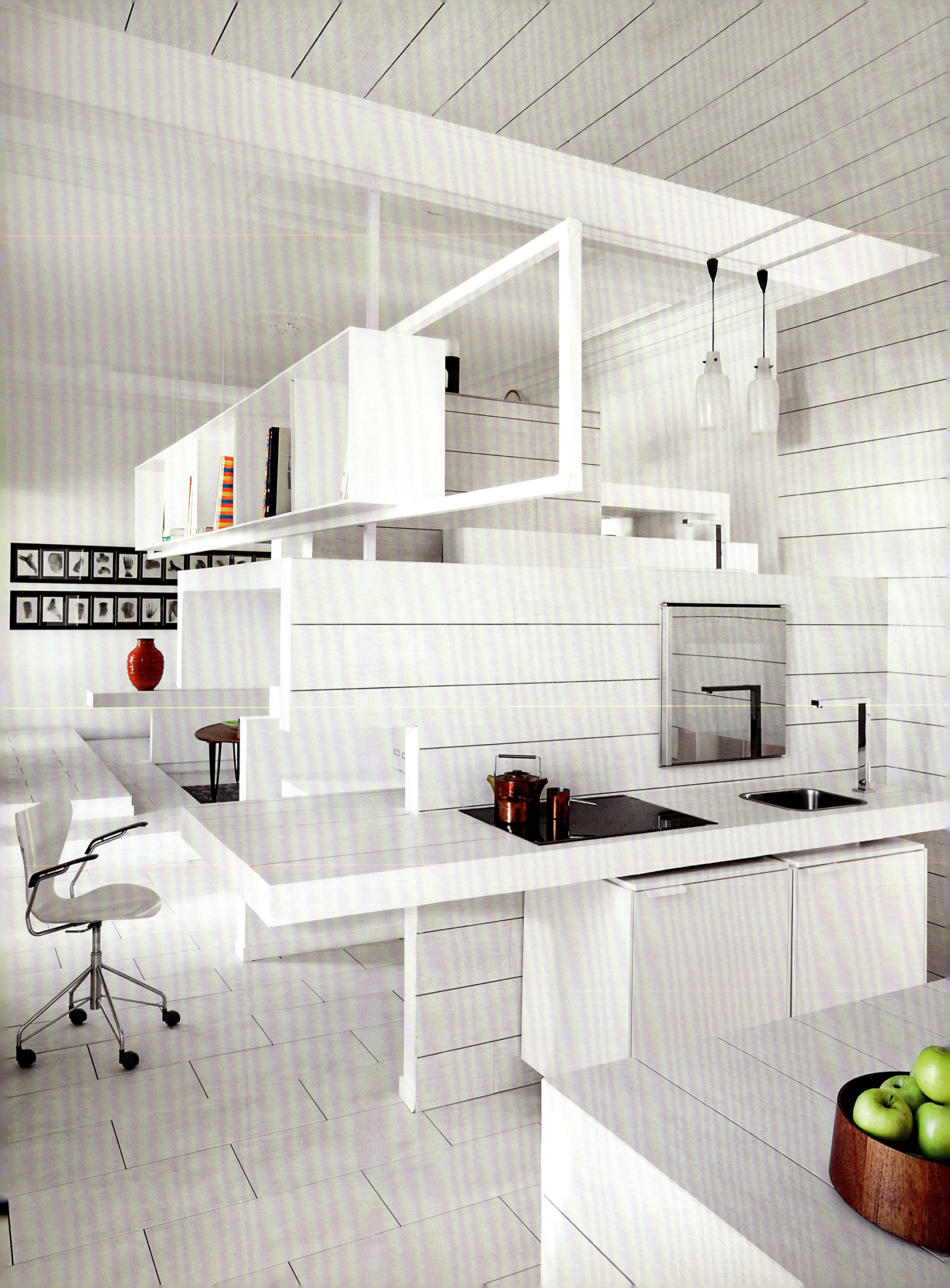

267–268 Snap-together ceramic tiles were used throughout for easy installation. "In small spaces, nothing should obstruct the sight lines to the windows," opines Ruiz Velázquez. Stairs lead up from the kitchen to a bed on the mezzanine—the typical functions of an apartment are assembled almost like Lego. • Fast alles hier besteht aus Keramikelementen zum Zusammenstecken „In kleinen Räumen sollte nichts die Sicht auf die Fenster verstellen", meint Ruiz Velázquez. Aus der Küche führen Stufen zum Schlafbereich auf der Empore: Die Wohnfunktionen wurden kombiniert wie Legosteine. • Des carreaux de céramique clipsables faciles à poser ont été utilisés partout. « Dans un petit espace, rien ne doit boucher la vue des fenêtres », affirme Velázquez. L'escalier mène de la cuisine au lit en mezzanine : les parties fonctionnelles typiques d'un appartement ont été assemblées comme un jeu de Lego.

▲ A 1950s Stilnovo floor lamp and two series of vintage X-rays were installed in the entrance. The ceramic vase adds a welcome burst of color. • Eine Stilnovo-Leuchte aus den 1950ern und zwei Reihen alter Röntgenaufnahmen im Eingangsbereich. Die Keramikvase ist ein willkommener Farbklecks. • Dans l'entrée, un lampadaire Stilnovo des années 1950 et deux séries d'anciennes radiographies. Le vase en céramique ajoute une touche de couleur.

270–271 Wood furniture by George Nelson, Hans Wegner, and Finn Juhl balances out the angular architectural forms and stark, off-white coloring. • Holzmobiliar von George Nelson, Hans Wegner und Finn Juhl dient als Gegengewicht zur kantigen Raumarchitektur in mildem Weiß. • Les meubles en bois de George Nelson, Hans Wegner et Finn Juhl adoucissent la rigueur architecturale et réchauffent l'atmosphère austère.

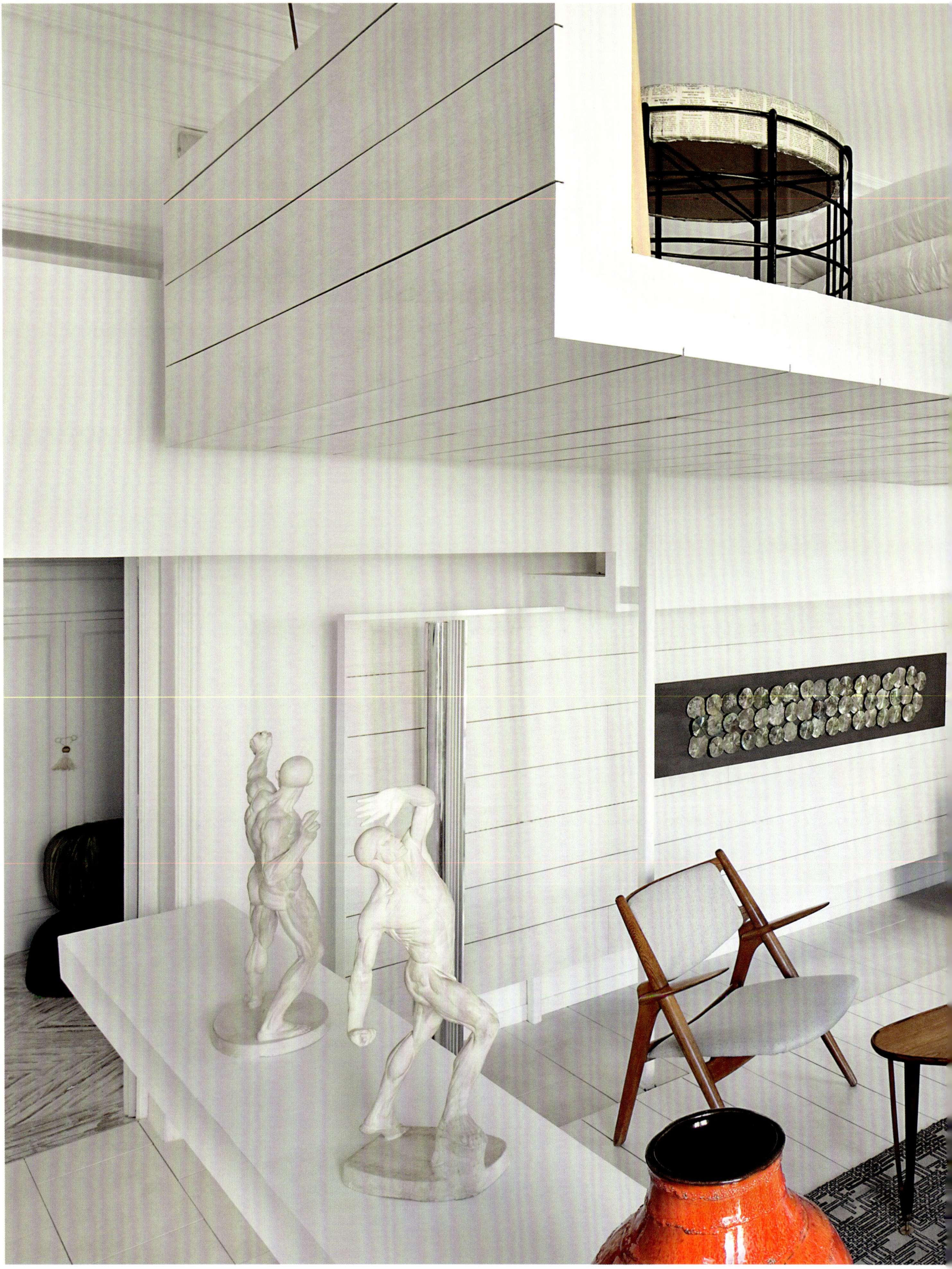

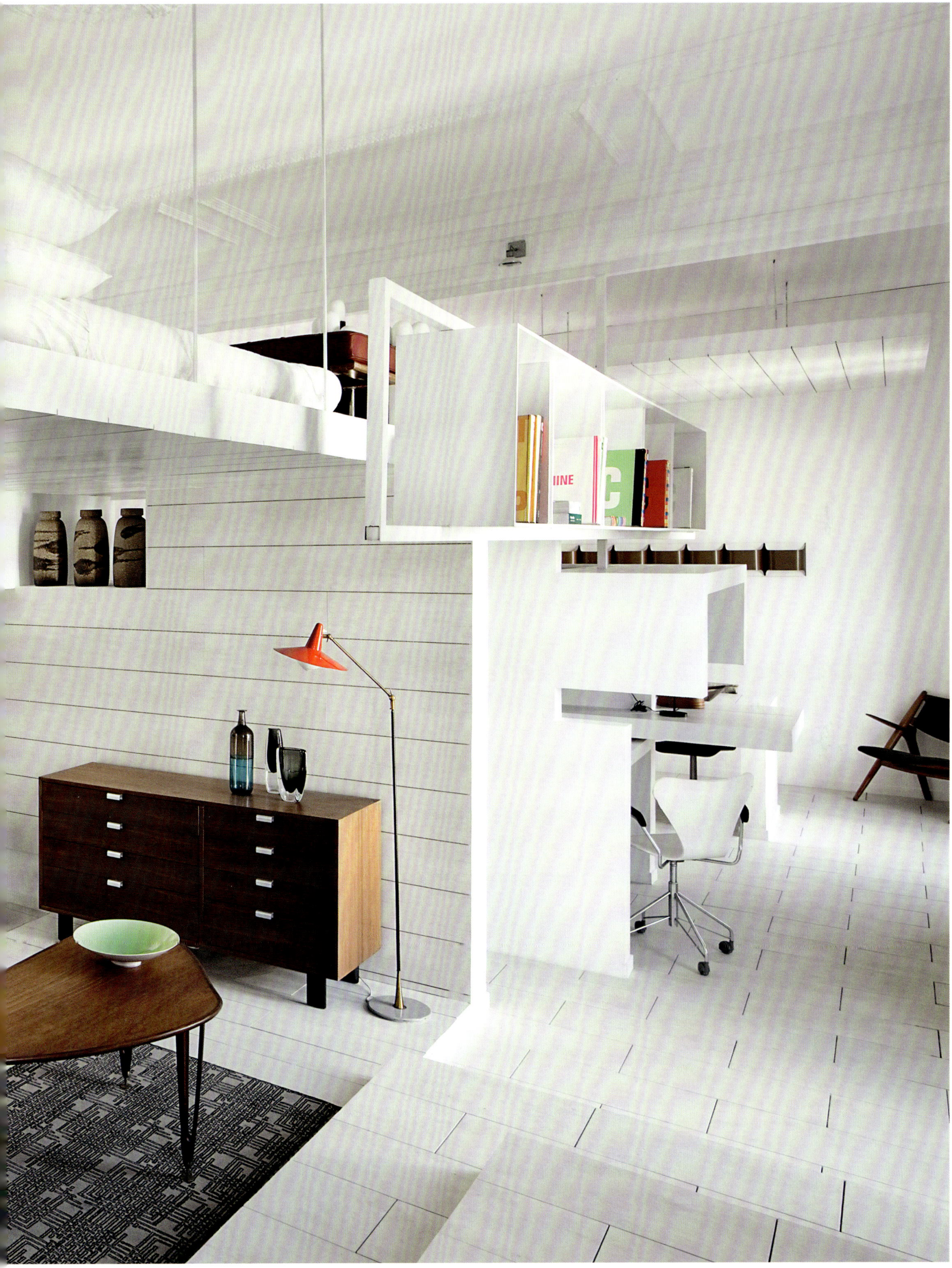

▲ The steel rods circumscribing the mezzanine level not only prevent people from falling out of bed, but also absorb vibrations on the platform. • Eine Einfassung aus Stahlstäben soll verhindern, dass man aus dem Bett fällt, außerdem vibriert die Plattform dadurch kaum. • Les barres d'acier autour de la mezzanine servent non seulement de garde-fou, mais atténuent également les vibrations de la plateforme.

▶ The toilet is sandwiched between the sitting area and kitchen. Ruiz Velázquez installed a tub and vanity diagonally above it. • Die Toilette versteckt sich zwischen Sitzbereich und Küche. Ruiz Velázquez installierte Wanne und Waschtisch diagonal darüber. • Les W.-C. sont pris en sandwich entre le salon et la cuisine. Au-dessus, Velázquez a réussi à placer en diagonale une baignoire et un plan vasque.

"THE PROBLEM IS THAT PEOPLE TEND TO BUY AN APARTMENT BY LOOKING AT THE NUMBER OF SQUARE METERS." HECTOR RUIZ VELÁZQUEZ

"They never think in cubic meters. But they should. That's how you make the best of a small space," concludes Ruiz Velázquez. When the architect was asked to develop this concept apartment for a Madrid trade show, his idea was "to use all the space you never use." He took advantage of the 3m 30 [10'10"] ceiling height to install the bed on a mezzanine level and created zones for cooking, working, and bathing on different levels. Each is assembled as if with building blocks. In fact, he used a total of 166 m² [1787 ft²] off-white ceramic tiles not only for the floors and walls, but also for elements like the dining table, and kitchen work surface. He then chose mainly vintage furniture in wood to mix in a bit of individual charm. For Ruiz Velázquez, the concept solves a common conundrum for many young Madrileños: "You don't have space to invite people for dinner." Here, he organized one for 25 people. PR executive Sandra Perez Gorris and her husband, Francesco, were particularly impressed. They asked him to install the very same concept in their apartment.

„Das Problem ist, dass die Leute ihre Wohnungen nach Quadratmetern kaufen", sagt Hector Ruiz Velázquez. „Dabei sollten sie eher in Kubikmetern denken, denn damit macht man das Beste aus kleinen Räumen." Als der Architekt ein Konzept-Apartment für eine Messe entwickeln sollte, war sein Leitgedanke, „all den Raum zu nutzen, den man sonst nie nutzt". Zugute kam ihm, dass die Decke 3,30 m hoch ist: Er stellte das Bett auf eine Zwischenebene und brachte Koch-, Arbeits- und Badzone auf verschiedenen Niveaus unter. Insgesamt verbaute er 166 m² mattweiße Keramikelemente – für Böden und Zwischenwände, aber auch für Esstisch und Küchenplatte. Vintage-Möbel aus Holz fügten individuellen Charme hinzu. In Velázquez' Augen löst sein Konzept ein Problem vieler junger Madrilenen: „Es fehlt an Platz, um Freunde zum Essen einzuladen." Hier organisierte er sogar ein Dinner für 25 Personen! Besonders beeindruckt waren PR-Beraterin Sandra Perez Gorris und ihr Mann Francesco: Sie baten ihn, das Konzept in ihrer eigene Wohnung zu wiederholen.

« Les gens ne comptent jamais en mètres cubes. Pourtant, c'est ainsi qu'on tire le meilleur profit d'un petit espace », explique l'architecte Hector Ruiz Velázquez. Dans cet appartement témoin conçu pour une foire madrilène, il a exploité « tous les espaces dont on ne se sert jamais ». Tirant profit des plus de 3 m de hauteur sous plafond, il a perché le lit sur une mezzanine et créé des zones pour cuisiner, travailler et se laver sur différents niveaux assemblés comme un jeu de cubes. Quelque 166 m² de carrelage en céramique revêt les sols, les murs ainsi que le plan de travail de la cuisine et la table à manger. De beaux meubles vintage en bois ajoutent une note de chaleur. Pour Ruiz Velázquez, ce concept résout le problème de nombreux jeunes Madrilènes : « Ils n'ont pas de place pour inviter des amis à dîner. » Ici, il a même organisé une réception pour 25 personnes ! Directrice des RP, Sandra Perez Gorris et son mari Francesco lui ont demandé de reproduire le même concept dans leur appartement.

SHAMIR SHAH

HIS MULTI-CONTINENTAL FLAT IN NEW YORK

WHO Yale-educated architect and designer based in New York. **WHAT** A 167 m² (1,800 sq. ft.), one-bedroom loft apartment that he shares with his partner, artist Malcolm Hill. **WHERE** A former 1930s printing press in Chelsea. Shah oversaw the interior renovation of the whole building. **URBAN HEAT** The day he first arrived in Manhattan, it was over 105°F (40°C). **COLD FEET** "I was worried about living in my own project, where there were going to be 50 clients as neighbors," he admits. So far, there have been no complaints. **GREEN DREAM** Shah was born into an Indian family residing in Nairobi for three generations. A keen equestrian in Africa, he rode at a racing stable, ascended Mount Kenya on horseback, and initially wanted to become a vet. **GREEN REALITY** His first encounter with Hill was in a salad bar. **RECENT COMMISSIONS** A loft on Lower Park Avenue; condominiums on the Upper West Side and in Los Angeles.

PHOTOGRAPHED BY MANOLO YLLERA STYLED BY PETE BERMEJO PORTRAIT BY GABRIELLE REVERE

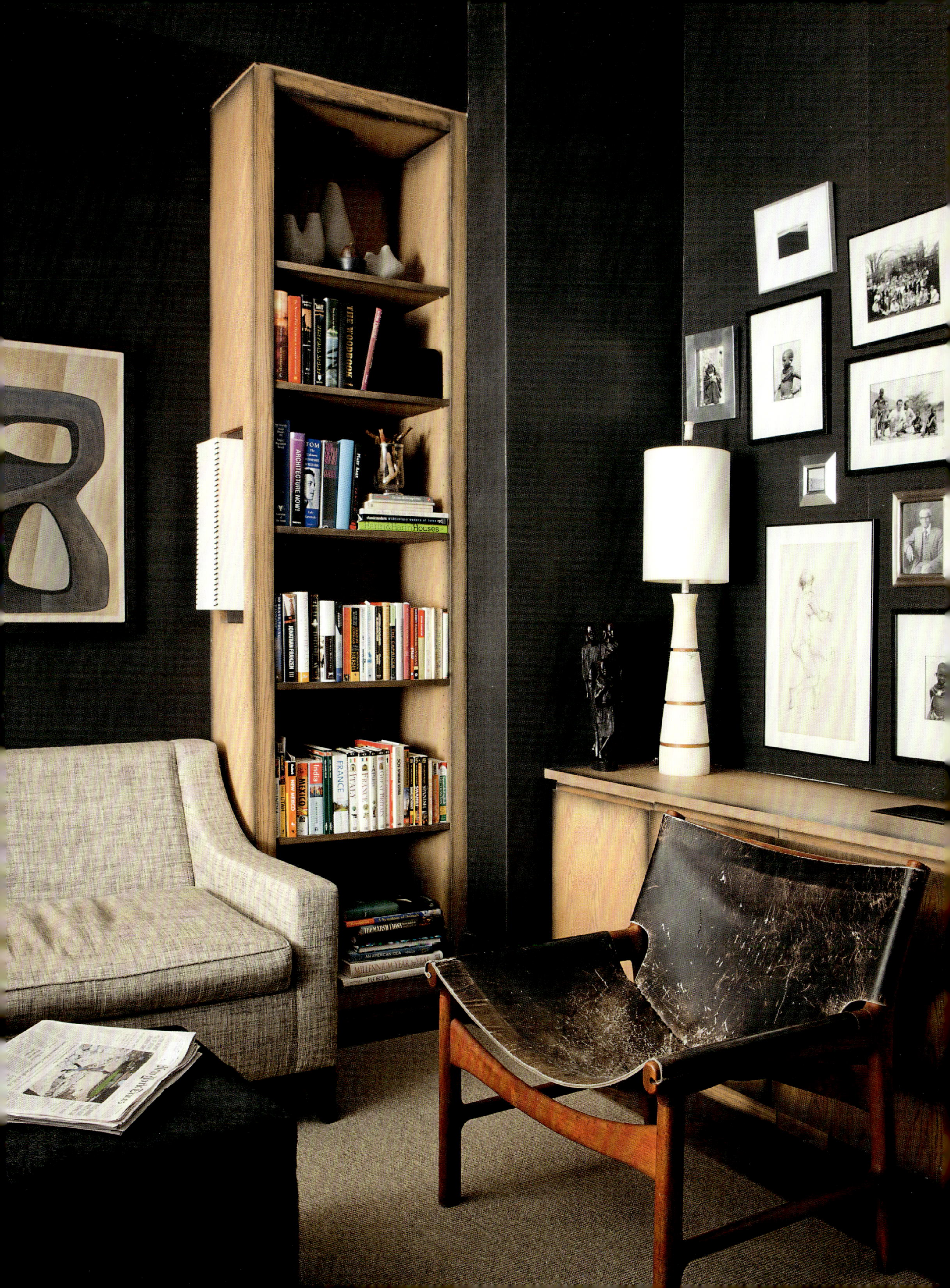

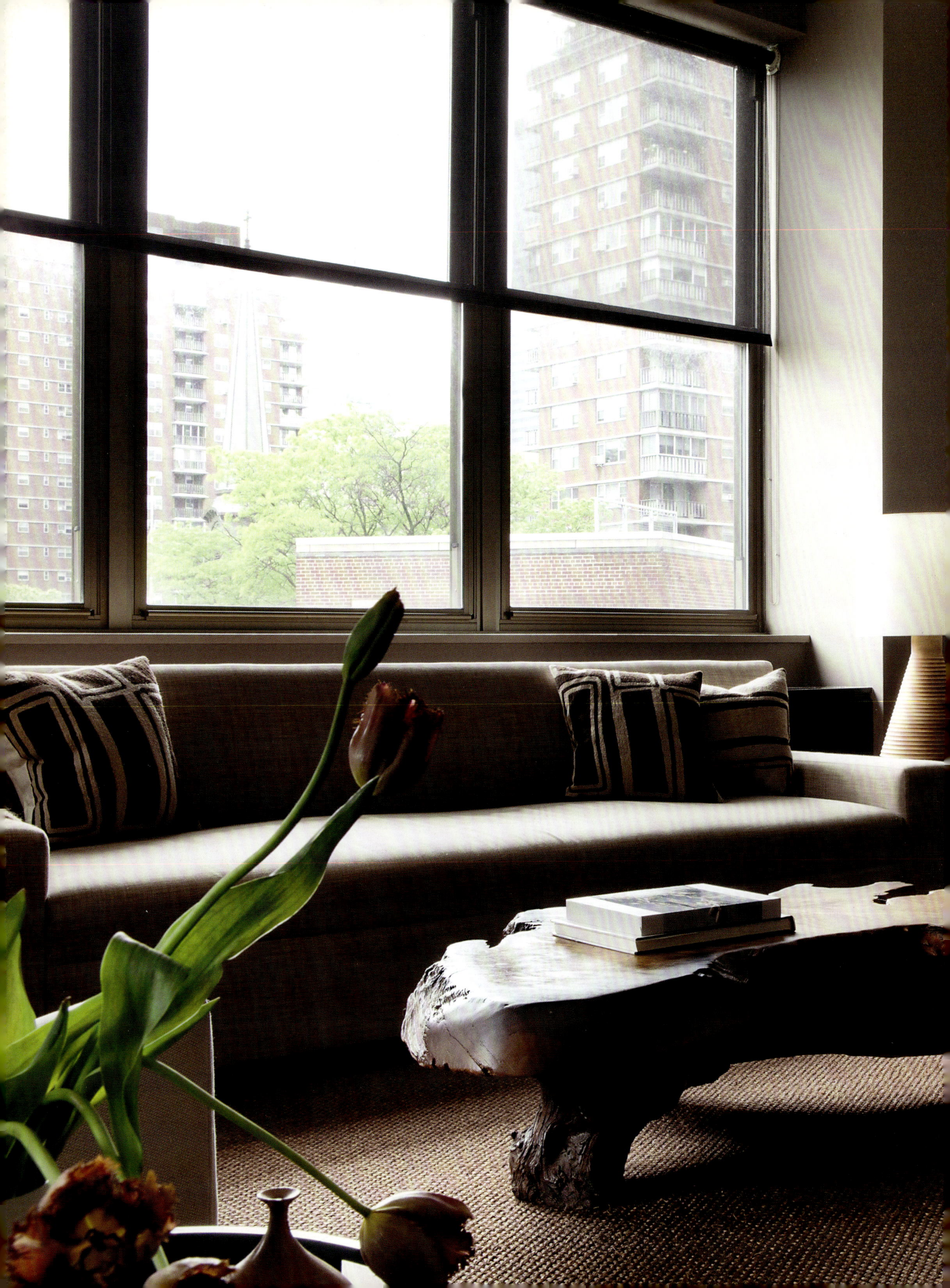

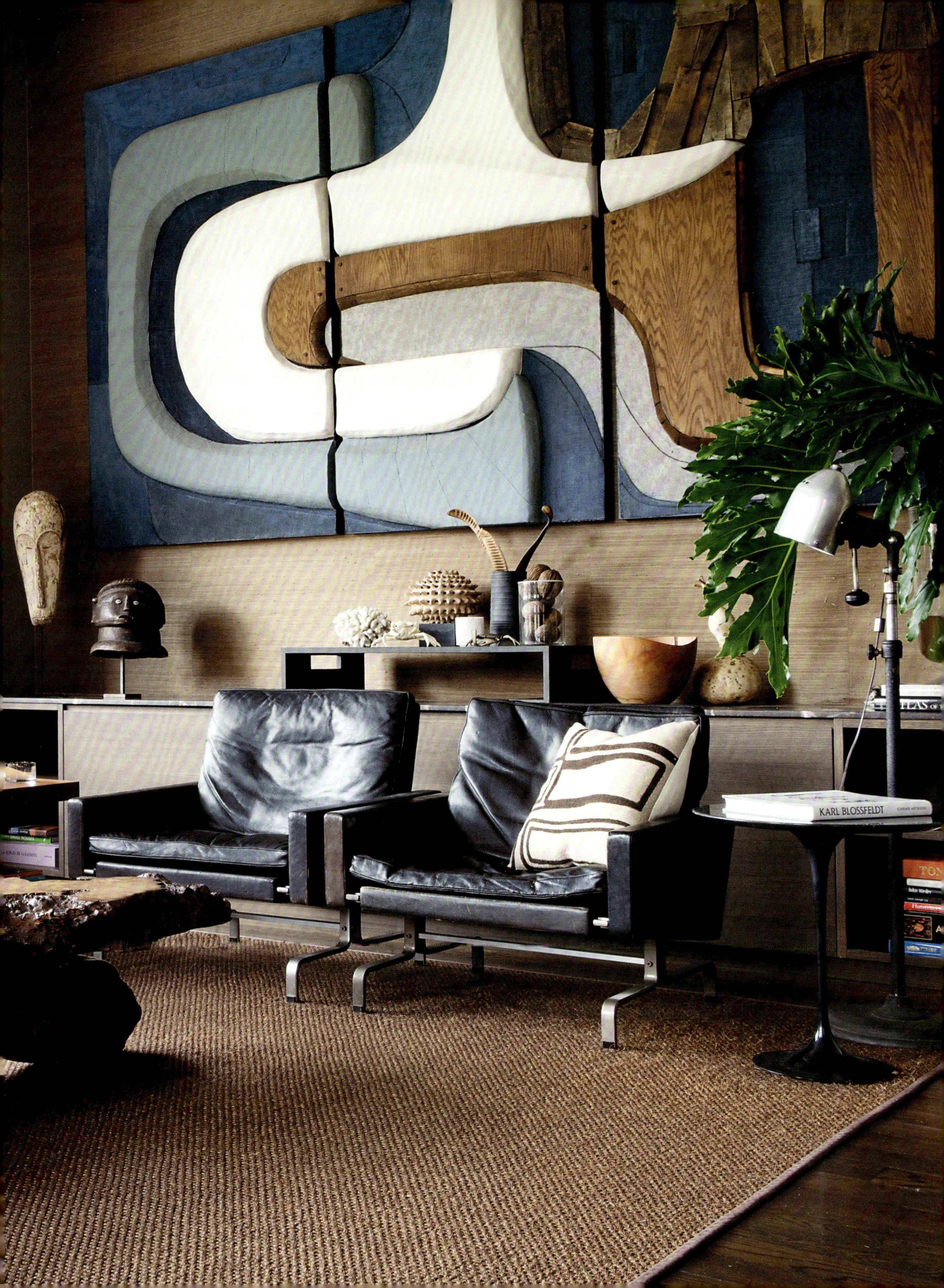
KARL BLOSSFELDT

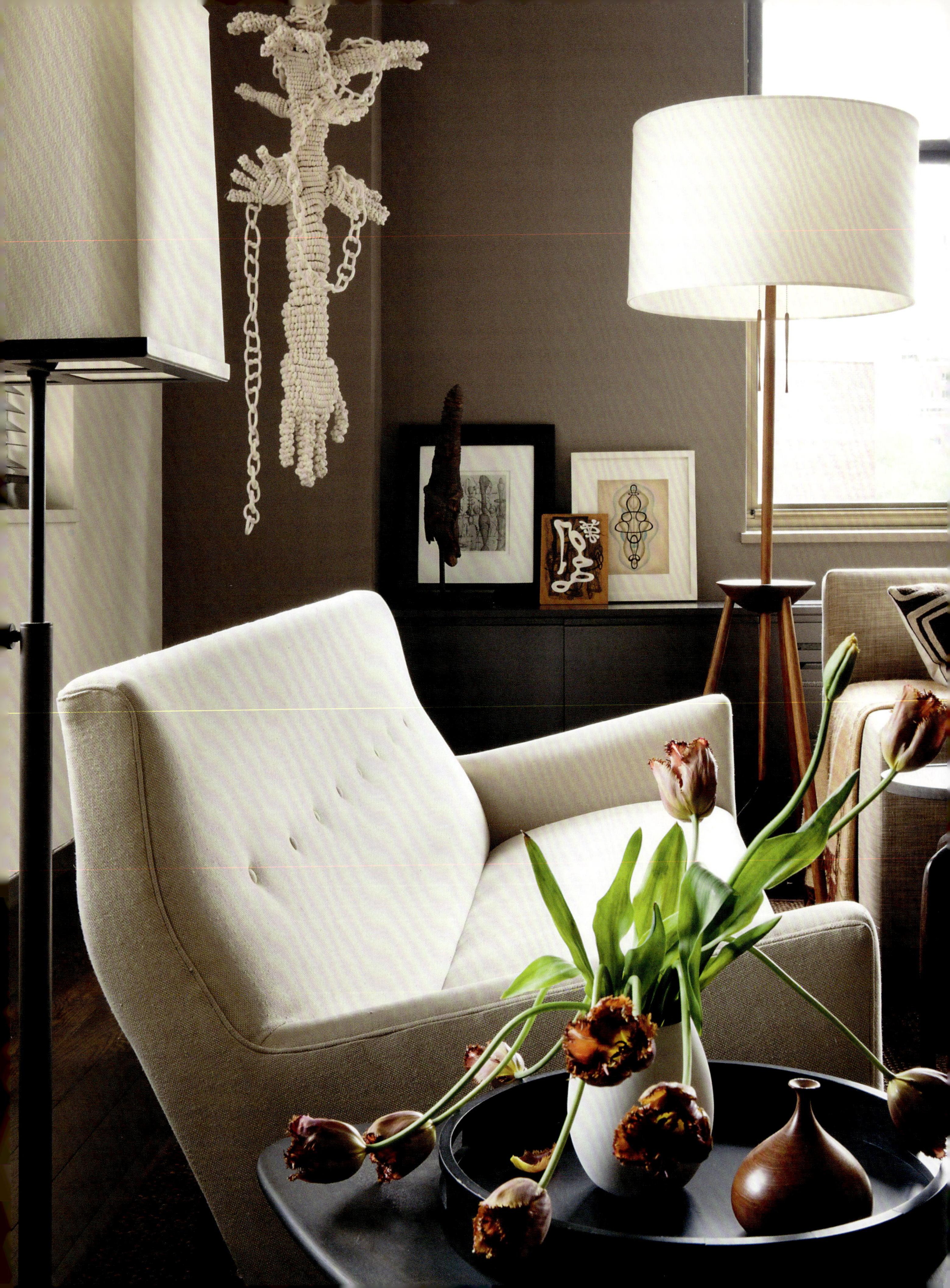

275 Shah covered the walls of the study in grass cloth. The midcentury chair was bought at Dansk Møbelkunst, while the sofa is his own design. • Die Wände des Arbeitszimmers bespannte Shah mit Bastgewebe. Den Midcentury-Sessel kaufte er bei Dansk Møbelkunst, während er das Sofa selbst entwarf. • Shah a tapissé les murs du bureau de toile végétale et a dessiné le canapé. Le fauteuil du milieu du 20ᵉ siècle a été acheté chez Dansk Møbelkunst.

276–277 His partner, Malcolm Hill, created the triptych on the living room wall from resin, recycled wood, and burlap. A vintage burl cocktail table sits on a sisal rug. • Sein Partner Malcolm Hill schuf das Triptychon aus Harz, Recycling-Holz und Rupfen im Wohnzimmer. Der Coffeetable aus Wurzelholz steht auf einem Sisalteppich. • Sur le mur du séjour, un triptyque de Malcolm Hill en résine, bois recyclé et toile à sac. La table en bois brut est posée sur un tapis en sisal.

◀ ▶ ▼ A Mary Hayslip macramé sculpture hangs above a Jens Risom sofa; antlers in the hallway; a bed throw made by Judy Ross, and Vinton the cat. • Über dem Jens-Risom-Sofa hängt ein Makramee-Objekt von Mary Hayslip; Geweihe im Flur; ein Bettüberwurf von Judy Ross und Kater Vinton. • Au-dessus du canapé de Jens Risom, une sculpture de Mary Hayslip en macramé ; des trophées de chasse dans l'entrée ; un jeté de lit de Judy Ross et Vinton le chat.

280 Shah customized the kitchen with smoky colors and designed the walnut-and-leather bench and stools. The black shooting target was found in California. • Shah gestaltete die Küche in rauchigen Tönen und designte Bank und Hocker. Die schwarze Silhouette ist eine Schießscheibe aus Kalifornien. • Dans la cuisine, Shah a opté pour des tons cendrés et a dessiné le banc et les tabourets. La cible silhouette a été trouvée en Californie.

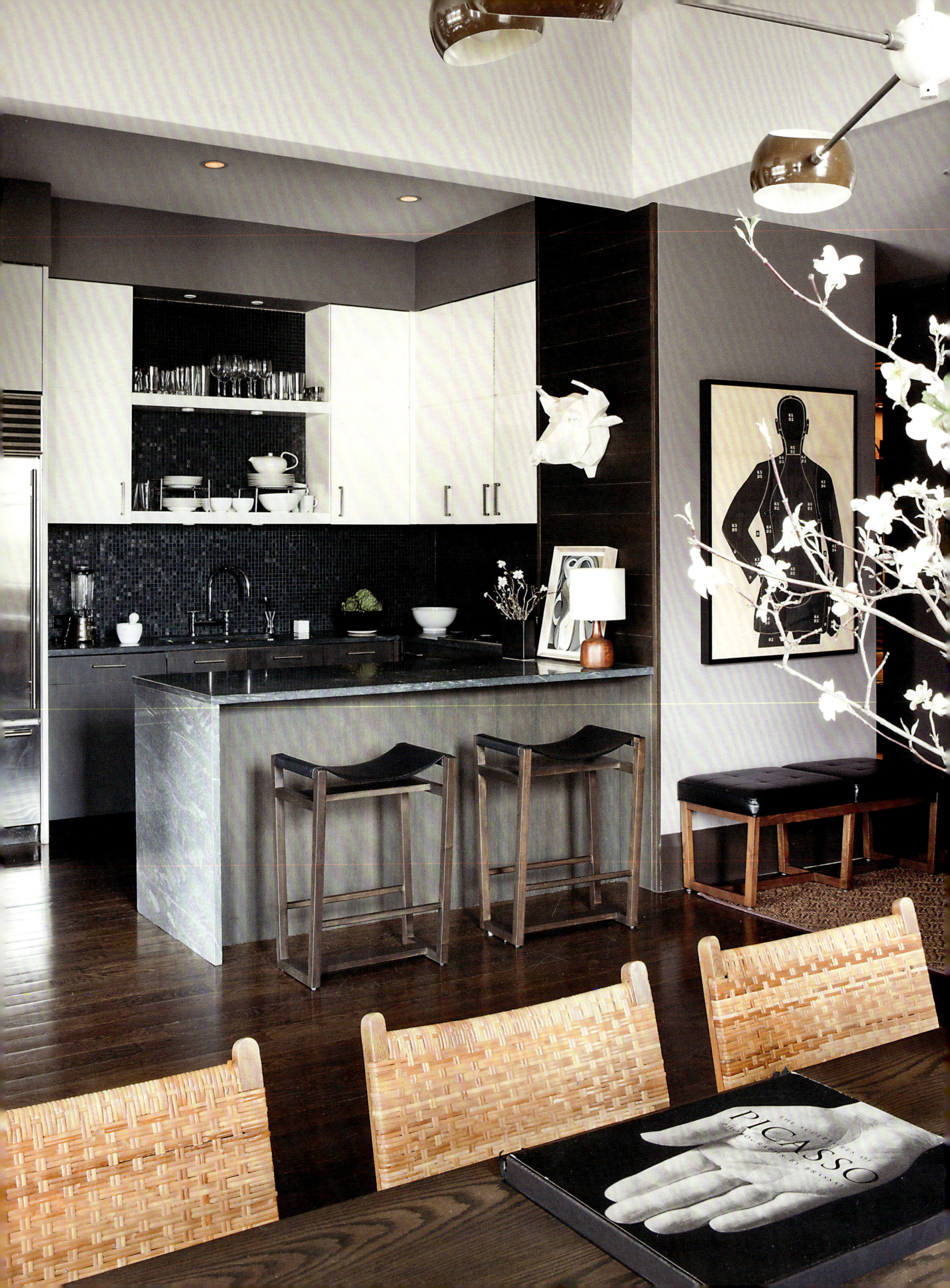
PICASSO

"I like things clean and spare, but not minimalist and not aloof. I would say I'm essentially a modernist at heart," professes Shamir Shah. Although he was commissioned to create the interiors of each unit of this residential renovation, when it came to furnishing his own unit, he opted for a certain amount of customization. Gravitating towards a darker palette (the flooring was originally "blond"), he also replaced doors, hardware, and cabinetry finishes. Shaw attributes his love of earthy tones to his native Africa and advocates interiors that impress with visual depth while still remaining approachable. "I think our work is not trendy," he opines. "It's very, very quiet." Which is not to say it's boring. In his home, custom designs and Scandinavian midcentury classics are enlivened by numerous works by his artist partner, Malcolm Hill, as well as a host of quirky souvenirs brought back from their travels. They include skulls from a vintage shop in Austin, Texas, a wooden gear found in Montana, and resin-encased insects that once made schoolgirls shriek in biology class.

„ICH MAG ES KLAR UND AUFGERÄUMT, ABER NICHT ABSOLUT MINIMALISTISCH ODER ELITÄR ABGEHOBEN." SHAMIR SHAH

„Im Grunde meines Herzens bin ich Modernist", fügt der New Yorker Interiordesigner hinzu. Für die Ausstattung aller Wohnungen dieses Hauses verantwortlich, variierte er sein Konzept im eigenen Apartment ganz nach persönlichem Geschmack. Er verwendete eine dunklere Palette (die übrigen Holzböden waren in „blond" bestellt), und veränderte Türen, Beschläge und das Oberflächen-Finish der Einbauten. Seinen Hang zu Erdtönen schreibt Shah seiner Kindheit in Afrika zu. Er mag optisch komplexe Interiors, die dabei zugänglich bleiben. „Ich denke, unsere Arbeit ist nicht trendy", sagt er. „Sie ist sehr, sehr zurückhaltend." Dabei jedoch keinesfalls langweilig: In seiner Wohnung werden Maßanfertigungen und skandinavische Midcentury-Klassiker aufgelockert von Werken seines Lebenspartners Malcolm Hill und einer Reihe skurriler Reise-Mitbringsel – darunter Schädel aus einem Vintage-Shop in Austin, ein hölzernes Zahnradgetriebe aus Montana und Insekten in Gießharz.

« J'aime les espaces dépouillés, sans être froids ni minimalistes. Je suis essentiellement un moderniste », déclare Shamir Shah. Le designer new-yorkais a décoré tous les appartements de cet immeuble, mais, dans le sien, il a fait du sur-mesure. Optant pour une palette plus sombre (le parquet était « blond »), il a remplacé les portes, la ferronnerie et les revêtements des placards. Shah attribue son amour des tons terreux à son Afrique natale et préfère favoriser la profondeur visuelle. Il déclare : « Mon travail n'a rien de branché. Il est très sobre. » Mais pas ennuyeux pour autant. Ses propres créations et des classiques du design scandinave du milieu du 20e siècle côtoient des œuvres de son compagnon, l'artiste Malcom Hill, ainsi que des souvenirs de voyages, parmi lesquels un crâne déniché chez un brocanteur d'Austin, au Texas, un engrenage en bois trouvé dans le Montana et des insectes piégés dans des blocs de résine qui arrachaient autrefois des cris de terreur aux écolières pendant les cours de biologie.

LAURENCE SIMONCINI

HER RHAPSODY IN GRAY NEAR PARIS

WHO Co-founder of the Parisian children's store Serendipity. She shares the space with her entrepreneur husband and two children. **WHAT** A 600 m² (6,458 sq. ft.), five-bedroom house in an early-20th-century steel factory. **WHERE** The Parisian suburb of Malakoff. **COLLABORATOR** Simoncini teamed up on the project with interior designer Valérie Mazerat, best known for the décor of the Paris concept store Merci. **WHY SERENDIPITY?** The aim behind the super-chic store, which Simoncini runs in tandem with Elisa de Bartillat, is "to offer furniture for children and playful objects you won't see anywhere else." **ALL CHARM** Serendipity's selection mixes vintage and contemporary design, placing an emphasis on one-off pieces and limited editions. Among Simoncini's favorite finds are Anne-Valérie Dupond's textile animal trophies. **ALL CHANGE** "I guess my next living space will be all white," she says with a smile.

PHOTOGRAPHED BY MADS MOGENSEN   PRODUCED BY MARTINA HUNGLINGER

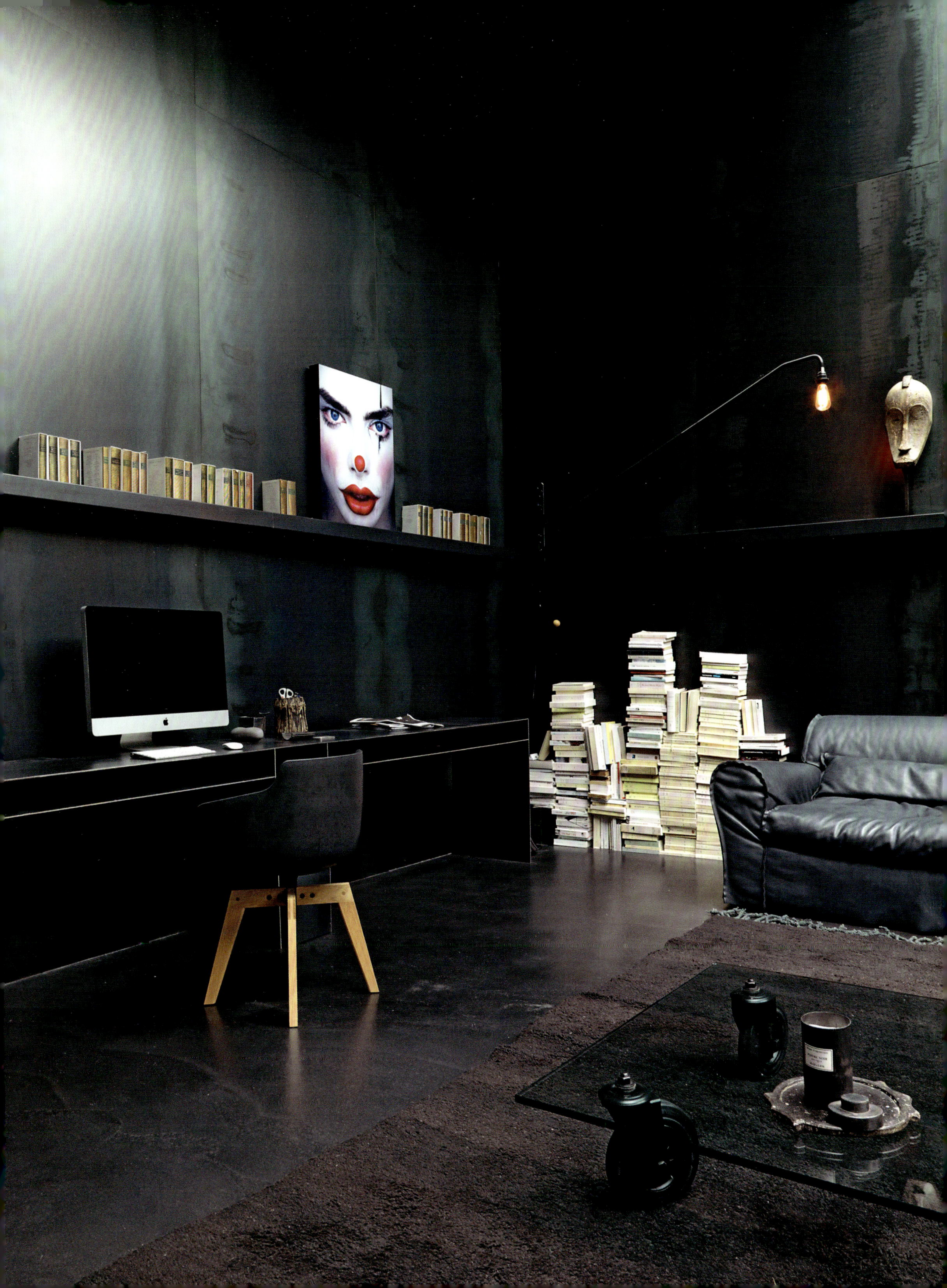

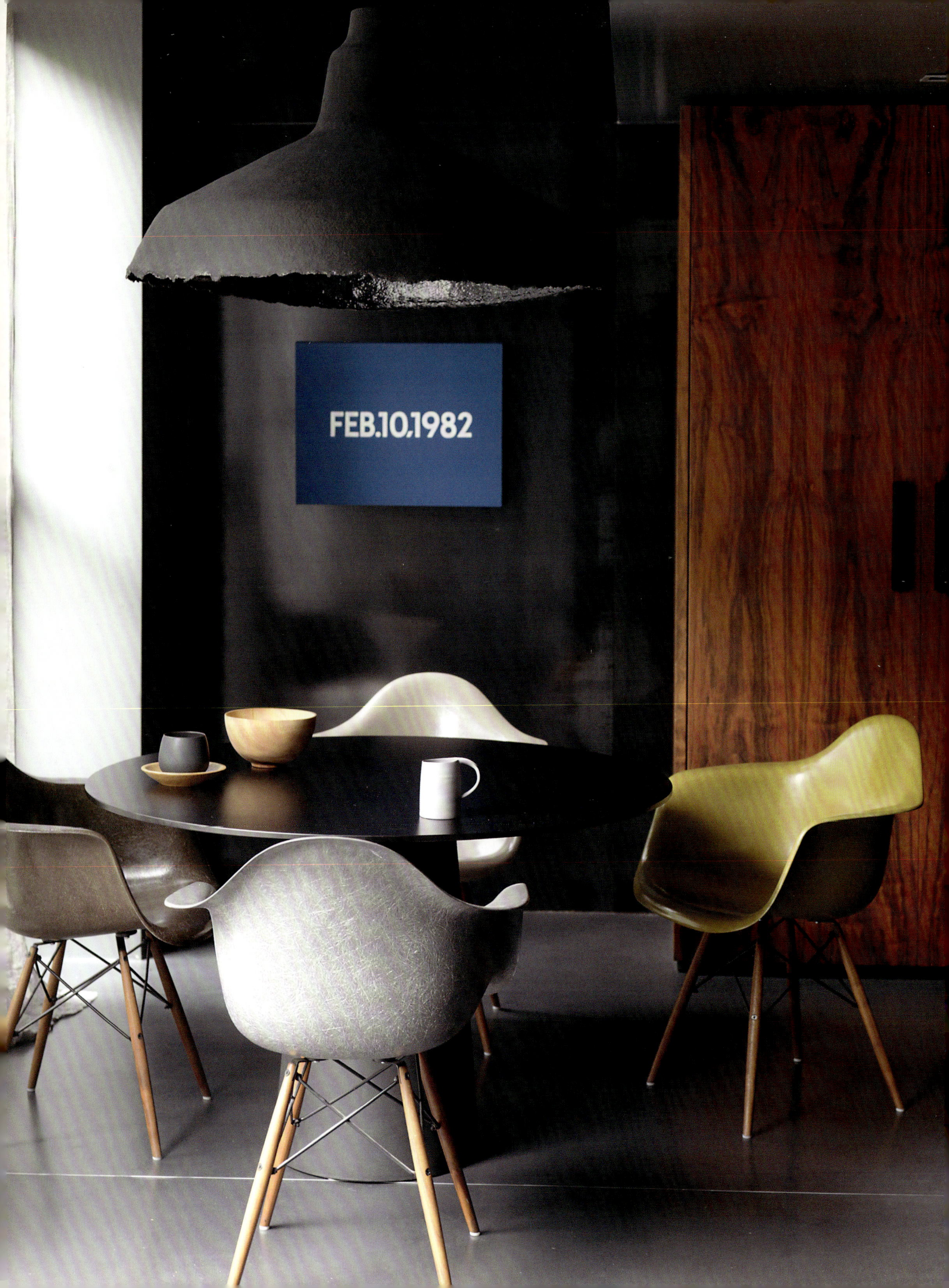
FEB.10,1982

283 The walls of Simoncini's husband's office are covered in sheets of steel. The photo is by Erwin Olaf and the desk chair by Jean-Marie Massaud. • Das Büro von Simoncinis Ehemann ist mit Stahlblech verkleidet. Fotografie von Erwin Olaf, Schreibtischstuhl von Jean-Marie Massaud. • Les murs du bureau du mari de Simoncini sont recouverts de plaques d'acier. Photo d'Erwin Olaf et fauteuil pivotant de Jean-Marie Massaud.

◄ A paper lamp from Jo Meester's Pulp collection hangs above Marcel Wanders's *Container* table in the kitchen. Date painting by On Kawara. • Eine Papierleuchte aus Jo Meesters Pulp-Kollektion hängt in der Küche über Marcel Wanders' *Container*-Tisch. Gemälde von On Kawara. • Dans la cuisine, un lustre en papier de la collection Pulp de Jo Meester est suspendu au-dessus de la table *Container* de Marcel Wanders. Tableau d'On Kawara.

▼ One thing that attracted Simoncini to the location was the garden. "We immediately had the impression of freshness and greenery," she enthuses. • Der Garten gehörte zu den Vorteilen, die Simoncini für den Ort einnahmen. „Wir hatten sofort das Gefühl von Frische und Grün", schwärmt sie. • Le jardin est l'un des attraits qui ont séduit Simoncini. « On se sent tout de suite entouré de verdure et de fraîcheur. »

▲ Part of the dining room wall is clad in tiles from Emery & Cie.: "Their reflections add more light." The custom table is made from steel and Dao wood. • Das Esszimmer ist teilweise mit Fliesen von Emery & Cie. verkleidet: „Sie reflektieren das Licht." Der Tisch wurde aus Stahl und Dao-Holz gebaut. • Un mur de la salle à manger est revêtu de carreaux de chez Emery & Cie. « Ils reflètent la lumière. » Table sur mesure réalisée en acier et bois de Dao.

FEB.10.1982

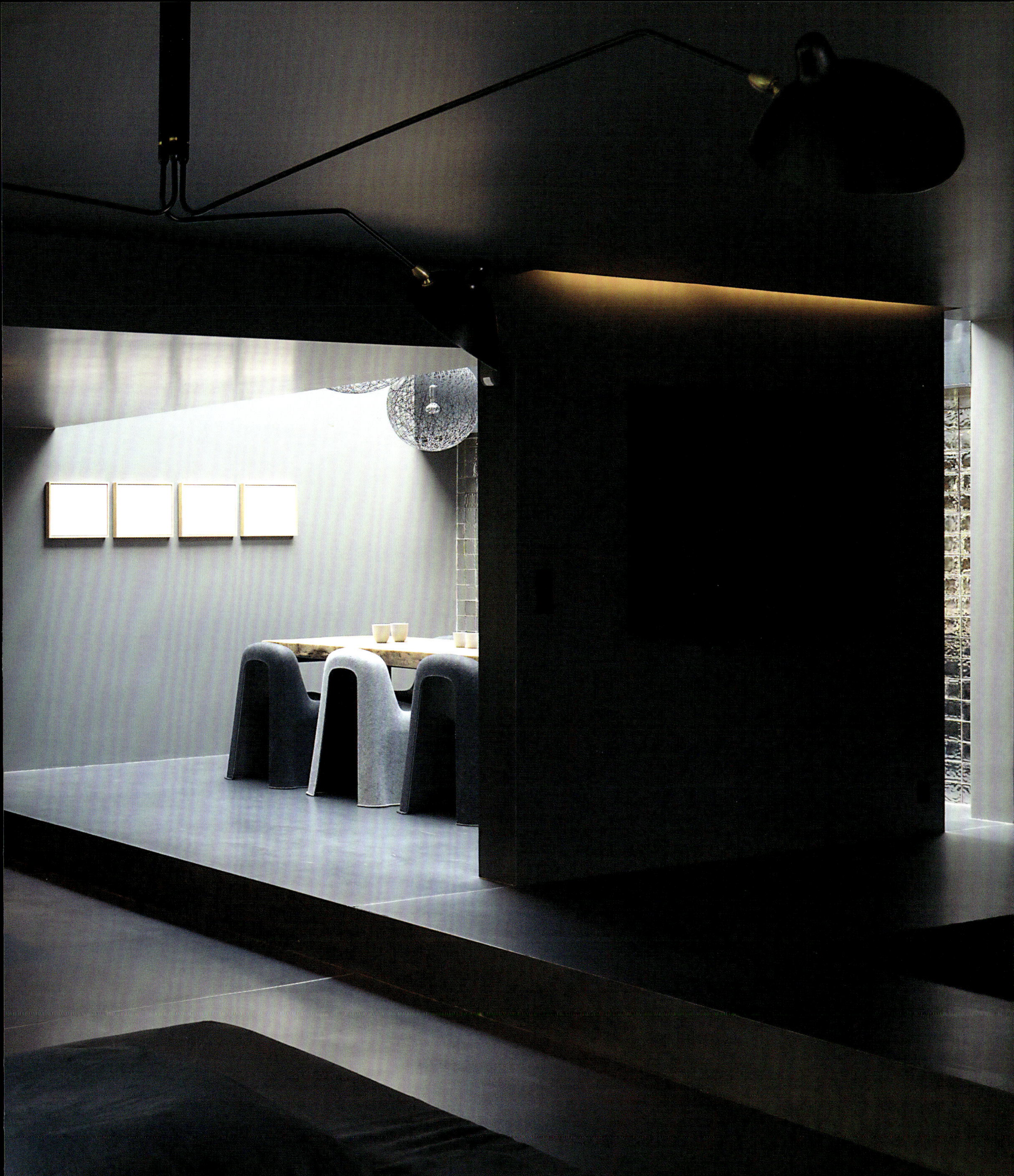

286–287 In the open cooking and dining area, the starkness of the metallic gray is offset by touches of warm yellow hues and the walnut surfaces of the kitchen cabinets. "It feels a little like a decompression chamber when I get home in the evening," remarks Simoncini. The central Bulthaup island is made from aluminum. • Im offenen Koch- und Essbereich wird das blanke Metallgrau durch warmes Gelb und die Nussbaumflächen der Küchenschränke ausbalanciert. „Wenn ich abends heimkomme, fühle ich mich hier ein wenig wie in einer Dekompressionskammer", sagt Simoncini. Die zentrale Bulthaup-Insel besteht aus Aluminium. • Dans la cuisine ouverte, l'austérité du gris métallique est adoucie par les tons chauds des placards en noyer. « C'est mon sas de décompression quand je rentre le soir », avoue Simoncini. L'îlot central en aluminium vient de chez Bulthaup.

▲ Loden on plywood: Perludi's *Amber in the Sky* bunk bed in the son's room. On the wall, Tintin's rocket is perched on the finial of an Indian column. • Loden auf Sperrholz: Perludis Stockbett *Amber in the Sky* im Zimmer des Sohns. Die Rakete aus *Tim und Struppi* steht auf einem indischen Kapitell. • Le fils dort dans un lit *Amber in the Sky* de Perludi en contreplaqué tapissé de loden. La fusée de Tintin est perchée sur un fleuron de colonne indienne.

▶ The two rectangles on the patio's far wall are a work commissioned from Herbert Hamak. Pebble-shaped table from Caravane. • Die beiden Rechtecke an der Patio-Wand sind eine Auftragsarbeit von Herbert Hamak. Kieselförmiger Tisch von Caravane. • Les deux rectangles sur le mur du patio ont été commandés à l'artiste Herbert Hamak. La table en forme de galet vient de chez Caravane.

▲ The corridor to the children's rooms entices with Oskar Zieta's *Plopp* stool and a hopscotch floor sticker by Marika Giacinti. • Im Flur vor den Kinderzimmern locken Oskar Zietas Hocker *Plopp* und ein „Himmel und Hölle"-Bodensticker von Marika Giacinti. • Dans le couloir menant aux chambres des enfants, un tabouret *Plopp* d'Oskar Zieta et une marelle en vinyle de Marika Giacinti.

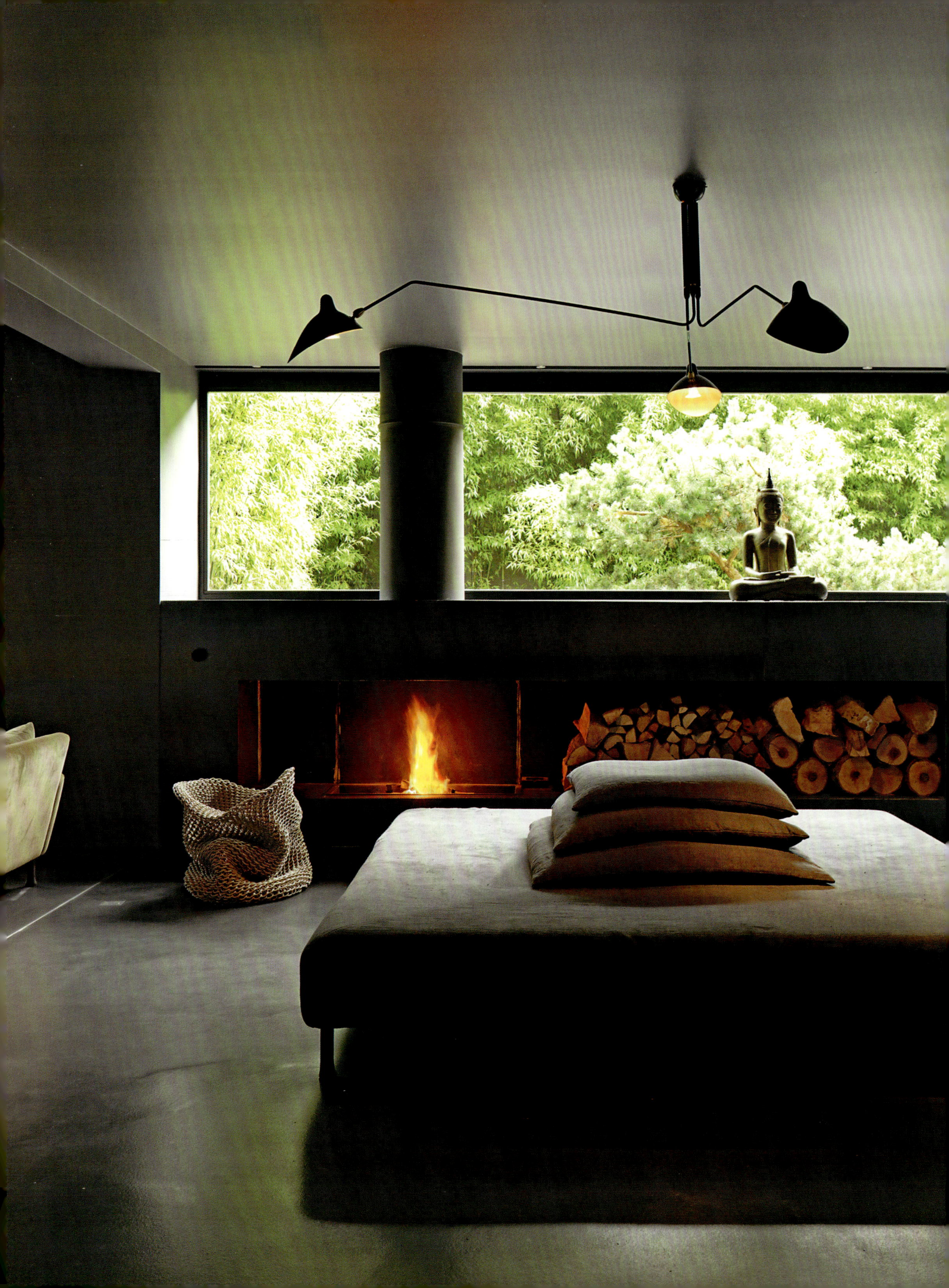

From the street, the former steel factory is rather unprepossessing. Step inside the courtyard and you enter a different world. "There are birds, bamboo, greenery," enthuses Laurence Simoncini. "It's like being in the country." Keen to create an equally restful interior, she painted all walls gray. "I find the unity soothing. One pink room, one green room is not for me," she explains. In keeping with the history of the immense space, Simoncini incorporated sheets of steel throughout and contrasted them with sensuous materials such as wood and felt. Furnishings were chosen with care. She hand-picked design classics by the likes of Eames and Serge Mouille, mixing them with contemporary pieces plus that essential dose of fun. A hopscotch outline was applied to a corridor floor, and Tintin's rocket placed on the finial of an antique Indian column. Items from her Paris store, Serendipity, found their place as well. Among them is her best seller: the *Amber in the Sky* bunk bed designed by Thomas Maitz from Austria. As she says, "I like to surprise with beauty that is not run-of-the-mill."

„WIR HABEN HIER VÖGEL, BAMBUS UND VIEL GRÜN. ES IST, ALS LEBTE MAN AUF DEM LAND." LAURENCE SIMONCINI

Von der Straße her sieht die ehemalige Stahlgießerei recht unspektakulär aus. Doch kaum betritt man den Innenhof, ist man in einer anderen Welt voll üppigem Grün. Für die Räume wünschte sich Laurence Simoncini eine ähnlich private Stimmung – und wählte dunkles Grau als Wandfarbe. „Diese Einheitlichkeit finde ich beruhigend. Ein Zimmer in Rosa, eins in Grün, das bin ich nicht", erklärt sie. Passend zur Geschichte der gewaltigen Räumlichkeiten spielt Stahlblech eine wichtige Rolle, wobei Simoncini sinnliche Materialien wie Holz oder Filz dagegensetzte. Klassiker von Eames, Serge Mouille und anderen Designgrößen mixte sie mit Zeitgenössischem, wobei die Spielfreude nicht zu kurz kommt. So thront die Rakete aus *Tim und Struppi* auf einem indischen Säulenkapitell, und im Flur lädt ein ein Hüpfrahmen zu „Himmel und Hölle" ein. Auch manches aus ihrem Pariser Laden Serendipity entdeckt man, darunter das Stockbett *Amber in the Sky*, ein Entwurf des Österreichers Thomas Maitz. Wie Simoncini selbst sagt: „Ich überrasche gern mit Schönem, das aus dem Rahmen fällt."

De l'extérieur, l'ancienne aciérie ne paie pas de mine mais, dès la cour, on pénètre dans un autre monde. « Il y a des oiseaux, de la verdure, des bambous. On se croirait à la campagne », déclare Laurence Simoncini. À l'intérieur, les murs gris sont reposants. « L'unité m'apaise. Je n'aime pas passer d'une pièce rose à une pièce verte. » Conformément à l'histoire du lieu, elle a incorporé dans le décor des plaques d'acier qui contrastent avec des matériaux sensuels tels que le bois et le feutre. Quelques classiques du design signés Eames ou Serge Mouille côtoient des meubles plus contemporains, le tout saupoudré d'une touche d'humour. Le sol d'un couloir est orné d'une marelle et la fusée de Tintin trône sur le fleuron d'une ancienne colonne indienne. Quelques pièces de sa boutique, Serendipity, y ont également trouvé leur place, dont le lit superposé *Amber in the Sky* de l'autrichien Thomas Maitz. « J'aime surprendre avec une esthétique hors des sentiers battus », explique-t-elle.

290 The ottoman in front of the fireplace is the family's favorite gathering spot. Basket made of knitted recycled paper from Best Before. • Die Ottomane vor dem Kamin ist der Lieblingstreffpunkt der Familie. Aus recyceltem Papier gestrickter Korb von Best Before. • La famille aime se réunir sur la banquette devant la cheminée. Panier en tresses de papier recyclé.

▲ A Tibetan goat pouf and a cowhide rug add warmth to Simoncini's office. The chandelier was made from terra-cotta beads by South African women. • Ein Pouf aus Kaschmirziegenfell und ein Kuhfell „wärmen" Simoncinis Büro. Den Lüster fertigten Südafrikanerinnen aus Tonperlen. • Un pouf en chèvre tibétaine et une peau de vache égaient le bureau de Simoncini. Des Sud-Africaines ont réalisé le lustre avec des perles en terre cuite.

◀ On the wall above her desk, Simoncini gathers an assortment of her children's drawings, invitations, and photos that catch her eye. • An der Wand über ihrem Schreibtisch sammelt Simoncini Zeichnungen ihrer Kinder, Einladungen und Fotos, die ihr auffielen. • Le mur devant son bureau est tapissé de dessins de ses enfants, d'invitations et de photos qui ont retenu son attention.

▶ Watching over a tiger wood table by Jérôme Abel Seguin is a gorilla that was created by British artist David Mach from 7,500 coat hangers. • Den Tigerwood-Tisch von Jérôme Abel Seguin hat ein Gorilla im Blick, den der britische Künstler David Mach aus 7500 Kleiderbügeln formte. • Un gorille créé par l'artiste britannique David March avec 7 500 cintres surveille une table basse en bois tigré de Jérôme Abel Seguin.

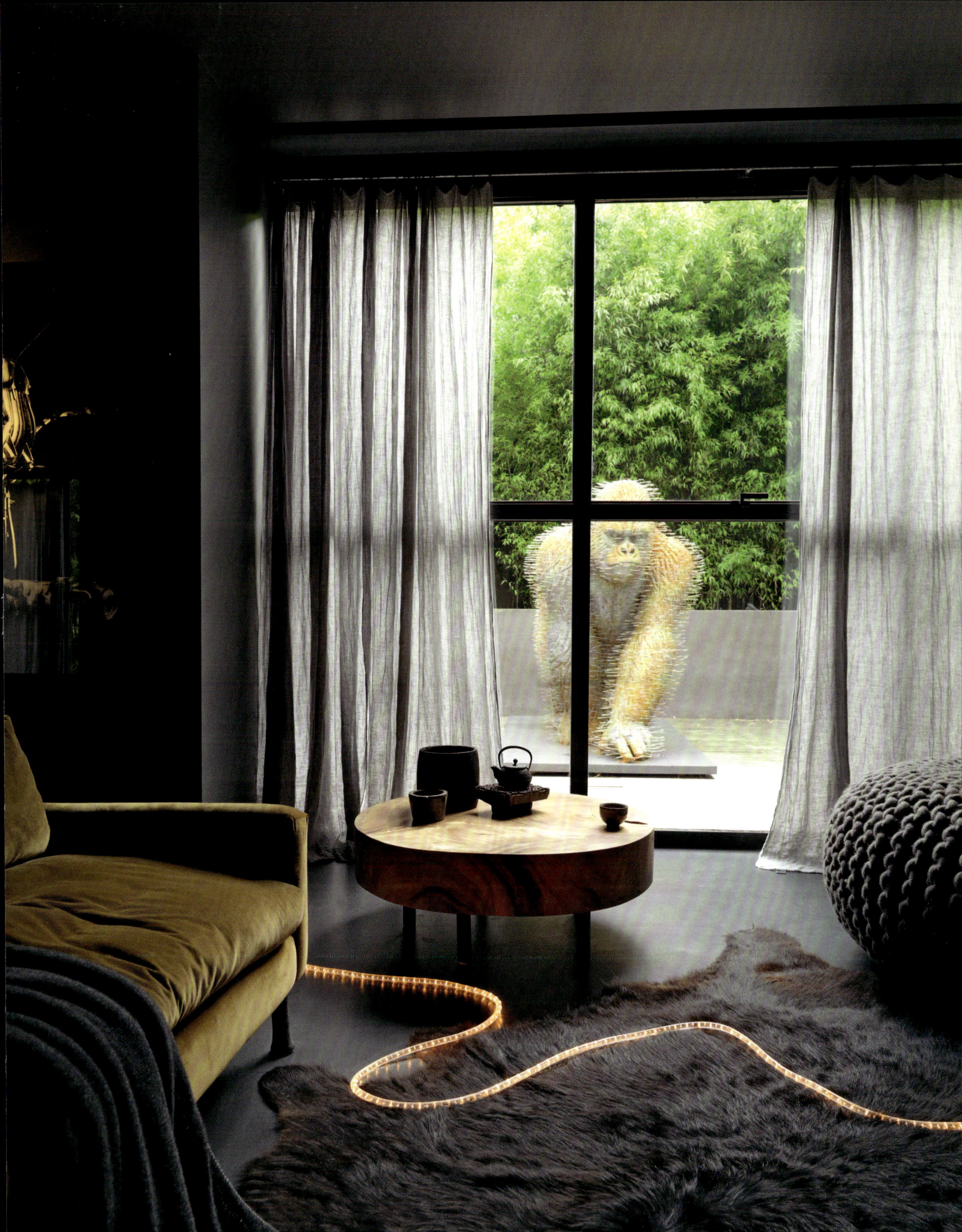

FAYE TOOGOOD

A SOPHISTICATED RENOVATION IN LONDON

WHO London-based designer. **WHAT** A 317 m² (3,412 sq. ft.), four-bedroom row house. **WHERE** One of the British capital's most sought-after neighborhoods. **THE CLIENTS** A fashion designer and a fashion photographer, both in their thirties. **COUNTRY-BRED** Toogood had a rural upbringing in the county of Rutland. **GETTING AHEAD** She made a name for herself as a stylist with her work for *The World of Interiors*. Clients have included Comme des Garçons, Kenzo, and Tom Dixon. **HEROES** Achille Castiglioni and Gio Ponti. **HOME TURF** All of Toogood's designs are produced in the U.K.—her *Cage for Birds* dressing table by a welder who normally works on motorcycles, and the wooden version of her *Spade* chair by a factory that also produces toilet seats. **RECENT PROJECTS** Limited-edition crystal pieces for Galerie BSL in Paris and a domestic interior in the north of London.

PHOTOGRAPHED BY BILL BATTEN   PORTRAIT BY RORY VAN MILLINGEN

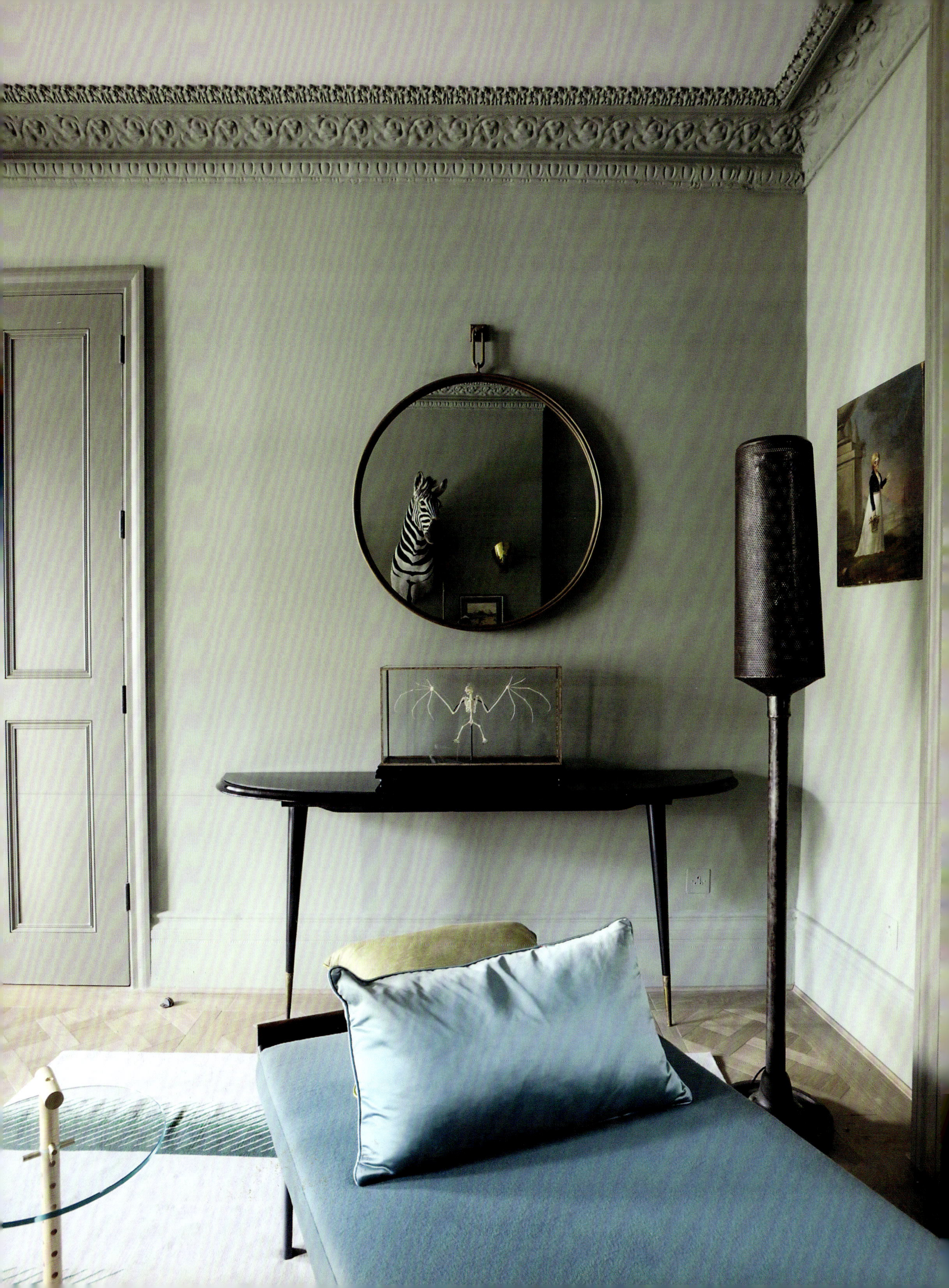

295 A bat skeleton and ebonized console table in the living room. Metal floor lamp from Philip Thomas. • Im Wohnzimmer steht ein Fledermausskelett auf einer ebonisierten Konsole. Metall-Leuchte vom Londoner Antiquitätenhändler Philip Thomas. • Dans le séjour, un squelette de chauve-souris est posé sur une console teintée couleur ébène. Le luminaire a été acheté chez l'antiquaire londonien Philip Thomas.

▼ Toogood installed the dining table in the kitchen. A 1950s Sputnik bulb chandelier and a trio of Hiroshi Sugimoto seascapes add to the ethereal atmosphere of the space. • Ein Sputnik-Lüster aus den 1950ern und *Seascapes* von Hiroshi Sugimoto geben der Essecke etwas Ätherisches. • La table de salle à manger est dans la cuisine. Un lustre « Spoutnik » des années 1950 et les photographies de mer de Hiroshi Sugimoto ajoutent à l'atmosphère « éthérée ».

▶ On the opposite end of the kitchen, a Michael Anastassiades *Tube Chandelier* over an Eames table and Prouvé chairs. • Am anderen Ende der Küche: Michael Anastassiades' *Tube Chandelier* über einem Eames-Tisch mit Prouvé-Stühlen. • À l'autre bout de la cuisine : un lustre *Tube Chandelier* de Michael Anastassiades suspendu au-dessus d'une table Eames avec des chaises Prouvé.

298–299 For the walls of the living room, Toogood chose an Emery & Cie green. Both the *Elements* coffee table and the rug are her own designs. • Für die Wohnzimmer wählte Toogood ein raffiniertes Grün von Emery & Cie. Coffeetable *Elements* und Teppich entwarf sie selbst. • Pour les murs du séjour, Toogood a choisi un vert raffiné d'Emery & Cie. Elle a dessiné la table basse *Elements* ainsi que le tapis.

TOOGOOD 297

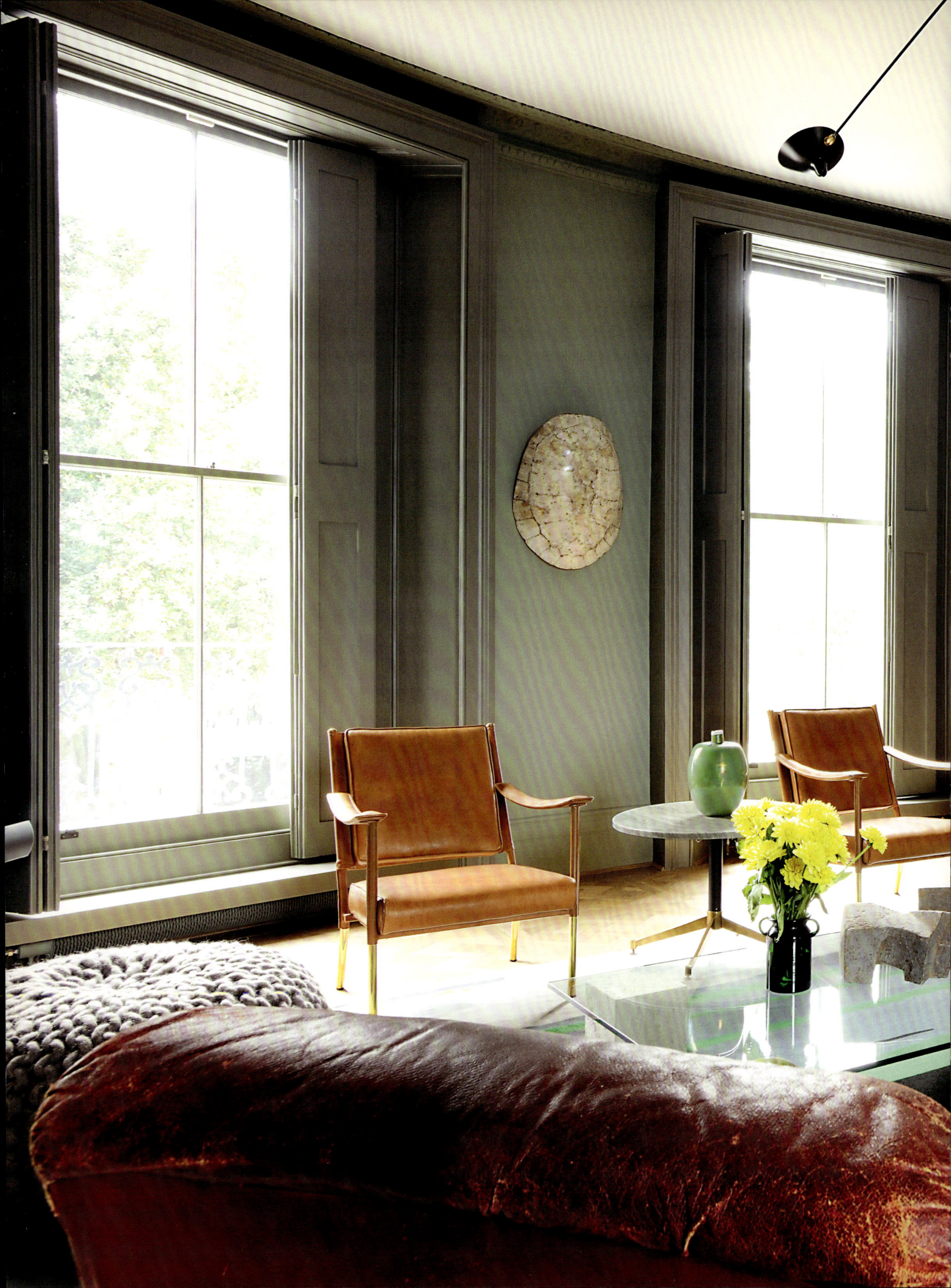

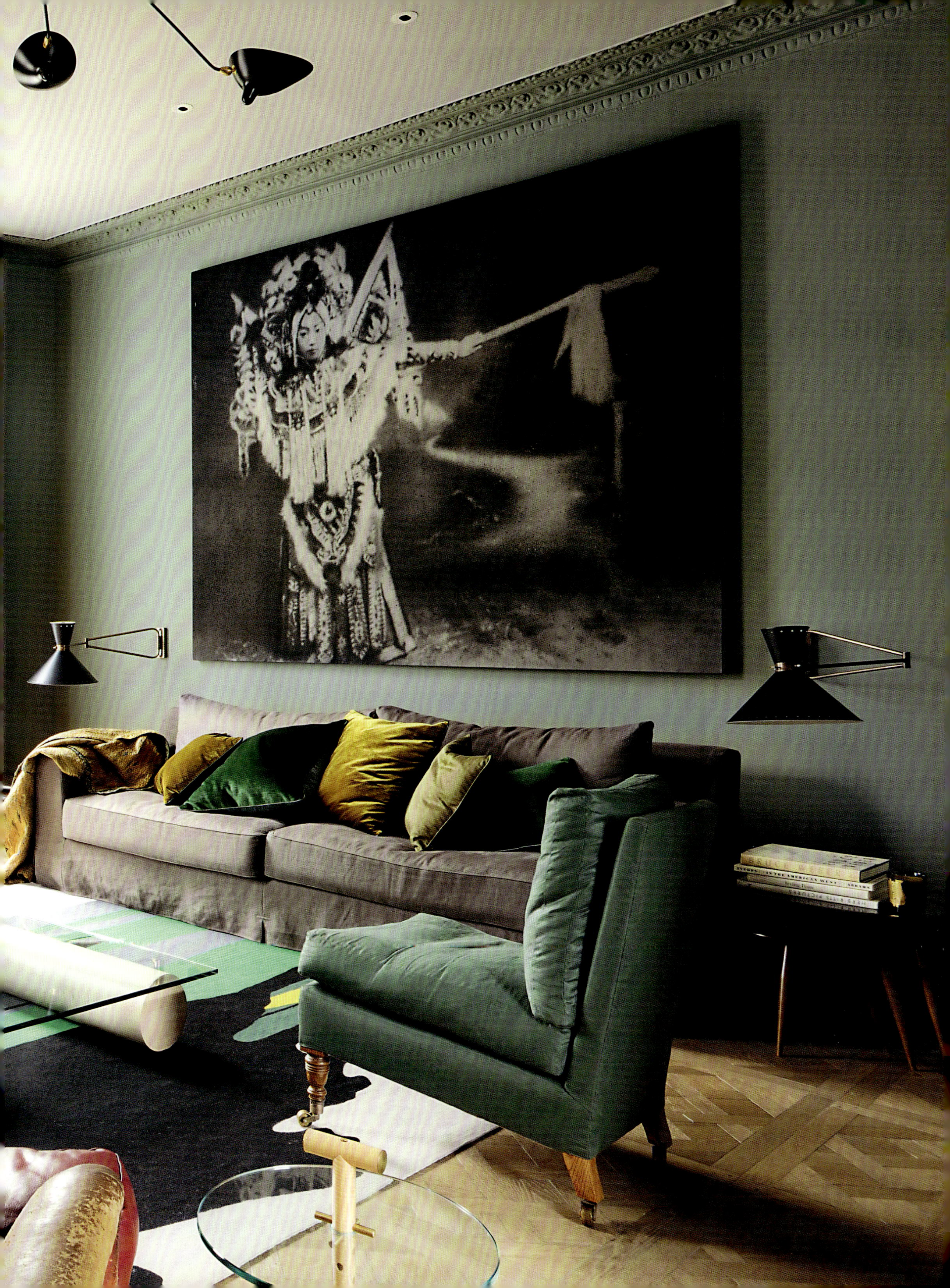

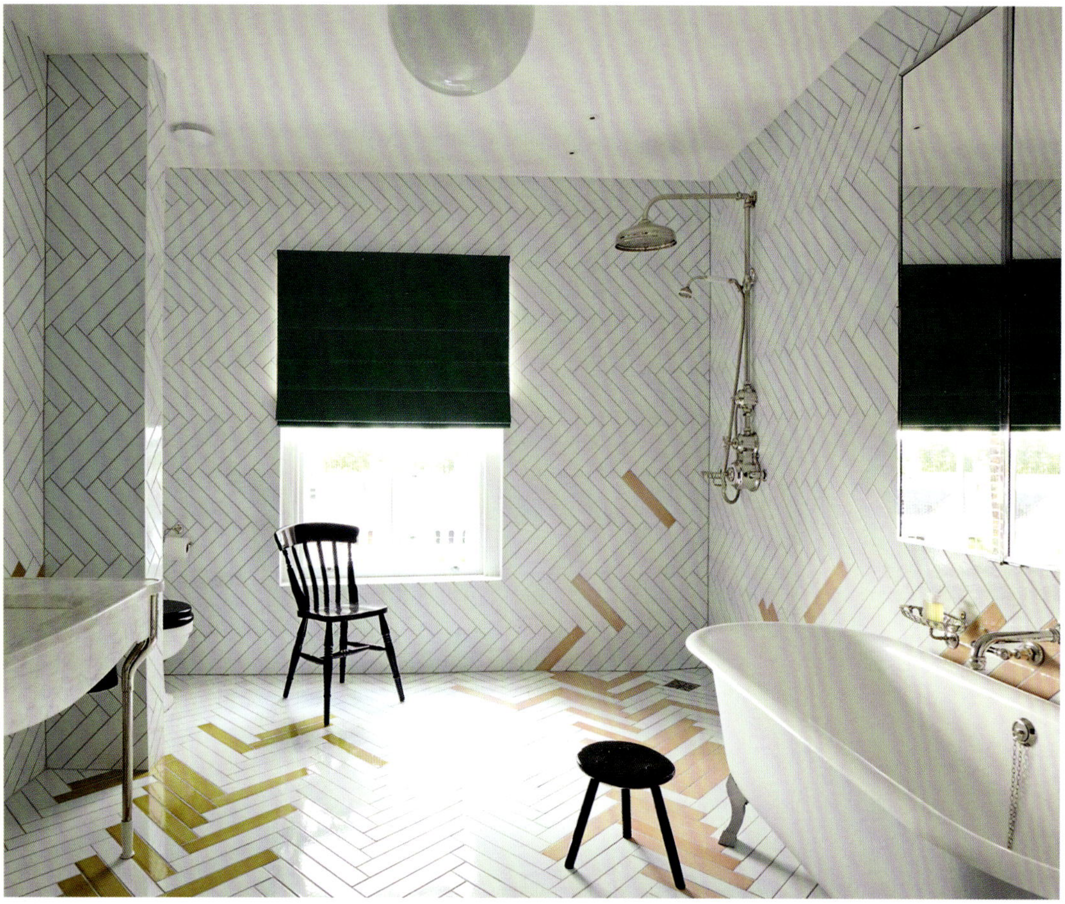

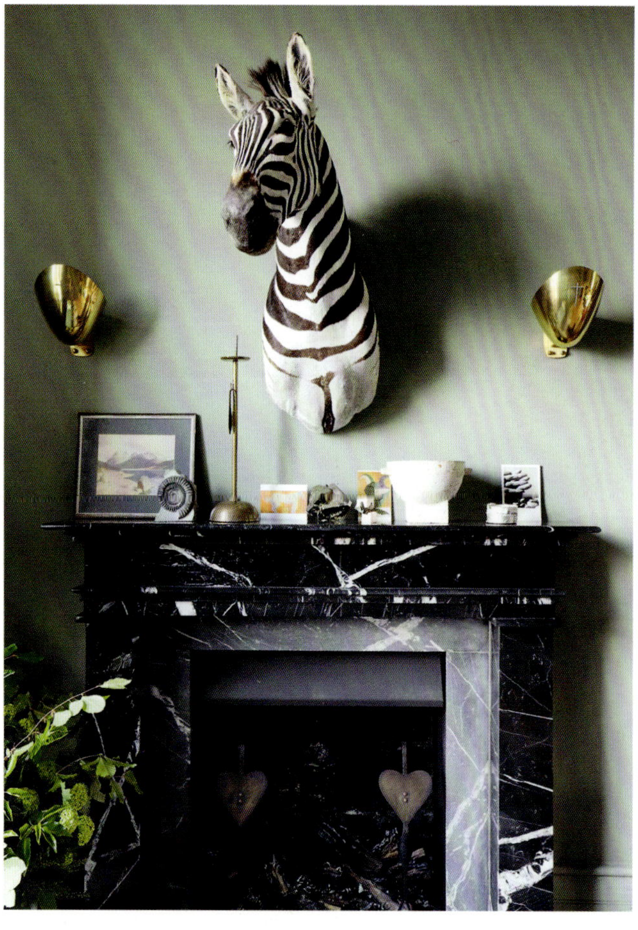

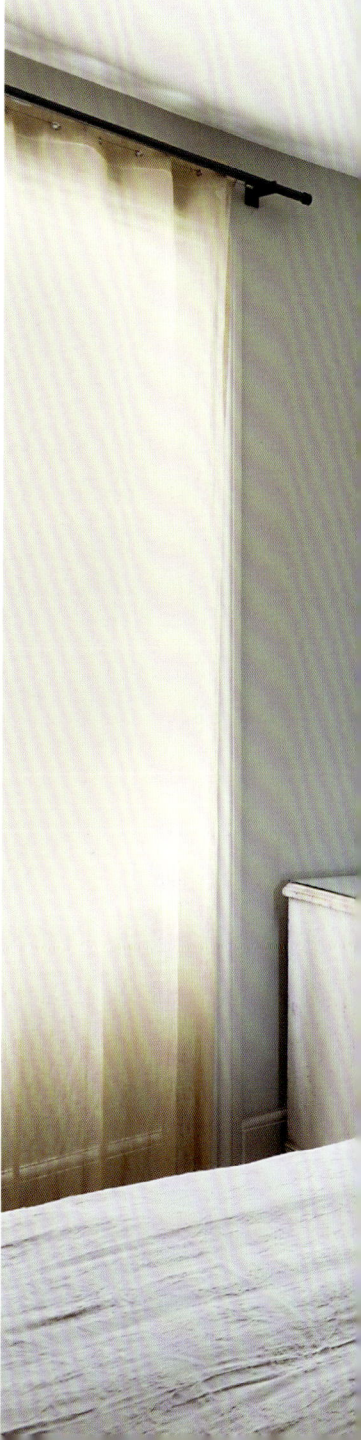

◀ Toogood used handmade, slightly irregular tiles in the bathroom. Main treading areas were highlighted with color. • Im Bad verwendete Toogood handgefertigte, leicht unregelmäßige Fliesen. Wo sie wie farbige Spuren wirken, liegen die Funktionsbereiche. • Soulignant les zones de grand passage avec de la couleur, Toogood a utilisé du carrelage fait main dans la salle de bains.

▶ In the living room, she refaced the fireplace with black marble and hung a zebra from Get Stuffed in Islington above it. • Den Kamin im Wohnzimmer ersetzte sie durch einen Eigenentwurf aus Marmor, darüber hängt ein Zebrakopf von Get Stuffed in Islington. • Elle a remplacé l'ancienne cheminée du salon par une autre en marbre noir veiné qu'elle a dessinée. Au-dessus, une tête de zèbre provenant de la boutique Get Stuffed à Islington.

▼ The chandelier in the bedroom is made of five *Selene* pendants from ClassiCon. Closets are covered in silk by De Gournay. • Im Schlafzimmer vereinen sich fünf *Selene*-Kugelleuchten von ClassiCon zum Lüster. Der Schrank wurde mit Seiden von De Gournay bezogen. • Le lustre de la chambre a été réalisé avec cinq plafonniers *Selene* de chez ClassiCon. Les placards sont tapissés de soies de chez De Gournay.

In the family room, two chairs from Caravane stand on a custom blue area carpet. *TWB* (Tailored Wood Bench) seat by Raw Edges for Cappellini. • Im Familienzimmer stehen zwei Sessel von Caravane auf dem blauen Maßteppich. Holzsitz *TWB* (Tailored Wood Bench) von Raw Edges für Cappellini. • Dans le séjour, deux fauteuils de chez Caravane sur un tapis bleu sur mesure. Le banc *TWB* (Tailored Wood Bench) a été créé par Raw Edges pour Cappellini.

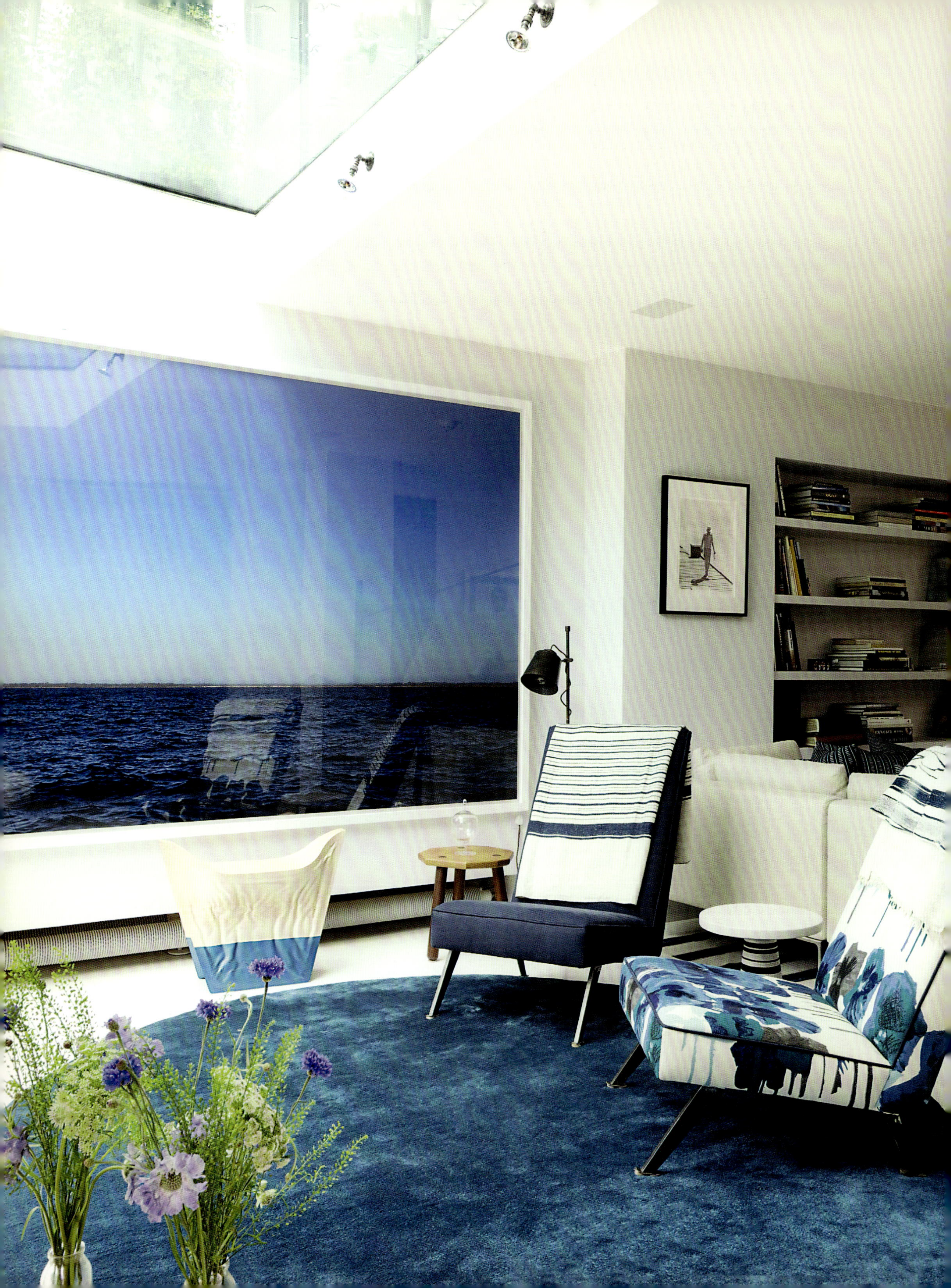

"I WANTED TO CREATE A SPACE THAT FEELS CONTEMPORARY, BUT ALSO EMBRACES THE FACT THAT THIS IS AN OLD HOUSE." FAYE TOOGOOD

Thus the London designer's aim with this, her first domestic interior, was quite clear. To achieve it, Faye Toogood revealed period features and removed unfortunate additions made in the late 1990s. "There was a lot of slightly green-tinged architectural glass going on," she cringes. The starting point for her color palette came from three photographic artworks her clients owned, as well as their love of Marni. Toogood used hues she associates with the Italian fashion brand: "slightly off colors," like fleshy rose or ochre or a moody green. The furnishings are a savvy mix of different periods and styles—"the modern, the Victorian, the rustic. I wanted the interiors to feel lived in, to feel layered." She also wanted them to be luxurious, as witnessed by the master bathroom clad in handmade enameled lava tiles. With that, she apparently drove the workmen crazy. "I gave them a specific map showing where each individual tile was to go," she recounts.

„Es sollten Räume werden, die sich zeitgenössisch anfühlen und doch das Alter des Hauses anklingen lassen", das hatte sich Faye Toogood für ihr erstes Privatprojekt vorgenommen. Also arbeitete die Londoner Designerin Details der Erbauungszeit heraus und entfernte unvorteilhafte Ergänzungen aus den 1990ern. „Wir hatten es mit einer Menge grünlichem Bauglas zu tun", stöhnt sie. Ausgangspunkt für ihre Farbwahl waren drei Foto-Arbeiten aus dem Besitz der Auftraggeber sowie deren Begeisterung für Marni. Immer wieder trifft man auf Nuancen, wie man sie von der italienischen Modemarke kennt – „leicht schräge Töne" wie Fleischrosa, Ocker oder ein verhangenes Grün. Die Möblierung mixt clever Epochen und Stile: „Das Moderne, das Viktorianische, das Rustikale. Alles sollte echt gelebt wirken, vielschichtig." Ein gewisser Luxus durfte auch nicht fehlen. So ist das Bad mit handgearbeiteten Lavasteinfliesen verkleidet, mit denen Toogood wackere Handwerker an den Rand der Verzweiflung trieb: „In meinem Plan war die Position jeder einzelnen Fliese vorgeschrieben."

« J'ai cherché à créer un espace contemporain tout en respectant l'esprit de cette vieille maison », déclare Faye Toogood à propos de son premier projet de décoration pour des particuliers. Dans ce but, elle a fait ressortir des détails d'origine et ôté des ajouts fâcheux datant de la fin des années 1990. « Il y avait beaucoup de verre architectural verdâtre », dit-elle avec une grimace. Pour sa palette de couleurs, elle s'est inspirée de trois photographies appartenant aux propriétaires ainsi que de leur passion pour Marni. Elle a repris des teintes légèrement passées propres à la marque italienne dans la chambre principale, tel que le rose chair et l'ocre. Dans le salon, elle a choisi un vert mélancolique. Le mobilier est un savant mélange d'époques et de styles : « Du moderne, du victorien, du rustique. Je voulais que ça ait l'air vécu. » Elle tenait également à ce que l'ensemble soit luxueux, comme en témoigne la salle de bains tapissée de carrelage en lave émaillée fait main. Les ouvriers ont cru devenir fous. « Je leur ai donné un plan précis indiquant l'emplacement de chaque carreau », explique-t-elle.

JORGE VARELA

A HOUSE IN MADRID THAT GIVES ORNAMENT A NEW LEASE ON LIFE

WHO Spanish architect and interior designer. **WHAT** A 250 m² (2,691 sq. ft.), three-bedroom house dating from the late 1920s that was remodeled in the 1950s. **WHERE** The El Viso neighborhood. **THE CLIENTS** A couple in their thirties, who both work in finance. **GOING DUTCH** Varela previously lived part-time in Amsterdam. He copied his old front door there and installed the result in this project. **SWISS HERO** His website is peppered with quotes from his favorite architect, Peter Zumthor. "I relate to the finesse of his thinking," he explains. "He always avoids show-off architecture and focuses on the details and atmosphere." **FRENCH GEMS** Varela was responsible for the scenography of "The Art of Cartier" exhibition at Madrid's Museo Thyssen-Bornemisza in winter 2012/13. **AMERICAN DREAM** He now has a house in Santa Marta on the Caribbean coast of Colombia. "It's really an amazing country," he enthuses.

PHOTOGRAPHED BY PABLO GÓMEZ-ZULOAGA

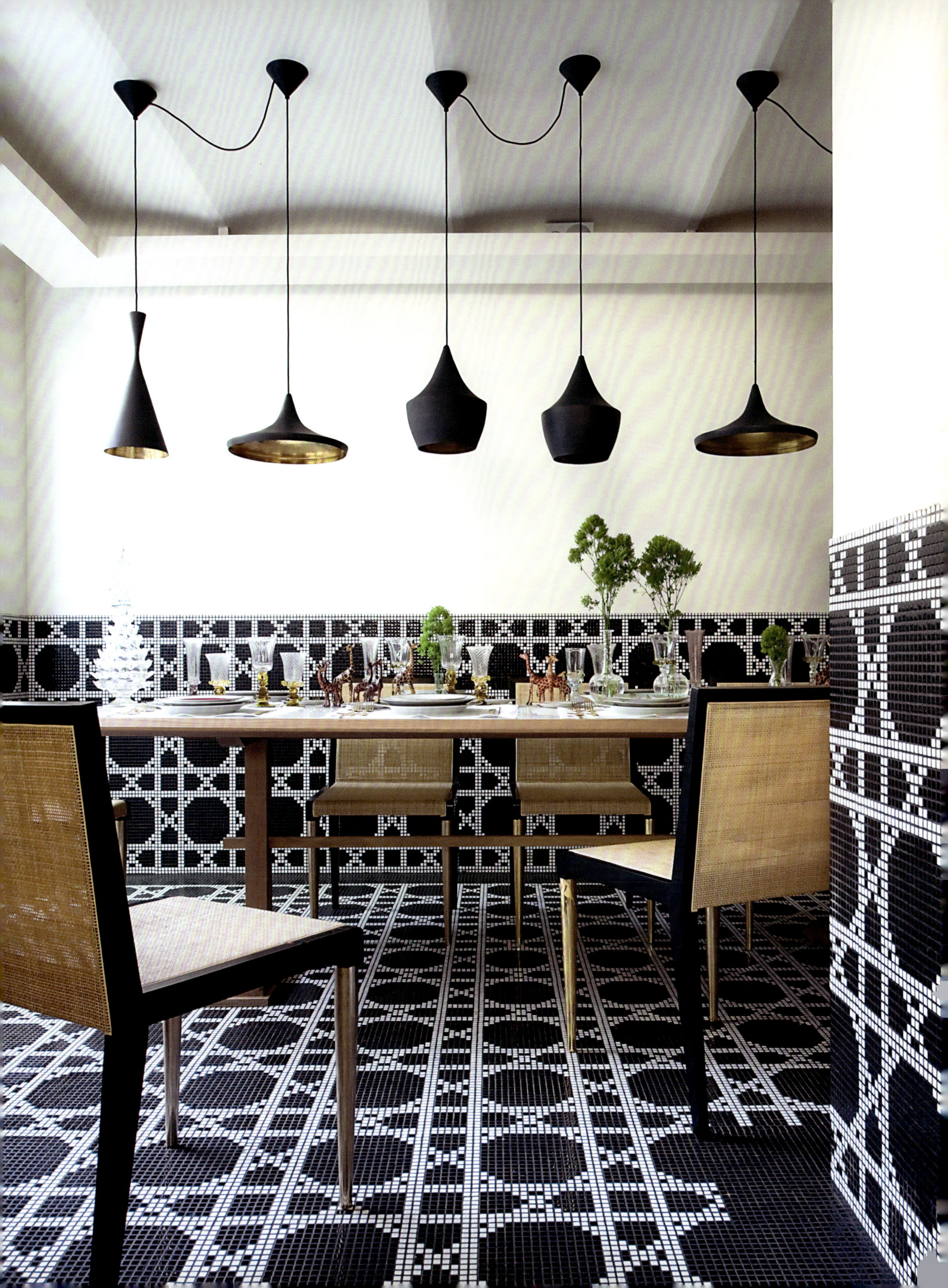

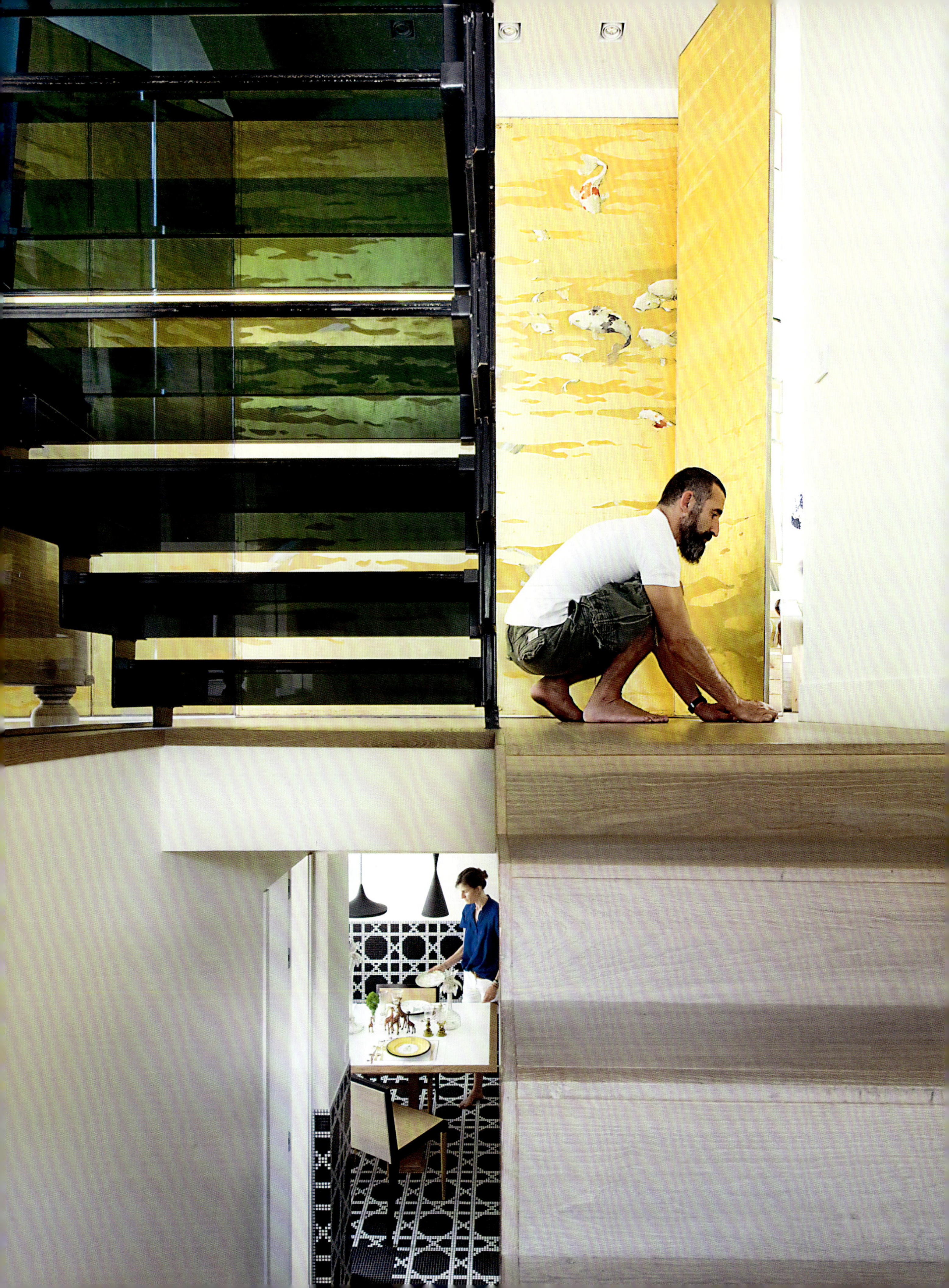

305 In the dining room, Tom Dixon pendants shine on a table and chairs by Varela. The mosaic is *Vienna* by Bisazza. • Für das Esszimmer in der früheren Garage ließ Varela den Boden ausheben, was mehr Raumhöhe brachte. Tisch und Stühle entwarf er selbst, die Lampen sind von Tom Dixon. Mosaik *Vienna* von Bisazza. • La salle à manger a été «creusée» dans l'ancien garage pour gagner de la hauteur. Les lampes sont de Tom Dixon, la table et les chaises sont des créations de Varela. Il a trouvé la mosaïque *Vienna* chez Bisazza.

◂ The architect unfolds the oil-and-gold-leaf screen, which is concealed in the living room's mirrored unit. • Der Architekt beim Entfalten des bemalten und mit Blattgold verzierten Wandschirms, der sich im Spiegel-Element des Wohnzimmers verbirgt. • L'architecte déploie le paravent peint à l'huile et doré à la feuille, intégré dans la cloison en miroir du séjour.

▲ An Aga stove stands out among aluminum-fronted cabinets in the kitchen. • In der Küche nimmt der dunkel glänzende Aga-Herd einen Ehrenplatz zwischen nüchternen Aluminiumfronten ein. • La cuisine sobre avec ses meubles revêtus d'aluminium. Une cuisinière Aga occupe la place d'honneur.

308-309 The mirrored partition is also functional: it hides two structural columns and contains a bar and TV. On the back wall is a José Manuel Ballester photograph; right, a Portuguese chest of drawers. • Der verspiegelte Raumteiler hat mehrere Funktionen: Er verhüllt zwei Stützpfeiler und enthält eine Hausbar und den Fernseher. An der Wand links hängt eine Fotoarbeit von José Manuel Ballester; vorn rechts steht eine portugiesische Kommode. • La cloison en miroir est fonctionnelle : elle cache deux colonnes porteuses, un bar et une télévision. Au fond, une photographie de José Manuel Ballester ; à droite, une commode portugaise.

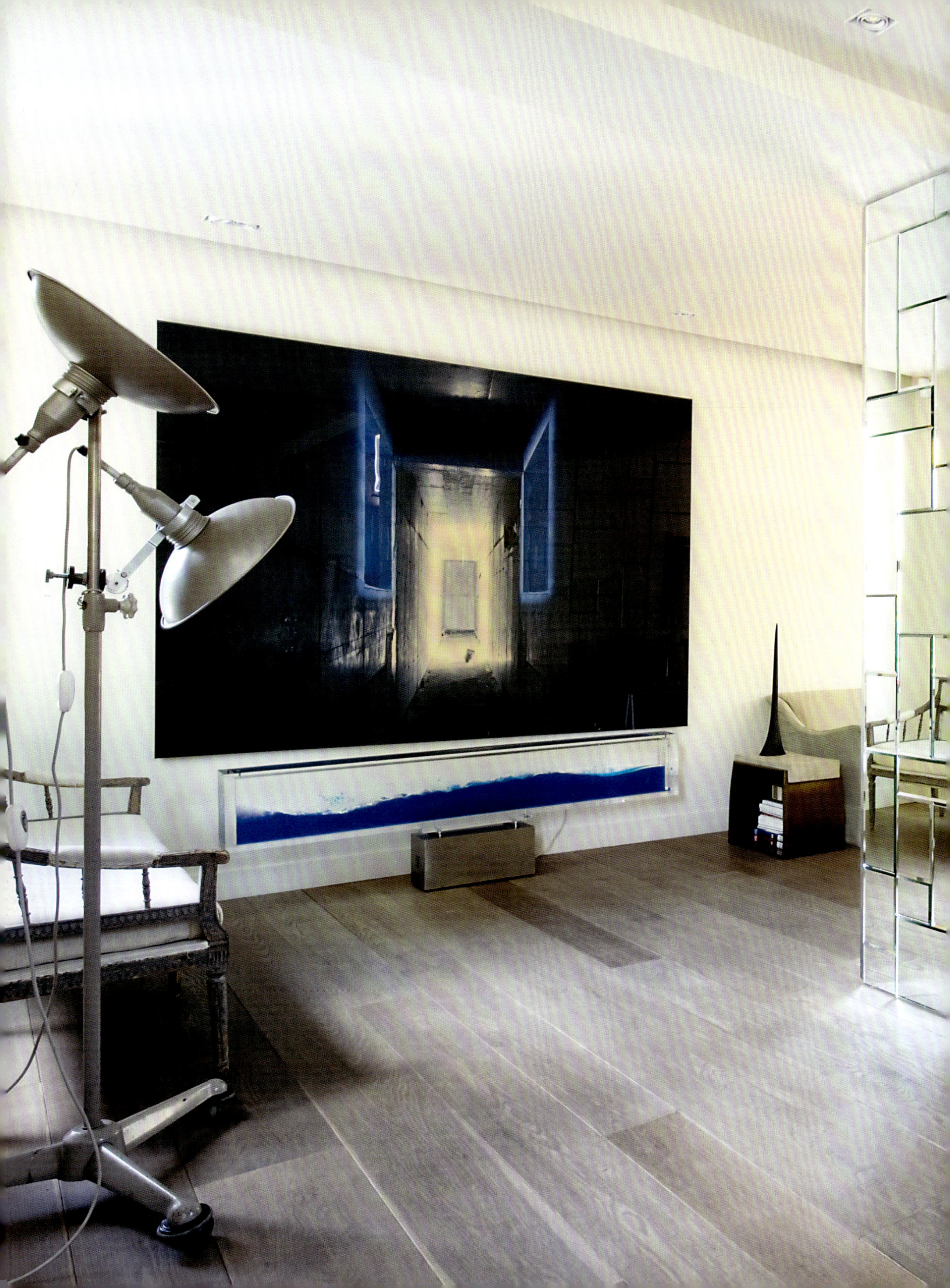

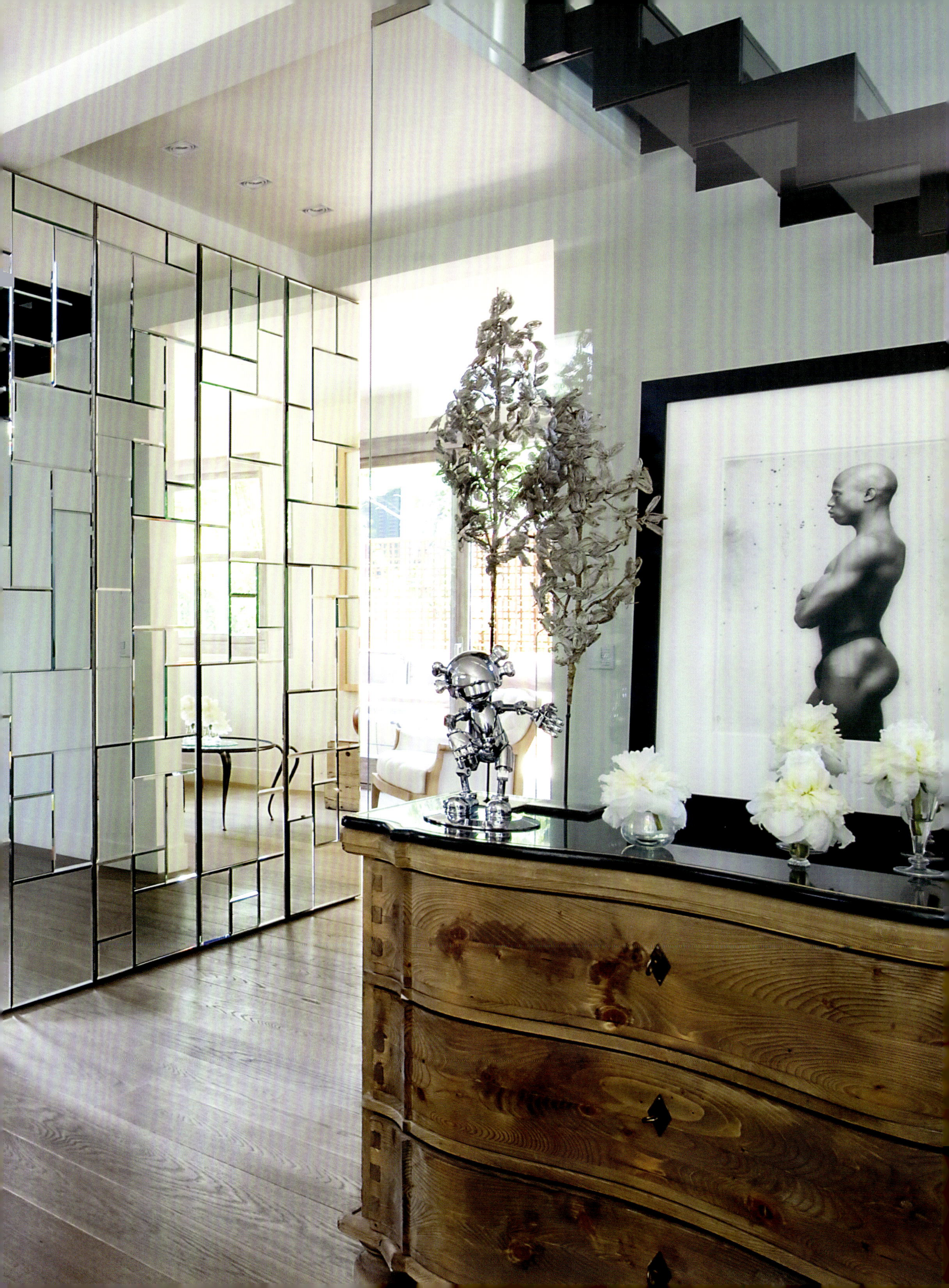

▲ In the pantry, an Alex Katz painting and a pair of 1950s Danish pendants are juxtaposed with a vintage French work table. • In der Pantry treffen ein Gemälde von Alex Katz, ein dänisches Leuchtenpaar aus den 1950ern und ein alter französischer Werkstatttisch aufeinander. • Dans arrière-cuisine, une paire de plafonniers danois des années 1950 est suspendue au-dessus d'une vieille table de travail française. Le tableau est d'Alex Katz.

▶ (clockwise) The walls in a guest room are in a striped cotton Kvadrat fabric; a sculpture by French artist Claire Rougerie sits on a c. 1900 leather chest originally used in safety deposit vaults; in the master suite, Carrara marble is paired with a custom mirrored vanity; the crisscross relief motif on the white dressing room doors is "a stylized version of patterns found on Moorish tiles at the Alhambra," explains Varela. The benches are made from bamboo. • (im Uhrzeigersinn) Gestreifter Baumwollstoff von Kvadrat dient im Gästezimmer als Wandbehang; eine Skulptur der Französin Claire Rougerie steht auf einem lederbezogenen Schränkchen, das ursprünglich im Tresorraum einer Bank stand; im Bad des Hausherrn umgibt Carrara-Marmor den maßgefertigten Spiegel-Waschtisch; die linearen Kerben auf den Einbauten der Ankleide „sind eine stilisierte Version von maurischen Fliesenmustern in der Alhambra", erklärt Varela; die Bänke bestehen aus Bambus. • (Dans le sens des aiguilles d'une montre) Les murs d'une chambre d'amis sont tapissés d'un tissu en coton rayé de chez Kvadrat ; une œuvre de la sculptrice française Claire Rougerie est posée sur un meuble en cuir (env. 1900) utilisé jadis pour entreposer des objets précieux dans la salle des coffres d'une banque ; dans la salle de bains principale, le marbre de Carrare est assorti à une coiffeuse en miroir sur mesure ; le relief sur les portes blanches du dressing est « une version stylisée des motifs de carreaux mauresques de l'Alhambra », explique Varela. Les bancs sont en bambou.

312–313 In order to open the house for natural daylight, Varela opted against draperies. Instead, he installed shutters in the master bedroom. The gilded bronze sconces date from the 1950s. • Um möglichst viel natürliches Licht ins Haus zu lassen, verzichtete Varela auf Vorhänge und entwarf stattdessen ein Raumkonzept mit Fensterläden für das Schlafzimmer. Die beiden Appliken aus vergoldeter Bronze sind aus den 1950er-Jahren. • Pour un maximum de lumière naturelle, Varela a décidé de ne pas utiliser de rideaux. Dans la chambre principale, il a posé des volets. Les appliques en bronze doré datent des années 1950.

314 A vintage bench from a school gymnasium stands next to an enameled iron tub in the master bathroom. • Vor der Wanne aus emailliertem Eisen im Masterbad steht eine Vintage-Bank aus einer Schulsporthalle. • Dans la salle de bains principale, un vieux banc trouvé dans le gymnase d'une école trône près d'une baignoire en fonte émaillée.

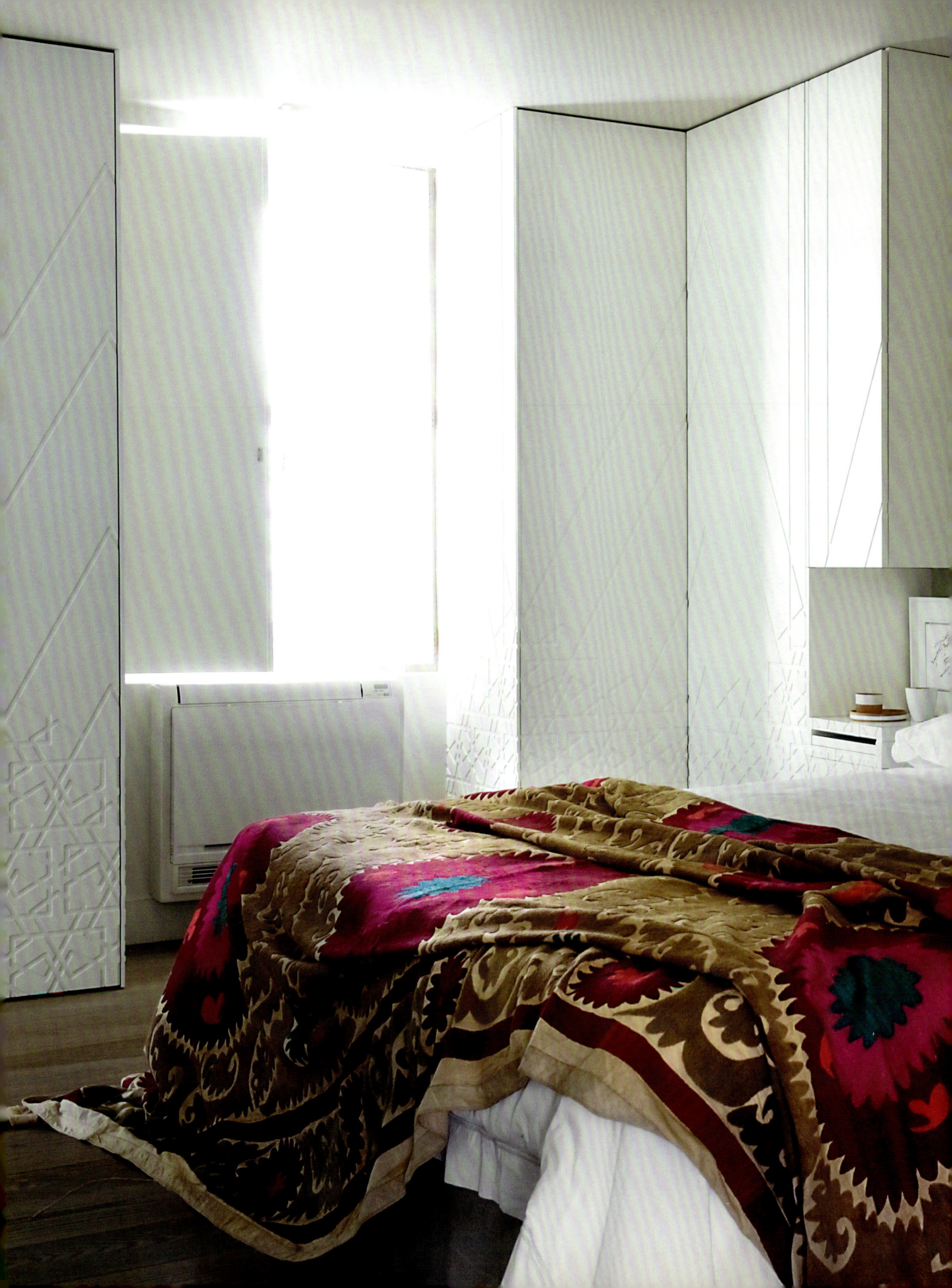

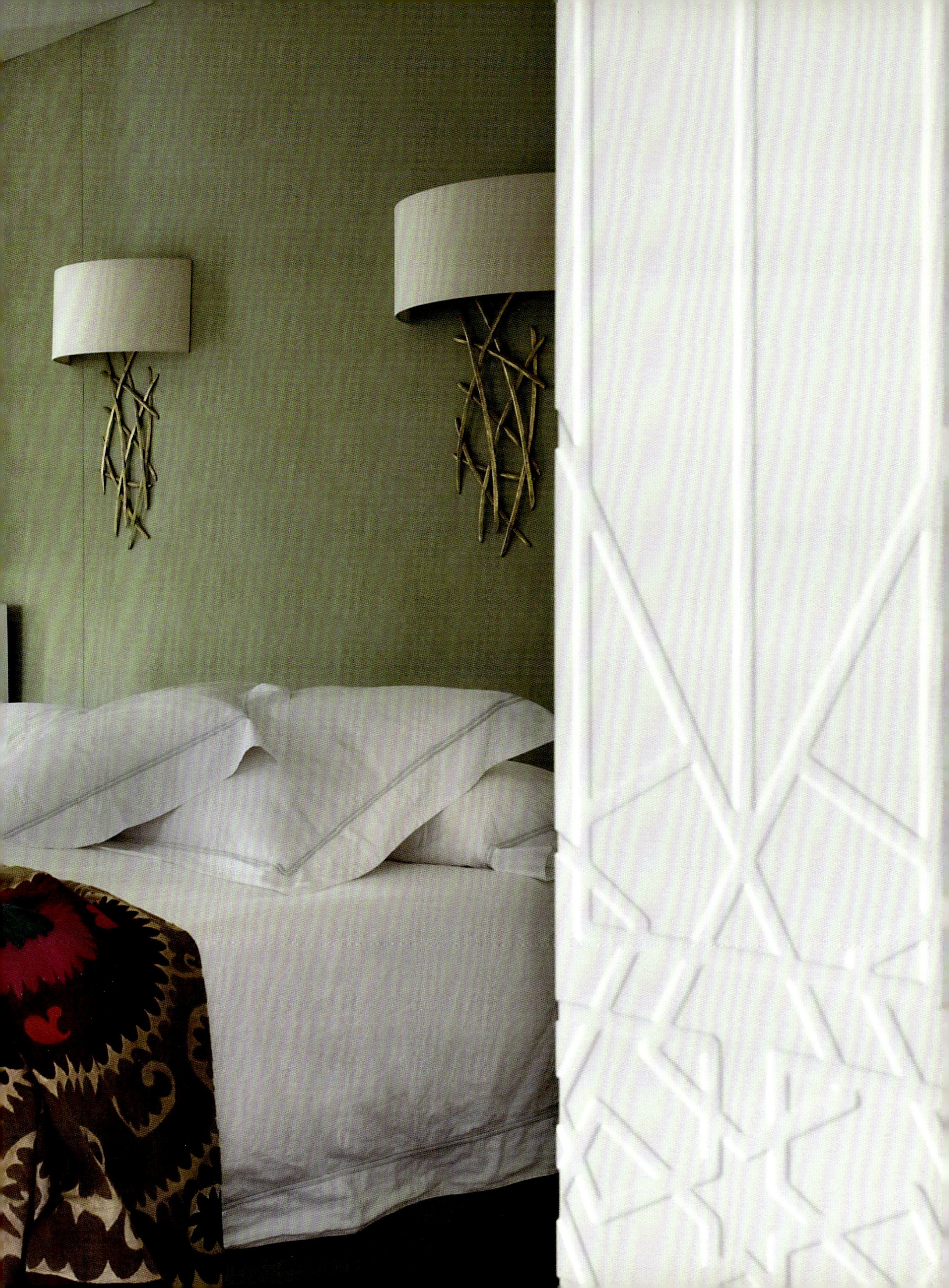

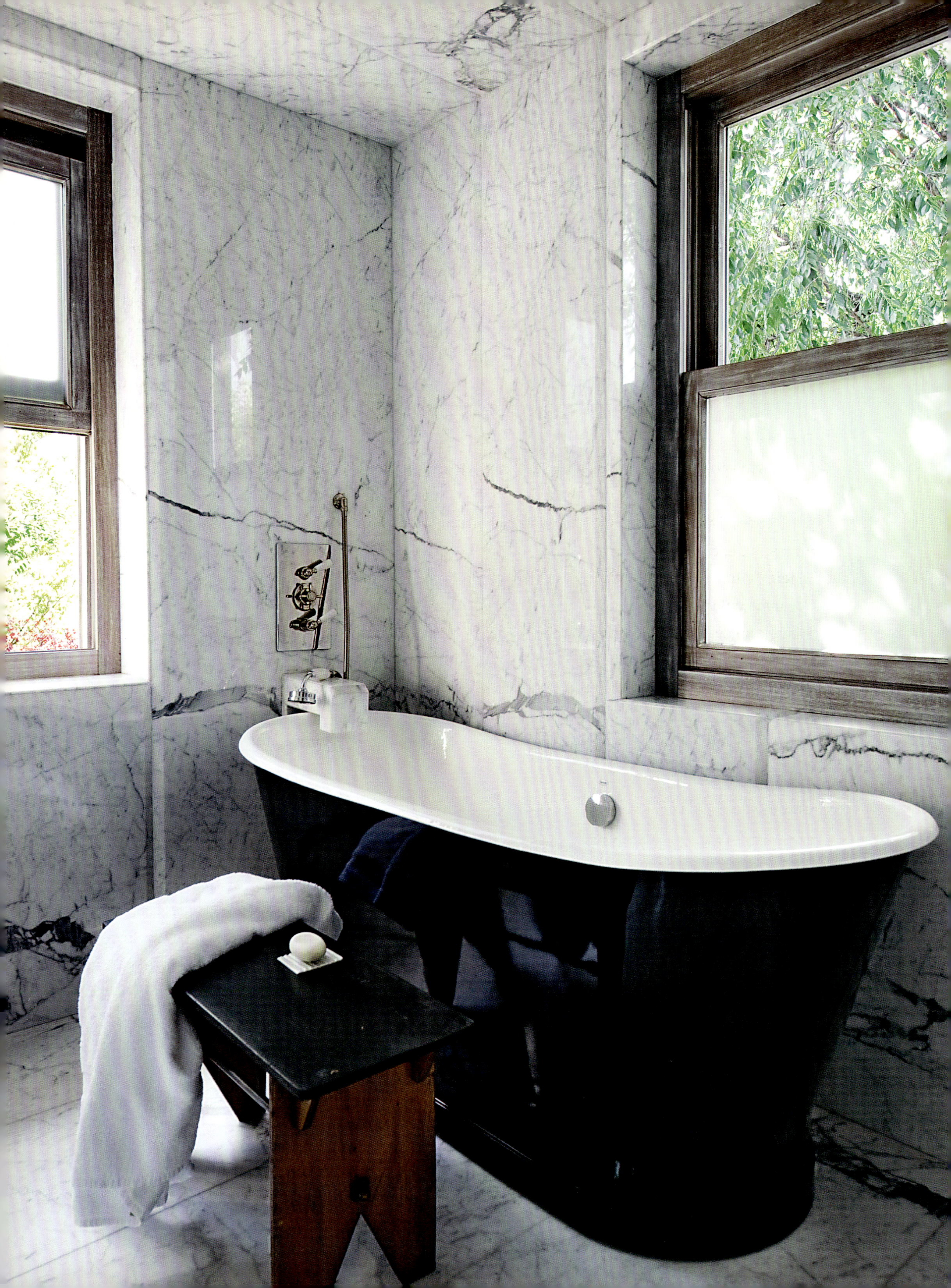

"It was a house pretending to be a mansion," declares Jorge Varela. "There were lots of moldings on the ceilings. It was very pretentious." Not surprisingly, his approach was to completely gut it. He was also keen to allow in as much natural light as possible. To this end, the Spanish architect opened up volumes, enclosed the stairwell linking the four floors in glass, and left the windows without draperies. The serene atmosphere he created is redolent of Belgian or Dutch interiors. "I'm quite attached to those textures, colors and materials," Varela admits. Yet, he also incorporated a few flourishes. One example is the tiled dining room in the basement. "It's like you're going into a hammam or maybe a pool," he opines. Another is the modular mirrored partition in the living room, which houses a gold leaf screen by Isabel Alonso that can be unfolded to close off the space from the entrance hall. Then, there are the relief motifs on the dressing room doors, inspired by the Alhambra in Granada. "I love Andalusian style," notes Varela. "For me, it's the most refined expression of artistic craftwork."

„Das Haus tat so, als wäre es eine herrschaftliche Villa", erzählt Jorge Varela. „Die Decken waren mit Gesimsen verziert, alles wirkte viel zu pompös." Kein Wunder, dass genau das verschwinden musste. Um möglichst viel natürliches Licht hineinzulassen, öffnete Varela dann einzelne Bereiche, verglaste die Treppe, die die vier Geschosse verbindet, und verzichtete auf Vorhänge. Die heiter-gelassene Atmosphäre, die nun herrscht, erinnert eher an belgische oder niederländische Interieurs. „Zu deren Tönen, Texturen und Materialien fühle ich mich hingezogen", gibt der Spanier zu. Ein paar flamboyante Fanfarenstöße setzte er als aber schon. Das mosaikverkleidete Esszimmer im Souterrain „erinnert an einen Hamam oder gar einen Pool". Ein Spiegelmodul im Wohnzimmer wiederum verbirgt einen blattvergoldeten Screen von Isabel Alonso; entfaltet, trennt er den Raum vom Entree ab. Zum Relief auf den Ankleideschränken ließ Varela sich übrigens von der Alhambra in Granada inspirieren. „Ich liebe den andalusischen Stil", erklärt er. „Er ist Kunsthandwerk in seiner raffiniertesten Form."

« C'ÉTAIT UNE MAISON QUI SE PRENAIT POUR UN MANOIR. » JORGE VARELA

« Les plafonds étaient surchargés de moulures. C'était très prétentieux », ajoute-t-il. Naturellement, il a tout repensé. Pour faire entrer le maximum de lumière, l'architecte a ouvert les espaces, entouré de verre la cage d'escalier qui relie les quatre étages et laissé les fenêtres sans rideaux. L'atmosphère pure et sereine ainsi créée évoque les intérieurs flamands. « Je suis très attaché à ces textures, ces couleurs et ces matières », avoue-t-il. Quelques fioritures ont été intégrées dans le décor, notamment le carrelage de la salle à manger en sous-sol. « C'est comme si on descendait dans un hammam ou une piscine. » Dans le séjour, il a aussi installé une cloison modulaire en miroir. Ce dernier accueille également un paravent doré à la feuille d'Isabel Alonso qui se déploie pour isoler la pièce de l'entrée. Sur les portes blanches du dressing et de la chambre, Varela a réalisé des motifs en relief inspirés de l'Alhambra de Grenade. « J'aime le style andalou », explique-t-il. « À mes yeux, c'est l'expression la plus raffinée de l'artisanat d'art. »

BERNHARD WILLHELM

A FASHION DESIGNER'S
ROSENHEIM PIED-À-TERRE IN PARIS

WHO German-born fashion designer Bernhard Willhelm. **WHAT** His 40 m² (430 sq. ft.), studio apartment in a 1972 building with a terrace the same size. **WHERE** In the 11th arrondissement near St. Ambroise church. **CONCEPT** "*Meine Welt*, my world, as will and representation, to quote Schopenhauer," states Willhelm. **HIS PARTNERS IN CRIME** Efe Erenler, a Berlin-based interior designer formerly of Erenler Bauer, who started to build things early on: "My father says, 'Efe, when you were three, you tried to take the drill out of my hands.' " Paris-based architect Caspar Muschalek praises the collaborative nature of the project: "Our role was to make sure that Mr. Willhelm's many ideas could settle, crystallize, and then be realized professionally." He and Erenler have also worked jointly on the interiors of the Sessùn boutiques in Paris and Berlin. **NO GO** Willhelm suggested lifting in the huge marble slab for his bathroom via helicopter. "I said, 'We'll need Daniel Craig as the pilot to get a permit for this,' " laughs Erenler. **LET THEM GROW** Stumping expectations, the wild 'n' wacky Willhelm has created a dainty rose garden on the terrace with the help of artist friend Nadine Stich.

PHOTOGRAPHED BY JAN BITTER   PORTRAIT BY JUERGEN TELLER

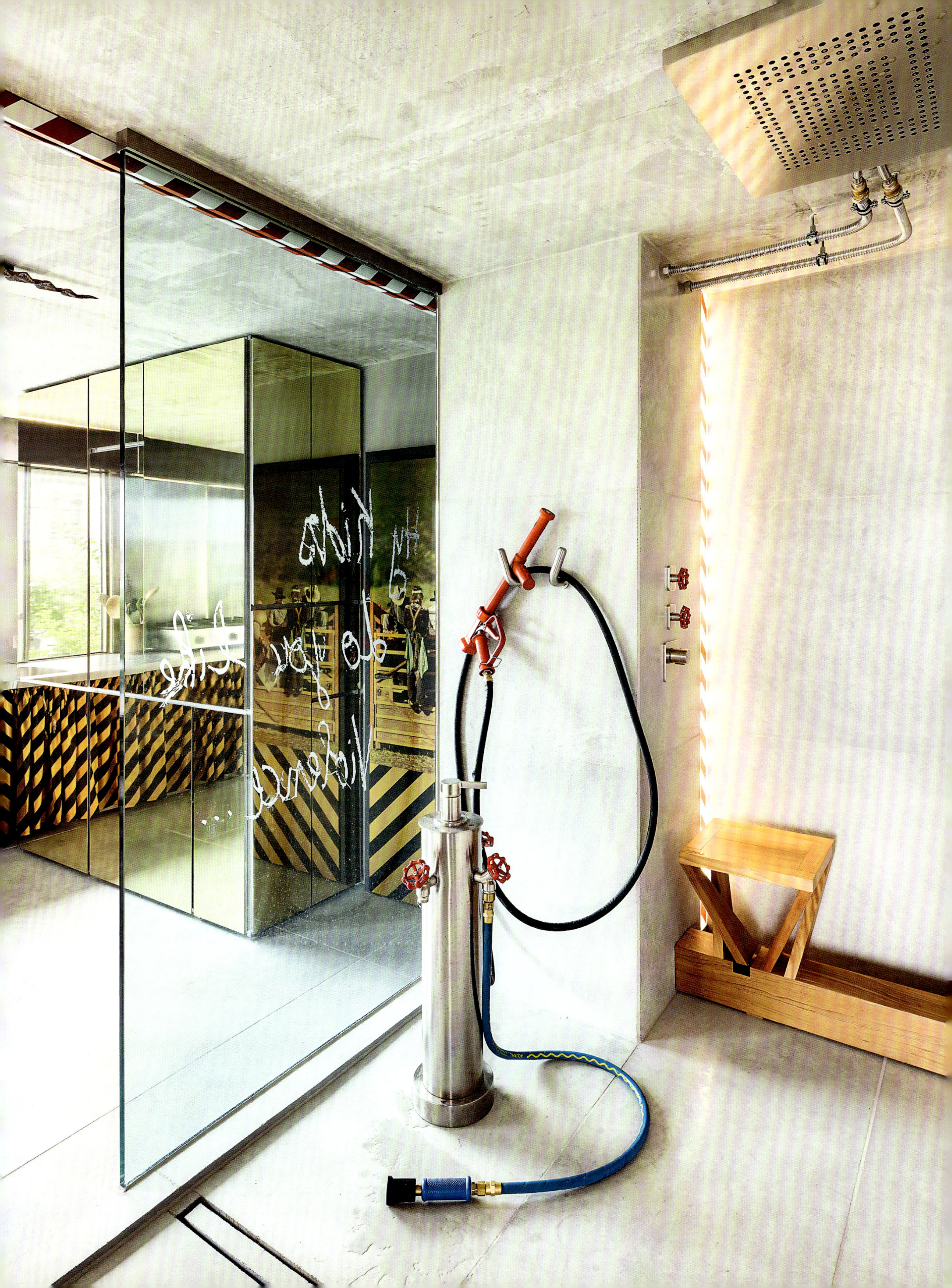

317 An advertisement for the Fire Brigade provided inspiration for the custom shower fixture, made from stainless steel and tubes normally found in the food-service industry. • Ein Werbemotiv der Feuerwehr war Vorlage für die stählerne Standbrause mit Schläuchen aus der Lebensmittelindustrie. • La douche, réalisée avec des tuyaux utilisés dans l'industrie alimentaire, s'inspire d'une publicité pour les pompiers.

▼ Marble sourced in Vienna was used on one of the bathroom walls. The bench is made from cedar. • Aus Wien importierter Marmor bedeckt eine Wand im Bad. Davor ein Sitz aus Zedernholz. • Un des murs de la salle de bains est recouvert d'un marbre importé de Vienne. Le banc est en cèdre.

▶ The building-site aesthetic is typified by the striped cotton skirt under the kitchen counter and the painted red-and-white rail. A platform with tatami matting serves as Willhelm's bedroom alcove. • Die gestreifte Baumwollschürze der Arbeitsplatte und die rot-weiße Deckenschiene verweisen auf Willhelms Baustellenthema. Ein Podest mit Tatami-Matten dient als Bettstatt. • La toile en coton rayé sous le comptoir de la cuisine et le rail de plafond peint de rayures rouges et blanches soulignent le style « chantier de construction ». L'estrade couverte de tatamis fait office de coin couchette.

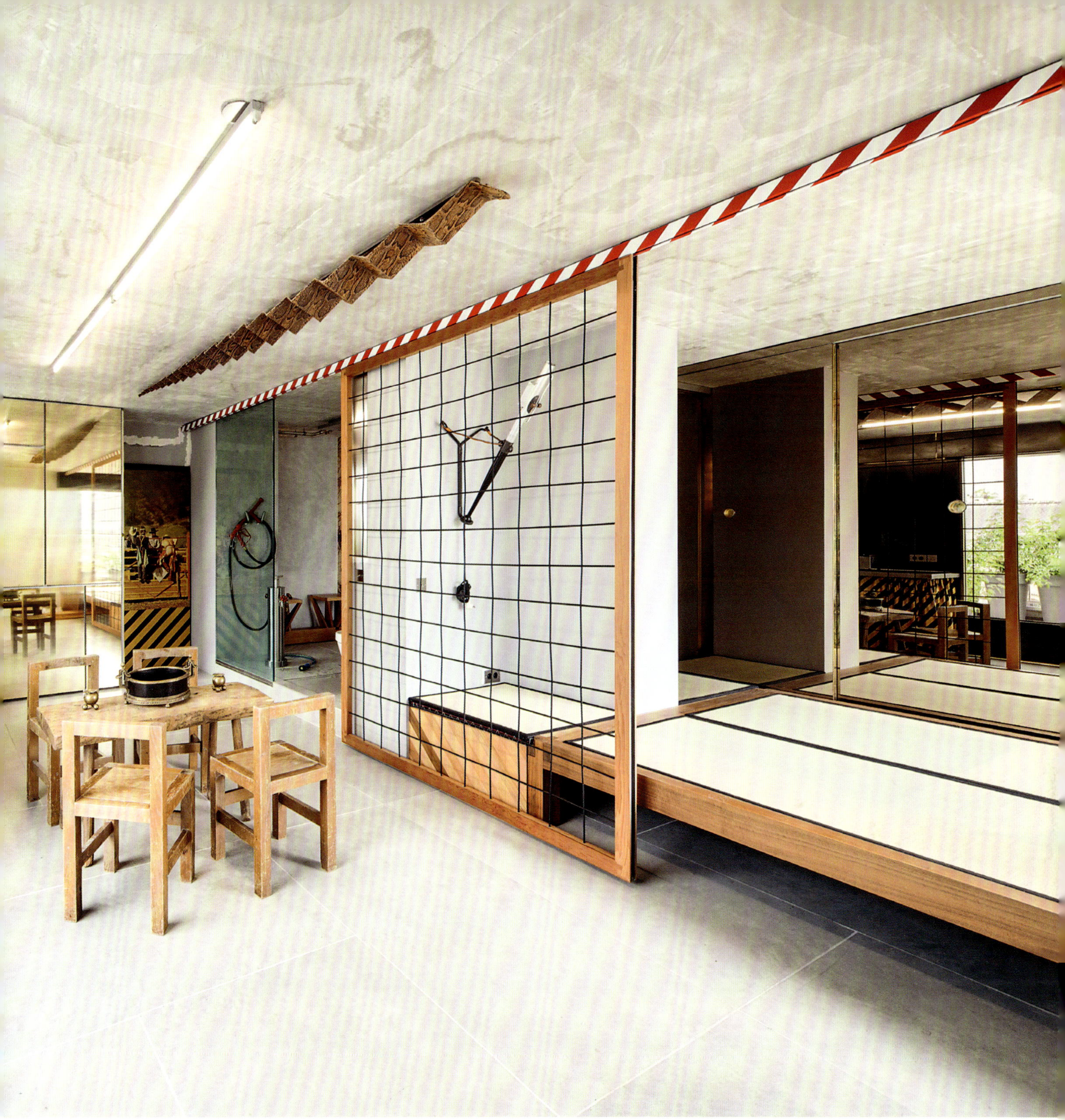

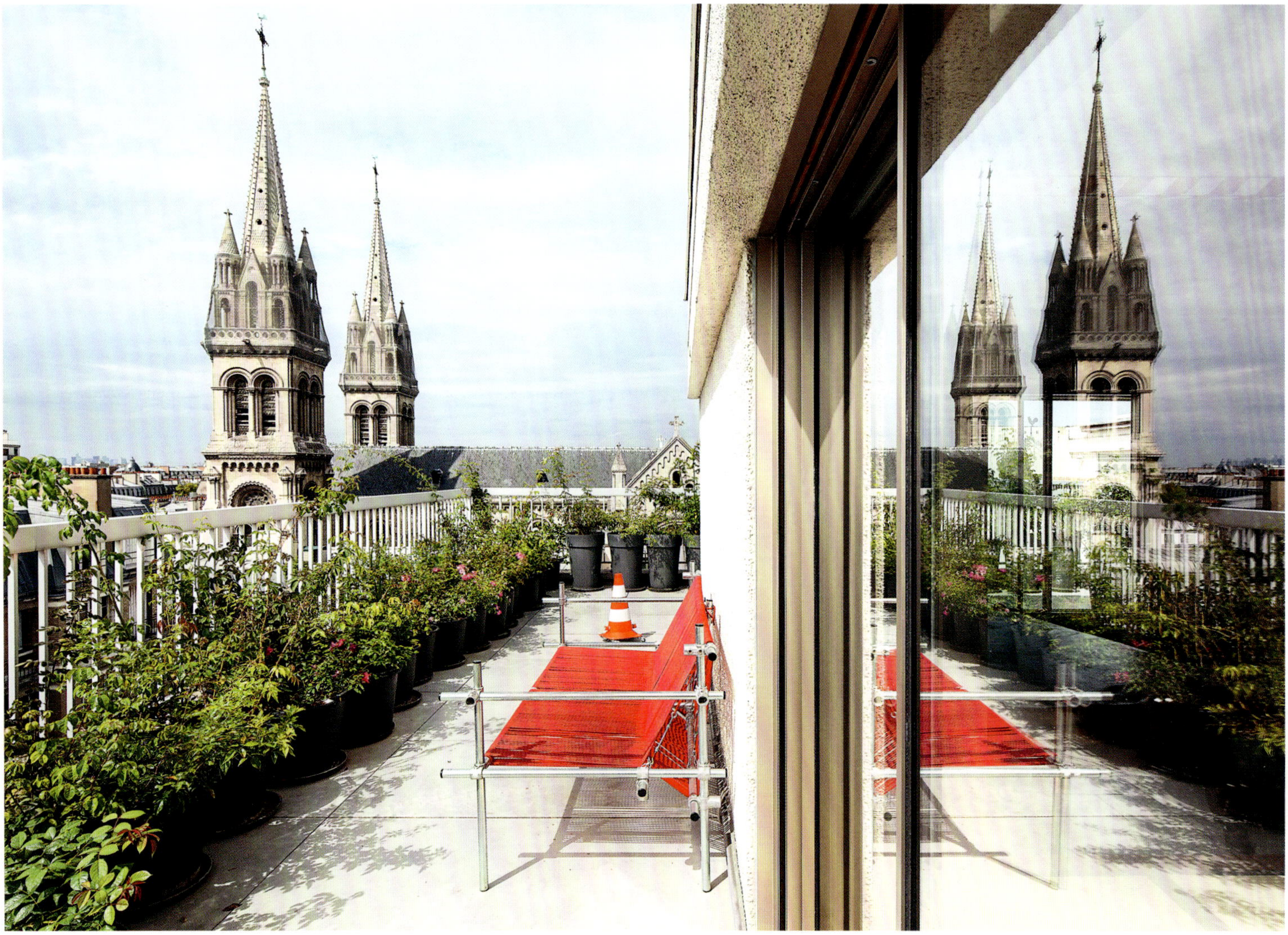

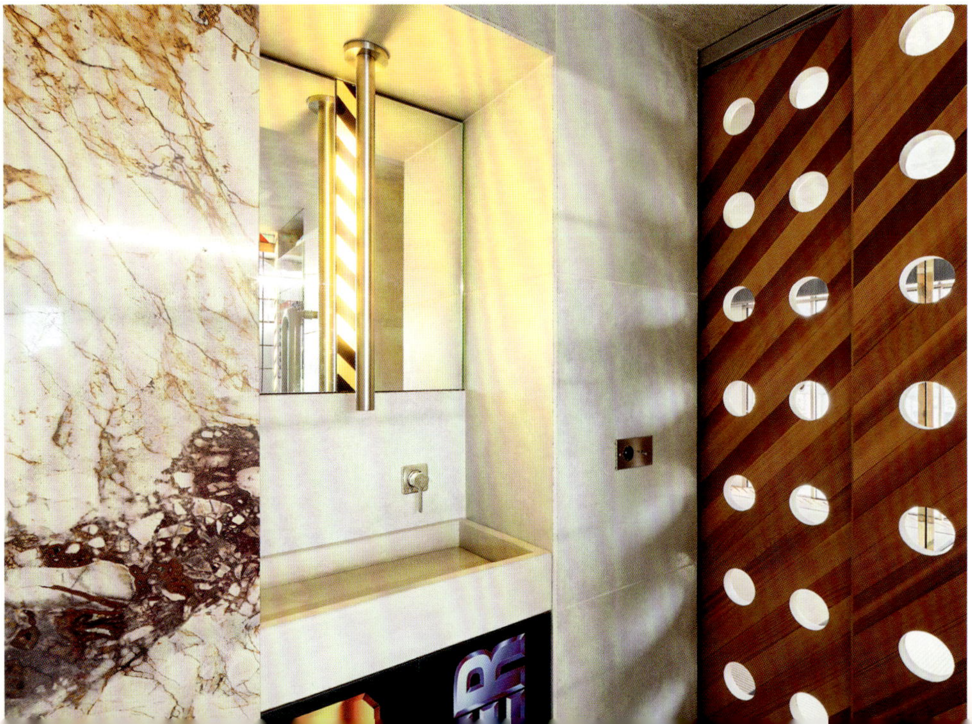

◄ Under construction: the cone and 1980s red-rope sofa on the terrace fit in perfectly with Willhelm's "work in progress" theme. • *Under construction:* Auch das Warnhütchen und ein Sofa aus den 1980ern auf der Terrasse passen perfekt ins Konzept. • Le cône de signalisation et le canapé rouge des années 1980 cadrent avec le style « chantier de construction ».

▶ Yellow-and-black stripes were applied to the glass of the halogen sconce above the custom concrete sink. The peekaboo panel provides glimpses through to the sleeping alcove. • Die Leuchte über dem Waschbecke aus Beton erhielt Warnstreifen. Durch die Bullaugen rechts blickt man in den Schlaf-Alkoven. • Des bandes noires et jaunes ornent la lampe au-dessus du lavabo en béton. La cloison ajourée donne sur le coin couchette.

▼ Owner Willhelm was adamant the toilet should not be hidden. "Otherwise, we'd have had to sacrifice the roominess of the shower," he explains. • Hausherr Bernhard Willhelm bestand darauf, die ins Bad integrierte Toilette nicht abzuschirmen. „Der Duschbereich sollte großzügig bleiben", erklärt er. • Bernhard Wilhelm tenait à ce que les W.-C. ne soient pas cachés « pour ne pas réduire l'espace de la douche ».

323 "Gib Techno keine Chance" is a nod to the slogan "Give Aids No Chance" in German. *Tubone* radiator from Antrax. • „Gib Techno keine Chance" spielt auf den Anti-Aids-Slogan an. Heizkörper *Tubone* von Antrax. • *Gib Techno keine Chance* est un clin d'œil au slogan de la campagne allemande « Ne laissez pas de chance au sida ». Le radiateur *Tubone* vient de chez Antrax.

"There's something that attracts me to the building-site aesthetic," declares fashion rebel Bernhard Willhelm. "I've used it in quite a few of my collections. It's very graphic, and the colors are really powerful." Yet this was only one of the themes he chose for his Paris abode—a space he refers to as "a little hamster cage" and "a playground." Others included Japanese teahouses, firefighters, and a touch of kink. "The question," admits interior designer Efe Erenler, "was, 'How can we merge all these ideas and not make it look like a theme park?'" He and architet Caspar Muschalek succeeded with bravura, most notably by creating a link between Japan and the construction world by putting down concrete floor slabs in a similar configuration to tatami mats. Willhelm also insisted on a hydrant-like shower fixture and solid materials. The glass partition in front of the bathroom is 2 cm (0.8 in.) thick and took eight people to install. Another whim was to have an open toilet. When asked what happens when friends come over, Willhelm replies, "I can always send them out on the terrace."

„DIE BAUSTELLEN-ÄSTHETIK HABE ICH SCHON IN MEHREREN KOLLEKTIONEN VERWENDET." BERNHARD WILLHELM

„Weil der Look sehr grafisch ist, mit kraftvollen Farben", fährt Willhelm fort. Auch andere Einflüsse entdeckt man in der Pariser Zweitwohnung, die der Modedesigner als „kleinen Hamsterkäfig" und „Spielplatz" bezeichnet: Dazu kamen Anklänge an japanische Teepavillons, Feuerwachen und ein guter Schuss *kinkiness.* „Die Frage war", resümiert Interiordesigner Efe Erenler, „wie können wir all diese Ideen verbinden, ohne dass ein Mini-Themenpark dabei herauskommt?" Ihm und Caspar Muschalek ist das gelungen, und zwar bravourös. Bestes Beispiel sind Betonplatten, die wie Tatami-Matten verlegt wurden – ein Link zwischen Japan und der Welt der Baustellen. Willhelm bestand zudem auf einer Dusche im Hydranten-Look und soliden Materialien. So ist die Glaswand vor dem Bad zwei Zentimeter dick, beim Einbau mussten acht Leute anpacken. Auch auf der offenen Toilette beharrte er. Und was, wenn Freunde zu Besuch sind? Auch das ist für Gastgeber Willhelm kein Problem: „Dann schicke ich sie eben kurz hinaus auf die Terrasse."

« Quelque chose m'attire dans l'esthétique des chantiers de construction », déclare l'enfant terrible de la mode Bernhard Willhelm. « Je m'en inspire dans mes collections. C'est à la fois graphique et coloré. » C'est aussi l'un des thèmes de son appartement parisien, qu'il décrit comme « une cage à hamster » et « un terrain de jeu ». Parmi ses autres inspirations : les maisons de thé japonaises, les pompiers et l'excentricité. Selon son décorateur Efe Erenler, « le problème était de combiner toutes ces idées sans en faire un parc d'attractions ». Avec Caspar Muschalek, ils y sont parvenus avec brio, notamment en disposant des dalles de béton sur le sol comme des tatamis. Willhelm voulait un combiné de douche en forme de bouche d'incendie et des matériaux robustes. Il a fallu huit personnes pour poser la cloison en verre de 2 cm d'épaisseur dans la salle de bains. Il tenait également à avoir des W.-C. ouverts. Et quand il reçoit des amis ? « Je peux toujours les envoyer sur la terrasse. »

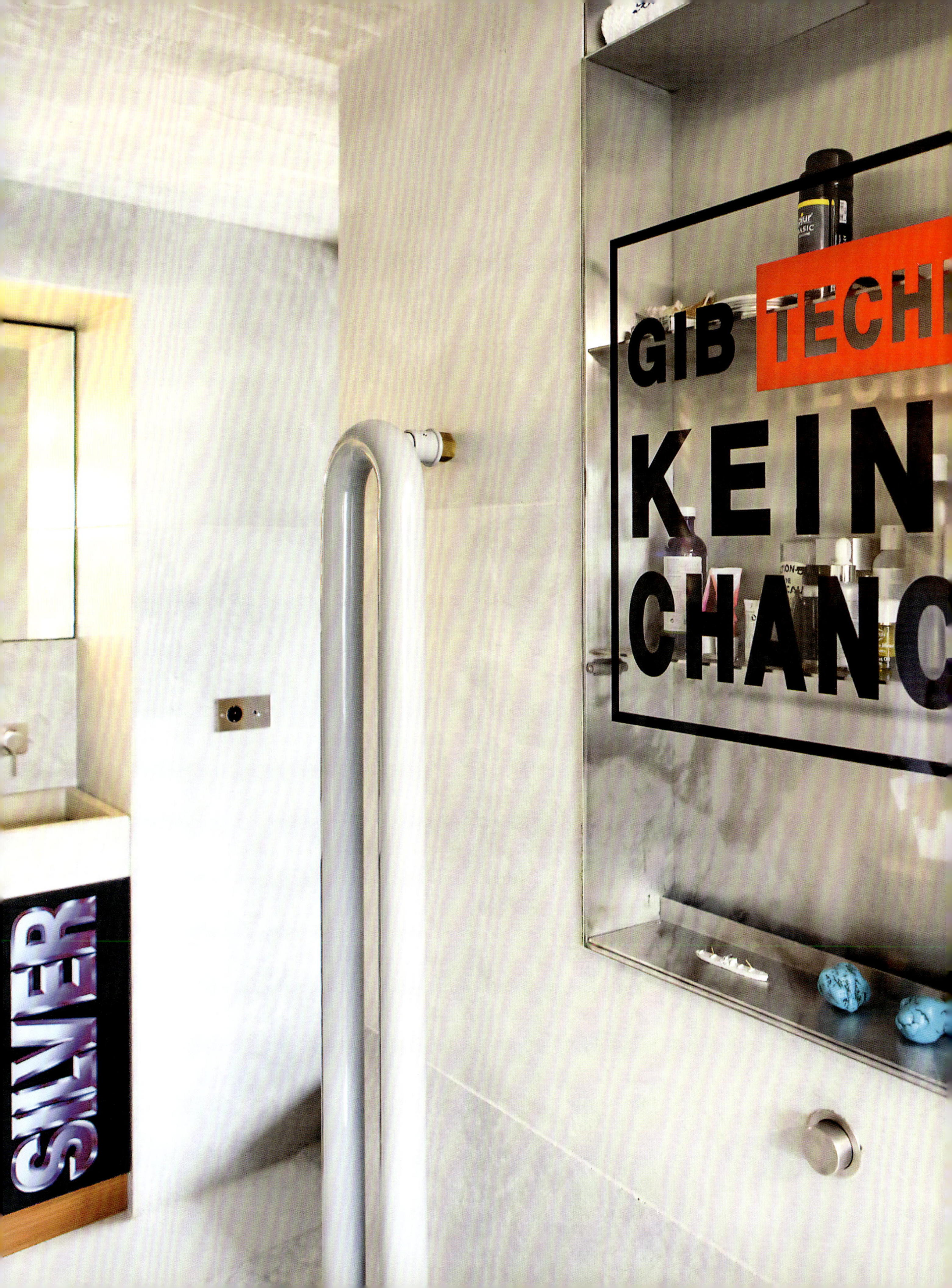
GIB TECH
KEIN
CHANC
SILVER

PIERRE YOVANOVITCH

HIS COOLLY SENSUAL APARTMENT IN PARIS

WHO Paris-based interior designer. **WHAT** A 210m² (2,260 sq.ft.), one-bedroom apartment in an 1890s town house. **WHERE** Directly on the Left Bank of the Seine. **SOLDIER OF STYLE** Yovanovitch carried out his civil service working for Pierre Cardin in Brussels, where he organized a Salvador Dalí exhibition. **IN THE LIMELIGHT** His Serbian father ran a firm that manufactured neon signs. One of his sisters, Sophie Menut, is a well-known food writer and TV presenter. **MENTOR** John Loring, the longtime design director at Tiffany. "He is quite phenomenally cultured," notes Yovanovitch. It was through Loring that he developed a passion for 20th-century American design. **HOSPITALITY** Yovanovitch's debut hotel project, the Hôtel de Marignan in Paris, opened in the fall of 2012. **CLOSET MINIMALIST** "Monk-like but comfortable," he once described his style. "If I listened just to myself, I'd live within white walls with nothing but a bench."

PHOTOGRAPHED BY STEPHAN JULLIARD/TRIPOD AGENCY   STYLED BY IAN PHILLIPS

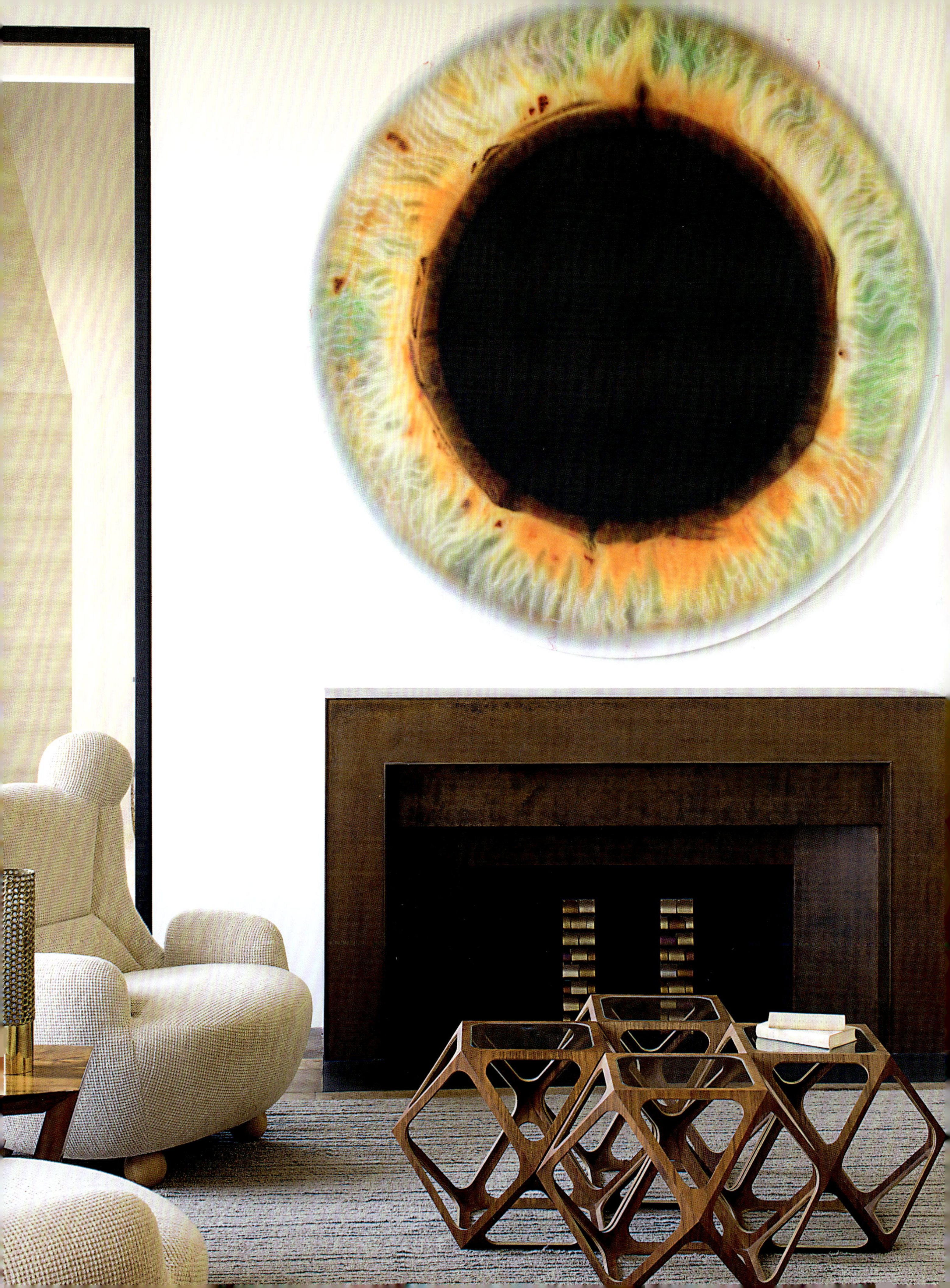

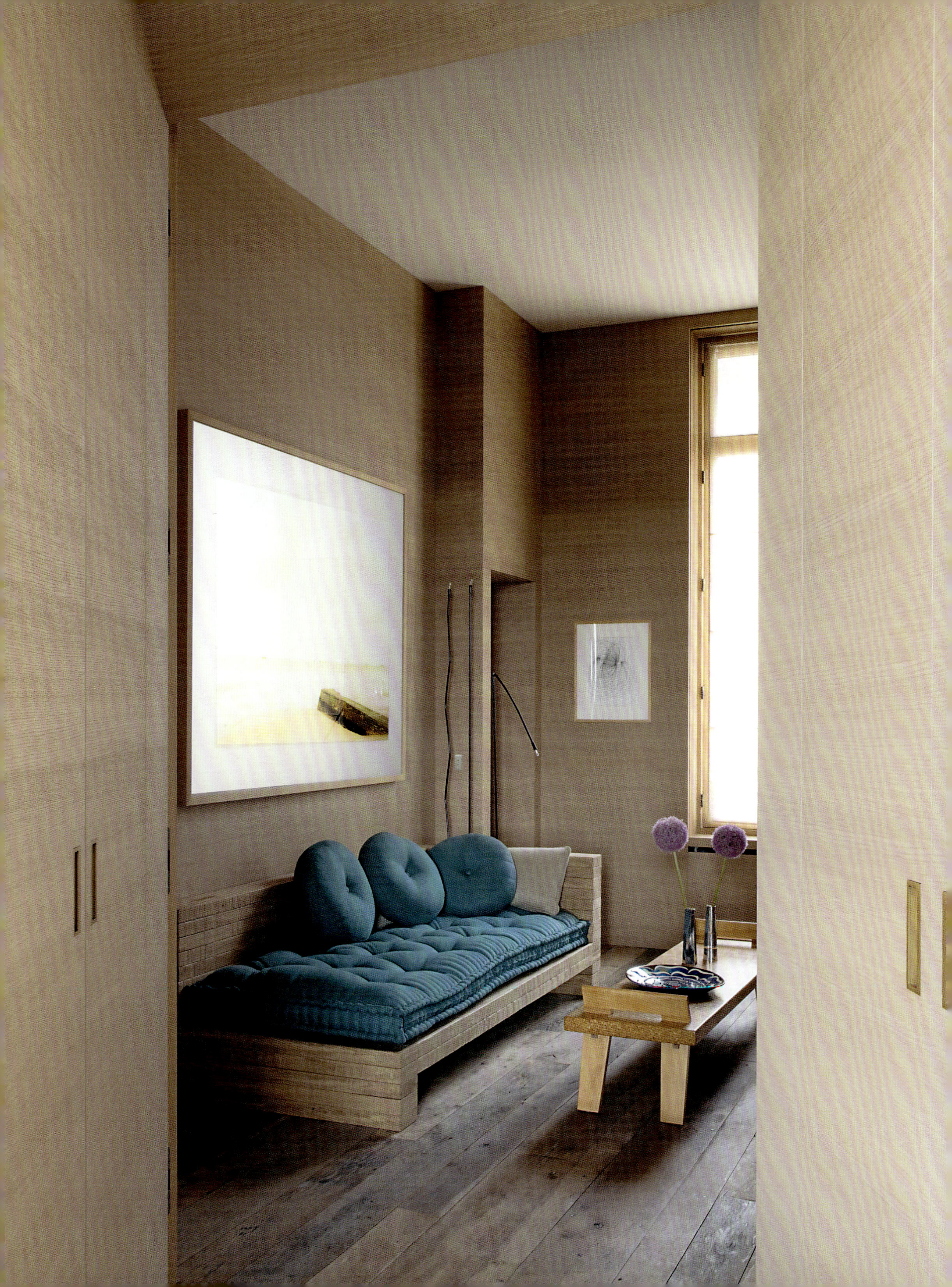

325 Above the iron fireplace in the living room hangs a painting from Marc Quinn's *Iris* series. The walnut-veneered plywood tables were created by Danish woodworker Rasmus Fenhann. • Ein Gemälde aus Marc Quinns Serie *Iris* hängt im Wohnzimmer über dem Eisenkamin. Tische aus nussbaumfurniertem Schichtholz von dem dänischen Holzdesigner Rasmus Fenhann. • Au-dessus de la cheminée en fer du séjour, un tableau de Marc Quinn de la série *Iris*. Les tables plaquées en noyer sont de l'ébéniste danois Rasmus Fenhann.

◀ In the small salon, Yovanovitch placed an Elger Esser photo above a custom daybed. The coffee table is by Paul Frankl. • Ein Daybed nach Maß mit Coffeetable von Paul Frank im kleinen Salon. Fotografie von Elger Esser. • Dans le petit salon, une photographie d'Elger Esser au-dessus d'un lit de repos créé sur mesure. Table basse de Paul Frankl.

▲ A set of 1940s James Mont chairs surrounds the Carlo Scarpa dining table. The window looks out directly onto the Seine and Tuileries Gardens. • Forties-Stühle von James Mont flankieren den von Carlo Scarpa entworfenen Esstisch. Durchs Fenster hat man die Seine und die Tuilerien im Blick. • Dans la salle à manger, des chaises des années 1940 de James Mont entourent une table de Carlo Scarpa. La fenêtre donne sur la Seine et le jardin des Tuileries.

329 The kitchen chairs are on casters and can be stored flush to the granite island. Above are a Sam Samore photo and Nendo's *Farming-Net* lamps. • Die Küchenstühle können passgenau unter die Granitplatte gerollt werden, darüber hängen Nendos *Farming-Net*-Leuchten. Foto von Sam Samore. • Dans la cuisine, les chaises montées sur roulettes se glissent sous l'îlot en granit. Luminaires *Farming-Net* by Nendo. Photographie de Sam Samore.

"TO ME, WHAT YOU SEE THROUGH THE MAIN WINDOWS OF YOUR HOME IS LIKE AN EXTRA ROOM." PIERRE YOVANOVITCH

In each of his apartments, Yovanovitch has attached particular importance to the view. The vista from his current abode is hard to beat: It looks out directly onto the Tuileries Gardens and Place de la Concorde. The interior was completely remodeled. The previous owner had bought it in the 1970s, but never lived there. "You expected to find the instruction manual still inside the oven," remarks the designer. He removed the 19th-century moldings and adopted a strict, architectural approach. Strong axes predominate, at times set deliberately at an angle and contrasted by sensual surfaces— nubbly fabrics, sandblasted oak, and a vintage parquet that was left raw. "I didn't want to sand it," Yovanovitch explains. "That would have destroyed its beauty." The furnishings very much reflect his fondness for 20th-century American and Scandinavian design. "I love the purity of the lines, the sobriety, and the choice of materials," he asserts. "They're both extremely sophisticated and simple."

„Was man durch die Hauptfenster der eigenen Wohnung sieht, ist wie ein zusätzlicher Raum", findet Pierre Yovanovitch. In seinem aktuellen Apartment ist das Panorama kaum zu schlagen: Man blickt direkt auf die Tuilerien und die Place de la Concorde. Der Vorbesitzer hatte die Wohnung in den 70ern gekauft, doch nie dort gelebt. „Ich wäre nicht erstaunt gewesen, wenn im Backofen noch die Gebrauchsanleitung gelegen hätte", sagt der Designer. Er gestaltete das Interieur komplett um. Nachdem der Stuck aus dem 19. Jahrhundert entfernt wurde, dominieren nun klare Achsen. Die strenge, architektonische Struktur konterkarieren sinnliche Oberflächen – grobe Stoffe, sandgestrahltes Eichenholz und rohe Vintage-Dielen. „Ich wollte sie nicht abschleifen", erklärt Yovanovitch. „Das hätte ihre Schönheit zerstört." Die Möbel spiegeln seine Begeisterung für amerikanisches und skandinavisches Design des 20. Jahrhunderts wider. „Ich liebe die Klarheit der Linien, die Nüchternheit und die Materialien. Das alles ist extrem raffiniert und schlicht zugleich."

Dans chacune de ses résidences, Yovanovitch a toujours attaché une grande importance à la vue. « Pour moi, ce qu'on voit des fenêtres principales est comme une pièce supplémentaire. » Celle de sa demeure actuelle est imbattable : elle donne directement sur le jardin des Tuileries et la place de la Concorde. L'intérieur a été entièrement rénové. L'ancien propriétaire avait acheté l'appartement dans les années 1970 et n'y avait jamais vécu. « On s'attendait presque à trouver le mode d'emploi encore dans le four », observe le décorateur. Il a ôté les moulures du 19ᵉ siècle et adopté une démarche rigoureusement architecturale. Les axes forts prédominent, parfois délibérément placés en diagonale et contrastant avec des surfaces sensuelles, des tissus texturés, du chêne sablé et un parquet ancien laissé brut. « Je n'ai pas voulu le décaper ; cela aurait détruit sa beauté », explique Yovanovitch. Le mobilier reflète son goût pour le design américain et scandinave du 20ᵉ siècle. « Ils sont tous les deux à la fois extrêmement sophistiqués et simples. »

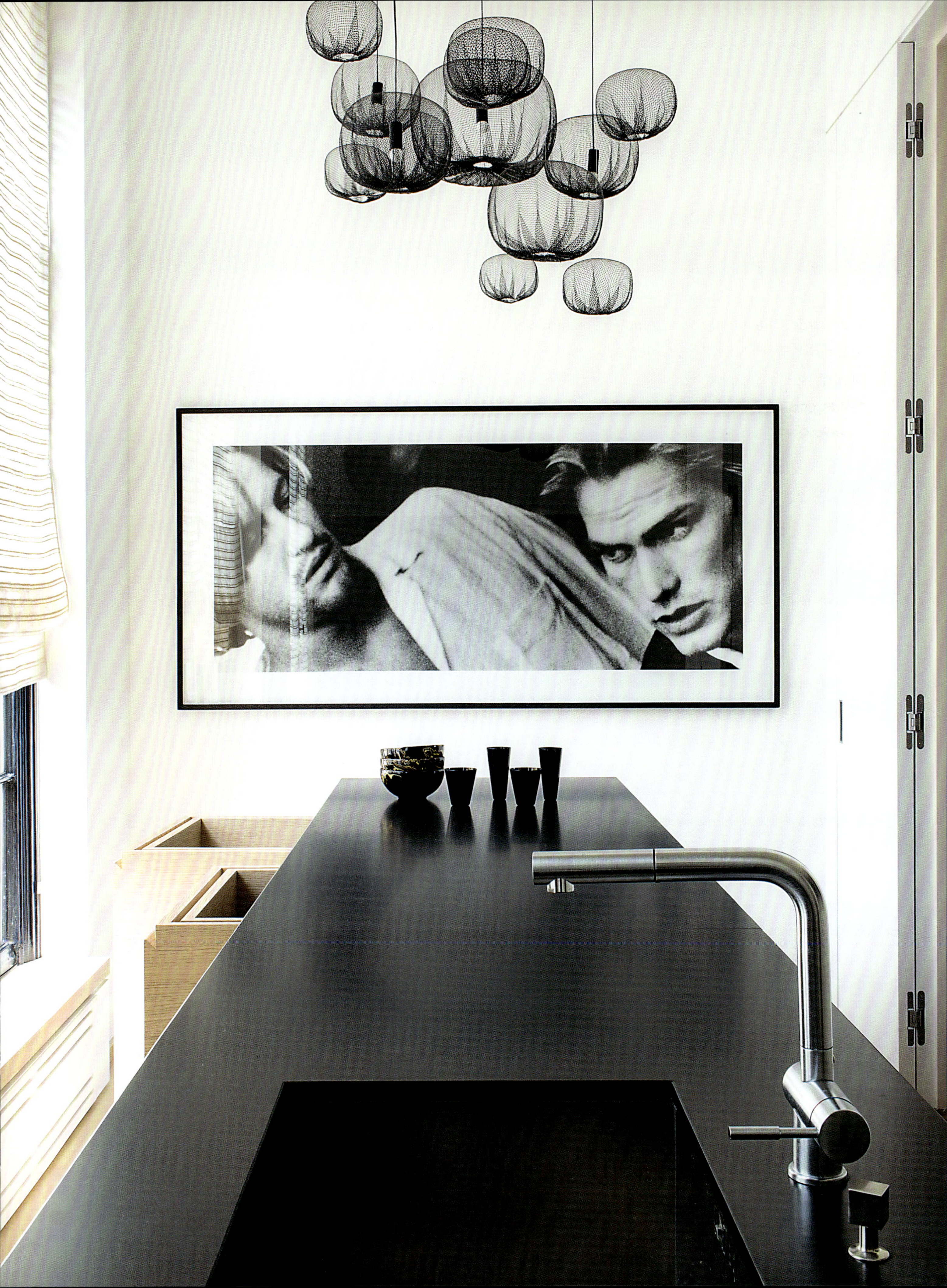

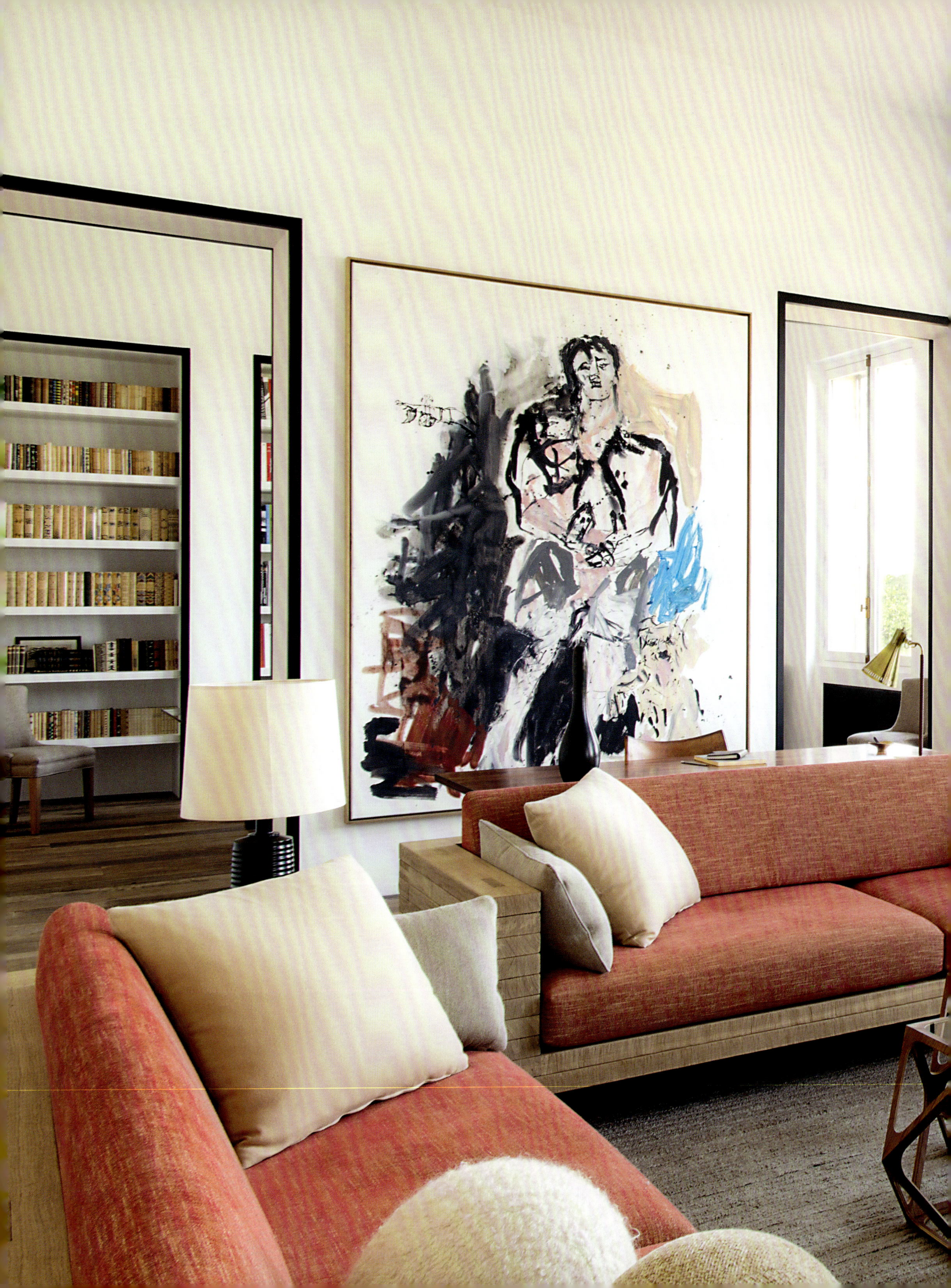

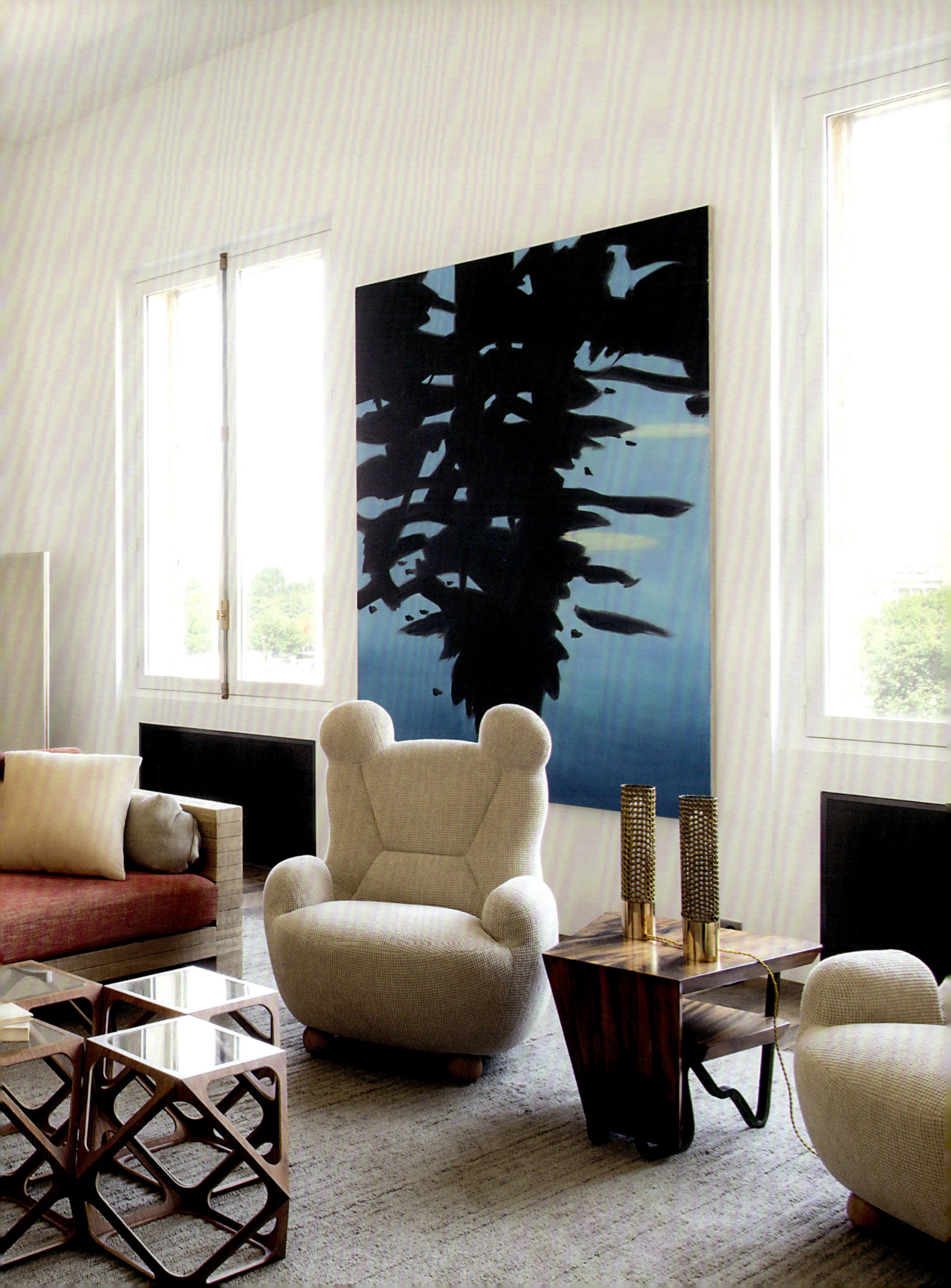

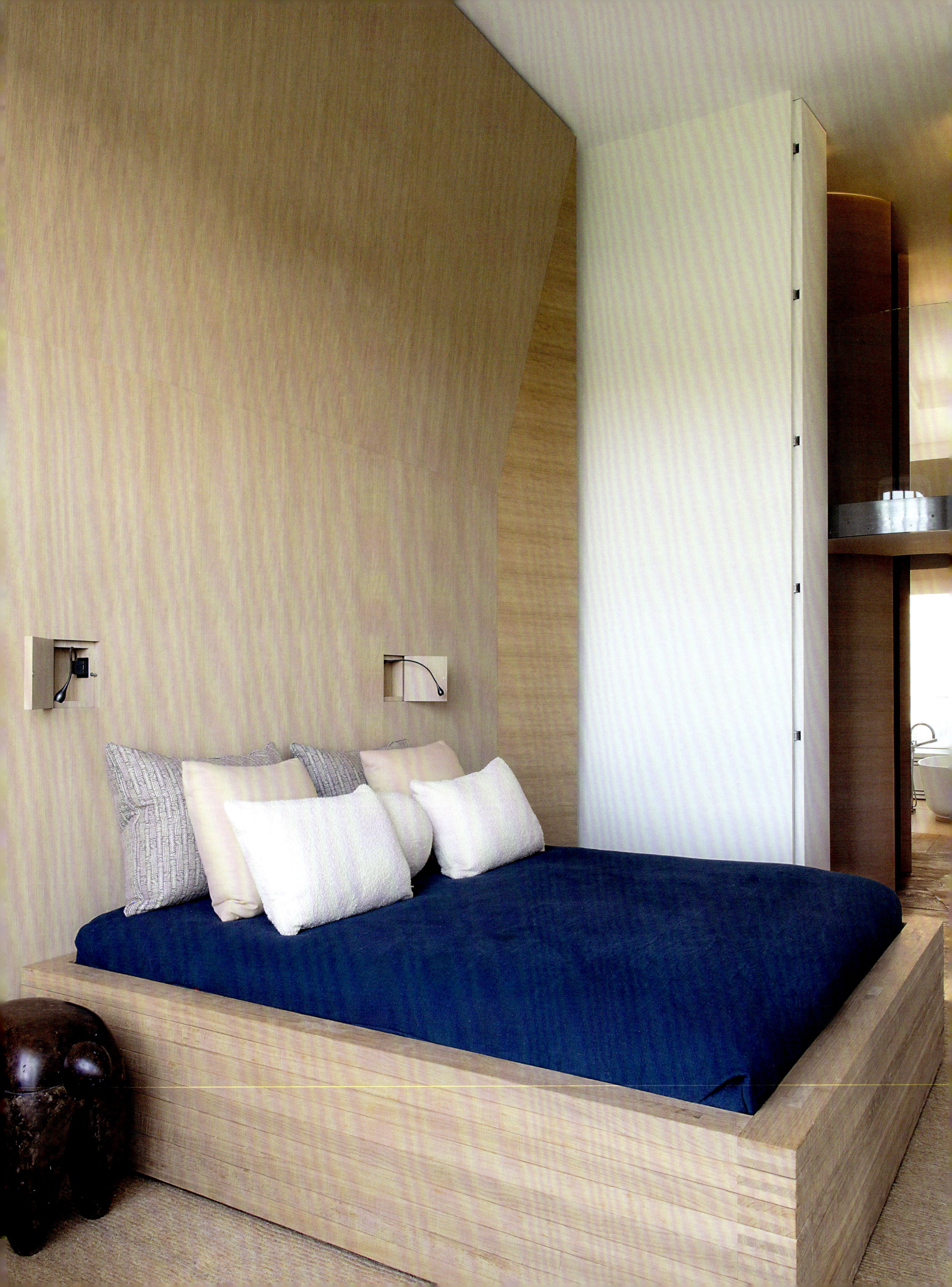

330–331 Furnishings in the living room include custom sofas and armchairs, a side table designed by Lloyd Wright (the son of Frank), and a pair of Pierre Forssell brass lamps. Paintings by Georg Baselitz and Alex Katz (right). • Neben eigens entworfenen Sofas und Sesseln steht im Wohnzimmer ein Beistelltisch von Lloyd Wright (Franks Sohn), darauf zwei Messingleuchten von Pierre Forssell. Gemälde von Georg Baselitz und Alex Katz (rechts). • Les assises du salon ont été conçues sur mesure. Table d'appoint de Lloyd Wright (le fils de Frank) et lampes en cuivre de Pierre Forssell. Le tableau à gauche est de Georg Baselitz ; celui de droite, d'Alex Katz.

◄ The Yovanovitch-designed oak bed was made by carpenter Pierre-Eloi Bris. • Das Bett ließ Yovanovitch von Schreiner Pierre-Eloi Bris aus Eiche bauen. • Le lit en chêne de Yovanovitch a été réalisé par Pierre-Eloi Bris.

▼ In between the master bedroom and bathroom, a patinated-steel spiral staircase leads up to a mezzanine dressing room. • Zwischen Schlafzimmer und Bad führt eine Wendeltreppe aus patiniertem Stahl hinauf zur Ankleide im Zwischengeschoss. • Entre la chambre principale et la salle de bains, un escalier en colimaçon en acier patiné mène au dressing en mezzanine.

▲ The bathroom features a *Baia* tub from Antoniolupi, Dornbracht faucets, and a custom vanity in Valverde marble. An opaque glass door conceals the toilet. • Antoniolupis Wanne Baia erhielt eine Standarmatur von Dornbracht, der Waschtisch wurde eigens aus Valverde-Marmor gefertigt. Eine Milchglastür verbirgt die Toilette. • Dans la salle de bains, une baignoire *Baia* d'Antoniolupi, une robinetterie de chez Dornbracht et un lavabo sur mesure en marbre de Valverde. Les W.-C. sont dissimulés derrière une porte en verre opaque.

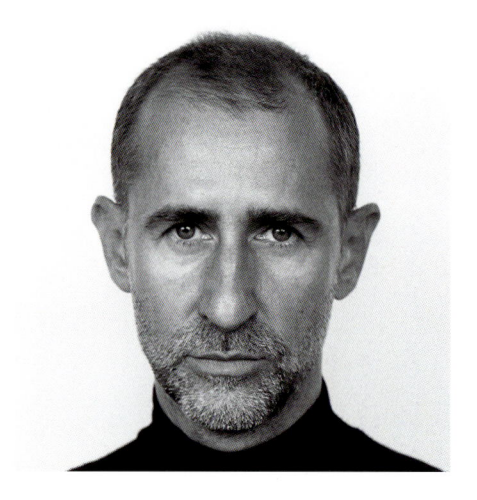

FABIO ZAMBERNARDI

HIS "METROPOLITAN RETRO" DUPLEX IN MILAN

WHO Creative director of Prada and Miu Miu. **WHAT** A 200 m² (2,153 sq. ft.) duplex on the top two floors of a 1959 building in Milan. Its architect, Giandomenico Belotti, is perhaps best known for his 1980 design, the *Spaghetti Chair,* which is part of the permanent collection at MoMA in New York. **WHERE** Near Milan's Piazza Sempione. **PAINFUL PAST** Before dedicating himself to edgy high style, Zambernardi was an assistant in a dental surgery. **MAN OF THE FIRST HOUR** Starting off with shoe designs, he has been working for Prada since 1981. **ON THE BOSS** "Miuccia Prada challenges people around her. She's always looking for something new, pushing herself to explore things she doesn't initially like." **FOR FRIENDS** Zambernardi has turned Belotti's former studio, on the ground floor of the same building, into a guest suite. **WITH FRIENDS** He co-produced the album *Little Happyness* for U.S. indie-pop band The Aluminum Group.

PHOTOGRAPHED BY GIULIO ORIANI   PORTRAIT BY BRIGITTE LACOMBE

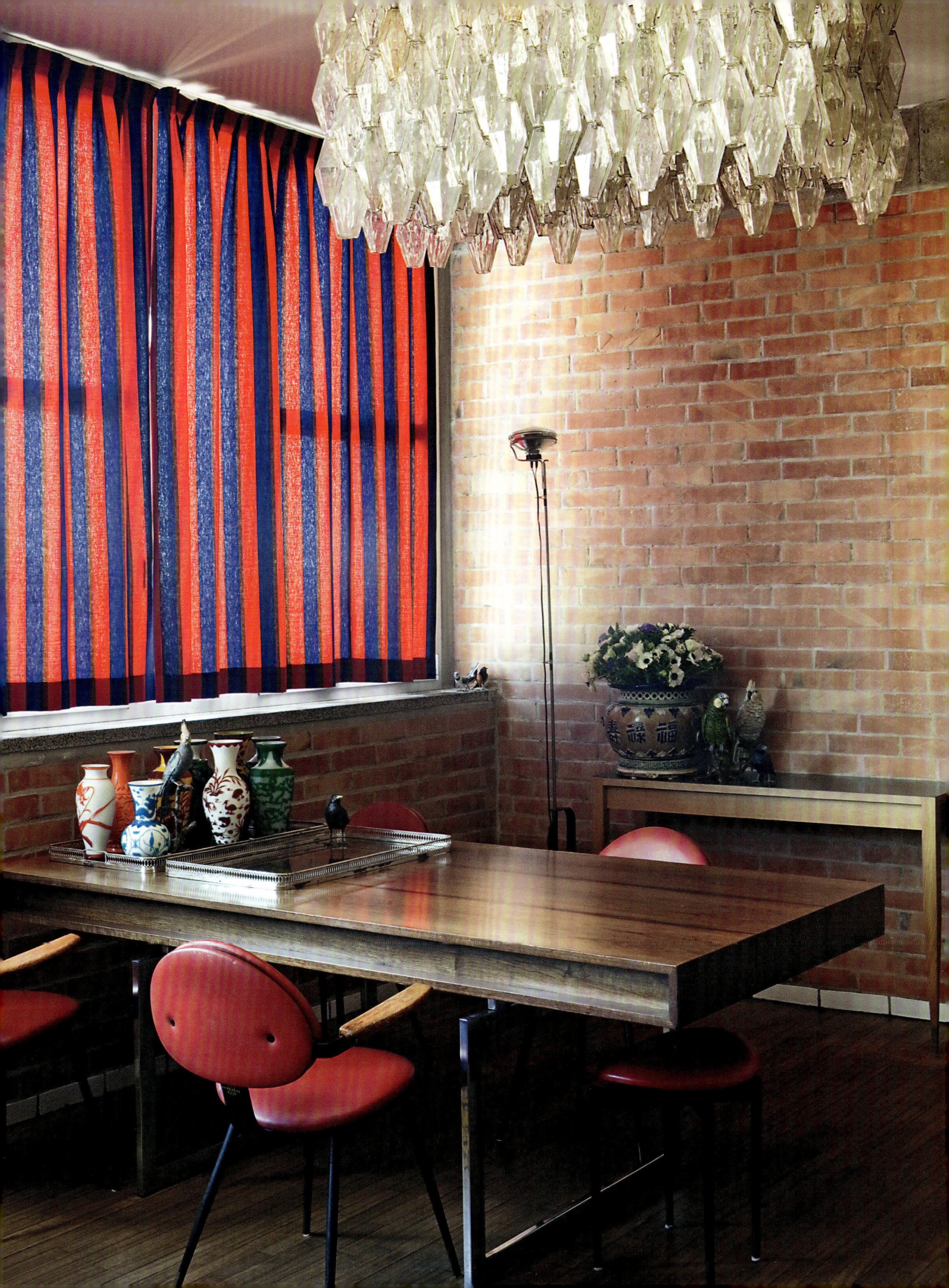

335 Nineteenth-century Chinese ceramics sit on the vintage Preben Fabricius and Jørgen Kastholm dining table. The chairs are by Carlo Mollino. • Chinesische Keramik des 19. Jahrhunderts steht auf dem Vintage-Esstisch von Preben Fabricius und Jørgen Kastholm. Die Stühle sind von Carlo Mollino. • Sur une table signée Preben Fabricius et Jørgen Kastholm, des céramiques chinoises du 19ᵉ siècle. Les chaises sont de Carlo Mollino.

▲▶ Zambernardi found his Prouvé bed in Paris. An Austrian antler chair is the only furniture he kept from his former apartment. The painting is one of several from Kathe Burkhart's *Liz Taylor* series that he owns (the others say HELL TO PAY and WHAT THE FUCK). This one's inspiration hangs around the corner in the master bathroom: a 1962 Bert Stern photo of Taylor in "Cleopatra" mode. Chrome-tile drawers by Paul Evans, c. 1970. • Sein Prouvé-Bett fand Zambernardi in Paris. Ein österreichischer Geweihstuhl ist das einzige Möbel aus seinem früheren Apartment. Das Gemälde gehört zu Kathe Burkharts *Liz Taylor Series* (er besitzt zwei weitere: HELL TO PAY und WHAT THE FUCK). Die Inspiration dafür hängt gleich um die Ecke im Bad: Bert Sterns Porträt von Taylor im „Kleopatra"-Look von 1962. Kommoden-Elemente mit Chromoberfläche von Paul Evans, um 1970. • Zambernardi a trouvé le lit Prouvé à Paris. Le fauteuil autrichien en bois de cerf est le seul meuble qu'il ait conservé de son précédent appartement. Au mur, l'une des œuvres de la série *Liz Taylor* de Kathe Burkhart qu'il possède (avec HELL TO PAY et WHAT THE FUCK). Celle-ci s'inspire d'une photo de Bert Stern de 1962, accrochée dans la salle de bains et représentant la star avec son look à la « Cléopâtre ». La commode aux tiroirs chromés a été conçue par Paul Evans vers 1970.

337

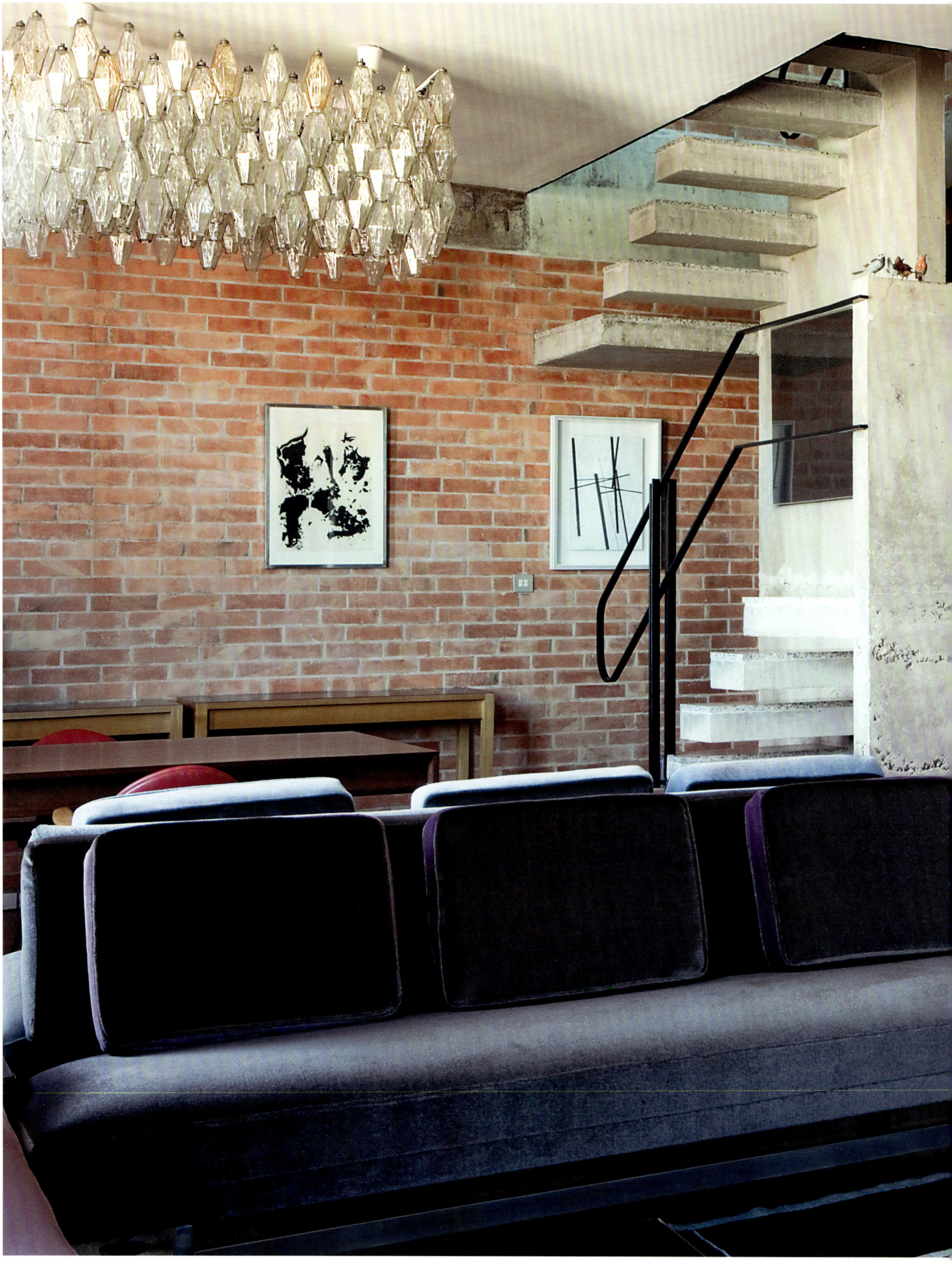

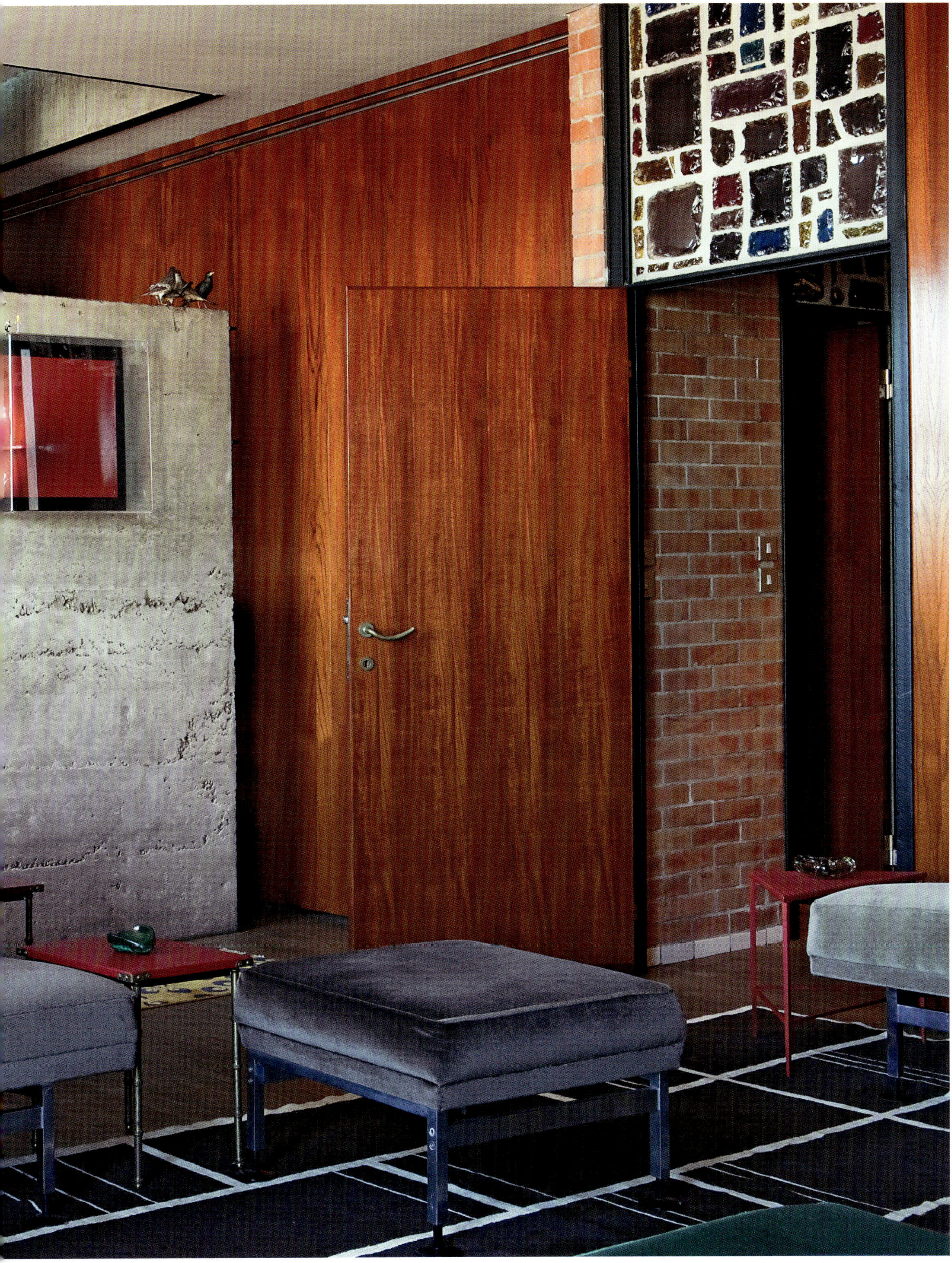

338–339 The 1960s sofa and ottoman originally belonged to government offices in Berlin. A raw-concrete staircase leads up to Zambernardis' terrace and veranda. • Sofa und Ottomane aus den 1960ern standen früher in einem Regierungsgebäude in Berlin. Eine Rohbeton-Treppe führt zu Terrasse und Wintergarten. • Le canapé et les poufs des années 1960 proviennent de bureaux gouvernementaux berlinois. Un escalier en béton brut mène à la terrasse et à la véranda.

◂▴ The veranda is home to numerous pieces of Scandinavian vintage design, including a 1960s dining suite and Artek's *A810* floor lamp by Alvar Aalto. Jean Prouvé's iconic daybed was given a lighter, somewhat American twist by reupholstering it with reproduced 1930s fabric. • Der Wintergarten steht ganz im Zeichen der skandinavischen Moderne, von der schwedischen Essgruppe aus den 1960ern bis zu Arteks Stehleuchte *A810* von Alvar Aalto. Der Bezug aus reproduziertem 1930er-Jahre-Stoff gibt Jean Prouvés ikonischem Daybed einen geradezu amerikanischen Twist. • La véranda fait la part belle au design scandinave, des meubles de la salle à manger suédoise des années 1960 au lampadaire *A810* d'Alvar Aalto pour Artek. Le célèbre lit de repos de Jean Prouvé a été tapissé d'une reproduction d'un tissu des années 1930 pour être « américanisé ».

342 In the living room, a Gianfranco Pardi painting hangs above a Paul Evans *Cityscape* sideboard. Porcelain monkey from the 18th century. • Im Wohnzimmer hängt ein Gemälde von Gianfranco Pardi über Paul Evans' *Cityscape*-Sideboard. Porzellanaffe aus dem 18. Jahrhundert. • Dans le séjour, une œuvre de Gianfranco Pardi au-dessus d'un buffet *Cityscape* de Paul Evans. Le singe en porcelaine date du 18ᵉ siècle.

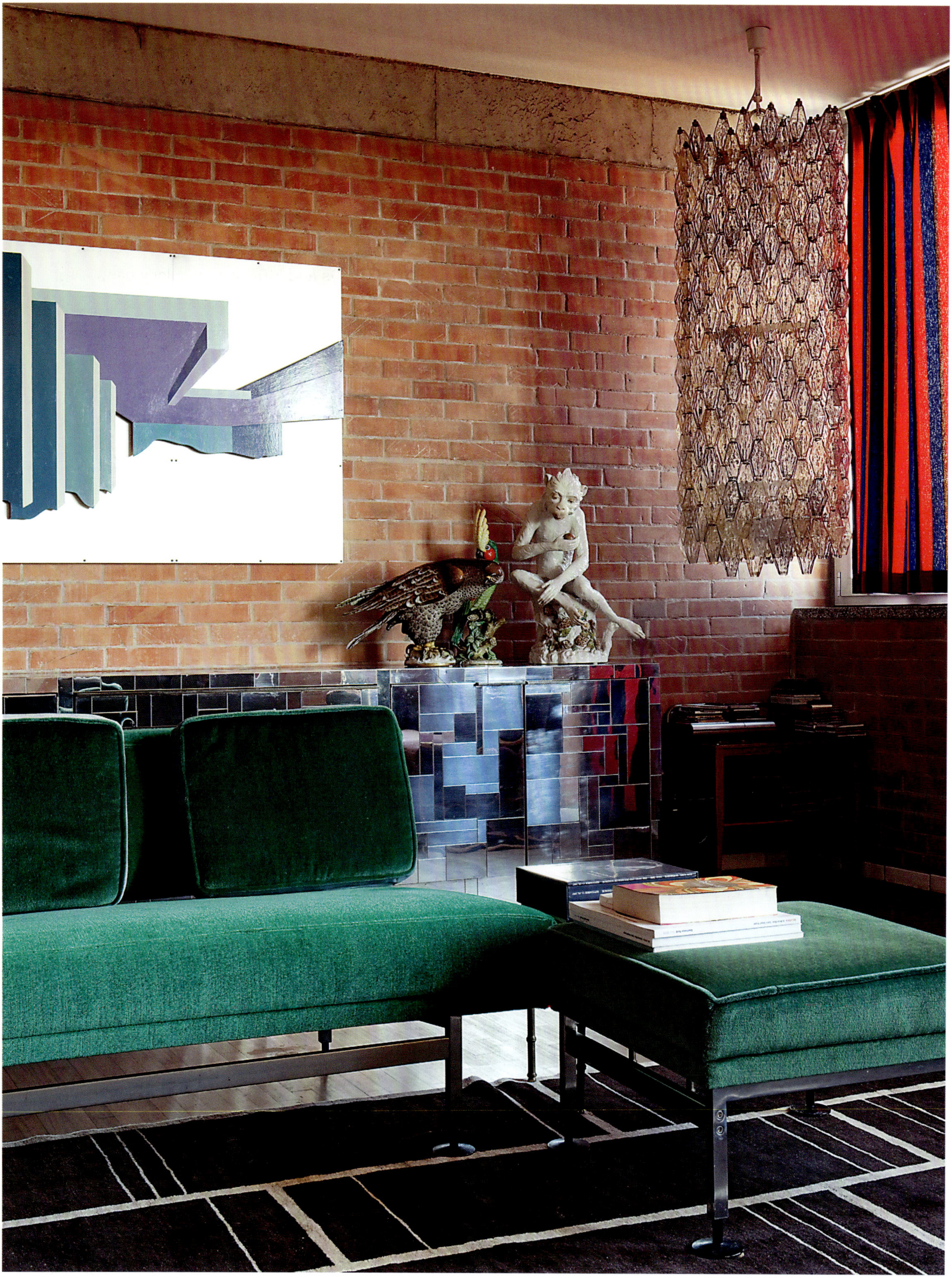

"The first thing the realtor told me was that I should cover up all the bricks," says Fabio Zambernardi, recalling his debut visit to the apartment he now calls home. "Everyone before me didn't like the place because of them." Yet it was precisely "the industrial, rough, and raw" materials that attracted him—not only the bricks, but also the exposed concrete and wrought iron doors. "I was very surprised by it all," he declares. "I'm from Milan, and I've never seen this kind of style here before." He updated the kitchen and bathroom and enclosed a veranda on the top floor, but otherwise "did the maximum possible to make the apartment look like it hadn't been touched." The interior features splashes of color and mostly vintage furnishings from the 1950s and '60s. A particularly happy find was his Jean Prouvé bed. "A special thing," Zambernardi says. "Plus, it fits perfectly. I don't like gigantic beds." Asked about the artworks depicting Liz Taylor by U. S. artist Kathe Burkhart, he readily admits to being a fan of the late actress: "But, mind you, in a really nonobsessive way."

„Als Erstes riet mir der Makler, all den Backstein zu verdecken", sagt Fabio Zambernardi, als er von seinem Besichtigungstermin hier erzählt. „Sämtlichen vorherigen Interessenten hatte die Wohnung deshalb nicht gefallen." Doch Pradas Kreativdirektor zogen gerade „die industriellen, rauen und rohen" Materialien an – die Ziegel, aber auch Sichtbeton und Schmiedeeisen-Türen. „Ich war wirklich verblüfft", erklärt er. „Ich komme aus Mailand, aber diesen Stil hatte ich hier nie gesehen." Er erneuerte Küche und Bad und fügte einen Wintergarten an. Ansonsten „tat ich alles, um die Wohnung unverändert aussehen zu lassen". Eingerichtet ist sie mit satten Farbakzenten und Vintage-Möbeln aus den 1950er- und 1960er-Jahren. Ein Glücksgriff war das Bett von Jean Prouvé. „Etwas ganz Besonderes", sagt Zambernardi. „Und es passt auch noch perfekt! Gigantische Betten mag ich nicht." Und was hat es mit den Liz-Taylor-Gemälden der US-Künstlerin Kathe Burkhart auf sich? Er sei ein Fan der verstorbenen Schauspielerin, gibt er zu. „Aber keine Sorge, zur Obsession reicht es nicht."

« LA PREMIÈRE CHOSE QUE M'A DITE L'AGENT IMMOBILIER, C'ÉTAIT QU'IL FALLAIT CACHER TOUTES CES BRIQUES. » FABIO ZAMBERNARDI

« Tous ceux qui avaient visité l'appartement avant moi n'en avaient pas voulu à cause de ça », ajoute le directeur de création chez Prada et Miu Miu. Or, ce sont précisément les matériaux « bruts, industriels » qui l'ont séduit : outre les briques, le béton nu et les portes en fer forgé. « Moi qui suis né à Milan, je n'avais jamais vu ce style auparavant. » Zambernardi a modernisé la cuisine et la salle de bains, créé une véranda au dernier étage. Pour le reste, il a fait son possible pour que le duplex « n'ait pas l'air d'avoir été touché ». Le décor parsemé de touches de couleur comprend principalement du mobilier des années 1950 et 1960. Parmi ses plus belles trouvailles : un lit de Jean Prouvé. « Une aubaine, d'autant plus qu'il était de la bonne taille. Je n'aime pas les lits géants », déclare-t-il. Quant à ses portraits de Liz Taylor par l'artiste américaine Kathe Burkhart, il avoue être un fan de la star en précisant : « Mais, attention, pas au point d'en être obsédé ! »

PHOTOGRAPHERS

BILL BATTEN

BRUCE BUCK

JOHN BESSLER

SERGE ANTON P. 98   While our location was quite the opposite, the Belgian photo star likes "places not yet inhabited by civilization." A big fan of Africa, his favorite shoot to date was taking portraits in Ethiopia. He is also a partner in *Toukoul*, a Brussels restaurant dedicated to the African country's cuisine. When not working for the likes of *Elle Decoration* and *Case da Abitare*, he does books on subjects as diverse as chocolate *(Pierre Marcolini: éclats)* and tribal rugs (the upcoming *Histoires de Désert*). serge-anton.com / *Portrait by Jules Spinash*

BILL BATTEN P. 294   Based between London and Suffolk, England, Batten has been described as "a Dickensian character with a dry sense of humor." He is a regular contributor to both *House & Garden* and *The World of Interiors*, for which he collaborated on stories for some 15 years with stylist Faye Toogood. "We had some jolly times," he recalls. Shooting her first-ever project as a decorator was also a treat. The resulting interiors, he asserts, are "very stylish—strong without being showy." *Portrait by Hugh Gilbert*

JOHN BESSLER P. 164   The stars of the shoot of John Loecke and Jason Oliver Nixon's house, Bessler told us, were the couple's dogs, Jasper and Weenie—"some of the best models ever!" The New Yorker works for *Traditional Home* and *Better Homes & Gardens* and has collaborated on two books—Nate Berkus's *Home Style* and *Edith Wharton: A House Full of Rooms*. He himself loves midcentury furniture, "but I am finding it hard to fit in my lakeside cabin in New Jersey." besslerphoto.com / *Portrait by Doug Todd*

SERGE ANTON

PIERO GEMELLI

MARINA FAUST

JAN BITTER

ADRIEN DIRAND

ANA PAULA CARVALHO

JAN BITTER P. 316 Ask this Berliner for the key ingredients to a successful interiors image and he replies "oppositions, life, chaos, and bustle." It's obviously a recipe that works. His photos have not only appeared in magazines like *A+U*, *Frame*, and *Interni*, but also in monographs about architects Daniel Libeskind and Sauerbruch Hutton. Although small, Bernhard Willhelm's Paris apartment apparently offered endless possibilities. "I've never taken so many pictures in one room," Bitter says. janbitter.de / *Portrait by Tina Brüser*

BRUCE BUCK P. 186 Although based near Manhattan, this regular contributor to *The New York Times* has worked extensively in the Caribbean. Buck is the principal photographer of three books—*Cuban Elegance*, *Caribbean Elegance*, and *French Island Elegance*—and says his best professional experience was shooting a resort on Anguilla. "My assistant and I each stayed in our own private villa and had a personal chef to prepare our meals," he recalls with a sigh. brucebuck.com / *Portrait by Charla Buck*

ANA PAULA CARVALHO P. 32 Having grown up in Angola and Mozambique, Carvalho studied in Maryland (USA). She now lives in her native Lisbon and works for the likes of *AD Spain*, *Casa Vogue Brazil*, and *Elle Decor Italy*. Her most memorable shoot to date took place one Saturday in January 2003: the studio of Oscar Niemeyer. Afterwards, she drank whisky with the late architect, whom she remembers as "very human and bohemian in his own way. A proud *carioca!*" anacarvalhophoto.com / *Portrait by Tiago Carvalho*

ADRIEN DIRAND P. 68 While shooting the Habita Hotel in Monterrey (Mexico) in 2009, Dirand spotted a silhouette passing through the frame of his viewfinder. "That mysterious figure," he declares proudly, "is now my amazing wife." The Paris-based son of legendary interiors photographer Jacques Dirand and brother of interior designer Joseph Dirand collaborates regularly with *The World of Interiors*, *Citizen K*, and *Air France Magazine*. adriendirand.com / *Portrait by Zanna*

MARINA FAUST P. 78 "There's a great luxury to shooting your own space," remarks the internationally renowned artist. "Yet, it's also a challenge to distance yourself from what you know…" Still, she likes to be tested: "For my own art performances, I often create demanding circumstances. They make you inventive." A vivid memory is a backstage shoot at a Martin Margiela show lit by 1,600 candles that generated a huge smoke cloud and almost set the place on fire. marinafaust.com / *Portrait by Pierre Weiss*

PIERO GEMELLI P. 196, 258 It was only after studying architecture in his native Rome that Gemelli took up photography in 1978. Today, he does many things, among them shooting interiors for *Marie Claire Maison*, *Ideat*, and *Casa Vogue Brazil*. The Paulo Mendes da Rocha house in São Paulo made a big impression on him. "I felt time and space were suspended while I was there," he says. "As if the house were protecting me from the outside world." pierogemelli.com / *Portrait by Beatrice Rossetti*

STEPHAN JULLIARD

FRANÇOIS HALARD

FRITZ BRUNIER, DAVID HIEPLER

INEZ VAN LAMSWEERDE, VINOODH MATADIN

ACHIM HATZIUS

GREGORY HOLM

PABLO GÓMEZ-ZULOAGA P. 304   When not taking care of his family—"three kids and two dogs"—the Madrileño collaborates with *AD Spain, Maison Française,* and *House & Garden.* The secret of his success, he says, is "my perseverance and patience." He also displays a certain bonhomie, as on the shoot with his good friend Jorge Varela. "We laughed a lot," he says. "And I think you can see the result of our connection in the pictures." *Portrait by Inés Sentmenat*

FRANÇOIS HALARD P. 144   Interiors are definitely in Halard's blood. His grandfather was the founder of Nobilis, and his parents created the Yves Halard home-furnishings brand. He himself works for *Vogue, W,* and *T Magazine,* and has produced numerous books (among them, the monographic *François Halard*). He was struck both by the modernity of Jon Rosen and Tiina Laakkonen's house and by Jon's motorbike—"the best-looking I've ever seen. I wish I could have driven it!" *francoishalard.com / Self-Portrait*

ACHIM HATZIUS P. 108   The Berlin-based photographer's most surreal commission was a shoot for Helsinki's Museum of Finnish Architecture—three days in an remote, unheated attic. When not sequestered, he works for magazines including *AD Germany, Monocle,* and *Apartamento.* Since first shooting Peter Heimer's flat he has developed a friendship with the art consultant. "Every now and then," he recounts, "I stop by to capture something new." *hatzius.com / Self-Portrait*

HIEPLER, BRUNIER P. 88   On each shoot, both David Hiepler and Fritz Brunier take photos "sometimes with and sometimes without consulting the other." Their clients include David Chipperfield Architects, Audi, and publications such as *AD Germany, Architectural Record,* and *Die Zeit.* For the Berlin-based photographic duo, the guest bathroom in art dealer Michael Fuchs's apartment is akin to "a small private gallery. We liked the Damien Hirst hanging over the toilet!" *hiepler-brunier.de / Portrait by Schnepp/Renou*

GREGORY HOLM P. 58   Splitting his professional time between shooting projects for architects and acting as artistic director of Detroit's 2:1 art space, Holm also creates large-scale installations. For his *Ice House Detroit* project in winter 2010/11, he sprayed an abandoned home with water—every six minutes, for 30 days. His work has been shown at The Cranbrook Art Museum in Michigan and Te Tuhi for the Arts in New Zealand. *gregoryholm.com / Portrait by Guy Campbell*

INEZ & VINOODH P. 152   After meeting during their studies in Amsterdam, the iconic Dutch duo began working together in the early 1990s and quickly achieved fame with their fashion images and portraiture. For them, the shoot of their New York loft was something new. "It's interesting to look at your own apartment from an architectural standpoint," they say. "To consider lines and shapes rather than individual objects." *vlmstudio.com / Self-Portrait*

JAMES McDONALD

PABLO GOMEZ-ZULOAGA

GIULIO ORIANI

MASSIMO LISTRI

MADS MOGENSEN

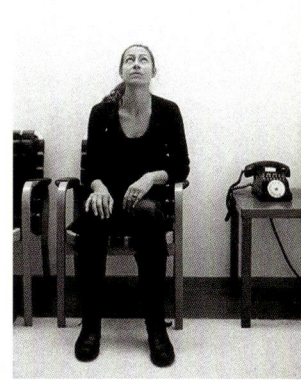

GAELLE LE BOULICAUT

STEPHAN JULLIARD   P. 238, 324   The Parisian's career got off to a flying start when an image from his first-ever shoot made the cover of the book, *Dealers Choice*. Since then, his work has been published regularly in the European and Chinese editions of *AD*, *Elle Decoration Russia*, and *Belle* (Australia). For the stories in this book, the keen traveler overcame seasickness on the boat to Capri, flew to L.A., and went to Pierre Yovanovitch's apartment in Paris by foot. *tripodagency.com / Portrait by Peter Lindbergh*

GAELLE LE BOULICAUT   P. 228   She claims her most hair-raising commission to date was "being rigged up on a cliff to shoot portraits of stunt girls in Sydney." Le Boulicaut's home may be Vannes, France, but she travels regularly to shoot stories for the international editions of *AD* and *Elle Decoration*. Of her trip to Mumbai, she has happy memories of the home-cooked curry and Cleo the Collie: "She wanted to be in every photo. So, the driver had to take her for a walk!" *gaelleleboulicaut.com / Portrait by Jeremy Callaghan*

MASSIMO LISTRI   P. 116   The Florentine photographer is nothing if not prolific. He is co-founder of the publishing house FMR and has worked on more than 60 books, including *Casa Mexicana*, *Grand Interiors*, and *Palazzi Italiani*. Listri has also been exhibited from Tokyo and Taipei to London and Lima, and produced a stunning series on empty museums. When asked for his favorite room at the Palazzo Margherita, he opts for Francis Ford Coppola's own—"the most intimate," he says. *massimolistri.com / Self-Portrait*

JAMES McDONALD   P. 218   The intrepid photographer chillingly recalls a shoot at Chillingham Castle in England: "The bedroom where I slept was haunted." As well as working for *The World of Interiors* and *House & Garden*, the Londoner wrote and photographed the book *Alnwick Castle: The Home of the Duke and Duchess of Northumberland*. For him, "a camera lens is just a piece of glass. Good images rely on the design and atmosphere of an interior." *jamesmcdonaldphotography.co.uk / Portrait by Giovanni Agresti Fiumara*

MADS MOGENSEN   P. 282   Based in both Copenhagen and Neviglie near Turin, the great Dane works for *A&W*, *Häuser*, and the international editions of *AD* and *Elle Decoration*. His first book, *A Sense of Place*, was published in 2008. Four years later, an unforgettable travel commission took the snow-lover 2,000 km (1,250 miles) north of Helsinki. His tips for a great interiors image? "Balanced light, classic composition, and fewer rather than too many objects." *madsmogensen.com / Portrait by Martina Hunglinger*

GIULIO ORIANI   P. 334   His most memorable commissions, claims Oriani, have been in the Middle East. His first interior shoot was a house in Sanaa, Yemen, and he also photographed a story on carpets in Bam, Iran. For Fabio Zambernardi's apartment, he didn't travel so far (he is based in Cernusco Sul Naviglio near Milan)—which doesn't stop him from being impressed by the designer's attention to detail and his veranda: "It gives you a great sense of freedom." *orianigiulio.it / Portrait by Moreno Belloni*

WILLIAM WALDRON

SIMON UPTON

RICHARD POWERS

MARK ROSKAMS

JONNY VALIANT

RICHARD POWERS P. 12, 136   Based in Antibes, lucky Powers travels the world for stories that appear in the likes of *Vogue Living, Elle Decor US,* and *AD France.* He has also collaborated on nine books (*New Paris Style, The Iconic Interior…*) and has several more in production. He describes the Mathias Kiss shoot as "another great day in the office" and Jonathan Adler's work as "just brilliant": "There's so much to shoot," he says. "Never a dull moment!" richardpowers.co.uk / Portrait by Mia Powers

MARK ROSKAMS P. 208   "What a trip!" says the New York-based photographer in reference to the "pop-up" apartment created by Doug Meyer. "It's genius!" His first book, *Masseria: The Italian Farmhouses of Puglia,* was published in 2011 and proved less stressful than a hotel shoot he once did in the Bahamas: "All my equipment was confiscated at customs, except the camera. I ended up building a tripod out of chairs." markroskams.com / Portrait by Miguel Correra

CHRISTIAN SCHAULIN P. 24, 126   fotografieschaulin.de

RACHAEL SMITH P. 42   "I was brought up in a house full of cameras," recounts Smith, whose father is a collector and keen amateur photographer. She herself lives in Stamford, England, and works for publications like *The World of Interiors* and *The Telegraph Magazine.* Her most memorable shoot to date? A portrait of designer Michael Young in Hong Kong "on the top of a skyscraper, at night, during a lightning storm." rachaelsmith.net / Portrait by Ade Rowbotham

SIMON UPTON P. 176   "The secret to a good interiors image," says Upton, "is making it about the room, not the photographer." He works for the likes of *The World of Interiors* and *Tatler,* and loves going from one world to another—"directly from the Seychelles to the Arctic Circle." After collaborating on some 20 books, including *London Interiors* by TASCHEN, he claims, "The more I see, the less I want. I try to keep my home simple and functional." simonupton.com / Portrait by Anne Becker

JONNY VALIANT P. 50   The globetrotting Valiant was born in the UK, brought up in Australia, and now resides in New York with his wife Julz, and sons Hunter (on motorbike) and Cash. He has worked for *Vogue Australia, Martha Stewart Living,* and *House Beautiful,* and shot his first book, *French Accents.* The most remarkable thing about the apartment of Christopher Coleman and Angel Sanchez, he asserts, is the use of color and pattern: "It's not often you come across a place so bold." jonnyvaliant.com / Portrait by Julz Valiant

WILLIAM WALDRON P. 250   The photographer's work may appear regularly in *Elle Decor US* and *Architectural Digest,* but his favorite shoot to date was for *German Vogue*—the studio of artist Kara Walker. The New Yorker's credits also include two books: *So Chic* by Margaret Russell and Jamie Drake's *New American Glamour.* For him, John Robshaw is "both original and daring—right down to his choice of neighborhood. In 30 years, I never photographed anything there before." williamwaldron.com / Portrait by Malene Waldron

MANOLO YLLERA

RACHAEL SMITH

MANOLO YLLERA P. 266, 274   The witty Spaniard declares his home is "supposedly Madrid, but I'm rarely there." He works mainly for Condé Nast (AD Spain, Russia, China…) and when asked about his most memorable shoots, replies, "Mainly those I'd like to forget." His recipe for a successful interiors image? "If you want to have a siesta on a sofa in the picture, it means it's working. And if the architect, designer, and magazine are happy, you're on a roll."
manoloyllera.com / Self-portrait with his Dachshund Taco

TASCHEN is indebted to all the photographers, interiors stylists, syndication representatives, and nimble assistants who have made this book possible. We would like to thank them, as well as the holders of various rights, for their generous support. Special thanks to Jon Rosen and his NYC company, Nucleus Imaging, for swift action in a moment of technical need. And thanks to Sara Teske in Paris, whose diplomatic skills helped us pull in Bernhard Willhelm's stunning apartment through stormy seas. In fashion, elegance may be refusal, as Diana Vreeland famously put it. In interiors, nothing beats perseverance.

TASCHEN dankt allen Fotografen, Stylisten, Syndication-Editors und flinken Assistenten, die dieses Buch möglich gemacht haben. Gleiches gilt für die Inhaber verschiedenster Rechte, auf deren Wohlwollen ein solches Projekt angewiesen ist. Ein spezielles *Thank you* geht an Jon Rosen und seine Firma Nucleus Imaging für unkomplizierte Unterstützung in einem Moment technischer Not. Und an Sara Teske in Paris, ohne deren Diplomatie es Bernhard Willhelms erstaunliche Wohnung wohl nicht in dieses Buch geschafft hätte. In der Mode mag gelten, was Diana Vreeland sagte: Eleganz ist die Kunst des Neinsagens. Bei Interiors dagegen geht nichts über die Kunst des Durchhaltens.

TASCHEN tient à exprimer sa gratitude à tous les photographes, stylistes, éditeurs affiliés et infatigables assistants qui ont rendu possible ce livre. Un grand merci à tous ainsi qu'aux détenteurs de droits divers pour leur généreux soutien. Nous remercions particulièrement Jon Rosen et sa compagnie new-yorkaise Nucleus Imaging pour la rapidité de leur intervention technique ; ainsi que Sara Teske à Paris, dont les talents diplomatiques nous ont permis d'inclure dans le présent ouvrage le fascinant appartement de Bernhard Willhelm malgré bien des vicissitudes. « Dans la mode, comme le dit si bien Diana Vreeland, l'élégance, c'est le refus. » En décoration intérieure, rien ne vaut la persévérance.

CONTACTS

A

ABC HOME New York City, abchome.com
ADAM MCCULLOCH adammcculloch.info, info@adammcculloch.info
AGA agaliving.com
ALAIN GILLES Brussels, alaingilles.com, info@alaingilles.com,
T. +32 497 41 50 89
ALEX COCHRANE ARCHITECTS London, alexcochrane.net,
mail@alexcochrane.net, T.+44 20 7352 1194
ANDREW MARTIN London, andrewmartin.co.uk, T. +44 20 7225 5100
ANGEL SANCHEZ New York City, angelsanchezusa.com,
angela@angelsanchezusa.com
ANN SACKS TILE & STONE annsacks.com
ANTONIO LUPI Stabbia, antoniolupi.it, lupi@antoniolupi.it,
T. +39 0571 586881
ANTRAX S.R.L. Resana, antrax.it, antrax@antrax.it, T. +39 0423 7174
ARMEL SOYER Paris, armelsoyer.com, contact@armelsoyer.com,
T. +33 1 42 55 49 72
ARTEK Helsinki, stores at: artek.fi, info@artek.fi
ARTIFORT Schijndel, artifort.com, info@artifort.com, T. +31 73 658 00 20
ASTON MATTHEWS London, astonmatthews.co.uk,
sales@astonmatthews.co.uk, T. +44 20 7226 7220
ATTILALOU attilalou.com, contact@attilalou.com
AXEL VERVOORDT Wijnegem, axel-vervoordt.com, info@axel-vervoordt.com

B

BAGCHEE ARCHITECTS New York City, bagcheearchitects.com,
info@bagcheearchitects.com, T. +1 718 384 0849
BAIXA HOUSE Lisbon, baixahouse.com, T. +351 919 090 895
BARBER WILSONS & CO. LTD. London, barwil.co.uk, info@barwil.co.uk,
T. +44 20 8888 3461
BDDW New York City, bddw.com, info@bddw.com, T. +1 212 625 1230
BERNHARD WILLHELM Paris, bernhardwillhelm.com,
info@bernhard-willhelm.com, T. +33 1 47 00 08 68
BEST BEFORE Paris, bestbeforeparis.fr, bestbeforeparis@gmail.com,
T. +33 01 42 74 23 05
BIENNALE INTERIEUR Kortrijk, interieur.be, interieur@interieur.be
BISAZZA S.P.A Alte (VI), bisazza.com, T. +39 0444 707511
BONALDO S.P.A. Villanova, bonaldo.it, bonaldo@bonaldo.it
+39 049 9299011
BRUSSELS FLEA MARKET Located at Jeu de Balle in Quartier Marolles,
open daily from 6 a.m.
BULTHAUP GMBH & CO. KG Bodenkirchen, bulthaup.de,
T. +49 800 1004190

C

CALDER FOUNDATION New York City, calder.org, contact@calder.org,
T. +1 212 334 2424
CAPPELLINI *Peacock Chair* by Dror Benshetrit, *Mr. B* by François
Azambour, and *TWB Seat* by Raw Edges. See cappellini.it
CARAVANE Paris, caravane.fr, info@caravane.fr, T. +33 1 44 61 04 20
CARLOS ROUTH WODEHOUSE CONSTRUCTION CORP.
Watermill, NY, wodehouseconstruction.com, wodehouse@optonline.net,
T. +1 631 537 1897
CHRIS COLEMAN Brooklyn, NY, ccinteriordesign.com,
info@ccinteriordesign.com, T. +1 718 222 8984
CHRISTOPHER SPITZMILLER, New York City, christopherspitzmiller.com,
T. +1 212 563 1144
CLASSICON GMBH Munich, classicon.com, T. +49 89 7481330
CLEMENS TISSI Berlin, clemenstissi.com, mail@clemenstissi.com,
T. +49 30 24724714
COBERTOS DE PAPA – blankets from the Beira region.
More information at: mobapi.co
COLE AND SON LTD. London, cole-and-son.com,
customer.service@cole-and-son.com, T. +44 20 7376 4628
COLEFAX & FOWLER London, colefax.com, T. +44 20 7244 7427
COR SITZMÖBEL HELMUT LÜBKE GMBH & CO. KG
Rheda-Wiedenbrück, cor.de, info@cor.de, T. +49 5242 41020
COWTAN & TOUT, New York City, cowtan.com, T. +1 212 647 6900

D

D. PORTHAULT dporthaultparis.com
D'APOSTROPHE DESIGN, INC. , New York City, dapostrophe.com,
info@dapostrophe.com, T. +1 212 965 1077
DANSK MØBELKUNST Copenhagen, dmk.dk, T. +45 33 32 38 37
DAUM Paris, daum.fr, T. +33 1 53 05 12 29
DESCIENCE LABORATORIES BY SIMREL ACHENBACH
Brooklyn, NY, desciencelab.com, simrel@desciencelab.com,
T. +1 718 383 0702
DINESEN WOODEN FLOORS Rødding, Denmark, dinesen.com,
info@dinesen.com, T. +45 74 55 21 40
DOMÉSTICO domesticodsd.com.ar, mail@domesticodsd.com.ar
DOUG MEYER dougandgenemeyer.com, contact@dougandgenemeyer.com

E

EDWARD BARBER & JAY OSGERBY London, barberosgerby.com,
mail@barberosgerby.com, T. +44 20 7033 3884
EFE ERENLER Berlin, efeerenler.com, T. +49 30 66301161
EMERY & CIE emeryetcie.com, mail@emeryetcie.com

EMMA SLOLEY emmasloley.com, emma@emmasloley.com,
T. +1 646 736 7737
ERICKSON ASSOCIATES Naples, Florida, eaarchitecture.com,
info@eaarchitecture.com, T. +1 239 431 7990
ESTABLISHED & SONS London, establishedandsons.com,
info@establishedandsons.com, T. +44 20 7608 0990

F

FAYE TOOGOOD London, fayetoogood.com, info@fayetoogood.com,
T. +44 20 7226 1061
FIAMMA COLONNA MONTAGU fiammamontagu@gmail.com
FROMENTAL London, fromental.co.uk, info@fromental.co.uk,
T. +44 20 3410 2000

G

GAGOSIAN GALLERY LONDON London, london@gagosian.com,
T. +44 20 7841 9960
GALERIE BSL Paris, galeriebsl.com, info@galeriebsl.com,
T. +33 1 44 78 94 14
GEORGE NAKASHIMA New Hope, Pennsylvania,
nakashimawoodworker.com, info@nakashimawoodworker.com,
T. +1 215 862 2272
GIANDOMENICO BELOTTI *Spaghetti Chair* and other designs
via architonic.com
GRAY ORGANSCHI ARCHITECTURE New Haven, Connecticut,
grayorganschi.com, info@grayorganschi.com,
T. +1 203 777 7794
GRÜNTUCH ERNST ARCHITEKTEN Berlin, gruentuchernst.de,
mail@gruentuchernst.de, T. +49 30 3087788

H

HARVEY WOODWARD ART & INTERIORS harveywoodward.co.uk,
mail@harveywoodward.co.uk, T. +44 7958 778488
HÉCTOR ESRAWE Mexico City, esrawe.com, studio@esrawe.com,
T. +52 55 5553 9611
HÉCTOR RUIZ VELÁZQUEZ ruizvelazquez.com, hector@ruizvelazquez.com
HERMÈS Global furniture store locations: lesailes.hermes.com/nl/en/mobilier
HISTORIC LIGHTING COMPANY historiclighting.co.uk,
hello@urbancottageindustries.co.uk, T. +44 20 7193 2119

I

ILLUMINARE STUDIO Los Angeles, illuminarestudio.com,
illuminare@sbcglobal.net, T. +1 323 930 1504
INEZ VAN LAMSWEERDE & VINOODH MATADIN
Represented by: The Collective Shift, contact@thecollectiveshift.com,
T. +1 212 226 1544, Galleries: Matthew Marks, matthewmarks.com,
info@matthewmarks.com, T. +1 212 243 0200; Gagosian Gallery, gagosian.com

J

JACQUES GRANGE INTERIORS Paris, T. +33 1 47 42 47 34
JARLA PARTILAGER Berlin, jarlapartilager.org, info@jarlapartilager.org,
T. +49 30 20188543
JEAN-MARIE MASSAUD Studio Massaud, Paris, massaud.com,
T. +33 1 40 09 54 14
JÉRÔME ABEL SEGUIN jeromeabelseguin.com, jeromeabelseguin@free.fr,
T. +33 6 14 61 60 82
JERSZY SEYMOUR jerszyseymour.com, hookmeup@jerszyseymour.com
JESÚS MORAIME Jardineiro Paisajista, Madrid, jesus@moraime.com,
T. +34 913 197 786
JO MEESTERS Eindhoven, jomeesters.nl, post@jomeesters.nl,
T. +31 6 54 22 31 88
JOAQUIM TENREIRO Furniture available at R Gallery, New York City,
r20thcentury.com, r@r20thcentury.com, T. +1 212 343 7979
JOHN DERIAN COMPANY online@johnderian.com, T. +1 212 677 8408
JOHN MINSHAW DESIGNS London, johnminshawdesigns.com,
enquiries@johnminshawdesigns.com, T. +44 20 7262 9126
JOHN ROBSHAW TEXTILES New York City, johnrobshaw.com,
info@johnrobshaw.com, T. +1 212 594 6006
JOHN ROSSELLI ANTIQUES & DECORATIONS New York City,
johnrosselliantiques.com, info@johnrosselli.com,
T. +1 212 750 0060
JONATHAN ADLER New York City, jonathanadler.com,
customerservice@jonathanadler.com, T. +1 212 645 2802
JORGE VARELA ARQUITECTURA & ARQUITECTURA DE INTERIORES
Madrid, jorgevareladesign.com, into@jorgevareladesign.com,
T. +34 915 190 679
JOSÉ ADRIAO ARQUITECTO Lisbon, joseadriao.com, ja@joseadriao.com,
T. +351 213 620 762
JOSEPH DIRAND ARCHITECTURE Paris, josephdirand.com,
jd@josephdirand.com, T. + 33 1 44 69 04 80
JUDY ROSS New York City, judyrosstextiles.com,
contact@judyrosstextiles.com, T. +1 212 842 1705
JULIA LOHMANN London, julialohmann.co.uk, julia@julialohmann.co.uk,
T. +44 7909 882545

K

KATJA BUCHHOLZ Berlin, buchholzberlin.com, buchholzberlin@gmail.com,
T. +49 179 2900438

KAZUHIDE TAKAHAMA Japanese Designer, 1930-2010 His *Suzanne* seating is produced by Knoll. See knoll.com
KVADRAT kvadrat.dk

L

L'ESCAUT Brussels, escaut.org, escaut@escaut.org, T. +32 2426 48 15
LE MANACH Paris, lemanach.fr, T. +33 1 47 42 52 94
LE MILL Mumbai, lemillindia.com, info@lemill.in, T. +91 22 23742415
LIBERTY LONDON London, liberty.co.uk, customerservices@liberty.co.uk
LIVING DIVANI S.R.L. Anzano del Parco, Italy, livingdivani.it, info@livingdivani.it, T. +39 031 630954

M

MAARTEN BAAS Hertogenbosch, maartenbaas.com, info@maartenbaas.com
MADCAP COTTAGE JOHN LOECKE AND JASON OLIVER NIXON Brooklyn, NY, madcapcottage.com, john@madcapcottage.com, jason@madcapcottage.com, T. +1 917 513 9143
MAGNUS LÖFGREN DESIGNS Sweden, magnuslofgrendesigns.se, info@magnuslofgrendesigns.se, T. +46 8 20 04 39
MALCOLM HILL GALLERY malcolmhillnyc.com, mh@malcolmhillnyc.com
MARC NEWSON London, marc-newson.com, pod@marc-newson.com, T. +44 20 7932 0990
MARCEL WANDERS Amsterdam, marcelwanders.com, joy@marcelwanders.com, T. +31 20 422 13 39
MARIE-HÉLÈNE DE TAILLAC Paris, mariehelenedetaillac.com, paris@mhdt.net, T. +33 1 44 27 07 07 / 08
MARIKA GIACINTI Paris, marikagiacinti.com, contact@marikagiacinti.com, T. +33 06 83 30 04 73
MARIMEKKO Helsinki, marimekko.com, info@marimekko.fi, T. +358 9 75871
MARINA FAUST marinafaust.com, marina@marinafaust.com
MARSTON & LANGINGER London, marston-and-langinger.com, T. +44 20 7881 5700
MATHIAS KISS mathiaskiss.com
MECOX GARDENS mecoxgardens.com, info@mecoxgardens.com
MELINDA RITZ INTERIORS Glendale, CA, melindaritz.com, info@melindaritz.com, T. +1 818 551 0071
MICASA São Paulo, micasa.com.br, micasa@micasa.com.br, T. +55 11 3088 1238
MICHAEL ANASTASSIADES London, michaelanastassiades.com, studio@michaelanastassiades.com, T. +44 20 7928 7527
MICHAEL FUCHS GALERIE Berlin, michaelfuchsgalerie.com, info@michaelfuchsgalerie.com, T. +49 30 22002550

MOEBEL HORZON Berlin, moebelhorzon@modocom.de, T. +49 176 6273 0874
MONTECLARO WOOD *Terminalia amazonia* syn. *T. obovata*, known as "Guayabo leon" (Colombia) or "Pau-mulato brancho" (Brazil)
MUMBAI CHOR BAZAAR Mohammed Ali Road in South Mumbai
MUSCHALEK ARCHITECTES Montreuil, France, muschalek.com, post@muschalek.com, T. +33 9 50 68 14 80

N

NEISHA CROSLAND neishacrosland.com, rugs available through: The Rug Company, therugcompany.com
NENDO Tokyo, nendo.jp, info@nendo.jp, T. +81 3 6661 3750
NICKY HASLAM DESIGN London, nh-design.co.uk, info@nh-design.co.uk, T. +44 20 7730 0808

P

PALAZZO MARGHERITA Bernalda, Italy, T. +39 0835 549060 coppolaresorts.com/palazzomargherita, info@palazzomargherita.com
PAOLA LENTI SRL Meda MB, Italy, paolalenti.it, info@paolalenti.it, T. +39 0362 344587
PERLUDI GMBH Graz, perludi.com, info@perludi.com, T. +43 316 815678
PETER HEIMER Berlin, peterheimer.com, info@peterheimer.com, T. +49 30 3121205
PHILIP THOMAS DESIGN London, pjthomas.com, info@pjthomas.com, T. +44 20 7229 4044
PHILIPPE STARCK starck.com, info@starcknetwork.com
PIERO GEMELLI Milan, pierogemelli.com, info@pierogemelli.com, T. +39 02 89125281
PIERRE EL-KHOURY ARCHITECTS Beirut, Lebanon, pelk@dm.net.lb, T. + 961 1 564 111
PIERRE JORGE GONZALEZ & JUDITH HAASE AAS, Berlin, gonzalezhaase.com, aas@gonzalezhaase.com, T. +49 30 25296181
PIERRE YOVANOVITCH ARCHITECTURE D'INTÉRIEUR Paris, pierreyovanovitch.com, info@pierreyovanovitch.com, T. +33 7 42 66 33 98
PIERRE-ÉLOI BRIS St Jean du Bruel, France, travelling-designer.com, bris@travelling-designer.com, T. +33 6 69 62 88 62
PIET HEIN EEK Eindhoven, pietheineek.nl, T. +31 40 285 66 10
PLINIO IL GIOVANE Milan, plinioilgiovane.it, info@plinioilgiovane.it, T. +39 02 55190210
PROJECT ALABAMA New York City, projectalabama.com, info@projectalabama.com, T. +1 646 438 6937

Q
QUARELLA S.P.A. Sant'Ambrogio di Valpolicella, Italy, www.quarella.com
QUI EST PAUL? qui-est-paul.com, e.michaud@rotodesign.fr,
T. +33 545 303034

R
RALPH LAUREN HOME ralphlaurenhome.com,
customerassistance@ralphlauren.com, T. +1 888 475 7674
RASMUS FENHANN Copenhagen, fenhann.com, rasmus@fenhann.com,
T. +45 35 38 81 24
RESTORATION HARDWARE restorationhardware.com, T. +1 800 910 9836
REWIRE GALLERY Los Angeles, rewirela.com, hi@rewirela.com,
T. +1 323 664 5254
RICHARD SCHULTZ available at Knoll. See knoll.com
RICHARD WRIGHTMAN DESIGN New York City, richardwrightman.com,
info@richardwrightman.com, T. +1 718 707 0217
ROBERTO BELLANTUONO Conversano, Italy, robertobellantuono.it,
adm@robertobellantuono.it, T. +39 080 4958708
ROOSHAD SHROFF Mumbai, rooshadshroff.com, info@rooshadshroff.com,
T. +91 22 22037745
ROSS LOVEGROVE London, rosslovegrove.com,
general@rosslovegrove.com, T. +44 20 7229 7104
RUD RASMUSSEN Copenhagen, rudrasmussen.de, mail@rudrasmussen.dk,
T. +45 35 39 62 33

S
S.M.OG MILANO Milan, smogmilano.com, info@smogmilano.com,
T. +39 02 26809414
SACHS & LINDORES Brooklyn, NY, sachslindores.net, T. +1 212 366 1040
SARA BENGUR INTERIOS New York City, sarabengur.com,
T. +1 212 226 8796
SERENDIPITY Paris, serendipity.fr, contact@serendipity.fr, T. +33 1 40 46 01 15
SERGE MOUILLE sergemouille.com
SHAMIR SHAH DESIGN New York City, shamirshahdesign.com,
info@shamirshahdesign.com, T. +1 212 274 7476
SKARSTEDT GALLERY New York City, skarstedt.com, info@skarstedt.com,
T. +1 212 737 2060
SOANE BRITAIN London, soane.co.uk, shop@soane.co.uk,
T. +44 20 7730 6400
SOCIETY Costamasnaga (Lecco), societylimonta.com, T. +39 031 857111
STAATLICHE PORZELLAN-MANUFAKTUR MEISSEN GMBH
Meißen, meissen.com, info@meissen.com, T. +49 3521 4680
STELLAN HOLM GALLERY New York City, stellanholm.com,
info@stellanholm.com, T. +1 212 627 7444

STUDIO MUMBAI ARCHITECTS Mumbai, studiomumbai.com,
contact@studiomumbai.com, T. +91 22 65777560
STUDIO TIM CAMPBELL Studios in Los Angeles and New York City,
studiotimcampbell.com, info@studiotimcampbell.com
SVENKST TENN Stockholm, svenksttenn.se, info@svenksttenn.se,
T. +46 8 670 16 00
SYLVIA HEISEL sylviaheisel.com, contact@sylviaheisel.com

T
TATIANA BILBAO S.C. Mexico City, tatianabilbao.com,
info@tatianabilbao.com, T. +52 55 8589 8822
TECNOLUMEN Bremen, tecnolumen.com, info@tecnolumen.de,
T. +49 421 4304170
THE HEVENINGHAM COLLECTION heveningham.co.uk,
T. +44 1489 893481
TIINA THE STORE Amagansett, NY, tiinathestore.com,
info@tiinathestore.com, T. +1 631 267 6200
TIM FURZER New York City, timfurzer.com, client@timfurzer.com,
T. +1 646 450 8059
TOM DIXON STUDIO London, tomdixon.net, sales@tomdixon.net,
T. +44 20 7400 0500

U
UGO – ATELIER DE INTERIORES E DECORAÇÃO
info@ugo.com.pt, T. +351 213 461 102

V
VITRA GMBH Weil am Rhein, vitra.com, T. +49 7621 7020

W
WATERWORKS waterworks.com, T. +1 800 899 6757
WELLS MACKERETH ARCHITECTS London, wellsmackereth.com,
hq@wellsmackereth.com, T. +44 20 7495 7055
WERKSTÄTTE CARL AUBÖCK Vienna, werkstaette-carlauboeck.at,
office@werkstaette-carlauboeck.at, T. +43 1 523663120
WILLY GUHL Loop chair available through Eternit: eternit.de,
info@eternit.de, T. +49 6224 7010
WOLF GORDON New York City, wolf-gordon.com, T. +1 212 319 6800

Z
ZIETA by Oskar Zieta, Zurich and Wroclaw, zieta.pl, info@zieta.pl

IMPRINT

© 2013 TASCHEN GMBH

HOHENZOLLERNRING 53, D-50672 KÖLN

WWW.TASCHEN.COM

To stay informed about upcoming TASCHEN titles, please subscribe to our free Magazine at www.taschen.com/magazine, find our Magazine app for iPad on iTunes, follow us on Twitter and Facebook, or e-mail us for a sample copy at contact@taschen.com. Delve in and enjoy!

INTERIORS NOW

EDITOR	MARGIT J. MAYER	**LITHOGRAPH MANAGER**	THOMAS GRELL
ART DIRECTOR	ANDRÉ M. WYST, BERLIN	**FRENCH TRANSLATION**	PHILIPPE SAFAVI, PARIS
AUTHOR	IAN PHILLIPS, PARIS	**GERMAN TRANSLATION**	KARIN JAEGER, MUNICH
PROJECT MANAGER	STEPHANIE PAAS	**EDITORIAL ASSISTANT**	FALKMAR K. FINKE

Front cover: The living room of Pierre Yovanovitch's apartment in Paris. Paintings by Marc Quinn and (on spine) Alex Katz.
Back cover: A Beverly Hills kitchen by Melinda Ritz with a portrait of TV chef Julia Child. Both photos: Stephan Julliard/Tripod Agency
Styling: Ian Phillips

© 2013 VG Bild-Kunst, Bonn for the works of Alvar Aalto, Fernando and Humberto Campana, William N. Copley, Elger Esser, Alain Gilles, Herbert Hamak, Leiko Ikemura, Pierre Jeanneret, Johannes Kahrs, Alex Katz, Yves Klein, Magnus Löfgren, Ludwig Mies van der Rohe, Serge Mouille, Charlotte Perriand, Jean Emile Victor Prouvé, Kirstine Roepstorff, James Rosenquist, Carl Strüwe and Bernar Venet
© 2013 The Willem de Kooning Foundation, New York / VG Bild-Kunst, Bonn
© 2013 Eames Office, Venice, CA, www.eamesoffice.com, for the works of Charles and Ray Eames
© 2013 The Estate of Jean-Michel Basquiat / VG Bild-Kunst, Bonn
© 2013 The Andy Warhol Foundation for the Visual Arts, Inc. / Artists Rights Society (ARS), New York

Printed in Italy
ISBN 978-3-8365-3857-2